W9-BOE-520

The Birder's Guide to Bed and Breakfasts
UNITED STATES AND CANADA

Peggy van Hulsteyn

Foreword by Roger Tory Peterson
Birding Consultant, Anna Appleby

John Muir Publications
Santa Fe, New Mexico

To David, my favorite bird-watcher

John Muir Publications, P.O. Box 613, Santa Fe, NM 87504

© 1993 by Peggy van Hulsteyn
Cover © 1993 by John Muir Publications
All rights reserved.
Printed in the United States

First edition. Third printing December 1994
Printed on recycled paper

Library of Congress Cataloging-in-Publication Data
van Hulsteyn, Peggy.
   The birder's guide to bed and breakfasts / by Peggy van Hulsteyn;
foreword by Roger Tory Peterson
    p.   c m.
   Includes index.
   ISBN 1-56261-106-2: $15.95
   1. Bird watching—United States—Guidebooks. 2. Wildlife viewing sites—United
States—Guidebooks. 3. Bed and breakfast accommodations—United States—Guidebooks.
4. Bird watching—Canada—Guidebooks. 5. Wildlife viewing sites—Canada—Guidebooks.
6. Bed and breakfast accommodations—Canada—Guidebooks. I. Title.
QL681.V35 1993
598'.0723473—dc20   93-2260
                                                              CI

Cover photo: Canada geese fall migration, Klamath Basin NWR, Canada
   © Renee Lynn
Cover inset: Allen House Bed & Breakfast Inn, Amherst, Maine
Back cover photo: Garrett Mansion (Daryl Black)
Printer: Malloy Lithographing
Typesetting: Richard Harris
Design: Ken Wilson
Typeface: Goudy Old Style
Map on page 4: Jim Wood

Distributed to the book trade by
W. W. Norton & Company
New York, New York

Contents

Foreword

Organized birding tours started in the late 1930s in Florida to help several birds that were in trouble, including the snail kite and the limpkin. The idea of the National Audubon Society was to fill the local hotels with bird watchers, thereby helping the local economy. If the residents of those towns saw money coming in from people who wanted to watch birds instead of shoot them, they would be willing to cooperate. It worked. Those endangered birds are now more secure in Florida, and the local citizens are proud of their role in saving them.

Nature, wildlife, and birding tours now reach a variety of individuals, including those who already have some knowledge of the natural world, those who want to expand their world knowledge, and some who are just discovering this world and its myriad beauties and who may become hooked on birds for life. The increased understanding of birds and their habitat offered by bird tourism or "ecotourism" fills the ranks of conservationists with people of intelligence and influence, people willing to act if they see things of which they do not approve.

Birders, photographers, and travelers have had an enormously beneficial impact on saving our birds. Any problems or negative aspects can easily be solved with common sense and a code of behavior that exemplifies a reverence for life.

This book will help you expand the breadth of your birding experience. Enjoy your travels and learning, and use them for the benefit of us all, especially the birds.

March 1993   —*Roger Tory Peterson*

Acknowledgments

I agree with Dorothy Parker who said, "I hate writing. I like having written," and even with Richard Nixon who said, "Writing is the toughest thing I've ever done." I am, therefore, particularly grateful to the following people who helped make the writing of this book easier. Special thanks go to all the innkeepers and birding experts who were so generous with their time and knowledge.

I am especially grateful to Anna Appleby, my feisty and knowledgeable birding consultant.

A special thank-you to Roger Tory Peterson for his inspiration and introduction.

Thanks to Gene Delgado, my assistant and Sherlock Holmes, for his wonderful work in tracking down bed and breakfasts and for keeping me organized.

Thanks to Rhoda Barkan and Ruth Holmes for their crackerjack research assistance, not to mention their encouragement and good humor along the way.

Thanks to Daryl Black for her excellent research and photography. Nedra Westwater gets a pat on the back for being a winning birding traveling companion and first-rate photographer.

Lisa and Jim O'Donnell helped introduce me to the joys of birding and gave able assistance along the way. And thanks to Joanne Guttman, another birding mentor.

I appreciate all the help Valerie Brooker, my good friend and favorite librarian, gave me. Thanks to my long-standing friend David Donoho for his superb photographer's eye.

Thanks to Jeanie Fleming, Deborah Lee, and Sarah Lovett for their sage advice during the writing of this book.

A tip of the binoculars to Carol Beardmore, Ann Mason, and Nadine Koenig.

Thanks to Sheila Berg for her excellent editing.

Fully aware of the irony, I want to thank Vanity, whose feline frolicking and cavorting kept me entertained during this project.

As always, my deepest gratitude goes to my husband, David, whose humor, encouragement, editing skills, and general loving care sustained me during this project.

—*Peggy van Hulsteyn*

First, I want to thank Peggy van Hulsteyn, a wonderful companion and collaborator, for making it possible to tie together good places to bird with good places to stay. A whiz with the pen, she made my sometimes dry information on the birding areas better than merely readable.

Without the cooperation and active help of the following people and organizations, the birding area information could not have been written: my husband, Thomas P. Harper; David Levinson; Roy Lerman, M.D.; the refuge managers and staff of all the Department of the Interior national wildlife refuges; the superintendents, naturalists, and staff of all the national, state, and provincial parks; the Canadian Wildlife Service for their overwhelming response and assistance; the Audubon Sanctuaries; the National Forest Service managers and staff; the Nature Conservancy, especially the individual state preserve managers and staff; Milan Bull, Connecticut Audubon Society, for sharing the state's ten hot spots; George Derkovitz, Jr., president of the Friends of the Indiana Boundary Prairies of Markam for his help and enthusiasm; the Professional Association of Innkeepers (PAII) and its president, Pat Hardy, for invaluable assistance in directing us to bed and breakfasts that not only met the standards of the association but also understood the needs of bird-watchers and outdoors people; Peggy Mitchusson, for her excellent birding information on Nebraska, Oklahoma, Iowa, and Kansas; the Socorro Public Library staff for maps and research assistance; the Vermont Institute of Natural Science; the chambers of commerce and departments of tourism of the states and cities we included; Paul Kerlinger, Director, Cape May Bird Observatory; Dave Kline, Regional Vice-President, National Audubon Society; Carol Jacobson, the Nature Conservancy; Chris Ellingwood and Rob Walker, Canadian Wildlife Service; Steve Hoffman, Hawkwatch International; and Robie Dailey, Bruce Amsden, Jerry Lindsey, Kris Fleming, Cathy Walters, Andy Thompson, Tim Williams, David Muth, Julie Henderson, Maggie Briggs, David Peters, Michael Tansy, Brian Winter, Kate Crowley, Dana Kokubun, and Fran McDermott.

—*Anna Appleby*

Introduction

"One touch of nature makes the whole world kin."
—*William Shakespeare*

"Never does nature say one thing and wisdom another."
—*Juvenal (A.D. 60-140)*

"It is always sunrise somewhere; the dew is never all dried at once; a shower is forever falling; vapor is forever rising."
—*John Muir (1838-1914)*

"To be a bird is to be alive more intensively than any other living creature.... [Birds] live in a world that is always the present, mostly full of joy."
—*N. J. Berrill (b. 1903)*

"In order to see birds it is necessary to become a part of the silence."
—*Robert Lynd (1879-1949)*

"Birds are to see, to hear, to store in memory."
—*Allan D. Cruickshank (1907-1974)*

"Although birds coexist with us on this eroded planet, they live independently of us with a self-sufficiency that is almost a rebuke. In the world of birds a symposium on the purpose of life would be inconceivable. They do not need it. We are not that self reliant. We are the ones who have lost our way."
"Nothing wholly admirable ever happened in this country except the migration of birds."
—*Brooks Atkinson (1894-1984)*

"Everything about a hummingbird is a superlative."
—*Tom Colazo*

"I go to Nature to be soothed and healed, and to have my senses put in tune once more."
—*John Burroughs*

"There are no wild animals till man makes them so."

—*Mark Twain*

"Every human being looks to the birds. They suit the fancy of us all. What they feel they can voice, as we try to; they court and nest, they battle with the elements, they are torn by two opposing impulses, a love of home and passion for far places. Only with birds do we share so much emotion."

—*Donald Culross Peattie*

"Without birds, where would we have learned that there can be song in the heart?"

—*Hal Borland*

One of the things I love about being a journalist is the opportunity to explore new worlds. Learning about birds has been a joyful experience. As Len Eiserer said, "We judge bird song not by its musical quality nor even by its creativeness but by its effect on the human spirit." Birds have had a wonderful effect on my spirit; they have taught me to see, hear, and feel in a new lyrical way. Listening to a loon call to its mate, hearing the whooshing sounds as hundreds of sandhill cranes fly by in magnificent V formations, watching an eagle soar, and looking into the playful face of a puffin—these have been powerful, thrilling moments in my life.

Getting to know bird-watchers has only served to enhance the experience. Birders are the most enthusiastic, caring, and dedicated people I have ever met. As a bed and breakfast devotee, I have enjoyed trying to create a marriage between birders and B&Bs. It is a happy union from my standpoint because birders make wonderful bed-and-breakfast company.

Louise Lee, owner of the Glasgow Inn in Cambridge, Maryland, recently observed, "Birders are the best guests. They are sensitive and tuned in to where they are. They walk around my acres and take time to see what is around them. Birders look with eyes that see and ears that hear. I think it is because birders are contented, peaceful people and know who they are and what they are about. Birders have a graciousness about them. In their quiet gentle way they are really turning their avocation into a national pastime."

Which brings me to the subject of the innkeepers themselves. I have been writing about country inns for some time, so this aspect of the research was not quite as complicated or novel to me as the esoteric subculture of birding. I have, for the most part, been impressed with the generosity and enthusiasm of the innkeepers. The vast majority were extremely helpful and eager to do anything they could to make their inns receptive to birders' needs.

No introduction would be complete without a caveat. Mine is that this is not a definitive listing of every birding hot spot in the country. I did not have the room, the youth, the time to list every birding spot in America. I hope this may be the first in a series. In the next edition, you will find information on birding refuges in New Hampshire and West Virginia.

Finding bed and breakfasts for some birding spots was a genuine challenge. Birds often like to nest in areas where there is no place for humans to nest. You will note that some of the inns are often an hour from the birding refuge; that is because I could not locate any places closer. They may exist, but they have escaped my eagle eye. In a few places, I had to resort to listing motels. Suggestions or comments from readers on new locations will always be appreciated.

In contrast, some birding hot spots were located in populated areas that had fifty or more bed and breakfasts; it then became a matter of trying to figure out which ones were the closest to the birding refuge or which ones would most appeal to birders. This culling process involved a complicated trade-off among convenience, cost, and comfort.

This is an audience participation book. If there are other birding refuges or bed and breakfasts you would like to see in the next edition, I reemphasize my interest in hearing from you. If there are some places I discussed that disgust you, this too would be invaluable information. It should be clear that a book of this scope, covering the United States and Canada, was a monumental task. So I, personally, could not visit each place listed. Furthermore, inns change; owners come and go. I was as meticulous as possible in selecting places, but deadlines dictated expedience in a few cases. That is why there is a blank page at the back of the book—for your comments.

Whenever possible, I tried to find bed and breakfasts in various price ranges. Many people who have never stayed in bed and breakfasts are surprised by how expensive some can be. There were certain locales that only had very expensive inns; in others, the prices were very modest.

For each listing, there is a factual description of the birding refuge, explaining how to get there, what type of birds you will see there, and which is the best season. Next to each refuge, I tried to find at least three bed and breakfasts where you could stay. Bear in mind that formulas work better in chemistry than they do in guidebooks. My main hope is that you will enjoy your visit to these Fly Inns and have a happy birding experience. If you have just begun, you are in for the adventure of your life, for, as Roger Tory Peterson puts it, "In a world that seems so very puzzling, is it any wonder birds have such appeal? Birds are, perhaps, the most eloquent expression of reality."

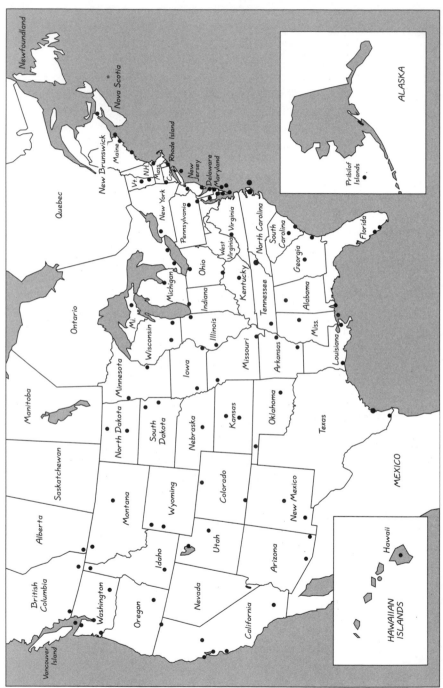

Birding Sites, U.S. and Canada

Bon Secour National Wildlife Refuge/ Dauphin Island Bird Sanctuary

NEAREST AIRPORTS: Mobile, Alabama; Pensacola, Florida.

LOCATION: From Mobile, drive west on I-10 to Route 59 south, then to Route 193 south. Route 193 crosses the bay to Little Dauphin and Dauphin Island. To reach Fort Morgan and the rest of Bon Secour refuge, you take an auto ferry the short distance from island to island. You can also take a passenger-only ferry from Fowl River on Route 59 to reach the Dauphin islands. From Pensacola, drive west on US 98 to Route 59 (on the east side of Mobile Bay), then south to Route 180 west until you reach the information center at the entrance to the refuge.

CONTACT: Bon Secour National Wildlife Refuge, P.O. Box 1650, Gulf Shores, AL 36542. (205) 968-8623.

BEST BIRDING: Spring, fall, and winter; summer for fledglings.

TOURS/WORKSHOPS: Contact refuge manager.

Encompassing a good portion of Alabama's remaining coastal habitats, the barrier islands refuge consists of 4,000 acres of beaches, dunes, pine and oak woodlands, shrubs, wildflowers, and other native plants. In mid-April, the songbirds start to arrive on their way north; commonly seen are Cape May, prothonotary, pine, yellow-throated, hooded, Kentucky, and black-and-white warblers as well as northern parulas. There is a chance you will be able to spot a golden-winged warbler here also. Both summer and scarlet tanagers are common, as are rose-breasted grosbeaks. Indigo buntings, painted buntings, and dickcissels nest on the refuge, along with Bachman's and seaside sparrows.

Raptors patrol the land and sea; osprey courting flights, nest building, and hatching all occur from April through July. In spring and fall, there is great diversity and large populations of shorebirds. During those seasons, lesser golden plovers, Wilson's plovers, American avocets, upland sandpipers, and short-billed dowitchers all search the shores for food; and elegant, royal, and caspian terns fly above scanning the waters for nourishment. The gull-billed tern can be seen as well. Numerous species of herons and egrets are also at home here, including great, little, blue, tricolored, and yellow-crowned night herons as well as flashy reddish egrets. Gliding across the skies, the magnificent frigate birds can usually be seen throughout the year.

BAYOU HERON MOTEL
P.O. Box 233, 1506 Cadillac Avenue W, Dauphin Island, AL 36528
(205) 861-5534

The Bayou Heron Motel is a pleasant place to stay on historic Dauphin Island. Just the name should get you in the proper mood for your visit to the lovely Dauphin Island Bird Sanctuary.

Guy and Cynthia Mead welcome birders. When I first called them, they told me with great enthusiasm, "There must be thousands of birds here. It's a beautiful sight." By staying right on the island, you can get an early start.

The Bayou Heron Motel offers large 2-bedroom efficiency apartments with private baths, private balconies, and fine linens.

There is an attractive area right around the motel with picnic tables, BBQ cookers, and a large wooded yard. You are right next to a fishing pier and a boat launch. Happy birding!

Rates: Seasonal, $35-$60 nightly (2-night min.); $175-$300 weekly
Credit cards: Visa, MC
No. of rooms: 6, each with 2 bedrooms
No. of baths: 6
Wheelchair access: 2 rooms
Pets: No
Smoking: Yes
Senior citizen discount: No
Directions: 40 minutes from the mainland. After crossing the bridge, 1 mile on your right behind seafood gallery.

GULF BREEZE MOTEL
P.O. Box 107, 1512 Cadillac Avenue, Dauphin Island, AL 36528
(205) 861-7344

Dauphin Island Bird Sanctuary is a major resting and feeding site for migrating songbirds. The 164-acre sanctuary is the first land many birds encounter in the spring after their northern flight across the Gulf of Mexico. There is birding galore, but we could not find any bed and breakfast where you can nest.

Not to worry! Try the Gulf Breeze Motel for very comfortable lodging. The 19-unit motel has spacious rooms conveniently located near the public beach, restaurants, shops, and an 18-hole golf course. Best of all, you are within a wing flap of the Dauphin Island Bird Sanctuary. Mike and Karen Tafra have run the motel since 1982 and will be happy to welcome you to their island. They offer single and double rooms as well as an efficiency apartment with 2 bedrooms, a living room (with sofa sleeper), and a fully equipped kitchen. Availability is limited in season, so call early for reservations.

Rates: Single $40; double $50; efficiency $60; extra person $5
Credit cards: Visa, MC, AMEX, Discover, Diners, Carte Blanche
No. of rooms: 19

No. of baths: 19
Wheelchair access: Yes
Pets: Yes, owner responsible
Smoking: Yes
Senior citizen discount: No

Directions: Highway 193 south from Mobile. On the island, make a right at the water tower, travel 1 mile, and make another right on Penalver Street.

MALAGA INN
359 Church Street, Mobile, AL 36602, (205) 438-4701, (800) 231-1586

The managers of the Malaga Inn will show you their flair for Southern living and comfort. You can sip a mint julep around the romantic courtyard, and the nicely landscaped, quiet, gaslit courtyard is the perfect spot for an elegant dinner. Octavia's Restaurant and Lounge serves regional seafood specialties.

The Malaga Inn, in the historic district of downtown Mobile, is the only hotel of its kind in Alabama. The hotel was originally two townhouses built in 1862 by two brothers-in-law when the war was going well for the South. The two homes have been restored around a quiet patio and garden.

Each of the 40 rooms has been furnished with a great deal of individuality, reminiscent of the finest Southern tradition. All the rooms are fully air-conditioned, each with private bath and many with original hardwood floors.

After a full day of birding at Dauphin Island Bird Sanctuary, relax at the enclosed swimming pool.

If you want to explore Mobile, the staff will make arrangements for you to see the city's most popular and historic attractions. The inn itself is listed in the National Register of Historic Places. The room rate includes complimentary coffee, newspaper, and free parking.

Rates: $59-$69
Credit cards: Visa, MC, AMEX, Discover, Diners
No. of rooms: 40
No. of baths: 40
Directions: Inn will send map.

Wheelchair access: No
Pets: No
Smoking: Yes
Senior citizen discount: No

Wheeler National Wildlife Refuge

NEAREST AIRPORT: Skycenter Airport between Huntsville and Decatur, Alabama.

LOCATION: North central Alabama. Drive west from the airport on I-565/Route 20 to I-65 south across the Tennessee River toward Decatur. Take I-67 west at the junction with I-65 until you reach the visitor center.

CONTACT: Wheeler National Wildlife Refuge, P.O. Box 1643, Decatur, AL 35602. (205) 353-7243.

BEST BIRDING: Spring and fall.

TOURS/WORKSHOPS: Contact refuge manager.

Backed up against the Tennessee River and its feeder creeks and larger tributaries is the Wheeler National Wildlife Refuge, a lush riparian habitat. This is an area of swamps, hardwood bottomlands, and pine woods on the drier uplands. A highly managed refuge, it has more than 3,000 acres of crops that help support the large number of waterfowl that migrate through and winter here, including greater white-fronted and snow geese; wigeons; lesser scaups; buffleheads; common goldeneyes; hooded and red-breasted mergansers; American black, ruddy, and at least 10 other species of ducks.

Hawks also are attracted to the more moderate climate; you should be able to observe broad-winged, sharp-shinned, Cooper's, and red-shouldered hawks and possibly even a bald eagle. Here shorebirds are equally numerous in the fall and spring. The warbler migration in the early spring will include the blue-winged, golden-winged, Tennessee, chestnut-sided, black-throated green, Canada, and Blackburnian among the 27 species observed. In addition, at this time you should be able to see orchard and northern orioles, purple finches, and bobolinks.

THE DANCY-POLK HOUSE
901 Railroad Street, N.W., Decatur, AL 35601, (205) 353-3579

When visiting the Wheeler National Wildlife Refuge, you will want to stay at the Dancy-Polk House Inn. This place is for the birds. That is, it is the perfect place for birders to stay, since it is so convenient to the Wheeler refuge. The Dancy-Polk House was built in 1829 in the Palladian style. It is on the National

Register of Historic Places and the Alabama Register of Landmarks and Heritage.

Two large, comfortable bedrooms, furnished with antiques, are available on the third floor. Each bedroom sleeps four people. A large bath, with doors opening onto the upper porch, is shared by both rooms.

You can enjoy a continental breakfast before heading off to Wheeler. Bring your children along as they are welcome at the Dancy-Polk. It is never too early for the next generation of junior bird men and women. You will all enjoy the August migration of purple martins or viewing bald and golden eagles in December.

Rates: Single $45; double $50; extra person $10
Credit cards: No
No. of rooms: 2
No. of baths: 1
Wheelchair access: No
Pets: No
Smoking: No
Senior citizen discount: No
Directions: 1 block on Highway 20, 6 blocks west of US 31.

The Dancy-Polk House

Denali National Park and Preserve

NEAREST AIRPORTS: Anchorage or Fairbanks, Alaska, usually through Seattle, Washington. Anchorage can also be reached by cruise ship from May to September. The ferry system from and to Anchorage is extensive and can easily increase the places for birding either before or after visiting Denali.

LOCATION: The 6 million acres of Denali National Park and Preserve are almost directly centered between Anchorage and Fairbanks. From Highway 3, drive 240 miles north from Anchorage or 120 miles south from Fairbanks to the park entrance. There are speed limits to protect the wildlife. You can also travel by rail or bus from either city. Either private tours or those led by the park naturalists are recommended (see Contacts).

In Fairbanks, stop at Creamer's Field Migratory Waterfowl Refuge (spring migration), 1300 College Road, (907) 452-1531. Reservations are recommended for either bus or vehicle passes at least one day in advance of your visit.

CONTACTS: Superintendent, Denali National Park and Preserve, P.O. Box 9, Denali Park, AK 99755. Public Lands Information Centers: (907) 451-7353 in Fairbanks and (907) 271-2737 in Anchorage. For a free list of maps and publications, contact the Alaska Natural History Association, P.O. Box 838, Denali Park, AK 99755.

BEST BIRDING: Late May to early September.

TOURS/WORKSHOPS: There are many naturalist hikes, tours, and workshops. Check bulletin boards, the park newspaper, and with rangers. Be sure to check for available "discovery hikes." Advance registration is required. You may also wish to contact Wilderness Birding Adventures, P.O. Box 10-3747, Anchorage, AK 99510-3747, (907) 694-7442.

The two major habitats in the park are taiga and tundra. Taiga is a Russian word meaning "land of little sticks," a term that aptly describes the sparse forests close to the Arctic. Tundra, where there is little soil (less than an inch), can be either moist or dry and supports wildflowers, dwarfed bushes, and trees. The treeline is between 1,000 and 2,000 feet. Stands of trees are usually found near protected streams or gravel bars. Valleys have forests of spruce, aspen, balsam, poplar, and birch. Wintering birds here include ravens, ptarmigans, magpies, and gray jays. The spring, summer, and fall seasons are short but active due to north and south migrations as well as courting and nesting. On the tundra, watch for tree sparrows, Lapland longspurs, shorebirds, short-eared owls, and harriers. Golden eagles can be seen flying over high ridges, and northern hawk owls and goshawks frequent the forested valleys. In all, 161 species are found here and can be watched at close range. In the forest, spruce geese and willow ptarmigans may pose for you long enough to study their behavior. In the same habitat, look for gray jays and merlins, as well as mew gulls, gyrfalcons, plovers, and black-billed magpies. Other raptors are sharp-shinned hawks, ravens, great gray owls, and boreal owls, while other mountain species are rock ptarmigans and great horned owls. Around Mount McKinley and nearby Wonder Lake, you can see wood warblers and shorebirds: ducks, terns, sandpipers, and possibly a long-tailed jaeger.

CAMP DENALI
P.O. Box 67, Denali National Park, AK 99755, (907) 683-2290
Winter: P.O. Box 369, Cornish, NH 03746, (603) 675-2248

Camp Denali, founded in 1951, is Alaska's original wilderness vacation lodge and nature center. It beautifully integrates serious appreciation of nature with the little indulgences that make a vacation a vacation.

The lodging at Camp Denali consists of individual log or frame cabins with a separate central dining room, a living room, and rest rooms/shower buildings, all within a few minutes walk of each cabin. Cabins are located along a ridge, each one private and each with an exceptional view of Mount McKinley. They are furnished with wood-burning stoves, gas hot plates for heating water, propane lights, and well-kept outhouses. The interior decor is country calico, with quilts crafted by the Camp Denali staff.

Birding is sensational at this rustic but scenic spot. Camp Denali is more for the roughing-it crowd than its sister facility, the cushier North Face Lodge. At Camp Denali, although you do not have to be capable of climbing Mount McKinley, you must be able to walk over uneven ground from your cabin to the public buildings.

Camp Denali is a hands-on place. There is a natural history resource center containing exhibits, a museum-quality herbarium, a dissecting microscope, a resource library, and a photographic darkroom. In addition to daily activities and evening interpretive programs led by their own naturalist staff, there are excellent special workshops. One that birders should enjoy is entitled "Natural History and Photography or Spring Wildflowers and Nesting Birds" led by David Middleton. Middleton has taught ornithology at the National Audubon Society's Maine Ornithology Camp and is currently on the ornithology teaching staff with the National Wildlife Federation's Summit program.

If you are looking for an adventure destination in your Alaskan experience, for the camaraderie of kindred spirits, for the freedom, simplicity, and solitude of wilderness living and unforgettable birding, Camp Denali is that special place.

Rates: $240 per night per person
Credit cards: No
No. of rooms: 17 guest cabins
No. of baths: No private baths; out-
houses, central shower
Wheelchair access: Dining room
only
Pets: No
Smoking: No
Senior citizen discount: No
Directions: 250 miles north of Anchorage, 90 miles west into center of Denali
National Park.

DENALI CROW'S NEST CABINS
P.O. Box 70, Denali National Park, AK 99755, (907) 683-2723

Denali Crow's Nest Cabins, just one mile north of the Denali National Park
entrance, is in a spectacular setting. Nestled on Sugar Loaf Mountain in
the heart of the Alaska Range, the cabins overlook beautiful Horseshoe Lake
and the wild Nenana River. *Frommer's Dollar Wise Guide to Alaska* calls the
Crow's Nest "the pick of the litter."

National park lodges are often like staying at a high-class adult summer
camp. The Crow's Nest is no exception. The rooms have all the warmth and
charm of an authentic log cabin.

You can eat well at the adjoining Overlook Bar and Grill. From 11:00 a.m.
to 11:00 p.m., try the fresh salmon and halibut, steaks, chicken, and burgers.
At the bar, sample the forty-seven varieties of beer.

Denali is a birder's delight with its 157 species of birds. If you have time
for any more Denali activities, the Crow's Nest can arrange tours such as the
Kantishna Wilderness Trails Tour, Tundra Wildlife Tour, Natural History
Tour, Alaska railroad, river rafting, flightseeing, or the ERA helicopter tour.

Rates: $225 per person per night
(min. 3 nights)
Credit cards: No
No. of rooms: 17 cabins
No. of baths: Central shower facility;
outhouses near each cabin
Directions: Inn will send map.
Wheelchair access: No
Pets: No
Smoking: No
Senior citizen discount: No

NORTH FACE LODGE
P.O. Box 67, Denali National Park, AK 99755, (907) 683-2290
Winter: P.O. Box 369, Cornish, NH 03746, (603) 675-2248

How best to see this magnificent but enormous park? To capture the true
essence of Denali, stay at North Face Lodge. It is one of two lodges at
Denali National Park within view of the spectacular 20,320-foot Mount

McKinley. It is designed for those who want more than just a glimpse of the Denali wilderness. On arrival day, guests are met at the park entrance and transported to North Face facilities. This 90-mile, 5½-hour "northern safari" features naturalists who give guests an excellent introduction to the park's plants, animals, birds, history, and geology. The leisurely pace allows time for photography and wildlife observation. Grizzly bears, Dall sheep, moose, and caribou are occasionally seen.

North Face Lodge was designed with the atmosphere of a comfortable north country inn with 15 modern guest rooms, a dining room, and a living room, accented by a native stone fireplace. The well-appointed guest rooms have private baths and central heating. Cozy down comforters adorn the rooms' twin beds.

Besides great scenery and magnificent wildlife, you will enjoy good food. Breakfasts and dinners include single choice main entrées, with local culinary traditions, such as lingonberry-topped Swedish oven pancakes, Cousin Jim's barbecued salmon, and mile-high vegetarian lasagne. Guests pack their own lunches from a variety of sandwich fillings, homemade bread, fresh vegetables and fruit, trail mix, and home-baked cookies that are set out each morning after breakfast.

Rates: $265 per night per person   **Wheelchair access:** Dining room only
Credit cards: No   **Pets:** No
No. of rooms: 15   **Smoking:** No
No. of baths: 15   **Senior citizen discount:** No
Directions: 250 miles north of Anchorage, 90 miles west into center of Denali National Park.

St. Paul, Pribilof Islands

NEAREST AIRPORT: Anchorage, Alaska.

LOCATION: Travel via Reeve Aleutian Airways 600 miles to Cold Bay, then north about 300 miles to St. Paul, the northernmost island in the Pribilofs. The islands are approximately 650 miles west of Anchorage and 250 miles north of Dutch Harbor in the Aleutians, directly in the middle of the Bering Sea and 600 miles south of the Arctic Circle.

CONTACT: St. Paul Island Tours, Reeve Aleutian Airways, 4700 W. International Airport Road, Anchorage, AK 99502-1091. (800) 544-2248, (907) 546-2248.

BEST BIRDING: Mid-May to August. Asian specialties mid-May to early June. Bring raingear, hats, and warm clothing. Spotting scopes are a must, as are good binoculars. For a treat, bring your camera with 200 mm to 500 mm lenses, as well as a macro lens for tundra wildflower shots. Here you can approach the cliffs closely for pictures without disturbing the colonies of birds.

TOURS/WORKSHOPS: Guide services are provided as part of the travel package. Informal "workshops" take place over dinner with other birders. Here is a chance to bird by day and converse about birding until late at night.

St. Paul is a small island, 14 miles by 8 miles, with a year-round population of about 500 Aleut natives. Aleuts were originally brought here by Russians during the height of the fur seal trade. In addition to the opportunity to see numerous exciting bird species on the island, you will have a chance to view unusual wildlife. On Crater Hill in the mist you may see the reindeer herd; or you may see an Arctic fox and its pups along the way. The large fur seal males, with their harems and kits, spread themselves out along the shoreline and rocky beaches. The tundra meadows and plateaus are covered with wildflowers, which manage to thrive on volcanic soil that is less than an inch deep.

Over 2 million seabirds visit the island each year. You can easily observe horned and tufted puffins; parakeet, least, and crested auklets; red-legged and black-legged kittiwakes; common and thick-billed murres; red-faced cormorants, northern fulmars, and rock sandpipers. Check here especially for the endangered Eskimo curlew. Other exciting birds to see among the over 220 species that have been identified here on this windswept and Irish-green island are the red-throated, Arctic, and yellow-billed loons; and common, king, and Steller's eiders. Some of the accidentals you might observe are falcated teals, spectacled eiders, far eastern curlews, Mongolian plovers, greenshanks, long-toed stints, Oriental cuckoos, Arctic warblers, Bohemian waxwings, Siberian rubythroats, Japanese hawfinches, and gray-cheeked thrushes.

KING EIDER HOTEL
St. Paul Island Tour, Reeve Aleutian Airways, Inc.
4700 W. International Airport Road, Anchorage, AK 99502-1091
(800) 544-2248

One of the nice things about visiting St. Paul Island on Alaska's Pribilofs is that you do not have to spend a long time debating about which hotel you will choose. There is only one hotel, the King Eider. Its rustic atmosphere adds to the adventure of visiting this remote part of the world. Rooms are cozy and warm, and bath facilities are shared. Pack a robe.

You will not have to consult the *Guide Michelin* or *Zagat's Restaurant Guide* to decide where to dine. Again, it could not be simpler. There is one restaurant, the King Eider. Located a short walk from the hotel, home-style dishes are served each night, with the specialty, halibut, prepared in a multitude of ways. The convenient buffet offers everything from fresh salads, sandwiches, and soup to steak and specialty meat dishes.

Rates: Tour package: $799 plus tax; $1,549 plus tax
Credit cards: Visa, MC, AMEX, Discover
No. of rooms: 4 singles; 19 doubles; 1 room with 1 double, 2 singles; 1 room with 1 double, 1 single; 25 rooms total
Directions: Approximately 5 miles from the landing strip.

No. of baths: Shared bath facilities
Wheelchair access: Very limited
Pets: No
Smoking: Only in the lobby
Senior citizen discount: No

Red-legged kittiwakes

Chiricahua Mountains, Cave Creek Canyon, Portal

NEAREST AIRPORT: Tucson, Arizona.

LOCATION: Near the New Mexican border in southeastern Arizona. The shortest route is from Tucson via I-10 east to US 80 south (at Benson, Arizona) through Douglas, looping back north to Portal (just southwest of Rodeo, New Mexico). Birding is generally good along the road all the way. A more circuitous route is from Tucson to Madera Canyon, then to Ramsey Canyon and Portal via Route 90 to Bisbee, connecting with Route 80 north.

CONTACT: American Museum of Natural History, Southwestern Research Station, Portal, AZ 85632. (602) 558-2396.

BEST BIRDING: May through September.

TOURS/WORKSHOPS: Most are through private tour groups, such as Victor Emmanuel Tours.

The entire Chiricahua Mountains region is an excellent birding area. From desert scrub and grasslands to spruce and fur forest, a broad range of systems support a great diversity of species. Creeks and small ponds provide riparian habitat, with scattered cattle tanks furnishing additional water in this dry land. These mountains are famous for their elegant trogons and reintroduced thick-billed parrots. Common resident hummingbirds in the late spring and summer are blue-throated, magnificent, black-chinned, and broad-tailed; Anna's, calliope, and rufous migrate through.

If you hike up the mountains on the south slope above Cave Creek, a variety of soaring raptors can be seen below, passing over the trees along the water; among them are zone-tailed, Swainson's, and Cooper's hawks as well as prairie falcons. Also look for scaled quail, with their crew-cut headdresses, and Gambel's quail, with their bobbing topknots. Strickland's and acorn woodpeckers are often easy to spot here, as are dusky-capped, brown-crested, and sulfur-bellied flycatchers. Bendire's, curve-billed, and crissal thrashers can be seen in several habitats within the canyon and in the outlying regions around Portal and Rodeo, while Hutton's and Bell's vireos can be observed in the arroyos and the riparian regions. In addition, the western specialty warblers can usually be seen, and 3 tanager species are frequently spotted: the hepatic, summer, and western.

AMERICAN MUSEUM OF NATURAL HISTORY
Southwestern Research Station, Portal, AZ 85632, (602) 558-2396

I had a chance to fulfill some of my research mystery fantasies recently by staying at the Southwestern Research Station of the American Museum of Natural History. I was mildly disappointed that there were no murders to solve, but that was my only regret. It was exciting being at a field research station where scientists from across the nation and overseas come to study many aspects of the incredible diversity of plant and animal life in the Chiricahua Mountains. When the researchers are not in residence, hikers, naturalists, and birders are welcome to stay at the Station.

If you like adult slumber parties, you can stay in one room with four or five single beds and an adjoining bathroom. If you prefer a bit more privacy, you can reserve the room just for yourself. All linens are supplied. After birding, you can take a refreshing dip in the swimming pool.

Meals are served promptly at 7:30 a.m., noon, and 6:00 p.m. You will meet fellow birders, as guests eat family style in the dining room or at outside picnic tables. For hardy early-birds who would rather be birding at 7:30, a cold breakfast of cereal and juice can be arranged with the cook the night before.

There are no telephones for incoming calls. If you cannot be away from the outside world, there are two public telephones available at the Station.

Rates: $92-$96; includes all meals. Tour rates also available.
Credit cards: No
No. of rooms: 13
No. of baths: 13
Directions: Request a brochure or a map.

Wheelchair access: Yes
Pets: No
Smoking: Discouraged
Senior citizen discount: No

PORTAL STORE
P.O. Box 364, Portal, AZ 85632, (602) 558-2223

The Portal Store, Café, and Bed & Breakfast is a small, cozy hostelry set in one of the most beautiful environments in the country. Cave Creek Canyon in the Chiricahua Mountains is a fascinating area of lovely vistas, imposing canyon walls, mysterious caves, and a diversity of plant and animal life that rivals any other in the United States.

The highlight of Cave Creek is having the opportunity to see the elegant trogon. Visitors from around the world travel to the Chiricahuas to see this magnificent bird in its splendid surroundings. You can also enjoy 330 other species of birds, including 14 species of hummingbirds and 12 species of owls.

The Portal Store has a clean, comfortable guest house with six bedrooms. There are spacious separate men's and women's shower rooms. Breakfast is served in the café where guests may choose their own full breakfast from the menu.

Portal Store offers home-cooked meals in the family-owned café, and breakfast, lunch, and dinner are served year-round. If you want snacks or a picnic lunch for birding, come to the Portal Store. You can pick up milk, bread, lunch meats, canned goods and sodas as well as maps and postcards.

Enjoy western hospitality and great birding at Portal, the gateway to the Land of Cochise.

Rates: Single $35; double $45; extra person $10
Credit cards: Visa, MC
No. of rooms: 6
No. of baths: 2
Wheelchair access: Yes
Pets: No
Smoking: Okay
Senior citizen discount: No

Directions: I-10 in Arizona to Roadforks, NM. Turn south on Highway 80. Travel 25 miles, then turn right to Portal and travel 7 more miles.

Mile-High/Ramsey Canyon, The Nature Conservancy

NEAREST AIRPORT: Tucson, Arizona.

LOCATION: Ninety miles south of Tucson in the southeastern corner of Arizona. Drive west from Tucson on I-10 to the junction of Route 90 south. Continue on Route 90 south through Sierra Vista to Route 92 south. Look for Ramsey Canyon Road on your right. Drive about 4 miles to the entrance of the preserve. Good Nature Conservancy shop and information.

CONTACT: The Nature Conservancy, Mile-High Ramsey Canyon, RR #1, Box 84, Hereford, AZ 85615. (602) 378-2785.

BEST BIRDING: April through September. Other very good birding areas are Carr Canyon, the next canyon down from Ramsey, and the San Pedro River preserve on the plain below the canyon. A front-wheel-drive or a four-wheel-drive vehicle is recommended for Carr Canyon Road.

TOURS/WORKSHOPS: Guided tours available by reservation through the conservancy.

One mile high, this tree-shaded, sun-dappled canyon, situated 5,100 feet above the heat of lower elevations, is the hummingbird capital of North America. Outside the cabins on the Nature Conservancy land and on the grounds of the Ramsey Canyon Inn are numerous feeders that attract up to 14 species of hummingbirds, including the who's who of the hummingbird set— broad-billed, white-eared, beryline, violet-crowned, blue-throated, and magnificent (Rivoli's). If you walk up the canyon, which remains green year-round due to the spring-fed creek, you may see red-faced warblers, painted redstarts, and 2 species of southwestern warblers, Lucy's and Grace's.

Across from the visitor center you can see nesting golden eagles, since the conservancy usually has spotting scopes focused on areas of the cliffs where they are known to nest. The sight of a parent eagle spreading its wings as it takes off to hunt for a fledgling makes for a truly good day. Gray, common black, and Harris's hawks may be a challenge to find, but they are here. Bridled titmice, with their striking face patterns, and greater peewees are found at similar altitudes in the canyon. Although they are difficult to locate, sulfur-bellied and buff-breasted flycatchers are easier to identify than most flycatchers.

At lower elevations and along the San Pedro riparian area, you are likely to find vermilion flycatchers and petite, scale-patterned Inca doves as well as shiny black phainopeplas and rufous-crowned sparrows. Check closely for Botteri's sparrows, which sometimes feed with Cassin's sparrows, and if you visit in spring, listen for the song of the varied bunting.

MILE HI CABINS
Ramsey Canyon Preserve, 27 Ramsey Canyon Road, Hereford, AZ 85615
(602) 378-2785

This is your chance to contribute to a wonderful cause and have a birding vacation at the same time. When you stay at the cabins at Mile Hi, all the proceeds go to benefit the Nature Conservancy.

At Mile Hi, there are six comfortable housekeeping cabins nestled along the lovely Ramsey Creek. Each cabin is heated and includes a completely equipped kitchen, and there is a barbecue and picnic area in the cabin yard. Linens, paper goods, and soap are also provided. The cabins are available year-round. You need to plan ahead to stay here because Mile Hi Cabins are booked two years in advance during hummingbird season.

Mile Hi serves as the Ramsey Canyon Preserve headquarters. You are in the perfect spot to get permits for the preserve's trails, learn about the preserve and the Nature Conservancy through interpretive exhibits, shop in the Mile Hi Bookstore, or simply enjoy the beauty of the lower canyon. Staying right in the midst of the preserve makes for an intimate experience.

Rates: Double $60; 1-bedroom cabin $60; 2-bedroom cabin $70
Credit cards: Visa, MC
No. of rooms: 6 cabins (housekeeping provided)
No. of baths: 6
Wheelchair access: No
Pets: No
Smoking: Discouraged
Senior citizen discount: No

Directions: From I-10, take S.R. 90 to Sierra Vista, continue south on bypass to S.R. 92, go south on S.R. 92 to Ramsey Canyon Road, go west 4 miles to preserve entrance (10 miles from Sierra Vista).

RAMSEY CANYON INN
85 Ramsey Canyon Road, Box 85, Hereford, AZ 85615, (602) 378-3010

"I live in a bird-watcher's paradise made for people who love nature and hiking," says Shirlene Milligan, the innkeeper of Ramsey Canyon Inn. She has reason to boast. Ramsey Canyon Inn is located in one of the prime birding regions in the country. Bird-watchers flock to this area because more species of hummingbirds have been recorded here than anywhere else in the

United States. The hummingbird population is very much in evidence in Shirlene's yard; a multitude of feeders hanging from the patio attract blue-throated and magnificent hummingbirds. Their brilliant rainbows of color were in evidence everywhere.

Milligan is a member of the Ramsey Canyon Preserve and the National Audubon Society. She could hardly help but love birds in this exquisite setting. Situated on a winding mountain stream and surrounded by large sycamore, maple, juniper, oak, and pine trees, Ramsey Canyon Inn is the perfect place to add hummingbirds to a life list.

In some circles, Milligan is known as the pie woman. She has won more than 100 blue ribbons at county fairs from Kenai Peninsula, Alaska, to her hometown Cochise County Fair. The day I was there she baked a blackberry and a coconut custard. Of course, I had to sample both.

As you might expect, breakfast is a treat. I relished the homemade bread and jams and jellies from Milligan's orchard. But bird-watchers need a big breakfast to get them through a long day of birding. How about Dutch pancakes with sliced strawberries and whipped cream? Or cooked apples, peaches, and blueberries? Or cranberry-pecan or banana muffins?

You will have a humming good time at this bird haven.

Rates: $75-$105 per couple
Credit cards: No
No. of rooms: 6 rooms and 2 house-keeping cottages
No. of baths: 6 and 2

Wheelchair access: No
Pets: No
Smoking: Restricted to patio
Senior citizen discount: No

Directions: From Sierra Vista, take Highway 92 south to Ramsey Canyon Road (approx. 6 miles), turn right, go 3.5 miles to the inn.

Wapanocca National Wildlife Refuge

NEAREST AIRPORT: Memphis, Tennessee.

LOCATION: About 4 miles west of the Mississippi River in the northeast corner of Arkansas near Turrell, Tennessee. To reach the refuge from Memphis, about 50 miles away, drive west and north on I-55 to Highway 42, and take the Turrell exit. From Little Rock, Arkansas, take I-40 east 120 miles to the junction of I-55, then proceed north as above.

CONTACT: Wapanocca National Wildlife Refuge, P.O. Box 279, Turrell, AR 72384. (501) 343-2594.

BEST BIRDING: Spring, fall, and winter. Other excellent birding farther north on I-55 at Big Lake National Wildlife Refuge near Blytheville, about 50 miles away.

TOURS/WORKSHOPS: Contact refuge manager.

The refuge lies in the Arkansas Delta area. Once a hunting club amid farmlands, the 5,500-acre refuge is an important staging and feeding area for the north and south migrations and for overwintering birds. Sixty percent of the ducks using the refuge are mallards; the remaining 40 percent includes many species that use the Mississippi Flyway, such as gadwalls, pintails, green and blue-winged teals, and ring-necked, black, redhead, ruddy, and canvasback ducks. The shallow Wapanocca Lake is a sure lure, surrounded as it is by cypress and willow swamps. Wood ducks are year-round residents, their tree nesting enhanced by many boxes built and placed by the refuge staff.

As the air becomes cooler, look also for egrets, herons, red-shouldered and broad-winged hawks, shorebirds, gulls, terns, barred owls, yellow-bellied sapsuckers, Carolina wrens, and Kentucky warblers. In the spring, when the winds are softer, many warblers, including the prothonotary, Swainson's, Tennessee, Nashville, northern parula, magnolia, cerulean, and bay-breasted, use bottomland hardwood forests. Common in spring also are cardinals, bobolinks, orchard and northern orioles, scarlet and summer tanagers, indigo buntings, American goldfinches, golden plovers, least sandpipers, short-billed dowitchers, bobwhite quail, and an occasional Mississippi kite.

THE SNOWDEN HOUSE
Box 486, Hughes, AR 72348, (501) 339-3414/339-2703

The Snowden House is only three miles from the Mississippi River and the Mississippi Flyway. Wonderful migratory birds visit the area, and owner Polly Brown told me that she frequently has white pelicans in the front yard. The old plantation-style house, built in 1919, was constructed in the Louisiana River style with wrought iron trimming. Guests enter a very large entry hall featuring a chandelier alleged to be from Napoleon's palace. There are three bedrooms, each with a private bath.

The Snowden House is the place for weary city dwellers to get away from it all. As Brown explains, "It's peaceful and quiet, out in the country. We are not fairly rural, we're very, very rural." Country living has wonderful advantages such as the beautiful natural wooded grounds around the bed and breakfast. There are fragrant magnolias and enormous boxwoods.

Guests are served refreshments on arrival. In the morning, before birding at Wapanocca National Wildlife Refuge, you can look forward to a full country breakfast including egg soufflé, fresh fruit, and homemade breads. "It's not elegant," says Brown, "but it is good country-style food that stays with you." Restaurant dinners are available on Friday and Saturday nights. The kitchen is staffed by a faithful cook who has been with the inn for many years.

For good fishing, boating, and bird-watching, the Snowden House is an excellent choice.

Rates: $70-$75; extra person $10   **Wheelchair access:** Limited
Credit cards: Visa, MC   **Pets:** No
No. of rooms: 3   **Smoking:** Yes
No. of baths: 3   **Senior citizen discount:** No
Directions: Take I-40 west out of Memphis, drive approximately 10 miles to the south exit on Highway 147, continue south on Highway 147 for 17 miles.

White River National Wildlife Refuge

NEAREST AIRPORTS: Pine Bluff and Little Rock, Arkansas.

LOCATION: The refuge, in the southeast corner of Arkansas, can be reached via Highways 1, 17, and 44. From Pine Bluff, drive northeast about 40 miles to Stuttgart, then south and east on Highway 165 to the junction of Highway 1 at Dewitt. Follow Highway 1 to the northern entrance of the refuge. The distance from Stuttgart to the southern portion of the refuge is about 40 miles. From Dewitt, continue south on Highway 165 to the junction of Highway 17 and continue east on Highway 17 to the refuge.

CONTACT: White River National Wildlife Refuge, 704 Jefferson Street, P.O. Box 308, Dewitt, AR 72042. (501) 946-1468.

BEST BIRDING: Spring and fall; overwintering flocks in the winter.

TOURS/WORKSHOPS: Contact refuge manager.

The White River runs through the refuge, joining with the Arkansas River and then flowing into the Mississippi. Parts of the refuge are lands rescued from overuse, now protected and managed for wildlife. The refuge is an average of 10 miles wide and 65 miles long. The habitats here include 101,000 acres of bottomland hardwood forest; 10,000 acres of lakes, streams, and impoundments; and more than 1,000 acres of croplands, which produce supplemental food for the wintering flocks of ducks and geese. Flooding occurs uncontrolled in the refuge, flushing out the lakes and marshes, propagating seeds, and nourishing fish. Wintering waterfowl arrive until December and January, when the peak population averages 225,000 birds. The early morning sounds transport one as the ducks burst from the waters to become silhouettes against the dawn sky.

Bald eagles, often found perched atop trees, are numerous in the winter. Also look for fox and vesper sparrows and the blood-red cardinals. Hermit thrushes, Carolina and winter wrens, Carolina chickadees, horned larks, eastern phoebes, barred owls, and black vultures can all be seen during the fall and winter. Spring is a very active season along the Mississippi Flyway; at this time, you may see shorebirds, gulls, hummingbirds, flycatchers, finches, warblers, and thrushes.

EDWARDIAN INN
317 Biscoe, Helena, AR 72342, (501) 338-9155

"Helena occupies one of the prettiest situations on the river," wrote Mark Twain in *Life on the Mississippi.* Although we do not know much of Mr. Clemens's birding abilities, we do recognize him as an expert on Big River sights and scenery. If your plans include travel to the mid-South, make a journal note of the Edwardian Inn at Helena. It is an enjoyable place to stay while birding at White River National Wildlife Refuge.

Long before Twain extolled the virtues of Helena, DeSoto actually crossed the Mississippi at this point, followed in 1763 by Marquette and Joliet. Trappers and traders came after, and by 1800, the first business, a river terminal, had been established. The county was named for Sylvanus Phillips, an early settler, and the county seat was named for his daughter, Helena. The town is noteworthy for its historical architecture, both antebellum and postbellum. It was the site of a Civil War battle fought on July 4, 1863. Many soldiers are buried in the Confederate cemetery overlooking the river on the north side of town.

In 1904, William A. Short, a cotton broker and speculator, hired the Clem brothers of St. Louis to build this family dream house. He spent more than $100,000 for construction of one of the most elaborate homes in Arkansas. This restored turn-of-the-century, 12-room mansion is a fine example of a melding of bygone tradition and charm with modern comfort and convenience. Each room has a private bath, color television, and telephone. Of special note are the interior architectural features, which include eight working fireplaces and handsome woodwork detailing.

Rates: $44-$60
Credit cards: Visa, MC, AMEX
No. of rooms: 18
No. of baths: 18
Wheelchair access: Yes
Pets: Very small pets only
Smoking: Certain areas
Senior citizen discount: No
Directions: The inn is located on Highway 49 Business.

CALIFORNIA

Big Morongo Preserve, The Nature Conservancy

NEAREST AIRPORTS: Riverside or Palm Springs municipal airports; Los Angeles International.

LOCATION: Approximately 95 miles east of Los Angeles, via I-10, then 10 miles north on Highway 62. Also drive this same route from Riverside.

From Palm Springs, travel Highway 62. Do not miss a trip to the Salton Sea while you are in this area. Take I-10 about 70 miles south and east, then turn onto Highway 111.

CONTACT: Preserve Manager, P.O. Box 780, Morongo Valley, CA 92256. (619) 363-7190.

BEST BIRDING: Year-round, with specialties during the spring.

TOURS/WORKSHOPS: 4-6 weeks prior notice for group tours or workshops; contact preserve manager.

This is an unusual place in the desert canyons of California that should not be missed. The many bird species here comprise an enchanting and improbable grouping. The varied habitat is both home to many and a lure to many that otherwise might ignore the sometimes harsh sands. During migration about 125 species have been observed, including the American redstart and the black-throated blue warbler. Although this is only a 6-mile-long canyon, more than 270 species have been documented. Since this is one of the ten largest oases in the state, there is a vital year-round water supply; cottonwoods, scrub brush, desert washes, and riparian woodlands are found in this varied and wild environment. In their natural habitats, you can see verdins, phainopeplas, cactus wrens, and Cassin's kingbirds as well as red-shouldered and Cooper's hawks. What better sight to find in your binoculars than a vermilion flycatcher or a brown-crested flycatcher?

Migrants in this area include the willow, Hammond's, dusky, gray, and scissor-tailed flycatchers; and up to 29 warbler species have been reported. Hummingbirds also abound, including Costa's, Anna's, and black-chinned. In addition to the many species of birds, there are numerous species of mammals and reptiles to watch for, including desert bighorn sheep, mountain lions, bobcats, blacktailed mule deer, gray foxes, raccoons, black-tailed hares, lizards, skunks, and snakes.

CASA CODY
175 South Cahuilla Road, Palm Springs, CA 92262, (619) 320-9346

If you are looking for relaxation, this is the right place. Casa Cody is a friendly, quiet hotel—fondly reminiscent of the original town of Palm Springs. Rich in romance and in local history, it is the second-oldest hotel in the area. It was founded in the flapper and jazz '20s by the beautiful Hollywood pioneer, Harriet Cody. It is nestled against the spectacular San Jacinto Mountains in the prestigious Tennis Club area, the very heart of Palm Springs Village. Casa Cody is a pleasant place to perch while birding at Big Morongo.

Decorated in Santa Fe style, Casa Cody has 17 ground-level units, consisting of hotel rooms, studio suites, plus one- and two-bedroom suites with private patios. Some accommodations include wood-burning fireplaces and fully equipped tile kitchens. In addition to cable television, air-conditioning, and private telephones, there is the luxury of two pools (where a delightful continental breakfast is served every morning) and a secluded, tree-shaded whirlpool spa. You are going to enjoy this trip, even if you have forgotten your Peterson's Guide!

Rates: $35-$160 depending on season **Wheelchair access:** Yes
Credit cards: Visa, MC, AMEX, **Pets:** Yes
Diners **Smoking:** Yes
No. of rooms: 17 units **Senior citizen discount:** 10%
No. of baths: 18
Directions: 2 blocks west of Palm Canyon and one-half block south of Tahquitz. In the heart of the village.

DESERT VIEW MOTEL
57471 Primrose Drive, Yucca Valley, CA 92284, (619) 365-9706

Looking for clean, comfortable, well-appointed air-conditioned rooms with cable television? Want to bask in the California sun, dip in a refreshing pool? The Desert View may be just what you are looking for.

This motor inn is very close to Big Morongo, one of the best birding locations in the state. It is also easily accessible to restaurants, shops, the Hi-Desert Native Museum, the Hi-Desert Playhouse, the Joshua Tree Railroad Museum, and parks. The Joshua Tree Monument offers a unique opportunity to experience a slice of history and tour of the Desert Queen Ranch. Rangers give free evening campfire programs and lead hikes. Picnicking and night-time star-gazing under incredible clear desert skies are other delightful activities to be enjoyed in the area.

Rates: Single $36.50; double $38.50-
$42.50; extra person $5
Credit cards: Visa, MC, AMEX,
Discover
No. of rooms: 14
No. of baths: 14

Wheelchair access: Yes
Pets: No
Smoking: 7 smoking rooms;
7 nonsmoking rooms
Senior citizen discount: 10%

Directions: 1 block east of Highway 62/247 intersection, then 1 block south on Airway.

OASIS OF EDEN MOTEL
56377 29 Palms Highway, Yucca Valley, CA 92284, (619) 365-6321

This is a comfortable and inexpensive place to stay while birding at Big Morongo. The rooms are spotless, attractive, and well appointed. Air-conditioning, color TV, and full baths are standard features. Other highlights include 24-hour telephone wake-up service, complimentary coffee, tea, and cocoa in the lobby, free weekend continental breakfast in the lobby, direct-dial telephones with free local calls, year-round 103-degree whirlpool spa, heated pool, and special senior citizen discounts.

For nonsmoking guests, the motel offers a number of units; among them the Orient, Ancient Rome, Deep South, Persian, and the Art Deco '20s rooms.

Rates: Single $38.75; double $42.75;
extra cot $5
Credit cards: Visa, MC, AMEX,
Discover, Diners, Carte Blanche
No. of rooms: 39
No. of baths: 39

Wheelchair access: Yes
Pets: Yes ($10 extra per night and
$25 security deposit subject to management approval)
Smoking: Yes
Senior citizen discount: Yes

Directions: Approximately 16 miles north of I-10 on Highway 62.

TRAVELLERS REPOSE
66920 First Street, P.O. Box 655, Desert Hot Springs, CA 92240
(619) 329-9584

A wonderful feature of the Travellers Repose is the panoramic view from each guest's room—from the desert floor to the 9,000-foot mountains.

Choose from three guest rooms. The first, Button & Bows, is decorated in shades of rose and features an iron and brass queen bed. Lace curtains adorn the bay window. The private bath is complete with pedestal sink and pull chain commode. The Pine Room is furnished with a queen cannonball bed, a dresser, and an armoire in honey pine. It shares a bath with the Heart Room, which is decorated in all manner of hearts, with a country theme. The quilt was made by innkeeper Marian Relkoff.

Before heading out for nearby Big Morongo, you can enjoy a continental breakfast of juice, fruit in season, and homemade scones, muffins, and breads. The parlor is open for reading, card playing, or just meeting fellow guests. Tea and refreshments are served mid-afternoon. The pool and spa are open until 10:00 p.m.

Joshua Tree National Monument and the General Patton Museum are within an hour's drive.

Rates: $55-$75   **Wheelchair access:** Limited
Credit cards: No   **Pets:** No
No. of rooms: 3   **Smoking:** Outdoors
No. of baths: 2   **Senior citizen discount:** No

Directions: I-10 to Palm Drive, then 5 miles to (Desert Hot Springs) Pierson Blvd. Turn right, go 3 blocks, and turn left.

Red-shouldered hawk

Elkhorn Slough

NEAREST AIRPORTS: San Jose and Monterey, California.

LOCATION: The slough and the surrounding region is about a 1½-hour drive from the San Jose airport. Travel across the Santa Cruz Grade west to Highway 1 south, and enjoy one of the area's most scenic highways; or drive Highway 101 directly south to Highway 156 west at Castroville. The entrance to the park is at Moss Landing, some 40 minutes north of Carmel and 20 minutes north of Pacific Grove/Monterey. Be sure to bird the entire region, including the areas along Elkhorn Road, the Nature Conservancy Preserve, the Salinas River National Wildlife Refuge, and especially the Moss Landing Wildlife area. All are within an hour drive and well worth the effort.

CONTACT: Elkhorn Slough National Estuarine Research Reserve, 1700 Elkhorn Road, Watsonville, CA 95076. (408) 728-2822 or (408) 728-0560.
Be sure to check which days the reserve and visitor centers are open, as they are not open seven days a week.

BEST BIRDING: Year-round.

Driving up to the visitor center, there is no indication of the varied habitat and birds to be encountered here. For instance, from my own experience I can relate a viewing of what I have come to think of as the porcelain-perfect shrike. I had been walking north toward the old dairy site when I saw, atop a bush, alone on the grassland, a loggerhead shrike so ideal as scarcely to be believed. Its mask was shining in the pearly gray body as it literally seemed to pose with the rays of the western sun full on its chest. I continued the walk and was rewarded by my first sighting of an Arctic loon floating in the banked water. This particular estuary, one of the few left relatively undisturbed in California, is on the Pacific Flyway, and six rare, threatened, or endangered species use the slough and the surrounding land; these are peregrine falcons, clapper rails, brown pelicans, least terns, sea otters, and Santa Cruz long-toed salamanders.
The slough reserve encompasses 1,400 acres, with a total of about 5,000 acres for the entire ecosystem. Of the 267 species in this small area, over 200 can be found on the research reserve. From November through February, one can commonly see red-throated loons, eared and western grebes, surf and white-wings scoters, short- and long-billed dowitchers, wrentits, purple finches, and the lesser goldfinches. In the spring, numerous among the mud flats are common loons, Clark's grebes, cinnamon teals, red-shouldered hawks, California quail, black-bellied plovers, and many shorebirds, such as red knots,

western sandpipers, and curlews. In the summer, the shorebirds are still here, as are black-shouldered kites, Caspian terns, burrowing owls, Nuttall's woodpeckers, Bewick's wrens, and Pacific Coast flycatchers. In fall, many of these species remain because of the mild climate found in this habitat of marshes, grasslands, riparian woodlands, beaches, and sand dunes.

DUNMOVIN
1006 Hecker Pass Road, Watsonville, CA 95076, (408) 728-4154

This quaint old English Tudor home, nestled among flower gardens and redwood trees atop Hecker Pass, offers a panoramic view of Monterey Bay, Salinas, the Pajaro Valley, and Santa Cruz. This is a reasonably priced and convenient place to stay when birding at Elkhorn Slough.

The East Wing (not necessarily a birding analogy) features a queen-size bed amid antiques, many restored by innkeepers Ruth and Don Wakefield. A separate entrance leads to the hot tub in the private garden. Adjoining the East Wing is the blue bedroom, also furnished with antiques and a brass double bed. This room shares the oak bathroom with the East Wing, if necessary. On the west side of the house is a bedroom/sitting room featuring a queen-size sofa sleeper and two extra-long built-in bunk beds. The rattan in this room is a remnant of the Wakefields' years in Hawaii.

The aroma of freshly ground coffee will greet you each morning in the Great Room. You will be served a full breakfast, featuring Ruth's wonderful home-baked goodies.

"At the end of the day, when guests watch the sunset, they can realize why we called our home 'Dunmovin' and why we like to share this special place," the Wakefields explain.

Rates: Queen room $75; double bed $70; sofa bed $65; extra person $20
Credit cards: No
No. of rooms: 3
No. of baths: 3

Wheelchair access: No
Pets: No
Smoking: Outside only
Senior citizen discount: No

Directions: Highway 101 south to 152 west; 7 miles from Gilroy; 7 miles from Watsonville; 10 miles east of Highway 1.

THE GATEHOUSE INN
225 Central Avenue, Pacific Grove, CA 93950
(408) 649-8436, (800) 753-1881

"**S**teinbeck Returns to Pacific Grove." The historic Gatehouse Inn not only offers stunning ocean views but several times a year its hosts present an adventure into the life and work of author John Steinbeck, focusing on the years he lived in Pacific Grove. It was here (just across the street, in fact) that many of his books were written. The marine environment and the colorful population of the Monterey Peninsula were an inspiration for Steinbeck.

The Gatehouse Inn is a restored Victorian summer "cottage" constructed in 1884 for Senator Benjamin F. Langford. The eight unique guest rooms are furnished with period antiques and touches of Art Deco. There are fireplaces, private baths with clawfoot tubs, and queen-size beds with down comforters.

An expanded continental breakfast may be enjoyed beside the downstairs fireplace with other guests or in the privacy of your own room. Tea, wine, and hors d'oeuvres are served each afternoon.

Close at hand are monarch butterflies, whales, sea otters, and bird-watching of world renown. Your birding destination, Elkhorn Slough, is close by. From the standpoints of comfort and area activities, it would seem that the Gatehouse Inn lacks for nothing.

Rates: $95–$170
Credit cards: Visa, MC, AMEX
No. of rooms: 8
No. of baths: 8
Wheelchair access: Yes
Pets: No
Smoking: Limited
Senior citizen discount: No
Directions: From Highway 1, take Pacific Grove/Pebble Beach exit (Highway 68 west). Follow the signs to Pacific Grove. Once in town, continue on Forest Avenue to Central and turn right; go 17 blocks to the Gatehouse Inn.

SEVEN GABLES INN
555 Ocean View Boulevard, Pacific Grove, CA 93950, (408) 372-4341

Robert Louis Stevenson called the Pacific Grove/Monterey area "the greatest meeting of land and water in the world." A charming place to enjoy this magical meeting is the Seven Gables Inn whose spectacular rocky point setting offers dramatic views of the ocean and coastal mountains from every room. The Flatley family will take you under their wing and point you toward Elkhorn Slough where you will enjoy wonderful birding.

Even though this inn is very elegant, it is very relaxing. Every afternoon, tea is served on the sun porch or outdoors on the patio. There are always Nora's homemade goodies—shortbread or perhaps some wonderful fudge—to munch on.

An inn specialty is the generous sit-down breakfast served with classic elegance in the grand dining room. Silver platters of fresh fruit, yogurt, and a variety of homemade breads, cakes, or apple cobbler are served along with fine teas and coffee.

If you are an antique aficionado, you will appreciate the Flatley family's collection of fine European antiques. All the guest bedrooms are bright and sunny, and each has its own private bath. The beds are first-rate, the reading lights are excellent, and the rooms are beautifully appointed. All have attractive sitting areas and ocean views.

If you have time to spare after visiting Elkhorn Slough, take advantage of the scenic wonderland that surrounds you. There is the 17-Mile Drive, Cannery Row and Monterey Bay Aquarium, Carmel-by-the-Sea, Big Sur and Point Lobos, and the spectacular migration of the gray whales (October through March). A special treat is the year-round presence of the frolicking sea otters.

Rates: $95-$185
Credit cards: Visa, MC
No. of rooms: 14 (all with close-up ocean views)
No. of baths: 14
Directions: Fly into Monterey Airport. Easy 15 minutes to the inn.

Wheelchair access: Some
Pets: No
Smoking: No
Senior citizen discount: No

Marbled godwits

Point Reyes National Seashore

NEAREST AIRPORTS: San Francisco or Oakland, California.

LOCATION: Fifty miles north of San Francisco on Highway 1, Pacific Coast Highway, is the town of Inverness. From Inverness, you can reach the Point Reyes Peninsula to the west; the seacoast runs north and south. There is also good birding at nearby Tomales Bay and Bolinas Bay. This drive encompasses some of the most glorious scenery in the world. The Pacific coastline here is wild and beautiful and far removed from the cosmopolitan city of San Francisco. You will pass through the Golden Gate National Recreational Area and Muir Woods, so prepare to bird-watch from the time you leave the airport. If it is autumn, be sure to stop at the Marin headlands to see the hawk migration. Check the local conditions on Highway 1 as portions of the road are sometimes washed away by the winter storms or damaged by mud slides. An alternate route is Highway 101 north to Petaluma; take D Street from Petaluma to the Point Reyes-Petaluma Road.

CONTACT: Point Reyes National Seashore, Point Reyes, CA 94956. (415) 663-8522.

BEST BIRDING: Year-round.

TOURS/WORKSHOPS: Interpretive displays at headquarters, the Bear Valley Visitor Center. Self-guided Woodpecker Trail. Naturalist programs year-round. Check with headquarters for schedules.

Creeping northward on the edge of the Pacific plate, the San Andreas Fault has formed a rift between the mainland and the coast, now called the Point Reyes Peninsula. More than 400 species of birds have been observed in the bays and ocean surrounding this spit of land jutting west 12 miles out into the Pacific. The peninsula measures 26 miles north to south. Weather conditions vary considerably in the region. Coastal areas can be windy, foggy, and stormy, while inland or around the bays the weather may be calm and sunny. The varied terrain of this 70,000-acre national seashore includes chaparral ridges, valleys with laurel trees, forests, meadowlands, cliffs, and islands.

Because of the peninsula's geographic location, many vagrants can be seen here. From April 1 through Thanksgiving, you can observe bird banding at the Point Reyes Bird Observatory. Around the lighthouse rocks in the fall there are numerous brown pelicans; in the spring, migrating common murres, pigeon guillemots, loons, scoters, and possibly tufted puffins can be seen. Snowy plovers nest at Abbotts Lagoon, so tread gently and observe with a strong spotting scope only.

Do not disturb the nesting birds; this is an endangered species. Fall and winter are excellent seasons for observing raptors, 3 species of scoters, owls, peregrine falcons, and black-shoulder kites. There are at least 13 areas specified on the Point Reyes Peninsula for excellent bird-watching. The Christmas count here is consistently one of the highest in the nation. So request the bird list and plan to spend more than one day here at any time of the year.

HOLLY TREE INN
Box 642, Point Reyes Station, CA 94956, (415) 663-1554

The heart of the Holly Tree Inn is a spacious, inviting living room that emphasizes quiet comfort. Overstuffed chairs and sofas upholstered in Laura Ashley prints, books, magazines, and a large brick fireplace provide a relaxed setting for conversation, a complimentary glass of wine, and a chance to do absolutely nothing. The Baloghs are gracious and hospitable and really seem to enjoy their guests. According to Diane, the inn is run like a European inn. The Baloghs live on the premises and do everything they can to make their guests comfortable.

The house has a nice subtle English ambience. The four bedrooms and two cottages are all delightfully different. A popular one is the Cottage in the Woods. Holly Tree is no cabin, however, but instead a private, magical two-room getaway furnished with lovely pear wood antiques. You can luxuriate in an old-fashioned bathtub and enjoy the view of the wooded hillside through a greenhouse window. The king-size bed, polished pine floors, small fireplace, and pullman kitchen add to the charm.

Breakfast is a treat and might typically include freshly squeezed orange juice, fresh fruit, homemade poppyseed bread, and a wonderful asparagus soufflé.

The birding at Point Reyes is sensational. Tom is enthusiastic about all the other activities in his backyard. Point Reyes is exceptional year-round. During January, the Point Reyes lighthouse is one of the best places to watch the gray whales migrate south to their calving grounds. Exquisite wildflowers bloom throughout much of the park in the spring, and Tomales Bay is warm enough for swimming during the summer. The expansive ocean beaches are marvelous for picnicking. Mushroom gathering is quite popular here, as are the miles of hiking, biking, and horseback trails that are enjoyed year-round.

Rates: Single $80; two persons $100-$125 (inn rooms) or $150-$175 (cottages); extra person $25
Credit cards: Visa, MC
No. of rooms: 4 rooms, 2 cottages
No. of baths: 6
Wheelchair access: No
Pets: No

Smoking: Outdoors
Senior citizen discount: Discount of $25 per night for a stay of 2 or more nights midweek (Mon.-Thurs.). Valid September through May. Restrictions apply; not valid during holiday or blackout periods.

Directions: 1 hour north of the Golden Gate Bridge; 1 mile north of the main (Bear Valley) visitor center to the Point Reyes National Seashore.

POINT REYES SEASHORE LODGE
10021 Coastal Highway 1, P.O. Box 39, Olema, CA 94950
(415) 663-9000

There is no need for you to wing it at the magnificent Point Reyes National Seashore. Instead, fly away to the Point Reyes Seashore Lodge, a re-creation of a turn-of-the century country lodge.

This is an upscale, luxurious place where you can enjoy this special corner of northern California. The twenty-one elegantly appointed rooms have private baths. All the rooms have direct-dial telephones, many have fireplaces, most have whirlpool tubs. All the tubs have a tranquil view of the pastoral surroundings and Mount Wittenberg.

If you want to pamper yourself, try any of the three specialty suites, the Sir Francis Drake, Gracia, or Audubon. Naturally I chose the Audubon, which has upstairs sleeping lofts with feather beds, a double whirlpool tub, a wet bar and refrigerator, a fireplace, a deck, and a sofa bed/sitting area. The final sybaritic touch is the continental breakfast delivered to one's room.

If you can actually tear yourself away from all this elegance, there is plenty to do in the area. Besides birding, you can explore the nearby towns; little has changed since the early 1900s. Browse the local shops and discover exciting handcrafted items and local produce. Or meander up the coast to visit the charming fishing villages and enjoy a freshly caught seafood meal. Wander up the road a bit to the scenic Samuel P. Taylor State Park and the giant redwoods.

The friendly folks at Point Reyes Seashore Lodge will be happy to arrange bike rentals and dinner reservations. As they put it, "Our primary concern is your comfort and enjoyment, and to this end, we have created a special place for your visit to a unique area."

Rates: Single $85; double $175
Credit cards: Visa, MC, AMEX, Discover
No. of rooms: 21
No. of baths: 21
Directions: Inn will send map.

Wheelchair access: Yes
Pets: No
Smoking: Limited
Senior citizen discount: 10%

39 CYPRESS
Box 176, Point Reyes Station, CA 94956, (415) 663-1709

The brochure provided by the inn says it all: "Let Thirty-nine Cypress adopt you—you'll feel you have found your own special country home. It's only an hour's drive from the Golden Gate Bridge but a million miles away from the hustle and bustle of everyday life!"

Owner Julia Bartlett provides a truly idyllic country retreat with breathtaking views of the upper reaches of Tomales Bay. Over a substantial breakfast of juice, fruit, eggs, homemade breads, and coffee, she will be glad to brief you on Point Reyes. She is a veritable font of information and an avid environmental advocate, as you will be able to tell from her concern for the birds as well as her concern for health (she cooks only natural, organic foods).

Bartlett will provide maps and point you in the right direction for hiking wooded trails at Point Reyes National Seashore. She will even pack a picnic lunch and offer books on birds and a list of the species.

As *Gourmet* magazine put it, "The thrill of finding Point Reyes is only deepened by return visits, when people there gradually reveal the sudden dramas that punctuate the pervasive calm. The charming guest house is set into a bluff above Tomales Bay north of Point Reyes Station. Julia Bartlett, who ran the natural history program for the Point Reyes National Seashore before turning to full-time innkeeping, lives close to the rhythms of Point Reyes and eagerly shares her knowledge of it. Flora, her prize-winning Australian cattle-dog, believes that Julia opens her former home to guests with the express purpose of providing her with playmates. And indeed it is nearly impossible not to succumb to the sheer fun and vitality of this little English-garden-style Dogpatch."

Rates: $100-$120
Credit cards: Visa, MC
No. of rooms: 3
No. of baths: 3
Directions: Inn will send map.

Wheelchair access: No
Pets: By arrangement
Smoking: Outside only
Senior citizen discount: No

Sacramento National Wildlife Refuge Complex

NEAREST AIRPORT: Sacramento, California.

LOCATION: Delevan, Sacramento, Colusa, and Sutter refuges, which comprise the complex, are located 50 to 90 miles north of Sacramento. Take I-5 northwest to Colusa National Wildlife Refuge, then proceed north to the Sacramento National Wildlife Refuge off I-5, where headquarters for the complex is located. Sutter and Delevan are closed to the public. This entire region along the Sacramento River is good birding terrain.

CONTACT: Sacramento National Wildlife Refuge Complex, Route 1, Box 311, Willows, CA. (916) 934-2801.

BEST BIRDING: Fall (beginning in August) and winter.

TOURS/WORKSHOPS: Group tours can be arranged with two weeks notice by contacting refuge headquarters.

Although hot, humid, and dusty during the summer months, in winter, the Sacramento valley glistens with blue skies and shimmering water. At that time the rice fields, ponds, marshes, and woods are filled with fall migration birds and flocks that spend the winter here. Ducks and geese carefully reconnoiter the land for hunters and will not land unless it is safe (hunting is allowed on special and separate portions of the refuge). The migration begins in August, and by December, the combined number of geese and ducks may exceed one million. At this time you may be one of the fortunate birders to spot the endangered Aleutian Canada goose. These highly managed wetlands and the surrounding area are among the most important wintering sites along the Pacific Flyway.

In addition to waterfowl, you may see black-shouldered kites, golden eagles, and peregrine falcons; white-fronted geese and Ross's geese are abundant in the fall. Tundra swans are common in both fall and winter. The woodpeckers mostly likely observed are the acorn and Nuttall's. Yellow-billed magpies are common, as are tricolored blackbirds. Rarities that might be observed are northern shrikes, Eurasian teals, bald eagles, and red-shouldered hawks. In the right habitat, you can see California quail, black phoebes, and brown towhees. This region is not only rich in birds but also supports many species of mammals, reptiles, and amphibians.

THE HARKEY HOUSE
212 C Street, Yuba City, CA 95991, (916) 674-1942

In the days of the wild and woolly west you might have had second thoughts about reserving a room at the Harkey House: it belonged to the sheriff of Sutter County. Upstanding citizens of today need have no fear. They can experience a distinct combination of Victorian romance and modern comfort at the ca. 1864 inn bordering the banks of the Yuba River.

Innkeepers Bob Jones and Lee Limonoff Jones are waiting to greet you with complimentary beverages. You may sip them by a wintertime cozy fire or under a clear summer sky on the outside patio and pool area.

Oriental rugs, original artwork, and wicker furniture can be found throughout the house. The Harkey Suite will delight you with its elegance. It features a queen-size brass bed, burgundy paisley wallpaper, armoire, remote television/VCR, a stove, and an adjoining library. Lush flowers compliment the guest rooms, and robes are provided.

The residence includes a pool, spa, basketball court, library, art gallery, antique piano, rose garden, and hammock.

A full continental breakfast is served in the glass-paned French country dining room. You'll be in fine shape to bird the day away at Sacramento National Wildlife Refuge.

Rates: Single $65-$90; double $75-$100; extra person $10
Credit cards: Visa, MC, Discover
No. of rooms: 4
No. of baths: 4

Wheelchair access: No
Pets: No
Smoking: On porch and patio only
Senior citizen discount: 10%

Directions: 50 minutes drive north of Sacramento; 2 hours from San Francisco; 2 hours from Lake Tahoe.

THE INN AT SHALLOW CREEK FARM
Country Road DD, Route 3, Box 3176, Orland, CA 95963, (916) 865-4093

The Inn at Shallow Creek Farm is a blissful retreat for city-weary folks who crave a serene, rural atmosphere. You will have a chance to play gentleman or gentlewoman farmer at this ivy-covered, turn-of-the-century farm house as you stroll around the 3.5 acres of citrus orchards where chickens, ducks, geese, and guinea fowl roam freely.

Shallow Creek is an inn for all seasons. In the spring, drink in the fragrance of orange blossoms and other lovely flowers. In the autumn, enjoy the colorful foliage and the remarkable flocks of migratory birds. In the winter, watch the orange harvest and indulge in quiet evenings by the fireplace. Save some time to select almonds, pistachios, honey, olives, kiwis, melons, and citrus from local growers; stroll along quiet country lanes or gaze at the Milky Way with no interference from city lights.

You'll enjoy the old-fashioned hospitality here. A large, airy suite on the first floor offers space and privacy; the two nostalgic rooms on the second floor are perfect for two couples. A separate four-room cottage is a perfect haven from the pressures of the world. It has a wood-burning stove, a queen-size bed, a sun porch, and a full kitchen.

Breakfast features local fruits and juices with home-baked goods served in the formal dining room or on the sun porch.

Rates: $55-75; extra person $15
Credit cards: Visa, MC
No. of rooms: 4
No. of baths: 3
Wheelchair access: No
Pets: No
Smoking: No
Senior citizen discount: No
Directions: Take Chico/Orland exit from I-5. Go west 2½ miles, turn right on Country Road DD. Go one-half mile, cross low concrete bridge, take next driveway on the right.

WILBUR HOT SPRINGS
Star Route, Williams, CA 95987, (916) 473-2306

For those of you who scorn pampering but want something more permanent than a campsite, the Wibur Hot Springs Hotel will be particularly appealing. Guests bring their own bedding and food and prepare meals in a large country kitchen. You are advised to provide towels, robes, soap, sandals, and a flashlight for moonlight dips in the wooden bathhouse. There three large pools offer soaks in tubs where the water temperature ranges from a gentle 98 degrees to a skin-blushing 112 degrees.

The hot mineral water, which you can partake of in the buff, has been flowing from the earth for thousands of years. Native Americans considered the springs sacred healing ground. In the 1800s, Wilbur was a stagecoach stop for gold-rushers and drew the attention of internationals as a "curing spa."

The hotel, with 19 private rooms, a private apartment, and a group room (housing 18 single beds), is surrounded by a comfortable veranda where guests may take their meals. Also available are pocket billiards, Ping-Pong, badminton, a music area, and a library. The area is surrounded by lakes, rivers for rafting, and hiking and mountainbike trails. Every day of the week Esalen/Swedish massages are available. Should you want Trager, Shiatsu, or Deep Tissue sessions, they can be arranged.

The hotel is a proven sanctuary for those who want a reprieve from life in the fast lane.

Rates: $40-$90

Credit cards: Visa, MC

No. of rooms: 21 private, 1 group

No. of baths: 6 shared bathrooms

Wheelchair access: Yes

Pets: No

Smoking: Restricted

Senior citizen discount: No

Directions: 5 miles north of the intersection of Highways 16 and 20.

Red-tailed hawk

San Francisco Bay Area National Wildlife Refuge Complex

NEAREST AIRPORTS: San Francisco and Oakland, California.

LOCATION: The refuge boundary encompasses the southern end of San Francisco Bay from Redwood City on the west to Alviso at the tip, to the Newark/Freemont area on the East Bay. Oakland Airport is on the east side and north of the refuge. The refuge visitor center is accessible from Oakland Airport on I-880 (Highway 17). You can continue south on I-880 to the Alviso Environmental Education Center for workshops and interpretive displays as well as for bird-watching. To reach the west side, cross the Dumbarton Bridge from Newark to Redwood City and drive either north or south for additional birding areas. If you travel south on Highway 101, be sure to cross the bottom of the bay to the Alviso Slough for excellent opportunities to bird. Travel time in this area will depend on traffic conditions; call the refuge for the best time to drive on the freeways.

CONTACT: San Francisco Bay Area National Wildlife Refuge Complex, P.O. Box 524, Newark, CA 94560-0524. (510) 992-0222.

BEST BIRDING: Fall and winter.

TOURS/WORKSHOPS: Alviso Environmental Education Center has a library, observation tower, trails, and boardwalks for self-study areas. The refuge newsletter, *Tideline*, lists activity schedules for all areas of the refuge. Many tours and field trips are available. (510) 792-4275.

Consisting of 23,000 acres, this is the largest urban refuge in the United States. Habitat for over 281 species of birds, it is critical to the survival of the California clapper rail. Three other endangered species use the bay: the California brown pelican, the California least tern, and the peregrine falcon. Mud flats, salt marshes, salt ponds, and open waters are home to 800,000 water birds, a number that increases to millions during peak migration periods. Throughout the year, you will be able to find eared and western grebes, snowy egrets, black-crowned night herons, lesser scaups, buffleheads, and ruddy ducks. Search carefully for magnificent black-shouldered kites since they look like many of the gulls you will see flying overhead. Along the shores, willets, whimbrels, marbled godwits, dunlins, and sandpipers dance across the sands and mud flats. Gulls that may be appreciated here are the California, mew, Thayer's, glaucous, and glaucous-winged, along with least terns, Caspian terns, and possibly an elegant tern. Snowy plovers can be seen in all seasons; semi-palmated plovers and lesser golden plovers have been observed in all seasons, but they are rare. In the winter, you can see peregrine falcons, greater white-fronted geese, surf scoters, white-winged scoters, sharp-shinned hawks, black-necked stilts, and American avocets as well as herring and Thayer's gulls. Also, it is not unusual to see common barn owls, burrowing owls, and short-eared owls, along with ruddy and black turnstones and red knots. The Audubon Societies in the Bay Area are very active. Contact either the San Francisco or the Santa Clara group for excellent information.

BEST HOUSE BED AND BREAKFAST INN
1315 Clarke Street, San Leandro, CA 94577, (510) 351-0911

The Best House, an oasis in the city, has a rich and colorful history. Built ca. 1880, it was originally the townhouse for the popular San Leandro civic leader, Joseph Dumont. In 1886, Dumont sold his house to pioneer Daniel Best, who developed the most popular agricultural tractor of the day. This machine became the model for the now internationally known Caterpillar tractor.

Each of the five bedrooms in this interesting house has its own unique personality. Donna's Room has an Art Nouveau-inspired brass queen-size bed. You can picture yourself at the turn of the century preparing for an evening turn about town in a classic horse-drawn carriage or surrey.

One of the most requested rooms is the Garden Room. From the fluffy quilted bed, you can enjoy a restful view of the meticulously tended garden estate as well as the arbor area, gazebo, waterwheel, and bordering walkway plantings.

Even if you are not on your honeymoon, consider Best's Parlor Bridal Suite. The suite is decorated with a clever mix of bygone period items, all accenting the ornate brass and opal queen-size bed. Completing this once-upon-a-time picture is a marble fireplace and an outfitted private bath with an enclosed marbleized tub.

A full breakfast is served in the dining room. If the weather is typical California sunshine, you can have breakfast in the gazebo, the arbor area, or on the deck outside the dining room.

Rates: $75-$85
Credit cards: Visa, MC, AMEX, Diners
No. of rooms: 5
No. of baths: 5

Wheelchair access: No
Pets: No
Smoking: No
Senior citizen discount: No

Directions: From Highway 880, go east on Davis 2 miles, turn right on Clarke. The B&B is located 1 block to the right, on the corner.

COWPER INN
705 Cowper Street, Palo Alto, CA 94301, (415) 327-4475

Situated at the corner of two tree-lined streets in Palo Alto is the Cowper Inn, a beautifully restored 1896 Victorian house. It re-creates the comfort and elegance of the period's best homes. Inside the parlor you will find several cozy conversation areas, a brick fireplace, and a piano. Each of the 14 bedrooms, uniquely shaped, is furnished with antiques, television, and private telephone.

Breakfasts, featuring still-warm breads, fresh fruits, and other options, are served in the paneled dining room. As in days gone by, sherry is offered in the late afternoon.

Just a five-minute walk away, there are restaurants, theaters, a library, shops, galleries, and a variety of business services. The Stanford University campus is less than a mile away.

Rates: $55-$105; extra person $10
Credit cards: Visa, MC, AMEX
No. of rooms: 14
No. of baths: 13

Wheelchair access: No
Pets: No
Smoking: No
Senior citizen discount: No

Directions: Highway 101 to University Avenue, west; turn left on Cowper, 2 blocks to the inn.

GARRATT MANSION
900 Union Street, Alameda, CA 94501, (510) 521-4779

You do not have to venture far to find a place that is for the birds. At the Garratt Mansion, you are close to the San Francisco Bay Area National Wildlife Refuge, and there is also an estuary at the mansion, which is nestled in the urban community of Alameda, just twelve miles from San Francisco and Berkeley.

This Colonial Revival residence was built in 1893 for W. T. Garratt, a turn-of-the-century industrialist. It has since had several owners and, for fifty of its years, was used as a boardinghouse.

Now that the mansion has been restored, you can see the many lovely architectural features that make this an outstanding example of Victoriana. There are six bedrooms to choose from, three with a shared bath. Gramma's features two twin beds, a window seat, a dressing table, a large reading chair, and a shared bath. The Attic offers a queen-size bed, two large reading chairs, a teddy bear motif, a telephone, and a private bath. The fanciest room is Diana's, which has a queen-size bamboo canopy bed, a fireplace, a sitting room with telephone, and a private bath with clawfoot tub and stall shower.

Other pleasant amenities are fresh flowers, feather pillows, and afternoon cookies. Breakfast is a cheerful affair, with freshly squeezed orange juice followed by a filling and nutritious breakfast.

It is also worth noting that if there are any lovebirds in your group, the mansion is an exceptional setting for an intimate wedding.

Rates: Single $75; double $125; extra person $15
Credit cards: Visa, MC, AMEX, Diners
No. of rooms: 6
No. of baths: 4
Wheelchair access: No
Pets: No
Smoking: Outside only
Senior citizen discount: No

Directions: From Highway 880, take the High Street/Alameda exit, left on High Street, cross bridge, right on Central Avenue, travel 1½ miles, turn left on Union Street.

VICTORIAN ON LYTTON
555 Lytton Avenue, Palo Alto, CA 94301, (415) 322-8555

I received such a charming letter from a friend of mine about the Victorian on Lytton that I cannot possibly improve on it. So here it is, verbatim.

"I have uncovered that rarest of gems—a marvelous bed and breakfast called the Victorian on Lytton. It's positively smashing. Close to the hubbub of Silicon Valley and San Francisco. One short block from Palo Alto's charming shops and street cafés. And, if I'm feeling academic, Stanford University is just across the way about a mile. Ideal, wouldn't you say? Of course, for you, my dear, the birding is terrific at nearby San Francisco Bay Area National Wildlife Refuge.

"The Victorian on Lytton was built in 1895. At the time, it must have been a monstrous old thing—the guest rooms are of immense proportion. Much larger than the shoeboxes one so often finds. Ten rooms in total, each with four-poster or canopy beds, fluffy down comforters, boudoir pillows, and private baths. All are furnished with grand period antiques and are impeccably clean.

"It seems the place was fully restored in 1986. And it's apparent that meticulous care was taken. Absolutely nothing has been overlooked. The English garden is glorious, a perfect respite from the day where I can relax with my books or enjoy the myriad rare and imported flowers and plantings.

"Every detail, right down to traditional Blue Willow china, reflects the charm and understated elegance of Victorian heritage. But of course, the true test of any B&B is in the service. The service I have received is nothing short of regal. Each morning I have been plied with a delightful continental breakfast—in my room! Fresh juices, croissants, teas, coffees. And this pampering is the same for every guest. There is also complimentary port and sherry in the parlor each evening.

"So there you have it. Toss a few things in your valise and steal away for a weekend of unsurpassed hedonistic pleasures. However, the Victorian on Lytton is such a splendid and delightfully charming inn, I may not check out at all!"

Rates: $98-$175
Credit cards: Visa, MC, AMEX
No. of rooms: 10
No. of baths: 10

Wheelchair access: Yes
Pets: No
Smoking: No
Senior citizen discount: No

Directions: From Highway 101, take University Avenue west, go 2 miles, turn right on Middlefield, left on Lytton Avenue, the inn is on the right side. Parking in rear.

American avocet

COLORADO

Alamosa/Monte Vista National Wildlife Refuges

NEAREST AIRPORTS: Municipal airports at Pueblo, Colorado, and Santa Fe, New Mexico. International airports at Denver, Colorado, and Albuquerque, New Mexico.

LOCATION: From Denver/Colorado Springs, drive south on I-25 to Highway 160, then west until about 6 miles east of Alamosa. Turn south on El Ranch Lane and proceed 2 miles to the refuge. Continue west on Highway 160 to reach Monte Vista. From Albuquerque, take I-25 north to Santa Fe and Highway 285 north and east from Santa Fe to Alamosa, then take Highway 160 west to Monte Vista; from there, drive 6 miles south on Highway 15 to the refuge.

CONTACT: Refuge Manager, Alamosa/Monte Vista National Wildlife Refuges, 9383 El Ranch Lane, Alamosa, CO 81101. (719) 589-4021.

BEST BIRDING: Spring (March through May) and fall (September through November).

TOURS/WORKSHOPS: Each March, the twin cities and the refuges hold a crane festival over two weekends. Birding and wildlife workshops and refuge tours are held both weekends. For dates, contact refuge headquarters.

Although these refuges are most noted as a stopover point for sandhill cranes and the flock of fostered whooping cranes in spring and fall, they also support a wide variety of other birds and mammals. As part of the riparian ecosystem of the San Luis Valley (a combined 25,000 acres), they provide protection for the floodplains along the Rio Grande (Alamosa) and managed wetlands for additional habitat (Monte Vista). In spring, you can see white-faced ibis, cinnamon teals, common mergansers, American avocets, black-necked stilts, sandpipers (including an occasional Baird's), Franklin's gulls, band-tailed pigeons, Say's phoebes, violet-green swallows, and sage thrashers. In fall, over 20 species of ducks can be observed, as well as possibly Ross's geese. Common raptors are sharp-shinned, Cooper's, Swainson's, and rough-legged hawks, and occasionally a ferruginous hawk is sighted. Bald eagles are numerous in fall and in winter, and golden eagles are found in suitable habitats. Loggerhead shrikes, yellow-rumped warblers, Audubon's races, western tanagers, Cassin's finches, and Brewer's sparrows are also likely to be seen. Accidentals and rares to look for are ospreys, tundra swans, white-fronted geese, peregrine falcons, and long-eared owls.

While in the area, be sure to visit Great Sand Dunes National Monument to the west and north of Alamosa, where it is possible to hike on the dunes or participate in naturalist activities held during the summer season.

COTTONWOOD INN BED & BREAKFAST & GALLERY
123 San Juan Avenue, Alamosa, CO 81101, (719) 589-3882

Half the reason for picking a bed and breakfast is looking forward to a really outstanding breakfast. At the Cottonwood Inn, you will not be disappointed. As a matter of fact, you will not probably be asking the owner/chef, Julie Modecai-Sellman, for her wonderful recipes.

Entrées include a delicious eye-opener of green chili strata, fresh peach, German apple, or Swedish pancakes served with homemade rhubarb/strawberry sauce or real maple syrup, crab-spinach quiche, and Southwestern-style soufflé made with fresh-roasted chiles and tucked into a flour tortilla. On the side, you can look forward to raspberry streusel muffins, fresh peach and cream cheese pastry, or blue corn or blueberry muffins. You cannot leave the table until you finish your fruit cup, orange juice, and fresh ground, French roast, cinnamon coffee.

After breakfast, you can relax over your last cup of coffee in the parlor, where you can browse through their library or chat with other guests. Later, you might want to check out the extensive movie library and VCR.

After a day of birding, hiking, biking, fishing, rafting, downhill and cross-country skiing, or riding the Cumbres and Toltec Scenic Railway, you will be ready for a little snack. In your room, you will find homemade chocolate chip or shortbread cookies. In the parlor, you can sip some afternoon wine or soft drinks. Then after dinner, a mint on your pillow awaits you.

The five guest rooms at the Cottonwood Inn are uniquely decorated with comfortable antiques and artwork by area artists.

The Rosa Room features a queen-size white iron bed with hand-painted flowers on the headboard. The bed is covered with a hand-stitched rose-colored quilt in the wedding ring pattern. There is a twin bed and a semi-private bath.

A red-carpeted stairway leads upstairs to four more guest chambers. The Azul Room has refinished pine wood floors with area rugs, a king-size bed, and a private bath. The Blanc Room, with a window looking toward Mount Blanca, displays a marriage between Art Deco and the Southwest. The Verde Room, a cozy attic hideaway, has a queen-size bed, a slanted ceiling, and an antique dresser. The Blanc and Verde rooms share a bath.

Finally, the Apartment Annex, next door to the inn, is a 600-square-foot 1920s apartment offering privacy and space. This charming complex features oak floors, clawfoot tubs, living room, bedroom, bathroom, and kitchen.

The owners, Julie and George Modecai-Sellman, both schoolteachers, are fonts of information about the San Luis Valley and can offer good advice along with their excellent breakfasts. This is an ideal spot to stay while birding at the Alamosa/Monte Vista National Wildlife Refuges.

Rates: Single $52-$71; double $56-$75 **Wheelchair access:** No
Credit cards: Visa, MC, Diners **Pets:** No
No. of rooms: 6 **Smoking:** No
No. of baths: 5 **Senior citizen discount:** No
Directions: From the east: Highway 160 west, right on Fourth Street, right on San Juan to Second Street. From the west: Highway 160 east, left on W Street, right on Second Street to San Juan. From the south: Highway 285 north through Main, which becomes west, then right on Second to San Juan.

GREAT SAND DUNES COUNTRY CLUB AND INN
5303 Highway 150, Mosca, CO 81146, (719) 378-2356

If you really want to get away from it all, try the Great Sand Dunes Country Club and Inn. It is a stunning secluded guest retreat situated at the heart of Colorado's legendary Zapata Ranch, high up in the San Luis Valley. Neighboring the inn is the Great Sand Dunes National Monument, a 55-square-mile swath of towering sand that changes its shape with every breath of wind, its color with every passing hour.

According to the *New York Times* (June 14, 1992), "The Great Sand Dunes Country Club and Inn is the brain child of a Japanese-American architect, Hisayoshi Oata, who is never seen at Zapata Ranch without his 10-gallon hat and boots. Hisa, as he is called by everyone, first came to the valley in 1988 as a self-professed 'burned-out professional.' He was deeply touched by the unspoiled wilderness, and his first look into the black, enigmatic eyes of a wild bison became a spiritual experience that he never got over.

"He envisioned a retreat where he could share his exhilaration with other harried professionals who had lost touch with nature and their own peace of mind. He formed Rocky Mountain Bison Inc. and purchased a 100,000-acre spread that included Zapata Ranch and the adjoining Medano Ranch. He also bought 800 head of buffalo, which he turned loose on his land. The herd has now grown to more than 2,000 head. Hisa's pride and joy is his pet buffalo, Amelia, who comes when she is called and follows him around like a dog."

The inn is casually elegant, featuring rough-hewn log cabin-type buildings. Much of the furniture was handmade by Berle, the ranch caretaker and master carpenter, and Barbara Lewis, his wife. There are nice appointments such as kachina dolls, western antiques, handmade quilts, and Navajo rugs.

You can go birding at the Alamosa/Monte Vista National Wildlife Refuges, tour the bison ranch, hike at Zapata Falls, go mountain biking, or stay at the ranch and golf, swim, or take advantage of the health spa.

Rates: Double $170; suite $210
Credit cards: Visa, MC, AMEX, Discover
No. of rooms: 15
No. of baths: 15
Directions: Inn will send map.

Wheelchair access: Yes
Pets: No
Smoking: No
Senior citizen discount: No

Cinnamon teal

Rocky Mountain National Park

NEAREST AIRPORT: Denver, Colorado.

LOCATION: There are two major entrances, one at Grand Lake and one at Estes Park. To reach Estes Park, take Highway 36 to Highway 34; this is about 65 miles northwest of Denver. From Cheyenne, Wyoming, take I-25 south to Highway 34 west. Be sure to check on road conditions and dates when each area of the park is open, as the main road through the park climbs to over 12,000 feet.

CONTACTS: Rocky Mountain National Park, Estes Park, CO 80507. (303) 586-2371 or (303) 586-2385.

BEST BIRDING: Spring, summer, and fall.

TOURS/WORKSHOPS: This park offers a full range of hikes, educational tours, and workshops, one of which is called "Hummingbirds to Eagles." In the summer, credit courses are available through the seminar coordinator, Rocky Mountain Nature Association, Estes Park, CO 80517, (303) 586-3565. Park-sponsored events are listed in the park newspaper, which can be ordered at the contact phone numbers.

Rocky Mountain National Park straddles the Continental Divide and includes many diverse habitats: marsh, forest, meadow, mixed wood and tundra, riparian, and shrub and bush.

Of special interest to bird observers are white-tailed ptarmigans, which are year-round residents here. In summer and winter, you can find blue grouse. Other residents in this more than 242,000-acre park are gray jays, dippers, pygmy nuthatches, and black-capped and mountain chickadees. Amid the riot of summer wildflowers on wide meadows will appear numerous sparrows, larks, broad-tailed hummingbirds, and woodpeckers. The tundra area supports water pipits, while western screech owls and green-tailed towhees inhabit the shrubs and bushes. The astute observer can see Cassin's finches and western tanagers in the forests and elsewhere, swallows, vireos, thrushes, flycatchers, warblers, and wrens. Raptors fly along the ridges and over the flatlands where prey is plentiful, and there are numerous owls in the coniferous forests and mixed wood regions.

THE ANNIVERSARY INN
1060 Mary's Lake Road, Moraine Route, Estes Park, CO 80517
(303) 586-6200

Owners Don and Susan Landwer specialize in romantic getaways for couples. The picture-postcard setting could turn even the most unimaginative types into Romeo and Juliet. The Anniversary Inn is nestled among tall fir and pine trees; in the winter, it is snowcapped like a wedding cake, and in the spring, it is surrounded by a ring of wildflowers.

All the guest rooms are named after Strauss waltzes. Imagine dancing around the upstairs Blue Danube Room gazing through the window at the beautiful mountain view or lounging on the upholstered fainting couch. You cannot help but succumb to l'amour in this room filled with white walls, sloped ceiling, blue wainscoting, and blue, red, and green hand-stenciling.

The Emperor's Room offers a queen-size bed, plum-colored balloon shade, off-white walls, lace curtains, and a private bath. The Vienna Woods room features a handmade pine bed, lace curtains, and antique furniture.

Breakfast is served on the enclosed wraparound sun porch. You will feast on anything from Eggs Benedict to fresh berry pancakes, accompanied by freshly baked muffins and breads and fruits and juices. If you get up early enough, you will wake to the aroma of newly baked bread.

The Anniversary Inn is a wonderful place to just relax. But, remember, you are here to go birding at Rocky Mountain National Park. If you are a non-birding spouse who thinks ornithology is for the birds, you can amuse yourself hiking at nearby Rocky Mountain National Park or Lake Estes, visit the historic MacGregor Ranch, go mountain climbing, horseback riding, rafting, sledding, snowshoeing, downhill and cross-country skiing, or play golf or tennis, shop, or sample neighborhood restaurants.

You can top off an idyllic day enjoying light refreshments before a warm fire.

Rates: Single $75-$115; double $85-$125
Credit cards: Visa, MC
No. of rooms: 4
No. of baths: 4

Wheelchair access: Yes
Pets: No
Smoking: No
Senior citizen discount: No

Directions: Route 36 or Route 34 to Estes Park. Follow Route 36 west through the town, approximately 2 miles to stoplight at Mary's Lake Road. Turn left. Entrance to inn will be 1/10 of a mile on the left.

BLACK DOG INN
650 S. St. Vrain, P. O. Box 4659, Estes Park, CO 80517, (303) 586-0374

There really is a black dog at the Black Dog Inn. She is a black lab named Sara and is, in fact, the namesake. But the inn is clearly people oriented with its sunny family room, large country kitchen, cozy dining room, and comfortable living room where you can relax, read, or watch a movie in front of a crackling fire.

Built in 1910, the Black Dog Inn was one of the earliest homes built in the burgeoning village of Estes Park. It is snuggled among towering pine and aspen on a rolling acre with an expansive view of Lumpy Ridge and the Estes Valley.

The house was remodeled in 1990 by Pete and Jane Princehorn, a Loveland, Colorado, couple who had always wanted to live in Estes Park. The Princehorns enjoy making their guests feel comfortable. They have a nice selection of games, guidebooks, and VCR movies. If you are a budding Vladimir Horowitz, there is a piano at your disposal. The work of local artists adorns the walls. Snacks are available in the kitchen to complement the iced tea and soft drinks.

The Princehorns hope to attract folks who like hearty gourmet breakfasts. A favorite breakfast is hollowed-out baked potato skins stuffed with eggs scrambled with green pepper, mushrooms, and tomatoes, with a dollop of sour cream on the top. Another popular breakfast is homemade bread, melon, juice, eggs scrambled with snow peas, squash, tomato, and mushrooms, and coffee or tea.

The four guest rooms have names in keeping with the surroundings: Mummy Mountain, Bighorn Mountain, Lumpy Ridge, and Mt. Olympus. Mummy Mountain, with an antique queen-sized mahogany bed, Oriental rug, private entry, and private bathroom, offers a panoramic view of Estes Valley and Mummy Mountain. Lumpy Ridge has a cozy courtyard room, an antique queen-sized walnut bed, a reading nook, and a shared bath.

A footpath, running in front of the inn, leads to nearby Estes Park attractions; a public pool, a dinner theater, a golf course, and restaurants are all within walking distance. You may choose to reserve one of the inn's bicycles to tour the town.

Nearby Rocky Mountain National Park offers cross-country skiing, hiking, snowshoeing, backpacking, rock climbing, llama trekking, whitewater rafting, fishing the Big Thompson River or high mountain streams and lakes, and, of course, wonderful birding.

Rates: Double $60-$70; group and off-season discounts
Credit cards: Visa, MC
No. of rooms: 4
No. of baths: 3

Wheelchair access: Yes
Pets: No
Smoking: No
Senior citizen discount: No

Directions: From Stapleton Airport, to Route 36 to Boulder, Lyons, and Estes Park. In Estes Park, Highway 36 to Highway 7, south ½ mile to the inn.

RIVER SONG INN
P.O. Box 1910, Estes Park, CO 80517, (303) 586-4666

Everything about this beautifully designed and decorated bed and breakfast is appealing. For a very special treat, try the Carriage House, which has a huge hot tub in front of a roaring fire. An oversize shower and skylight add to the overall charm.

Another popular cottage is the Indian Paintbrush, hidden among tall pine trees. This getaway is furnished entirely in Southwestern decor and includes handwoven Navajo wall hangings, a love seat, a Jacuzzi, and a queen-size bed suspended from the ceiling by heavy white chains and placed before a rose-tiled fireplace.

You will wake up to the delicious smells of apples baking in nutmeg and cinnamon sauce. A leisurely breakfast might include one of these delectables: corn fritters topped with Vermont maple syrup or apple pandowdy or blueberry cobbler topped with vanilla yogurt.

For a special weekend treat, consider booking an elegant candlelight dinner. You and your one and only will be seated at a beautifully set table with owner Sue Mansfield's heirloom silver, crystal, and china. Celebrated chef and pastry specialist Carol Graham might serve an avocado topped with fresh tomato, red onion, and feta cheese, basil chicken, brown and wild rice pilaf, Japanese eggplant, and amaretto torte. Bring your own gypsy violin, and you will be in for the evening of your life.

At some point, of course, you will want to go birding at the magnificent Rocky Mountain National Park, but you may find it hard to tear yourself away from the River Song. There's plenty to appeal to the five senses at this lovely hideaway, situated on 27 wooded acres next to the Big Thompson River. You can hike through this woodland and talk to elk, deer, eagles, owls, chipmunks, and squirrels, or sit and gather wool at the restful gazebo by the river.

Rates: $85-$160
Credit cards: Visa, MC
No. of rooms: 9
No. of baths: 9

Wheelchair access: 2 rooms
Pets: No
Smoking: No
Senior citizen discount: No

Directions: From Denver Airport, 1½ hours north via I-25. Three miles from south entrance to Rocky Mountain National Park.

CONNECTICUT

Audubon Center/Audubon Fairchild Garden/National Audubon Society

NEAREST AIRPORTS: La Guardia and White Plains, New York.

LOCATION: Northwestern corner of Connecticut at the border with New York. From New York, drive north on I-684 to Exit 3N. Turn north on Route 22, and go to the first traffic light. Then turn right on Route 433. Proceed 2 miles to a stop sign at John Street. The Audubon Center entrance is on your left. The Fairchild Garden is on North Porchuck Road 1 mile from the Audubon Center.

CONTACT: National Audubon Society, Audubon Center in Greenwich, 613 Riversville Road, Greenwich, CT 06831. (203) 869-5272.

BEST BIRDING: Spring and fall; the center is open 9:00 a.m. to 5:00 p.m. Tuesday through Sunday; it is closed on holiday weekends and Mondays. The Fairchild Garden is open daily.

TOURS/WORKSHOPS: See below.

The National Environmental Education Center for the Audubon Society is located here in the midst of 280 acres of open woodlands, meadows, ponds, and streams. It sponsors both local and national programs for visitors as well as for environmental professionals. The summer resident ecology workshop for adults uses the diverse habitats of the sanctuary and garden for hands-on learning experiences. Other adult education programs are conducted at summer camps in Maine, Connecticut, and Wyoming. Other courses offered by the center include natural history, ecology, and nature center planning. Teacher/naturalists are your interpretive hosts as you explore the center, the sanctuary, and the garden.

In the spring and summer, you can walk along the 8 miles of trails surrounded by many varieties of trees, wildflowers, and birds. Bird blinds are located on Mead Lake. Look for blue-winged, black-and-white, Kentucky, and worm-eating warblers; American redstarts, rose-breasted grosbeaks, northern cardinals, and indigo buntings enliven the meadows and forests like small colorful banners. You may also observe stiff-tailed wrens and gravity-defying red-breasted and white-breasted nuthatches, which spiral down the trees hunting for food. Chickadees, tufted titmice, wood thrushes, eastern wood peewees, and bluebirds are other species you may see at various times of the year.

In fall when the leaves change color, it is time for hawk-watching, since thousands of raptors migrate south through the garden and the sanctuary; the best place to view hawks is at Quaker Ridge. Overall, 160 species of birds share this area with 35 species of mammals and 900 species of flowering plants and ferns. Complete maps, trail guides, and plant and animal lists are available at the environmental book and gift shop at the center.

THE HOMESTEAD INN
420 Field Point Road, Greenwich, CT 06830, (203) 896-7500

Set among graceful and noble old trees and sweeping lawns, the Homestead Inn's elegant facade invites the traveler to pause a moment and savor the joys of a simpler time and place. The inn began its life as a New England farmhouse, homestead of Augustus Mead, the judge and gentleman farmer who built it in 1799. In 1859, it was sold to innkeepers, undergoing its change from Colonial to the distinctive "Carpenter Gothic" of the Victorian era.

In 1978, when Lessie Davison and Nancy Smith first saw the inn, it was in total disrepair. Only its grand old bones and indestructible grace remained intact. In September 1979, the stately old structure was reborn.

A welcome addition is LaGrange, the inn's restaurant. The only evidence of its days as a barn are the exposed two-hundred-year-old beams. The restaurant is worth a trip in itself. In this rural setting, Parisian chef Jacques Theibeult, formerly sous-chef at LeCirque in New York City, brings a refreshing contemporary touch to classic French specialties. The excellent wine list enhances his cuisine. A wide array of desserts are prepared daily by the inn's own pastry chef. The Homestead Inn has been described by the *Denver Post* as the best country inn in America and by the *New York Times* as a triple-star dining experience.

There are wonderful nooks and crannies in which to hide away at the Homestead. On summer afternoons, you can curl up with your favorite book on the front porch of the Main House, lean back in the comfortable, blue-cushioned, white wicker settees, or enjoy a little sport in the Backgammon Room, which in winter is warmed by a softly glowing fireplace. You can drop in for a quiet drink at the Chocolate Box.

Each of the inn's bedrooms in the three historic buildings reflects the romance and style of another era. No two rooms are alike; many have canopy beds, and all are decorated in a simple but elegant fashion. The rooms are nicely appointed with antiques but also include such civilized amenities as electric blankets, good "reading in bed" lights, color television, clock radios, and a private bath.

The Homestead Inn is a pleasant environment to enjoy while birding at nearby Audubon Center in Greenwich and Fairchild Wildflower Garden.

Rates: $87-$175
Credit cards: Visa, MC, AMEX,
Discover, Diners
No. of rooms: 23
No. of baths: 23
Directions: ½ mile from I-95, 1 mile from the Merritt Parkway.

Wheelchair access: Yes
Pets: No
Smoking: Yes
Senior citizen discount: No

THE STANTON HOUSE INN
76 Maple Avenue, Greenwich, CT 06830, (203) 869-2110

The Stanton House Inn is a finely proportioned former mansion designed by renowned architect Stanford White. The inn has a rich and varied history. It was built on land granted to the Reverend Richard Sackett when he was pastor of the Second Congregational Church in 1717. Mary A. Seaman and her husband, Charles H., lived in the house until 1899. The house was then purchased by Edward and Susie Brush. The Brushes were prominent and contributed to some of the more interesting buildings in town—the Greenwich Library, Greenwich Hospital, Greenwich Academy, and the Brush Memorial Chapel.

Perhaps the most interesting former occupant was Mrs. Nora Stanton Barney, who bought the inn in 1937. She called it the Stanton House, in honor of her grandmother, Elizabeth Cady Stanton, the noted American feminist and social reformer. For the next quarter century, the Stanton House was a popular gathering spot for travelers and residents alike.

In 1983, Doreen and Tog Pearson restored the inn to its present splendor as a bed and breakfast. Their goal is to provide a comfortable home-away-from-home environment for their guests.

The inn is furnished with period antiques that blend well with Stanford White's classic architectural lines. The 25 bedrooms feature air-conditioning, color television, and telephone. One room has a working fireplace. Twenty-three rooms have private baths, while 2 have a shared bath.

The continental buffet breakfast is served in the dining room from 7:00 to 9:30 a.m. weekdays and 8:00 to 10:30 a.m. weekends and holidays.

If you want to try your wings at activities other than birding at the Audubon Center in Greenwich and Fairchild Wildflower Garden, you are within walking distance of shops and restaurants and a mere 32 miles from the Big Apple.

Rates: Single/double $75-$125; extra person $10
Credit cards: MC, Visa, AMEX
No. of rooms: 25
No. of baths: 25 (2 rooms shower/bath)

Wheelchair access: No
Pets: No
Smoking: No
Senior citizen discount: No

Directions: From the Merritt Parkway, take Exit 31. Turn toward the Greenwich Business District. Go approximately 4 miles to where the road intersects with Maple Avenue. Turn left and go about 150 yards. The Stanton House is on the right. From the Connecticut Turnpike (I-95), take Exit 4, Indian Field Road. If coming from NYC, turn left; from New Haven, turn right. Follow Indian Field Road for about ¾ mile to the Post Road (Putnam Avenue). Make a left-hand turn and go about 1 mile to Maple Avenue (the Second Congregational Church will be on your right). Make a sharp turn to the right before the church and go approximately 150 yards. The Stanton House Inn is on your left. By train, Manhattan to Greenwich, takes 35 minutes (Metro-North Express from Grand Central Terminal); 24-hour taxi at Greenwich station.

Ten Connecticut Hot Spots

NEAREST AIRPORTS: New York City; New Haven and Hartford, Connecticut.

LOCATION: See below.

CONTACTS: Connecticut Audubon Society, 2325 Burr Street, Fairfield, CT 06430, (203) 259-6305; Connecticut Ornithological Society, 314 Unquowa Road, Fairfield, CT 06430; Stewart B. McKinney National Wildlife Refuge, P.O. Box 1030, Westbrook, CT 06498, (203) 399-2513.

BEST BIRDING: See below. Other good birding areas are found throughout the Stewart B. McKinney National Wildlife Refuge in addition to Milford Point listed below.

TOURS/WORKSHOPS: Write or call contacts.

Milan Bull of the Connecticut Audubon Society has prepared a list of 10 hot spots that will be useful to birding enthusiasts. These birding areas center around four regions of the state. Bull's favorite areas are Milford Point and River Road; the other hot spots listed by him, along with the types of birds to concentrate on at each location, are the following:

Northwest:

1. Nesting warblers and migrants, River Road, Kent. Take Route 7 north to the monument at Kent Center. Turn left on Route 341 immediately. Make a right turn over the bridge onto Skiff Mountain Road. Drive 1 mile and bear right to the road that follows the river. Walk or drive the road.

2. Migrant warblers and wetland species, West Cornwall Road, Sharon. Drive north on Route 7 to the covered bridge in Cornwall. Just 100 feet beyond the bridge, turn left up the hill on West Cornwall Road. Set your trip odometer and drive 2.5 miles and park just before the beaver pond. Walk to the next pond, about 2 miles.

3. Spring and summer land and marsh birds, White Memorial Foundation, Litchfield. From Litchfield Center drive west on Route 202 toward Bantam. Turn left at the sign and bear right to the headquarters building. Detailed maps are available for the varied habitats.

South-Central:

4. Spring migrants and rare nesters, Devil's Hopyard, East Haddam. From Hartford, drive south on I-91 to Route 9. Go south to Route 82 at Tylerville. Cross the Connecticut River to East Haddam. Turn right at the Hopyard sign,

then drive 3.3 miles to the park entrance. Walk the stream edges and trails toward the picnic area and hillsides.

5. Spring and summer rails, water birds, and migrants, Durham Meadows, Durham. From either New Haven or Hartford, take I-91 to the junction with Route 68. Drive east on Route 68 to Durham. Turn left on Route 68 and go to Route 147, then turn left. Continue about 1 mile on Route 147 to the turnout under the power lines.

Coastal:

6. Shorebirds, ducks, terns, hawks, and waders, Milford Point, Milford. From I-95 take Exit 34 to Route 1. Turn right at the traffic light and proceed to Milford Point Road, then turn right. Continue 2 miles past the tennis courts and bear right, then left to the stop sign. Turn right on Seaview Avenue and drive to the sanctuary. Scan the marsh on the right; then follow the path to the beach and west to the point.

7. Migrant warblers and land birds, East Rock Point, New Haven. Take I-91 through New Haven to the Willow Street Exit. Turn right on Willow Street. At the second traffic light, turn right onto Mitchell Drive, and go past the light to the stop sign. Turn right on Livingston Street to East Rock Road Junction, about 0.4 mile. Park in this area.

8. Fall migrants, water birds, and hawks, Hammonasset State Park, Hammonasset. From New Haven take I-95 east to Exit 62 and continue driving to the park. For good birding, observe in and around the cedar trees on East Beach Road, on Willard's Island, and at Meig's Point.

9. Good migrants, winter ducks, and spring and fall shorebirds, Barn Island, Stonington. Driving east from Hammonasset on I-95, exit Highway 1 at Groton and drive to Stonington. From Stonington, head north on Route 1. At the traffic light, turn right onto Greenhaven Road 1.8 miles from the intersection with North Main Street. Take an immediate right on Palmer Neck Road and drive 1.7 miles to the boat ramp and parking area. Bird the impoundments east and west.

Northeast:

10. Northern nesters, winter finches, and ducks, Bigelow Hollow, Union. From Hartford, drive northeast on I-84 to Exit 105/Route 90. Go right on Route 105 for 1.8 miles to Route 171. Turn right on Route 171 and drive 1.5 miles to the park entrance. The trails to the upper and lower lakes are especially good for birding.

THE GRISWOLD INN
36 Main Street, Essex, CT 06426, (203) 767-1776

There is an art to being unique, and the owners of the Griswold Inn have mastered it. Their guest house, at the foot of Main Street, sits on the bank of the Connecticut River in the charming village of Essex. Stepping into this country hotel, you quickly discover it offers much more than comfortable beds, extraordinary meals, and superb drinks.

The inn embodies a spirit of bygone days. It is a kaleidoscope of nostalgic images that may touch you as you warm up to the potbelly stove, peruse myriad Currier and Ives prints, visit a taproom once described as the most handsome barroom in the United States, scan a library of firearms dating from the fifteenth century, or study the historic collection of marine art by Antonio Jacobsen. These can be found in a group of small, inviting dining rooms named Covered Bridge, the Steamboat, the Library, and the Green Room. Marvelous aromas will arouse your appetite. The Griswold Inn is famous for prime rib, seafood, meat pies, and its own 1776 sausages.

There are 25 guest rooms, including standard rooms, petite suites, and luxury suites. All have air-conditioning, private baths, telephones, and piped-in classical music. Some have fireplaces. A complimentary continental breakfast is served to overnight guests.

The Griswold Inn is close to your destination, Devil's Hopyard State Park in East Haddam, Connecticut.

Rates: Double $80-$165; extra person $10
Credit cards: Visa, MC, AMEX
No. of rooms: 25
No. of baths: 25
Directions: Inn will send map.

Wheelchair access: No
Pets: Yes
Smoking: Yes
Senior citizen discount: No

HIDDEN MEADOW
40 Blood Street, Lyme, CT 06371, (203) 434-8360

If you do not believe there are perfect places in this imperfect world, you must visit Hidden Meadow; this is a country home that has, over the years, been owned by a prominent Lyme family, a Broadway actor, and an author specializing in New England historic houses and barns.

Situated in the beautiful Connecticut River Valley, this lovingly restored Colonial house with Georgian entry was built in 1760. It is surrounded by long-established lawns, stately trees, small orchards, a reflecting pool, stone walls, terraces, and a perennial garden. A small barn can accommodate your horse should you arrive equestrian style.

Tim Brossard, a marketing/advertising executive and professional old-house renovator, and his wife, Karen, a United States Pony Club riding instructor, started their B&B in 1991. They love to spoil their guests with fine china, silver, linens, and fresh flowers in a dining room decorated with antiques, chintzes, and still life paintings. They make maps and offer touring suggestions to nearby Old Lyme Village, Essex, Mystic, and Stonington.

With only three bedrooms, each with attached bath, personal, friendly service is given. Homemade bread, muffins, brandied French toast, farm-fresh eggs with country sausage or bacon, pancakes, and walnut waffles are a few of the delightful breakfast offerings.

After a full day at your birding destination, Devil's Hopyard State Park, you will enjoy the late afternoon tea, sherry, or lemonade accompanied by homemade cookies. In July, the Brossards invite you to share their raspberry crop.

Rates: 2 double rooms with private baths (king-sized bed or twins) – $110 each; cot $25; 1 double room, private bath (queen-sized bed) – $90
Credit cards: No
No. of rooms: 3
No. of baths: 3
Wheelchair access: No
Pets: Depends
Smoking: Outside
Senior citizen discount: No

Directions: From Boston/Providence, I-95 south to Exit 70 (Old Lyme) through light at end of ramp, straight across onto Halls Road past another light to next light, which is Route 156. Go right on 156 North. Proceed 2.1 miles to Bill Hill Road on the right. Follow Bill Hill to stop sign. Continue straight 150 yards to Blood Street on the right. Hidden Meadow is the fourth driveway on left. From New York/New Haven, I-95 north to Exit 70 (Old Lyme), turn left at end of ramp onto Route 156 north. Proceed as above. From Hartford/Middletown, Route 91 south to Route 9. Route 9 south to I-95 north. Take Exit 70 (Old Lyme), turn left at end of ramp onto Route 156 north. Proceed as above.

DELAWARE

Bombay Hook National Wildlife Refuge

NEAREST AIRPORTS: Dover and Wilmington, Delaware.

LOCATION: From Dover, drive north on Route 13 to Route 42 east, then to Route 9 at Leipsic. Continue on Route 9 for 2 miles to Road 85, which ends at the refuge entrance, approximately 8 miles. From Wilmington, take Route 13 north to Route 42, then continue as above. Total distance is about 40 miles.

CONTACT: Refuge Manager, Bombay Hook National Wildlife Refuge, RD 1, Box 147, Smyrna, DE 19977-9764. (302) 653-9345.

BEST BIRDING: Spring and fall.

TOURS/WORKSHOPS: Some conducted by refuge staff for groups by request. Check with refuge manager.

Situated on the western shore of Delaware and the eastern shore of Delaware Bay, the 15,000-acre refuge is about three-fourths tidal salt marsh. The Leipsic River flows through the refuge on its way to the bay, and two islands, Kent and Kelly, provide additional protected habitat for breeding and staging during migrations. Other ecosystems are freshwater impoundments, wooded swamps, grass and timber uplands, and croplands that provide supplemental food for waterfowl and migrants. Bald eagles hatch and fledge from March through May, which is also the peak of the waterfowl and shorebird migration. Glossy ibis, snow geese, wood ducks, buffleheads, ruddy ducks, black-bellied plovers, willets, ruddy turnstones, red knots, white-rumped sandpipers, sanderlings, dunlins, and American woodcocks are common. Also look for rails, gulls, barred owls, red-bellied woodpeckers, wood thrushes, and more than 20 species of wood warblers.

Raptors that can be observed here are bald eagles, northern falcons, harriers, red-tailed and red-shouldered hawks, kestrels, peregrines, and ospreys. Mergansers are common, as are the avocets that delicately shovel under the water for food. There is abundant waterfowl throughout November, including tundra swans, teals, American black ducks, gadwalls, wigeons, scaups, and scoters. Veery, blackpoll, and palm warblers, seaside and sharp-tailed sparrows, and white-throated sparrows are all easily observed in the right habitat.

THE INN AT MEETING HOUSE SQUARE
305 South Governor's Avenue, Dover, DE 19902, (302) 678-1242

The Inn at Meeting House Square is a mother-daughter production. Sherry and Carolyn DeZwarte run this small, friendly bed and breakfast. The two-and-a-half-story house built in 1849 is conveniently located across the street from the Delaware State Museum, formerly the 1790 Presbyterian Church, which stood on "Meeting House Square."

Traditional decor features memorabilia collected on family travels. Guests seem to congregate at the swinging bench on the brick-enclosed sun porch. The four rooms, all with private baths, are attractively furnished with antiques. There is one king-size bed, one queen-size. Some of the antiques in the parlor are family heirlooms.

You can arise before 6:00 a.m., drive the 10 miles to Bombay Hook National Wildlife Refuge for some bird-watching, and return to the Inn at Meeting House Square for a wonderful breakfast. The breakfast is worth putting down your binoculars for. You can select your fare the night before from an array of eggs Benedict, French toast with sausage, walnut bread, sticky buns, or blueberry, apple, cherry, or peach French tarts, all with perfectly flaky crusts. If you would like any of these dishes made with low cholesterol eggs, just let your hostesses know.

There is plenty to do in Dover besides birding, and the DeZwartes will be happy to point you in the right direction. Right across the street are the local state museums. From June through September, you can attend the weekend auto races. Every Tuesday and Friday the Amish arrive in their buggies and hold Spences Bazaar, a charming mix of vegetables, fruits, and old and new treasures. You might find the perfect antique for your house or a Christmas present for your neighbor. You are just minutes away from the historical Green of Dover, the Legislative Mall, and many restaurants.

Rates: Single $35-$60; double $42-$68; extra person $8
Credit cards: Visa, MC, AMEX, Discover
No. of rooms: 5
Directions: Inn will send map.

No. of baths: 5
Wheelchair access: No
Pets: No
Smoking: Yes
Senior citizen discount: Yes

Prime Hook National Wildlife Refuge

NEAREST AIRPORTS: Dover, Delaware; Baltimore, Maryland.

LOCATION: South of Bombay Hook National Wildlife Refuge on the coast of Delaware Bay and the Atlantic Ocean, Prime Hook National Wildlife Refuge can be reached by ferry from Cape May, New Jersey, via Cape Henlopen State Park and the city of Lewes. From Dover, Delaware, drive south on Highway 113 to the junction of Route 1 south and to the refuge entrance, about 22 miles. From Baltimore, Maryland, drive east on Route 2, across the bay bridge, and east on Highway 50 to Route 404 until you reach Georgetown. Drive Highway 9 east to Route 1 north and proceed to the refuge entrance. The distance from Baltimore is approximately 80 miles. Other birding areas are Cape Henlopen State Park, 1 mile east of Lewis, and Cape May, New Jersey, across Delaware Bay by ferry.

CONTACT: Refuge Manager, Prime Hook National Wildlife Refuge, Road #1, Box 195, Milton, DE 19968, (302) 684-8419.

BEST BIRDING: Spring and fall.

TOURS/WORKSHOPS: Contact refuge manager. Also Cape Henlopen State Park, 42 Cape Henlopen Drive, Lewes, DE 19958, (302) 645-8983.

The horseshoe crab not only gives life to more horseshoe crabs but its millions of eggs give sustenance to countless shorebirds that descend on the Delaware Bay in spring and early summer. In May and June, the coastal wetlands of Prime Hook are literally overrun by red knots, ruddy turnstones, and sanderlings; semi-palmated, least, and spotted sandpipers; and dunlins and willets. Dowitchers, snipes, and woodcocks, along with plovers and gulls, are also found there.

In this refuge, you can also canoe through 15 miles of ditches and streams for quiet observation of birds and mammals. With over 8,000 acres, primarily coastal wetlands but also freshwater marshes, timber and brush, grasslands, and croplands, many other bird species also find nurturing habitats here. Look for vireos and warblers, thrushes and thrashers, sparrows and finches. In the fall, the large concentrations of waterfowl arrive at the refuge; some use it for temporary staging and feeding, while others remain for the entire winter. Hunting is permitted on the refuge, so check with headquarters for schedules. Look for snow and Canada geese, wood ducks, blue- and green-winged teals, mallards, pintails, and ring-necked ducks. Red-shouldered hawks are common at this time, as are many raptor species migrating south.

THE INN AT CANAL SQUARE
122 Market Street, Lewes, DE 19958, (302) 645-8499, (800) 222-7902

How about this for something off the beaten path? Your own houseboat docked in front of the inn on your own canal. The toney two-story, two-bedroom houseboat offers a lovely living room, a small kitchen, and patio doors that open onto the cool water breezes in the summer. You even have your own view of the canal. What you do not have is noisy neighbors. The houseboat affords total privacy.

If living on the high seas is not for you, you can overlook the water by staying at any of the nineteen rooms that feature balconies. All rooms offer a queen- or king-size bed, eighteenth-century reproductions, and private baths.

Birders will be in seventh heaven as soon as they enter the lobby. There are two giant parrots to serenade you with a variety of sounds. In the summer, they are housed in the outdoor aviary.

Breakfast is casual, with continental fare served in the lobby. Most guests fix themselves trays of fresh fruits, homemade breads, and coffee and sit outside reading the complimentary *Wall Street Journal*.

There is plenty to keep you busy in historic Lewes. One interesting choice is the Zwaanendael Museum. It was built in 1931 by the state of Delaware in memory of the ill-fated Dutch settlement of 1631. It contains permanent and loaned exhibits dealing with the history of Lewes and Delaware as well as Dutch gifts and exhibits.

Lewes is a charming town in its own right. It dates from the year 1631 and has an interesting history. The saying goes that Lewes is to Delaware what Plymouth is to Massachusetts and Jamestown is to Virginia. After their first ill-fated attempt, the Dutch established a trading post at the site, which the British took over in 1682, renaming it Lewes after a village in Sussex, England.

Rates: Double $100-$150; extra person $15
Credit cards: Visa, MC, AMEX, Discover, Diners
No. of rooms: 19

No. of baths: 19
Wheelchair access: Yes
Pets: No
Smoking: Yes
Senior citizen discount: No

Directions: Delaware Route 1 to Route 9 east. Left at Front Street.

KINGS INN
151 Kings Highway, Lewes, DE 19958, (302) 645-6438

Staying at the historic King's Inn is another good reason for visiting Lewes. Built in 1888, it was originally the William F. Marshall House. The high-ceilinged rooms are filled with stained glass and evoke a more elegant, simpler era.

You can enjoy the front porch swing, or rock away your woes on the rocking chairs, curl up with your favorite book on the backyard swing in the wisteria arbor, or play volleyball or badminton in the backyard.

The King's Inn offers a relaxing Jacuzzi bath, video, cable television, and a stereo and classical, operatic, and jazz music collection. The owners, Leon and Patricia Rockett, have thought of your every need.

There are four bedrooms, all with ceiling fans. The largest is the Brown Room, which has a queen-size bed, a brown wicker table and chairs, a reading chair, and a large bookcase full of books bound in yellow, orange, beige, and brown. A favorite room is the Frog Room, so named because of the frog wall-paper. This room is a bibliophile's delight, having once served as the old library. It is crammed full of books and offers two reading chairs.

Breakfast is served in the plant-filled sun room. The inn serves a full Victorian breakfast with fresh-ground Swedish coffee.

First, you will want to go birding at Prime Hook. If you want to explore historic Lewes, the Rocketts can point you in the right direction and tell you more about Lewes' interesting history. You can take a walking tour and see historic houses, ride the Cape May Ferry, or take an excursion to Atlantic City. Other options are beaching, boating, fishing, crabbing, bicycling, antiquing, wind-surfing, and golfing.

Rates: $60 (no bath); $65 (with bath); $75 (triple)
Credit cards: No
No. of rooms: 5
No. of baths: 5

Wheelchair access: No
Pets: Yes
Smoking: No
Senior citizen discount: No

Directions: Route 1 to 5 points; left on Savannah Road parallel to Kings Highway; right on 4th.

THE NEW DEVON INN
Second and Market, P.O. Box 516, Lewes, DE 19958
(302) 645-6466, (800) 824-8751

Before you visit the Chesapeake area, be certain to read James Michener's *Chesapeake*. It will help make the area come alive for you. It was a big influence on Dale Jenkins, one of the owners of the New Devon Inn. As a matter of fact, Jenkins named the inn Devon in honor of the mythological island in *Chesapeake*.

There is nothing mythological or old-fashioned about the service at the New Devon. Each of the 24 rooms is individually decorated with antique beds, fine linens, and fluffy towels. All have hardwood floors. Particularly lovely touches are turned-down beds, chocolates on the pillow, and cordials at the bedside.

The guest parlor, furnished in 1920s Art Nouveau style, was my favorite room. Fortunately, I had a chance to visit it every morning because it is the breakfast area. I enjoyed sitting by the grand piano and quietly reading the paper while sipping my coffee and eating freshly baked pastries and muffins.

The lobby, which has two ornately carved elephant chairs from Taiwan, is another interesting place to relax and read the paper. The downstairs sitting area holds the inn's television. In the same area is a small music room with an antique bellows-operated organ.

The four innkeepers, Julie Diem, Bud Andrew, Dale Jenkins, and Bernard Nash, all know the area well and are happy to give suggestions on what to do and directions on how to get there. They might suggest visiting the small private gardens of Lewes during the annual garden weekend or renting a bicycle and peddling out to the beach.

Rates: Single $60-$95; double $70-$105; extra person $20

Credit cards: Visa, MC, AMEX, Diners

No. of rooms: 24 standard rooms, 2 suites

No. of baths: 26

Wheelchair access: Yes

Pets: No

Smoking: Yes

Senior citizen discount: No

Directions: Follow Savannah Road (Route 9) into Lewes, turn left on Second Street. The inn is located on the corner of Second and Market streets.

FLORIDA

Corkscrew Sanctuary/ National Audubon Society

NEAREST AIRPORT: Naples, Florida.

LOCATION: About 20 miles from Naples (on the west coat of Florida). Drive north on I-75 to exit 17 (Immokalee Road) and follow signs to the sanctuary. Or take US 41 north to County Road 846, then drive east until you reach the entrance.

CONTACT: Chief Naturalist, Corkscrew Swamp Sanctuary, Rt. 6, Box 1875-A, Sanctuary Road, Naples, FL 33934. (813) 657-3771.

BEST BIRDING: Year-round. Check with the Audubon Society for nesting times of storks and limpkins. Summer is green and wet; winter is colder and drier. This is a subtropical area, so bring insect repellent, sunscreen, and a hat.

TOURS/WORKSHOPS: Groups of ten or more, with one-month notice, can arrange a guided tour at no extra charge. There is a nominal admission charge. Contact the National Audubon Society at the sanctuary for information.

If you have never been to Florida, you will be surprised by the intensity of the bright blue skies and white sands; tinted glasses are not a luxury here. Houseplants of the north grow to the size of gigantic trees in the moist, warm soil of Florida, becoming ideal habitats for birds. This Audubon sanctuary is most famous for its nesting wood storks, limpkins, and barred owls; however, almost 200 species of birds use this protected place. In this wilderness swamp the water flows slowly through the wetlands and the largest virgin bald cypress stands in the United States, much as it did before the arrival of Old World explorers.

A boardwalk has been built in the sanctuary, allowing easy but controlled access to the cypress forest and wetlands; most birds can be viewed from this path. Watch for the American anhinga diving for fish or spreading its wings to dry in the sun. The heron family is well represented here, including the little blues, tri-colored, and yellow-crowned night. Glossy and white ibis are often seen on branches above the water, along with the only North American stork, the wood stork. Looking like a bandit when perched and a dancer in flight, the swallow-tailed kite can be observed in the boardwalk area. Throughout the seasons, you can see white-eyed vireos, purple gallinules, prairie warblers, pine warblers, boat-tailed grackles, wood ducks, ospreys, and bobwhites.

INN BY THE SEA
287 Eleventh Avenue South, Naples, FL 33940, (813) 649-4124

There is a wonderful part of Florida that most tourists never see. Hidden behind the condominiums and pink flamingos there exists an old Florida, a return to Southern graciousness, a gentler pace. Such a feeling is perfectly exemplifed in the Inn by the Sea Bed and Breakfast.

Built in 1937 of yellow heart pine, the house that is Inn by the Sea was one of Naples' first guest houses and is now on the National Register of Historic Places. Pine floors and ceilings, tin roofs and ceiling fans, and brass and iron beds all take you back to the good old days.

The inn is only 700 feet from the Gulf of Mexico in a quiet residential neighborhood of quaint "Old Florida" cottages. Surrounded by coconut palms, white bird of paradise and bougainvillea, an orange tree, and many other exotic plants, the Inn by the Sea is a veritable tropical paradise. The interior decor is wicker with cheerful floral print fabrics, making for a light, airy seascape feeling.

The South Florida Chapter of the American Society of Interior Design selected the Inn by the Sea for the site of its prestigious 1989 Designer's Showcase. The place is tastefully decorated with artwork emphasizing seascapes, beach scenes, and, best of all, birds. If you want to take a representative souvenir back home, consider buying one of these objets d'art, most of which are crafted by local artists.

The owner, Elise Sechrist Orban, is a one-woman preservationist committee. She is involved in encouraging the preservation of old homes in Naples and has become absorbed in the interesting history of her own inn. She tries to share her interest in South Florida history by naming each of the guest rooms for a local island. These lyrical names, such as Sanibel, Captiva, Gasparilla, Keewaydin, and Bokeelia, immediately convey a sense of the area's past.

Captiva is cool and refreshing with its white eyelet bedspread superimposed against the green-and-white striped walls and drapes. The ceiling fan gives the feeling of being deep within the tropics.

Breakfast keeps that tropical feeling alive with its fresh vine-ripened fruit, freshly squeezed Florida orange juice, natural cereals, homemade muffins and breads, and imported teas and coffee. You can enjoy this treat on the sun porch or take picnic breakfast down to the beach.

Besides birding on Corkscrew Swamp Sanctuary, there is plenty to keep you busy. You can play golf, tennis, go boating, fishing, sailing, windsurfing, snorkeling, beachcombing, bicycling, shelling, or swimming or try some shopping. For other options, you can visit Sanibel and Captiva islands, Everglades National Park, the Greyhound Race Track, or Thomas Edison's House. If time allows, you might explore the charming seaside community of Naples with its seven miles of fabulous beaches, gourmet restaurants, museums, and art galleries.

Rates: 5/93-12/21/93 – $65-$85;
12/21/93-5/1/94 – $95-$130
Credit cards: Visa, MC
No. of rooms: 5
No. of baths: 5
Directions: Inn will send map.

Wheelchair access: No
Pets: No
Smoking: No
Senior citizen discount: No

Inn by the Sea

J. N. "Ding" Darling National Wildlife Refuge

NEAREST AIRPORT: Fort Meyers, Florida.

LOCATION: From the airport, drive west about 20 miles; take Daniels Road to Summerlin Road and then Route 867 across the causeway to Sanibel Island and continue on the Sanibel-Captiva road. This road stretches along the entire length of the refuge. If you are driving from Fort Meyers, take I-75 south to Daniels Road (15 miles). From Naples, drive north on I-75 or US 41 to the same exit (28 miles), then follow the same directions as from the airport.

CONTACT: J. N. "Ding" Darling, 1 Wildlife Drive, Sanibel, FL 33957. (813) 472-1100.

BEST BIRDING: Fall, winter, and spring.

TOURS/WORKSHOPS: Canoe adventures and birding tours to the barrier island chain: (813) 472-5218. Guided interpretive tours, tram, and canoe: (813) 472-8900. Many nature trails, auto, biking, and hiking. Also contact the Sanibel-Captiva Nature Center for guided tours as well as refuge headquarters for their sponsored programs.

On this 12-mile-long barrier island, sand dollars are scattered along beaches, fish swim among the roots of ancient mangroves bordering the shore, and sunset colors highlight roseate spoonbills flying over to roost for the night. Numerous species of warblers pass through here on their way to more temperate nesting grounds. In the mangrove areas, you should be able to see black-whiskered vireos and Tennessee, blackpoll, and prothonotary warblers. Although shorebird species are very diverse here, perhaps the most exciting thing about this area is the number of year-round species, which include pelicans, anhingas, reddish egrets, mottled ducks, ospreys, red-shouldered hawks, Wilson's and snowy plovers, sandwich terns, mangrove cuckoos, smooth-billed ani, and fish crows.

Some of the species that can be observed in fall and winter are wood storks, American oystercatchers, red knots, white-crowned pigeons, gray kingbirds, and painted and indigo buntings. This is a premier birding area you will not want to miss. There are always surprises here; at the right time and in the right place you may see monk, green, or canary-winged parakeets, roseate terns, black rails, or peregrine falcons.

SANIBEL RESORT GROUP
1539 Periwinkle Way, Sanibel Island, FL 339570-4596
(813) 472-1833/472-1001

The Sanibel Resort Group offers old-style Florida accommodations for you to choose from when visiting J. N. "Ding" Darling National Wildlife Refuge. Here are three affordable, clean, and comfortable places for you to consider.

KONA KAI MOTEL
1539 Periwinkle Way, Sanibel Island, FL 33957-4596, (813) 472-1001

Kona Kai Motel offers motel rooms, efficiencies, and two-bedroom efficiencies, completely furnished, from linens to kitchen utensils. Here you can enjoy cable television and grill out by the large freshwater pool. The convenient location allows you to walk to island shops and restaurants and along the beautiful Sanibel River, which is just a few steps from your room.

Rates: $35-$74 off-season; efficiency $45-$84; rates are seasonal; bird-watchers discount
Credit cards: MC, Visa, AMEX
No. of rooms: 12

No. of baths: 12
Wheelchair access: No
Pets: No
Smoking: Yes
Senior citizen discount: Fall only

Directions: Within 5 miles of Ding Darling; 14 miles west of Ft. Myers.

BLUE HERON MOTEL
642 E. Gulf Drive, Sanibel Island, FL 33957, (813) 472-1206

This quiet resort is hidden among the lush palms across the street from the Gulf of Mexico. Most rooms open onto a screened lanai and pool. Whether shelling or swimming across the street in the gulf or fishing for snook, redfish, or trout off the canal docks, you will enjoy this island hideaway. There is color cable television in the fully furnished air-conditioned rooms.

Rates: $49.50-$116 depending on the season
Credit cards: Visa, MC, AMEX
No. of rooms: 9
No. of baths: 9

Wheelchair access: Yes
Pets: No
Smoking: Yes
Senior citizen discount: No

Directions: Coming off the Causeway, proceed to a 4-way stop, continue on Lindgren Blvd. to a stop sign, turn left on E. Gulf Drive. Blue Heron Motel is on the left.

DRIFTWOOD MOTEL
711 Donax, Sanibel Island, FL 33957, (813) 472-1852

Nestled less than a block from one of the island's most popular shelling beaches, the Driftwood offers easy access to the island's best restaurants and shops. Enjoy central heat and air-conditioning and color cable television.

Rates: Seasonal, $49.50-$165; bird-watcher discounts
Credit cards: Visa, MC, AMEX
No. of rooms: 4, two-bedroom suites
No. of baths: All rooms

Wheelchair access: Limited
Pets: No
Smoking: Yes
Senior citizen discount: Fall only

Directions: 14 miles from Fort Myers. Within 5 miles of Ding Darling.

'TWEEN WATERS INN
Captiva Island, FL 33924, (813) 472-5161, (800) 223-5865

Living up to its name, 'Tween-Waters Inn on Captiva Island is indeed nestled between the waters of the Gulf and the Bay.

Captiva Island is a tropical paradise of beauty, charm, and historical lore. Tucked neatly along Florida's west coast, this friendly island boasts acres of lush foliage, rare tropical birds, and a seemingly endless bounty of seashells. It is an ideal setting for visiting the birding hot spot, J. N. "Ding" Darling National Wildlife Refuge. The biggest draw in paradise, besides the birds, are the spectacular sunsets over the Gulf of Mexico.

At 'Tween Waters Inn, you can choose to stay in the new modern accommodations or in quaint cottages. You can take advantage of the large pool complex and tennis, bocce, and shuffleboard courts or try the surrounding natural waters. The full-service marina provides dockage, and boat, canoe, and even bicycle rentals, along with professional fishing and shelling guides.

The Old Captiva House, a favorite island eatery for over fifty years, serves fresh fish. If you are in a more informal mood, try 'Tween-Waters Crow's Nest, an island pub.

Rates: $130-$255
Credit cards: Visa, MC, Discover
No. of rooms: 126
No. of baths: 126
Directions: Inn will send map.

Wheelchair access: Yes
Pets: Limited
Smoking: Yes
Senior citizen discount: No

GEORGIA

Piedmont National Wildlife Refuge

NEAREST AIRPORTS: Atlanta, Georgia, International; Macon Municipal.

LOCATION: Due north of Macon, Georgia, in the center of the state. From Macon, drive north on I-75 to exit 61 in Forsyth, then east on Juliette Road to the refuge entrance. Or drive north on Highway 11 to Round Oak. At the fire-tower, take the paved road west for 3 miles to the refuge office. Atlanta is 84 miles north of Macon on I-75.

CONTACT: Piedmont National Wildlife Refuge, Rt. 1, Box 670, Round Oak, GA 31038. (912) 986-5441.

BEST BIRDING: Spring, fall, and winter.

TOURS/WORKSHOPS: Contact refuge manager.

In this refuge, Georgia pine, oaks, grasses, open meadows, creeks, lakes, and wetlands have replaced 35,000 acres of land once devastated by deforestation, erosion, and soil depletion resulting from poor farming techniques. Here, the staff has built up and maintains the old growth forest needed for the nesting of the red-cockaded woodpeckers; the Red-Cockaded Trail on the refuge leads to a colony of successful breeding pairs. At Allison Lake, the wood ducks use nesting boxes built for them, and their broods can be seen in spring and summer along the lakeshore. The Little Rock Wildlife Drive, one of the best trails for species variety, takes you through diverse habitats: pond, pine forest, crop-lands, flooded oak stands, and bottom and upland hardwoods. In the spring, listen and look for bobolinks as they join meadowlarks and blackbirds in the fields. The varied species that can be observed at that time also include Bachman's sparrows and orchard orioles. In addition, 19 species of warblers, including the golden-winged warbler, can be seen during migration.

1842 INN
353 College Street, Macon, GA 31201, (912) 741-1842

The 1842 Inn delivers a continental breakfast to your room, complete with flowers and a paper. And in the best European tradition, the inn offers a fine brandy to sip by your bedroom fire before retiring. There is also a turn-down service with imported chocolate mints on your pillow and shoeshines while you slumber.

This Greek Revival antebellum house will give you the illusion of having been transported to a plantation, but the twentieth-century creature comforts will bring you back to reality. There are sound-insulated walls that provide absolute privacy. Blackout linings in the draperies will be appreciated by late sleepers. Some rooms even have a second television to view while you relax in a whirlpool bath.

All 22 rooms offer an eclectic blend of Oriental rugs, fine antiques, and luxe linens and towels. It is a winning combination. The beds are all king- or queen-size period reproductions with custom-made mattresses.

Judge John J. Gresham, cotton merchant and founder of the Bibb Manufacturing Company, built this charming house in 1842. The house has been beautifully restored and features elaborate mantels, crystal chandeliers, graceful columns, and oak parquet floors inlaid with mahogany. The place is elegantly run, thanks to the owner, Aileen Hatcher.

Remember, birding is only a short distance away at Piedmont National Wildlife Refuge. Afterward, you could stroll over to Macon's Historic District, take a walking tour, attend the Cherry Blossom Festival in March, or just sip a mint julep in the Taft State Room at your elegant inn. The message is, "Enjoy."

Rates: $65-$105; extra person $10   **Wheelchair access:** Yes
Credit cards: Visa, MC, AMEX   **Pets:** No
No. of rooms: 21   **Smoking:** Yes
No. of baths: 21   **Senior citizen discount:** AARP 10%
Directions: Exit 52 on I-75 (request brochure for exact directions).

Great horned owl

Savannah Coastal Refuge Complex/ Pinckney, Savannah, Tybee, Wassaw, Harris Neck, Blackbeard, and Wolf National Wildlife Refuges

NEAREST AIRPORTS: For northern refuges, Savannah, Georgia; for southern refuges, Glynco Jetport near Brunswick, Georgia.

LOCATION: Six of the seven refuges in the Savannah Coastal Refuge are along the Georgia coast from Savannah to Darien. The seventh refuge, Pinckney, abuts Savannah National Wildlife Refuge to the east in South Carolina. Typee and Wolf are closed to the public. The largest refuge, Savannah, which is located 4 miles north of Port Wentworth on Highway 17, includes land in both Georgia and South Carolina. From Savannah, drive north on I-95 to exit 19, then to US 17 north. Wassaw Refuge, accessible only by water, can be reached by driving from Savannah to Coffee Bluff or Isle of Hope, where boats can be rented or charters arranged. The Harris Neck Refuge is midway between Savannah and Brunswick via I-95. Take the south Newport River exit 12 to US 17; travel south 1 mile to Highway 131, then east for 7 miles. The Blackbeard Refuge can only be reached by water; boats can be rented at Shellman's Bluff. From Savannah, drive south on I-95 to the Eulonia exit east. At the junction of US 17, drive north to Shellman's Bluff Road and east to the city.

CONTACT: Savannah Coastal Refuge Complex, Federal Court Building, 125 Bull Street, P.O. Box 8487, Savannah, GA 31412. (912) 944-4415 or (912) 652-4415/4416. A partial listing of marinas offering transportation can be provided on request.

BEST BIRDING: Year-round; migration peaks are in spring and fall.

TOURS/WORKSHOPS: Contact refuge complex headquarters.

More than 100 miles of Georgia coastline are protected by barrier islands, many of them wildlife refuges and state parks. Here you can see stately historic plantations and expansive rice fields or walk forest trails and dikes between freshwater impoundments.

In this area, look for woodcocks, hermit and gray-cheeked thrushes, and brown-headed nuthatches. American swallow-tailed and Mississippi kites nest here, as do bald eagles, purple gallinules, barred owls, yellow-throated vireos, and painted buntings. Closer to the coastline and on the islands (Harris Neck, Wassaw, and Blackbeard), winter visitors such as red-throated loons, northern gannetts, greater white-fronted geese, golden eagles, yellow-bellied sapsuckers, and up to 26 species of ducks can be observed. Rich in the natural foods and habitats necessary for a great diversity of species, this region attracts a wide range of residents, including wood ducks, black vultures, ospreys, sharp-shinned hawks, king rails, American oystercatchers, American avocets, ruddy turnstones, black skimmers, red-cockaded woodpeckers, pine warblers, and Bachman's and seaside sparrows. Overall, the complex lists 299 bird species and is active with migrating or resident birds most months of the year. The songbird migration is in March; in April, the shorebirds peak; fall migration occurs in September and October; and the waterfowl population peaks in November. Hunting is allowed on the complex, so also check on those schedules.

BALLASTONE INN
14 East Oglethorpe Avenue, Savannah, GA 31401
(912) 236-1484, (800) 822-4553

There is something about Savannah that exudes charm, hospitality, and those things that represent the best of the old South. The Ballastone Inn typifies the best of Savannah. The minute you walk in the door, you will be handed a glass of sherry. Shoes left outside your door will be polished overnight, and you will find a cozy terry-cloth robe in the bathroom. Every night, chocolates and cordials magically appear at your bedside. The well-trained staff will serve your breakfast at whatever time you choose, in your room, in the double parlor, or in the courtyard. They will arrange everything from restaurant reservations and theater tickets to sightseeing tours and airline flights. With this type of service, you may never want to go home.

Bride and *Glamour* magazines voted the Ballastone one of the most romantic bed and breakfasts in the nation. Paul Newman, who once stayed here, wrote in the guest book, "A delightful slice of the old South. A gentle reminder that all does not necessarily go well with the Yankees."

The ceiling fans, rice poster and canopy beds, marble-topped tables and dressers, chavall mirrors, and comfortable love seats are elegant reminders of the genteel past. Modern conveniences such as air-conditioned rooms, 24-hour service from the concierge, and an elevator have not been overlooked. As the Ballastone brochure promises, if you stay here, you will "return to the romance of the old South."

Rates: $95-$200
Credit cards: Visa, MC, AMEX
No. of rooms: 21
No. of baths: 21
Wheelchair access: Yes

Smoking: Yes
Pets: Small pets only
Senior citizen discount: Depending
on season

Directions: The inn is centrally located in the historic area of Savannah.

THE ELIZA THOMPSON HOUSE
5 West Jones Street, Savannah, GA 31401
(912) 236-3620, (800) 348-9378

There are two things I love about visiting the South: one is the sense of history, and the other is the graciousness. The Eliza Thompson House in Savannah scores on both counts.

According to Civil War lore, the beautiful, red-haired Eliza was one of Savannah's most highly regarded hostesses. Her reputation apparently caught the attention of General Sherman. One story has it that Eliza was one of the reasons Sherman spared Savannah on his infamous "March to the Sea." Another is that Sherman dealt leniently with Savannah to offer it to President Lincoln as a gift. Whatever the reason, you will be glad that this lovely house in this gem of a city was saved.

The graciousness of the Eliza Thompson House is certainly intact. You can imagine yourself in a bygone era sitting in the beautifully landscaped courtyard next to a flowing fountain while taking afternoon tea. You can enjoy civilized conversation with fellow guests during the wine and cheese reception from 5:00 to 7:00 p.m.

The inn is a warm melding of the traditions and charms of the last century coupled with the comforts of today. The blend of old and new is evident in the rich elegance of gleaming heart pine floors and period furnishings combined with the comforts of direct dial phones, color television, and a private bath. This is the best of both worlds.

The main house has twelve stately guest rooms; Miss Eliza's Carriage House contains twelve more rooms. You will be sure to dine in style. Every morning, a complimentary newspaper is provided with the deluxe continental breakfast. Save room for lunch, because one of Savannah's star attractions, Mrs. Wilkes, serves a Southern lunch fit for Rhett Butler.

Rates: $88, $98, $108; extra person
$10
Credit cards: Visa, MC, AMEX
No. of rooms: 25
No. of baths: 25
Directions: Inn will send map.

Wheelchair access: Yes
Pets: No
Smoking: Yes
Senior citizen discount: No

FORSYTH PARK INN
102 West Hall Street, Savannah, GA 31401, (912) 233-6800

You will probably find fancier inns in Savannah but none more cheerful and friendly. Owners Virginia and Hal Sullivan capture the epitome of gracious Southern hospitality. Every evening, they will invite you to join them on the patio or parlor for a visit and offer a nice wine chilled in an elegant silver bucket.

The Forsyth is located in Forsyth Park, Savannah's largest and most opulent park, containing moss-laden oaks, blooming azaleas, scented magnolias, lighted monuments, and a sparkling fountain.

The inn is just a hop, skip, and jump from the historic Riverfront and its antique shops, museum homes, and many good restaurants.

The rooms at the inn take you back to the proper pampered life-style of the landed gentry of the nineteenth century. All nine rooms feature period furnishings with four-poster king- and queen-size beds, unique fireplaces, antique marble baths or whirlpool tubs, and carefully preserved architectural details. Love birds may prefer the private carriage cottage nestled in the courtyard.

Rates: Single $60-$85; doubles $85-$145; extra $15
Credit cards: Visa, MC, AMEX, Discover
No. of rooms: 10
No. of baths: 10
Wheelchair access: No
Pets: No
Smoking: Yes
Senior citizen discount: 10% at certain times of year

Directions: Exit 17A on I-95 onto I-16; go 9 miles to end of I-16; at first traffic light, turn right onto Liberty Street; at next traffic light, turn right onto Whitaker Street; go ½ mile. Inn is on the corner of Whitaker and W. Hall across from the city park.

MAGNOLIA PLACE
503 Whitaker Street, Savannah, GA 31401
(912) 236-7674 , (800) 238-7674

In Atlanta, folks ask, "What's your business?" In Macon, they inquire, "What's your religion?" In Augusta, they want to know what was your grandma's maiden name? But in Savannah, they immediately ask, "What do you want to drink?" Who could not be beguiled by a town with such a charming tradition?

Located in the heart of the city's famed historic districts on fashionable Forsyth Park, Magnolia Place Inn retains the graceful ambience of the original Magnolia Hall. The inn, built in 1878 in the Victorian style of the period, features sweeping verandas overlooking the park and tall windows to capture the afternoon breezes.

Each room is beautifully appointed with English antique furnishings and prints and porcelains from around the world. The butterfly collection in the parlor is famous.

High tea is served every afternoon in the elegant parlor. You will be treated to imported teas, wine, and benne seed cookies. Benne, a type of sesame, is supposed to be a seed of good luck. As you sip your tea, drink in the surroundings of Chinese porcelains and artfully placed pieces of Japanese cloisonné. Note the fireplace, rimmed with hand-painted tiles from Portugal.

All the 13 bedrooms have queen- or king-size four-poster beds, many completely outfitted with canopies and side drapes. Several offer luxurious Jacuzzi baths and working gas fireplaces.

Morning coffee and tea are served from an antique silver service. Continental breakfast is served in the parlor, garden, or veranda overlooking the park.

While you are dining at one of Savannah's fine restaurants, maybe 45 South or the Pirates House, the staff at the Magnolia will be turning down your bed and putting hand-rolled truffles and cordials in your room.

Save some time to stroll around Savannah. As one of our tour guides put it, "Savannah is like a beautiful baby. Everyone loves her."

If you want a perfect birding adventure (not to mention alligators, dolphins, and horseshoe crabs), try naturalist Cathy Sakas's one-day cruises to the magnificent barrier islands. Call Spartina Trails, (912) 234-4621.

Rates: $89-$195   **Wheelchair access:** No
Credit cards: Visa, MC, AMEX   **Pets:** No
No. of rooms: 13   **Smoking:** Yes
No. of baths: 13, some with Jacuzzis   **Senior citizen discount:** No
Directions: 15 minutes east of the airport via I-60; in the heart of the Historic District overlooking Forsyth Park.

HAWAII

The Hawaiian Islands have a very fragile ecosystem, and many areas are closed to the public to preserve the threatened and delicate flora and fauna. Inquire about the restrictions governing those lands that are open, and walk carefully. Good birding ethics are especially necessary here.

Many national wildlife refuges require special use permits for public access. Check before you leave. Nature Conservancy preserves require advance arrangements. Leave mainland seeds and dirt at home; clothing and shoes should be cleaned before setting foot on the islands since nonnative plants are devastating to the ecosystems here.

NEAREST AIRPORT: From the North American mainland, most flights arrive at the Honolulu Airport on the island of Oahu. Commuter flights to each of the other islands are easily available from here.

LOCATION: The largest island lies closest to the equator in a northwesterly curve. The other main islands are, in order, Maui, Molokai, Oahu, and Kauai. Since you will be able to bird Hawaii from just about any location on the island, no specific area is discussed here. You can determine where you want to bird according to your preference for urban or rural locations.

CONTACT: Natural Area Reserves System, 1151 Punchbowl Street, Honolulu, HI 96813. To obtain good general maps of all parks and refuges or for more specific data, contact Division of State Parks, 75 Aupuni Street, Hilo, HI 96720; Superintendent, Hawaii Volcanoes National Park, Hawaii Volcanoes National Park, HI 96718; Division of Forestry and Wildlife, 1648 Kilauea Avenue, Hilo, HI 96720; Hakai Au Forest National Wildlife Refuge, 154 Waianuenue Avenue, Room 219, Hilo, HI 96720; National Audubon Society, Hawaii State Office, 212 Merchant Street #320, Honolulu, HI 96813. (808) 522-5566.

Hawaii's Birds, edited by Robert S. Shallenberger (Honolulu: Hawaii Audubon Society, 1984), lists the following places for good birding on the Big Island.

Marine Birds: Hawaii Volcanoes National Park (coastline and Halemaumau Crater), Kahinahina (dark-rumped petrels), southwest rift of Mauna Loa (dark-rumped petrels).

Water Birds: Waipio and Waimanu valleys, Kaloko Pond, Aimakapa Pond, Opaelula Pond, Hilo Ponds (Waiakea, Lokoaka, Mohouli).

Forest Birds: Hawaii Volcanoes National Park (Olaa Tract, Kalapana Extension, Thurston Lava Tube, Kilauea Iki Trail, Kipuka Puaulu Trail, Manuna Loa Strip Road), Mauna Kea (Pohakuloa, Puu Lauu), Puu Huluhulu (Saddle Road), Upper Hamakua Ditch Trail.

Upland Birds: Saddle Road Ranchlands, Mauna Loa Strip Road, Puu Waawaa, Puu Anahulu.

The islands are a lush wonderland for birds. Along the Saddle Road look over the Ohia Forest canopy for apapanes, iiwis, and amakihis; with careful observation and luck, you might even spot an akepa. In the forests, the flickering reds of omaos and elepaios can usually be seen. You will need permission from the Department of Land and Natural Resources to enter the Puu Laau area; call 933-4221 for information. The dry forest habitat of mamane trees here is the exclusive food source for the palila. The pueo feeds along the road, and you may also catch a glimpse of the Mauna Kea elapaio.

Marine birds frequenting the coastline, ponds, and wetlands include sleek Hawaiian nobody with its white cap, as well as red-tailed and white-tailed tropic bird. The long-legged waders feeding along the shores are Hawaiian stilts, wandering tattlers, Pacific golden plovers, and ruddy turnstones. Hawaiian geese can only be found on Maui and Hawaii, while regal Hawaiian hawks can only be found on the Big Island where they soar gracefully above grasslands in search of prey.

Hawaii Volcanoes National Park

CHALET KILAUEA AT VOLCANO
P.O. Box 998, Volcano, HI 96785, (808) 967-7786
(800) 937-7786 from the mainland

Two very un-chicken-looking bantam chickens—Ramona and Snookums—are the greeters and official mascots for Chalet Kilauea at Volcano, a unique and beautiful bed-and-breakfast inn 1.5 miles from the entrance to Hawaii Volcanoes National Park. These are just two of the birds you will see on the grounds, where bird feeders are liberally placed and the surroundings encourage visitation by feathered friends and humans alike.

Hosts Lisha and Brian Crawford believe in service and it shows, from the attention to detail (monogrammed bathrobes, flowers in every room, and welcome chocolates) to the variety of environments from which guests can choose for their stay. Among the eight units available, the Crawfords offer three theme rooms and one suite. The Continental Lace Room is for the hopeless romantic. Lace curtains, French oil paintings, and wicker furniture make this the ideal room for a honeymoon couple. There is also the Out of Africa Room, filled with baskets, masks, and other African pieces collected during the Crawfords' travels. You could choose the Oriental Jade Room, a delightful space where black, rose, and jade comprise the color scheme and antique Chinese screens enhance the atmosphere. Then there is the Tree House Suite, which includes a two-story unit with a king-size bed and color cable television; you look over hundreds of trees from the upstairs window.

Attention to detail shows in the two-course full gourmet breakfasts served at the Chalet as well. The first course includes juices and fruits of the season, and a second course might be smoked salmon and bagels, Indian curry with grilled tomato, or Hawaiian sweet bread French toast. Top this off with Kona coffee and a selection of international teas and you will be ready for a day at the volcanoes. If you return to the inn between 4:00 and 5:00 p.m., afternoon tea awaits you, and you can top that off with a dip in the Jacuzzi on the premises.

Lisha says that the Thurston Lava Tube in Hawaii Volcanoes National Park is a great birding place, as is Devastation Trail inside the park. She also recommends Bird Park, three miles from the Chalet on the Mauna Loa Strip Road. However, one of the best places to spot the Hawaiian goose, the nene, is on the golf course. Many birds do seem to collect on the courses because of the constant source of water, grass, and probably a spare insect here and there.

The birds are here, the service is here, and the Crawfords are here to offer their corner of the Big Island to you.

Rates: $75-145; extra person $14   **Wheelchair access:** No
Credit cards: Visa, MC, Discover   **Pets:** No
No. of rooms: 9   **Smoking:** No
No. of baths: 7   **Senior citizen discount:** No
Directions: Route 11, between mile markers 26 and 27, turn onto Wright Road (also called Route 148), go ¾ mile to Chalet Kilauea sign. The parking lot is directly beyond on the right.

COUNTRY GOOSE BED AND BREAKFAST
P.O. Box 597, Volcano, HI 96785, (808) 967-7759
(800) 238-7101 from the mainland

The Country Goose Bed and Breakfast Inn is at the gateway to Hawaii Volcanoes National Park. Each guest room is supplied with books on birds, Hawaiian culture, fish, hiking, and volcanoes.

This is a small inn with two rooms, each with a private entrance and bathroom. There is a common area where people can gather and discuss Hawaii and birds. Full breakfasts are served. Owner Joan Earley says some guests have stayed for 15 days, and they have never been offered the same breakfast twice. Given advance notice, she will even bake pizzas for your nighttime journey to the lava flow, just 21 miles from the property.

Your host recommends visiting Hawaii Volcanoes National Park and taking the Mauna Loa Strip Road, which offers great views of old craters as well as an ideal picnic site. She also recommends an excursion to Bird Park, 4 miles from the bed and breakfast, and to Punaluu, the black sand beach. Fresh water flows into the beach area, attracting ducks and geese in addition to saltwater fowl.

Joan is partial to this part of the world. She makes visitors welcome, not only by providing hospitality but by being a font of information. The best part is that she is willing to share it with her guests.

Rates: $65-$125
Credit cards: No
No. of rooms: 2 rooms, 3 vacation rentals
No. of baths: 2 private baths (one in each room); all vacation rentals have at least 2 baths
Wheelchair access: Yes
Pets: No
Smoking: No
Senior citizen discount: 10%
Directions: 2 miles from Hawaii Volcanoes National Park; 26 miles from Hilo; 92 miles from Kona.

East Island

LIHI KAI
30 Kahoa Road, Hilo, HI 96720, (808) 935-7865

Those who are familiar with islands know that on each there is a windward, the windy and frequently rainy side, and a leeward, or dry, side. Visitors to the Big Island are very lucky because the contrasts between the east and west coasts are great and wonderful. To enjoy the lush climate and the wildlife it attracts in the Hilo area, the windward side, visit Amy Gamble Lannan at the Lihi Kai.

Lannan explains that Lihi Kai means "edge of the sea," and her bed and breakfast is right on a seacliff near the famous Honolii surfing beach. A five-minute walk in the opposite direction, across a bridge, is one of the abundant waterfalls in the area. The verdant surroundings wrap you in warmth and freshness. While taking a breakfast of fresh juices, breads, and local preserves on the lanai, you will see cardinals at the feeder and myna birds having "domestic arguments out in the yard." Lannan is happy to tell you which places to explore and where you might find an albino turkey, pheasant, and mourning doves.

The Lihi Kai has two rooms and one and one-half bathrooms available for guests as well as a teahouse enclosed with shoji screens for those who like to sample the more casual island feeling. A swimming pool is also available for vacationers who may want to just stay put for a while. Activities outside the area might include an excursion to Hawaii Volcanoes National Park, 29 miles into the island's interior, or, believe it or not, skiing! This may be the ultimate vacation destination—birding in the morning and surfing or skiing in the afternoon. Take a walk on the edge of the sea and see the real Hawaii.

Rates: Single $45; double $50; $5 premium for less than 3 nights
Credit cards: No
No. of rooms: 2
No. of baths: 1½
Wheelchair access: Yes
Pets: No
Senior citizen discount: No

Directions: From Hilo airport, take Route 11 and turn right (traffic lights); continue on Route 11 until you come to Route 19; turn left and continue until you see second set of traffic lights and veer off to the right onto bayfront highway. You will be on the bayfront instead of Kam Avenue and will be following the oceanfront on your right for about 3 miles. Take first right turn after mile marker 4. When you see a large cemetery on your left (Alae Cemetery), slow down so you can spot Alae Point (Alae on stone wall) on your right. Turn right (Nahala Street) one block; turn right onto Kahoa Road and take second turn down on left; this is still Kahoa Road and a cul-de-sac. 30 Kahoa Road is at the bottom of the street on the right (red birds on the mailbox).

West Island

DOC BOONE'S BED AND BREAKFAST
Box 666, Kealakekua, HI 96750, (808) 323-3231

The drive from the main street of Kealakekua to Doc Boone's is an excursion into a spacious, almost rural residential setting, through neighborhoods and houses belonging to people who appreciate the perfect and peaceful climate. The 2,000 additional feet of altitude keep it warm but not hot during the day and cultivate cool evening breezes.

Another bonus is the many vegetables and fruits almost exclusive to the mainland which can be grown here in addition to the "tropicals." Doc Boone and his wife, Jeannie, have 27 different kinds of fruit and vegetables on the property—apples, tomatoes, pomeloes (a type of grapefruit), guava, papaya, avocados—and they use these deftly in their homemade breakfasts. Breakfast usually begins with a freshly squeezed juice and continues with a lovely bowl of oatmeal. Different breads, made of home-ground ingredients and spread with homemade jams and jellies, are provided each day.

After breakfast, Jeannie or Doc will give you a guided tour of their garden, where you will discover the simple joys of the area. Avid cyclists, the Boones are intimately familiar with the area and can help plan itineraries for the mode of transportation of your choice. On hand in their B&B are books with local information, including books on the birds of Hawaii.

In the evening, your home away from home awaits. Three upstairs rooms and the apartment downstairs offer different settings for different needs. Small groups can be housed in the downstairs apartment, with a private entrance, small kitchen, and bathroom. When I was there, one couple from Canada, another from the eastern United States, and a group of scuba divers returning from Fiji were the occupants.

The Boones enjoy people and sharing their corner of the world and are the consummate hosts for your Hawaiian visit.

Rates: $55, $60, $70
Credit cards: No
No. of rooms: 4
No. of baths: 2
Directions: 20 miles south of the airport.

Wheelchair access: Yes
Pets: No
Smoking: No
Senior citizen discount: No

DRAGONFLY RANCH
P.O. Box 675, Honaunau, HI 96726, (808) 328-2159/9570

Located on the "sunny" or Kona side of the Big Island is a place that exemplifies the fantasies of many mainlanders. The Dragonfly Ranch is that unusual combination of yesterday's pace and today's conveniences wrapped up in a rambling treehouse of the tropics.

Available to guests are four sections that offer different life-styles on the same property. The Redwood Cottage is a complete house with deck, hammock, and double dragonfly swing under a monkeypod tree. A honeymoon suite provides an outdoor waterbed in the midst of lush vegetation with a bay view. It is joined with an indoor room so that you can also "come in from the jungle." For those who yearn for an atmosphere of creativity, the Recording Studio is the place, with its treehouse feeling and view of the meadow and ocean. Each suite includes a wet bar and refrigerator, bathroom, outdoor shower, stereo, and cable television. There are also rooms available in the main house as well as a library with Hawaiiana literature. Leisurely complimentary continental breakfasts are included.

Your hosts will be happy to help you arrange excursions to different parts of the island, including the nearby City of Refuge, great snorkeling at Kealakekua Bay and Captain Cook's Monument, and even a full moon flight over the volcano in the Dragonfly Helicopter. Of course, they can always take you on a walk around the Dragonfly Ranch gardens and provide information on the local bird population.

Many guests of the Dragonfly Ranch will tell you that the 40-minute drive from the Keahole Kona Airport is a drive into a tropical fantasy. It takes time to absorb the wonder. Perhaps this is why the owners offer reduced rates for weekly or longer visits. Perhaps this is also why people return again and again to absorb the smells and sounds and wonder of Paradise.

Rates: $60-$160
Credit cards: Visa, MC
No. of rooms: 6
No. of baths: 6

Wheelchair access: No
Pets: No
Smoking: Outside only
Senior citizen discount: No

Directions: South on Highway 11 to Highway 160, west 1½ miles to bend in road below Wakefield Garden and Restaurant; gate on right with sign of the Dragonfly.

MERRYMAN'S BED AND BREAKFAST
Box 474, Kealakekua, HI 96750 (808) 323-2276, (800) 545-4390

Take two people from Alaska and move them to Hawaii, and what do you get? Two very happy and friendly bed-and-breakfast owners, Penny and Don Merryman. They built their own sunny, cedar home on an acre of land twelve years ago. The wood floors and 16-foot ceilings are features that make the place special. The ocean view adds to the enchantment. The grass surrounding the house is dotted with palms, papayas, passion fruit, and banana trees replete with luscious little bananas. These are attractive not only to visitors but also to the cardinals and finches that frequent the garden. The broader surrounding area is planted in coffee and macadamia nut trees, which gently slope up the mountains from the sea.

The Merrymans provide a fine breakfast with Kona coffee and have a refrigerator available for guests to keep snacks and goodies for the day. They recommend taking the Saddle Road—over the island and through the mountains—between Mauna Kea and Mauna Loa as a good bird-watching trip. It is a less-traveled road that provides spectacular scenery and a view of Hawaii not often seen by mainlanders. They can also point you in the direction of the best snorkeling, horseback riding, and, yes, shopping. This peaceful bed and breakfast on the lush country slopes of Kealekekua is just minutes away from it all.

Rates: Single $55-$75; double $65-$85; extra person $15
Credit cards: No
No. of rooms: 4
No. of baths: 2 rooms with private bath
Directions: 20 miles south of the airport on Highway 19.

Wheelchair access: No
Pets: No
Smoking: Out on deck
Senior citizen discount: No

Merryman's Bed and Breakfast

Waipio Valley

WAIPIO WAYSIDE BED AND BREAKFAST INN
P.O. Box 840, Honokaa, HI 96727
(808) 775-0275, (800) 833-8849 from the mainland

Imagine for a moment that you are living in a 1938 sugar plantation manager's house, lying in a double hammock on the large lanai, and staring across at the cane fields on a perfect day in Hawaii. You can do exactly this if you stay at the Waipio Wayside Bed and Breakfast Inn. Guests are immersed in one of the most historically rich areas on the island of Hawaii.

Just a 10-minute drive on Highway 240 is the spectacular mile-wide Waipio Valley and the nearby Kohala Mountains. This peaceful piece of geography is the traditional home of Hawaiian rulers and was one of the most densely populated sections of the island prior to European settlement. It is brimming with mythology and contains many unexcavated archaeological sites. Birds abound in the Kalopa State Park, a native Hawaiian forest 20 minutes from the bed and breakfast. Owner Jacqueline Horne says that in addition to viewing an abundance of birds, it is not unusual to see wild horses about as you hike on the great trails woven throughout the valley or on the beautiful black sand beach minutes from the property.

Horne offers incredible full breakfasts. She loves to cook and has had so much demand for her recipes that she may publish a cookbook. Her breakfasts might include smoothies made with tropical fruits, waffles, omelets, soufflés, and cranberry muffins and other assorted breads. Although she prepares mostly vegetarian cuisine, she will also cook other meals at the guest's request.

The Waipio Wayside Bed and Breakfast Inn has five rooms available, two with full baths, one with a half bath, and two with shared bathrooms. An ample lanai has double hammocks looking out on one and one-half acres of land, surrounded by cane fields. To end the day, guests can stroll among the orchids and out to the gazebo to watch the sunset.

Horne's property, near the northernmost point on the island, is appealing not only for its historical, agricultural, and wildlife riches but also for its beauty as a little slice of the old Hawaii.

Rates: $50-$95, some restrictions
Credit cards: Visa, MC
No. of rooms: 5
No. of baths: 2 private, 1 half bath, 2 shared
Wheelchair access: Yes
Pets: No
Smoking: Outside only
Senior citizen discount: No

Directions: Northeast of Saddle Road. From Hilo, 55 minutes via Highway 19.

IDAHO

Snake River Birds of Prey Natural Area

NEAREST AIRPORT: Boise, Idaho.

LOCATION: Approximately 35 miles south and west of Boise and 60 miles south and east of Boise. Use Exit 44 on I-84 to Kuna, then take Swan Falls Road south to reach the main entrance.

CONTACTS: Bureau of Land Management, Boise District, 3948 Development Avenue, Boise, ID 83705. (208) 384-3300.

BEST BIRDING: Mid-March through June.

TOURS/WORKSHOPS: Available from local outfitters and guides. Check for rafting and canoeing opportunities on the Snake River for viewing of raptors.

The Snake River Birds of Prey Area encompasses over 482,000 acres of public land along 81 miles of the Snake River Canyon. This ecosystem contains the most densely known nesting population of birds of prey in North America. It is also home to wintering raptors that do not nest in the area. The combination of rugged cliffs, riparian vegetation, and prairie and rangeland above the cliffs provides protected nesting sites and abundant prey species.

The common raven as well as 14 species of raptors nest here in the spring: American kestrels, ferruginous hawks, golden eagles, northern harriers, prairie falcons, red-tailed hawks, Swainson's hawks, burrowing owls, common barn owls, great horned owls, long-eared owls, short-eared owls, western screech owls, and turkey vultures. Good binoculars, spotting scopes, and telephoto lenses are necessary for bird-watching and photography as approaching the nesting areas too closely could prevent the birds from reproducing. Wintering and migrant raptors include bald eagles, Cooper's hawks, merlins, northern goshawks, ospreys, peregrine falcons (rare), rough-legged hawks, and sharp-shinned hawks. Other spring and summer birds that inhabit this region are black-throated sparrows, sage sparrows, lark buntings, yellow-headed blackbirds, rock wrens, canyon wrens, and California quail.

IDAHO HERITAGE INN
109 West Idaho Street, Boise, ID 83702, (208) 342-8066

If you are a history or politics buff, you will want to stay at the Idaho Heritage Inn. The inn was built in 1904 for Henry Falk, one of Boise's early merchants. It remained in the Falk family until 1943, when it was purchased by then-Governor Chase A. Clark. Clark enjoyed a prestigious career in public service that culminated in his appointment as a federal judge. The home was used by the Clarks' daughter, Bethine, and her husband, Senator Frank Church, as their Idaho residence during Church's tenure in the Senate. The home remained in the Clark/Church family until 1987, when it was purchased and lovingly restored by Tom and Phyllis Lupher.

Let the Idaho Heritage Inn take you back to a more leisurely time of grace and elegance when stress was not the predominant word in everyone's conversation. Forget your job and family worries and enjoy the antique fixtures and furniture, interesting items of nostalgia, and fine period wall coverings.

When you enter the inn, you step into the main floor with its spacious, ornate entry, formal dining room, and bright airy sun room, featuring diamond-paned French doors, oak flooring, Oriental carpets, and plentiful, comfortable seating. The sun room provides guests with VCR and television.

All the guest bedrooms have period furniture and private baths. If you are a would-be politician, you will love the names of the rooms: Governor's Suite, Senator's Room, Judge's Chamber, Mayor's Study, and Executive Suite. I fancied myself the gubernatorial type, so I settled into the Governor's Suite with its white wicker rockers, love seat, oak sleigh bed, antique dresser, and enclosed sun porch.

The Judge's Chamber has Victorian furnishings, a private bath, and access to the covered veranda.

Whichever room you choose, you will be pampered by being served breakfast in your room. Your hand-delivered tray will consist of freshly squeezed juice, fresh fruit, oven-warmed breads, such as Phyllis's popular sour cream coffee cake, muffins served with homemade jams and preserves, fresh-ground coffee, and the daily newspaper. In the evening, if you step into the parlor, you can find a goblet of wine, a good book, and some friendly conversation.

The birding is splendid at Snake River Birds of Prey Natural Area. A nearby birding alert: wild geese and ducks make their home year-round at the beautiful Greenbelt on the sparkling Boise River.

Rates: $55-$75
Credit cards: Visa, MC, AMEX, Discover
No. of rooms: 5
No. of baths: 5

Wheelchair access: No
Pets: No
Smoking: No
Senior citizen discount: No

Directions: From I-84, take the Broadway exit north to Idaho Street, turn left on Idaho Street and drive for 2 blocks. The inn will be toward the left.

THE IDANHA HOTEL
10th & Main Street, P.O. Box 1538, Boise, ID 83701, (208) 342-3611

How can you not love discovering a hotel in the middle of Idaho that has a four-star continental restaurant complete with an Austrian chef? Peter Schott's Continental Restaurant in the Idanha Hotel is a visual treasure containing Louis XIV chairs, brass rails, white lace-over-linen tablecloths, bouquets of red carnations, candlelight, and waiters in black-tie. And the food lives up to its surroundings. The wine list is impressive, and entrées include filet of beef Madagascar. For dessert, you might choose fresh blueberries Grand Marnier over French vanilla ice cream. A French-speaking sommelier, soft chamber music, and hot, damp towels for after-dinner hands add to the overall pleasant ambience.

When the Idanha was opened in 1901, it was the state's largest building and the most expensive and elegant hotel in town. Distinguished guests of another era have included Teddy Roosevelt, John and Ethel Barrymore, Buffalo Bill, Clarence Darrow, and Pablo Casals.

The wonderfully restored lobby reflects this age of elegance. The Art Deco chandelier from the famous Astor Hotel in New York, the 1896 brass statue lamps, and the Alaskan marble entrances pay tribute to a simpler and more beautiful life-style.

The exterior of this interesting hotel is worth several snapshots. The ivory-turreted, red-brick château is more reminiscent of San Francisco or the French countryside than Boise.

There are 44 bedrooms, all with air-conditioning and private baths, in this city castle. A breakfast of orange juice, sweet rolls, coffee, and the daily paper is served in the cheerful sun room. Other complimentary services include free off-street parking and free transportation to the airport. You will want to give yourself plenty of time to bird at the interesting Snake River Birds of Prey Natural Area.

Rates: $45.75-$111.75
Credit cards: Visa, MC, AMEX, Discover, Diners
No. of rooms: 45
No. of baths: 45
Wheelchair access: No
Pets: Restrictions apply
Smoking: Nonsmoking rooms available
Senior citizen discount: 15%

Directions: From I-84, take City Center exit, which turns into Main Street. The hotel is at the corner of 10th and Main.

Kootenai National Wildlife Refuge

NEAREST AIRPORT: Spokane, Washington.

LOCATION: In the Idaho Panhandle 110 miles east and north of Spokane. On Highway 95 approximately 80 miles north of Coeur D'Alene, 30 miles north of Pend Oreille. The refuge is about 5 miles west of the city of Bonners Ferry and only 20 miles from Canada. If you have time, be sure to visit the Creston Valley Wildlife Management Area, 40 miles north in Canada (see British Columbia). Glacier National Park is only 5 hours drive east in Montana.

CONTACT: Refuge Manager, Kootenai National Wildlife Refuge, HCR 60, Box 283, Bonners Ferry, ID 83805. (208) 267-3888.

BEST BIRDING: Spring, fall, and summer, in that order. Other places to bird and observe wildlife nearby are the McArthur Wildlife Management Area, Dawson Lake, and Sinclair Lake/Moyie River Loop.

TOURS/WORKSHOPS: Check with refuge manager or the Bonners Ferry Chamber of Commerce, P.O. Box 375, Bonners Ferry, ID 83805.

The panhandle of Idaho sparkles with lakes, marshes, rivers, waterfalls, and mountains. In the midst of this wealth of wetlands and wildlife is the Kootenai National Wildlife Refuge. In the spring (March through May) you can observe snipes "winnowing" and ruffed grouse "drumming," and the pintail and mallard migration is at its peak. Waterfowl, ospreys, songbirds, and bald eagles begin nesting in the late spring. According to the refuge manager, the same pair of bald eagles has been nesting on the refuge for nine years and has just finished rebuilding its nest after it was totally destroyed by a major windstorm. Nesting bald eagles are making a comeback in this region and can also be seen in large numbers at nearby Pend Oreille Lake and Coeur d'Alene. Other spring visitors include tundra swans, red-necked grebes, wood ducks, Vaux's swifts, calliope hummingbirds, golden-crowned kinglets, American redstarts, and red crossbills. The refuge has several songbird trails for walking and observation. Fall (September through November) is the time of the duck migration, which peaks in early November; the most prominent species are Canada, mallard, and pintail. Bald eagles also arrive in autumn to feed on the rivers and marshes and to prey on the injured or sick ducks. Hunting is allowed in this refuge, so be sure to check with the manager regarding the dates of hunting season and park hours. Other wildlife on the refuge includes 22 species of fish, 7 species of amphibians, 7 species of reptiles, and 45 species of mammals. The area is rich in history, and the pristine surrounding landscape is attractive to photographers and painters.

ANGEL OF THE LAKE BED AND BREAKFAST
410 Railroad Avenue, Sandpoint, ID 83864, (208) 263-0816

If you are a movie aficionado, this is the bed and breakfast for you. Scene one: Enter the Angel of the Lake Bed and Breakfast and act out your favorite flick by picking one of the inn's four classic motion picture theme rooms.

Take One: Gone with the Wind Room. Frankly, my dear, you won't be able to tear yourself away from this bedroom, with its oversize antique bathtub and Mediterranean feeling.

Take Two: Casablanca Room. You'll want to stay again and again in this play-it-again-Sam room with its plants and lace canopy.

Take Three: African Queen Room. Pretend you are Katherine Hepburn in this room filled with artifacts and mosquito netting.

Take Four: Blazing Saddles Room. If you are full of beans, you will want to stay in this room, known for its Old West hotel ambience.

Even if you are not the Hollywood type, however, you will enjoy this bed and breakfast. The 100-year-old inn is located in a peaceful waterfront setting on Pend Oreille Lake.

You may want to take advantage of the Angel of the Lake's flambé dinners for two on your own veranda or in your room. These romantic dinners feature such items as Caesar salad, Steak Diane, Prawns Provencal, and crepes suzette.

Nearby Kootenai National Wildlife Refuge offers wonderful birding opportunities. If time permits, you can also fish, sail, water-ski, swim, golf, or hike. In the winter, you can visit Schweitzer Mountain for cross-country or downhill skiing, sleigh riding, ice fishing, and ice skating.

Rates: Double $65 (shared bath), $75 (private bath); $10 less for single; extra person $10
Credit cards: Visa, MC
No. of rooms: 4
No. of baths: 3 (2 with private baths; 2 with shared bath)
Wheelchair access: Yes
Pets: No
Smoking: No
Senior citizen discount: 10%
Directions: From 1st Street (Highway 95N), turn right onto Bridge Street, then turn left onto Railroad Avenue. Train riders: the inn is next to the Sandpoint Amtrak Station.

DEEP CREEK RESORT
Rt. 4, Box 628, Bonners Ferry, ID 83805, (208) 267-7578

If you want a quick culinary trip around the world without leaving the States, try the Deep Creek Resort. The new owners, Lorenz Caduff and Theo Kaufmann, recently moved from Switzerland to Bonners Ferry. They brought with them their delicious Swiss cuisine. A favorite is Fondue Bourguignonne. They also brought Greek, French, and Italian specialites.

If you are red, white, and blue to the core, Deep Creek Resort offers old-fashioned American steaks, prime rib, and chicken fried steak with homemade gravy. Vegetarians have their own menu. Children have their own selection of spaghetti with cheese, fish and chips, and chicken strips with French fries.

As for accommodations, Deep Creek offers something for everyone. You can stay at cabins along the creek, rent tent and trailer spaces, or hook up your RV.

Bonners Ferry is an outdoors paradise. You can picnic at Roman Nose Lake and hike its mountain trails, pick a bucket of huckleberries, hike to the historic West Fork Cabin, photograph the beautiful Selkirk Mountains, or view the fabulous Kootenai Valley from Katka Overlook. Perhaps you would prefer to tour a working fire lookout on Black Mountain, raft on the waters of the Moyie River, mountain bike through the Kootenai River dikes, or sight-see at the Anheuser Busch hop fields. You could also visit the Kootenai tribal white sturgeon fish hatchery, swim at the Bonners Ferry City Pool, explore the old growth forest of Long Canyon, hike to one of several unique waterfalls, watch the moose wade at McArthur Lake Wildlife Reserve, go horseback riding on mountain trails, or search for Boulder City Ghost Town.

Rates: $25-$42
Credit cards: Visa, MC, AMEX, Discover
No. of rooms: 10
No. of baths: 10

Wheelchair access: No
Pets: Yes
Smoking: Yes
Senior citizen discount: No

Directions: Take Highway 95 north toward Canada, turn left at the Naples, Deep Creek, exit. The resort is located on old Highway 95. Approximately 65 miles from Coeur d'Alene.

ILLINOIS

Indian Boundary Prairies/ Markham-Gensburg, Paintbrush, Sundrop, Dropseed

NEAREST AIRPORT: Chicago, Illinois.

LOCATION: From Chicago, drive southeast on I-57 to the interchange with Highway 6, then east on Highway 6 to Kedzie Avenue, north; follow Kedzie Avenue north to 15th Street. Drive east on 15th Street to the entrance of the Markham-Gensburg Prairie. Or, from Chicago, take I-294 to the interchange with Highway 6; drive Highway 6 west to Kedzie Avenue, and continue as above. The other prairies are short distances away, and maps are available at the Markham-Gensburg office.

CONTACT: Friends of the Indian Boundary Prairies, P.O. Box 394, Markham, IL 60426. (302) 346-8166.

BEST BIRDING: Spring, summer, and fall.

TOURS/WORKSHOPS: Many throughout the year. A calendar is published in the *Paintbrush Prairie Newsletter* by the friends of the Indian Boundary Prairies organization.

Located a few miles from Chicago's city center, the Indian Boundary Prairies consist of patches of tall, green grass punctuated with blazing star, blue gentian, and purple prairie clover. This is a special place where the original ecosystem of prairie grasslands and birds, such as bobolinks, Henslow's sparrows, meadowlarks, and yellow rails, still survive. From April to November, birding among the wildflowers and butterflies will give you a glimpse of the land as it was 8,000 years ago when the glaciers receded.

The largest part of the remnant prairie is the 100-acre Markham-Gensburg section about 25 miles south of the Chicago Loop, in the suburb of Markham. In spring, gold finches, indigo buntings, and yellow-breasted chats are abundant. This is also a haven for nesting sparrows; look for savannah, swamp, field, vesper, song, and chipping sparrows as well as dickcissels. Listen for the scolding of the kingbirds and the whistles and trills of the red-winged blackbirds and meadowlarks. This is a suitable habitat for raptors as well; species such as the American kestrel and the red-tailed hawk both mate and raise their broods here. In the wetter areas, look for short-billed marsh wrens, green-backed herons, American bitterns, mallards, and soras. Other wildlife that inhabit the prairie lands are white-tailed deer, gray foxes, Franklin's ground squirrels, rare moths, butterflies, and snakes.

BED AND BREAKFAST LINCOLN PARK/SHEFFIELD
2022 N. Sheffield Avenue, Chicago, IL 60614, (312) 327-6546

The Lincoln Park area is an enjoyable and convenient neighborhood to stay in while birding at the Indian Boundary Prairies. The neighborhood is the home of DePaul University and is renowned for its tree-lined streets, renovated homes, and excellent restaurants, theater, and music. The attractive Victorian building at 2022 North Sheffield offers the following lodging options:

1. A one-bedroom suite with living/dining room combination with a small refrigerator/freezer and microwave. The bedroom can be set up with one king bed or twin beds, with a pull-out double sleeper in the living room. The bathroom has a bathtub/whirlpool combination.

2. A two-bedroom apartment with a fully equipped kitchen—a double bed in one bedroom and a queen bed in the other, with an additional pull-out queen sleeper in the living room.

3. A two-bedroom apartment with a fully equipped kitchen—a double bed in one bedroom and twin beds in the second bedroom. There is also a cot available.

4. A guest room with an adjoining bathroom in the host's home which has a queen-size contemporary four-poster bed.

Each of these units has cable television, telephone, answering machine, coffee maker, and self-serve continental breakfast. Enjoy.

Rates: $55-$65; extra person $10; also 1-bedroom apartment $75, 2-bedroom apartment $115
Credit cards: Visa, MC
No. of rooms: 6
Directions: Inn will send map.

No. of baths: 4
Wheelchair access: No
Pets: No
Smoking: Yes
Senior citizen discount: No

RAPHAEL HOTEL
201 E. Delaware, Chicago, IL 60611, (312) 943-5000, (800) 821-5343

During a recent visit to the Indian Boundary Prairies, a wonderful birding habitat 20 miles from the Chicago Loop, I made myself at home at the European-flavored Raphael Hotel.

My room was a two-room suite, bigger than most New York apartments. A lovely king-size bed, a nice bath with excellent soaps and gels, and a comfortable sitting room with television provided a cozy setting. After a full day of birding, I wrapped myself up in my terry cloth robe and helped myself to some wine and cheese from the convenient mini-bar.

The Raphael's Gothic architecture and high-ceilinged lobby with chandeliers put me in mind of one of my favorite small hotels in London. I enjoyed the complimentary newspaper at my door every morning and the turn-down service at night.

If you want to take a few extra days to see Chicago, you will appreciate the location of the Raphael, which is just one block east of the Magnificent Mile, next to the Water Tower and the John Hancock Building in the historic Gold Coast district. For those not in the know, the Water Tower is a shopping heaven. But for those with loftier goals, you might prefer to spend your time at the fabulous Art Institute of Chicago with its wonderful impressionist collections and the intriguing Mrs. Thorne's miniature rooms. The Raphael, incidentally, provides free passes to the Institute. Another interesting excursion is a tour sponsored by the Chicago Architecture Foundation. Chicago is truly an architectural wonderland.

Rates: $95-$150
Credit cards: Visa, MC, AMEX, Discover, Diners
No. of rooms: 172
No. of baths: 172

Wheelchair access: Yes
Smoking: Yes
Pets: Yes
Senior citizen discount: No

Directions: 13 miles from Midway Airport, 25 miles from O'Hare.

Mark Twain National Wildlife Refuge Complex, Gardner Division

NEAREST AIRPORTS: Springfield, Illinois; St. Louis, Missouri.

LOCATION: The refuge complex is situated on the west central border of Illinois, along the Mississippi River. From Springfield, Illinois, drive west on Highway 36 to Highway 336 north; continue until you reach Highway 24 west and go a few miles to the city of Quincy (distance approximately 120 miles). From St. Louis, Missouri, travel north about 100 miles via I-70 west to US 61 north. Cross the Mississippi on Highway 24 east and proceed to Quincy. The Mark Twain Refuge Complex meanders with the Mississippi and Illinois rivers for more than 250 miles and consists of four divisions. The Gardner Division is near the center of the complex. Good birding exists along the entire corridor, but island birding in the Gardner Division requires that you have your own boat or that you rent one in one of the major cities, since they are not available in Quincy. Plan your trip to include both the Missouri and Mississippi sides of the river, as well as part of Iowa.

CONTACT: Refuge manager, Mark Twain National Wildlife Refuge Complex, Suite 100, 311 N. 5th Street, Quincy, IL 62301. (217) 224-8580.

BEST BIRDING: Spring and fall migration; winter for bald eagles.

TOURS/WORKSHOPS: Contact refuge headquarters, especially for "Eagle Days."

The refuge complex covers 23,500 acres, situated like stepping-stones along the Mississippi River. The varied habitats of bottomlands, islands, fields, marshes, sloughs, ponds, old growth and mixed forest, croplands, lakes, and levees all exist in the four districts of Gardner, Brussels, Anadna, and Wappello. The birds listed here can be found in all of the divisions; send for a bird list for district specialties. From March through May, green and little blue herons, black-crowned and yellow-crowned night herons as well as Canada, white-fronted, and snow geese are common, along with 18 species of ducks and an occasional whistling swan.

Raptors along the flyway are sharp-shinned, Cooper's, red-tailed, red-shouldered, broad-winged, and rough-legged hawks as well as bald and golden eagles, which can be viewed especially well near Belair in the Anadna District. Great blue herons and ospreys are joined by merlins and kestrels. Sandpipers, gulls, rails, soras, and bobwhites abound; Acadian flycatchers, swallows, and warblers migrate through the region. On fall birding expeditions, many of the same species can be seen. Look also for old-squaws and mergansers. American woodcocks are common, as are yellow-billed cuckoos, screech-owls, horned larks, rusty blackbirds, indigo buntings, and dickcissells. Overall, the bird list contains 235 species, some of which only occur on one of the refuges.

BUELTMANN GASTHAUS
1680 Maine Street, Quincy, IL 62301, (217) 224-8428

The Bueltmann Gasthaus offers gracious hospitality, baby-sitting, and piano music on request. You and your children will enjoy climbing the grand staircase to your room. The antique-furnished bedrooms include fireplaces, private baths, and queen-size beds. Victorian lace curtains purchased in Germany and family heirloom rockers add to the character of the spacious guest rooms.

Before heading off for birding at the Mark Twain National Wildlife Refuge Complex, you will relish your breakfast feast of homemade pastries and jams, cheese, and fresh fruits.

If you have plenty of time and are a museum aficionado, try the Quincy Museum of Natural History and Art, the Gardener Museum of Architecture and Design, and the Lincoln-Douglas Valentine Museum.

Rates: $40-$45; extra person $10
Credit cards: No
No. of rooms: 4
No. of baths: 3
Wheelchair access: No
Pets: No
Smoking: No
Directions: Southwest corner of 18th and Maine.

THE KAUFMANN HOUSE
1641 Hampshire Street, Quincy, IL 62301, (217) 223-2502

Pamper yourself in the beautifully decorated Kaufmann House. It is the perfect stopping-off place for the magnificent Mark Twain National Wildlife Refuge Complex whose headquarters are in Quincy. At the Kaufmann House, you can sleep in an intimate Victorian bedchamber or slumber on a charming painted iron bed among brightly pieced quilts. You will enjoy the simplicity of an Early American atmosphere. One room has a private bath, while the other two rooms have a shared bath.

Wake up to the delicious aroma of piping hot homemade rolls and coffee or tea, complemented by chilled fresh fruit. You will be served this treat either on the stone-terraced patio or in the antique-filled Ancestor Room.

Quincy itself is an attractive town with wide, tree-lined streets and magnificent architecture. However, be sure to give yourself plenty of time for birding.

Rates: Single $40-$60; double $45-$65; 10% discount for 3 or more nights
Credit cards: No
No. of rooms: 3
Directions: Inn will send map.

No. of baths: 2
Wheelchair access: No
Smoking: No (permitted on porch)
Pets: No
Senior citizen discount: No

Indiana Dunes National Lakeshore and State Park

NEAREST AIRPORT: Chicago, Illinois.

LOCATION: Approximately 93 miles south and east of O'Hare Airport. Take I-94 east to Indiana 49, then north to US 12. The Visitor Center is located on the southwest corner of Kemil Road. From there, the seashore continues 26 miles in the direction of Michigan City. The state park, 2,182 acres, lies within the national seashore at the eastern end.

CONTACTS: Indiana Dunes National Lakeshore, 1100 North Mineral Springs Road, Porter, IN 46305, (219) 926-7561. Indiana Dunes State Park: Park Office (219) 926-1952; Nature Center (219) 926-1390.

BEST BIRDING: Spring and fall.

TOURS/WORKSHOPS: Write to the Park Service for a schedule of ranger guided activities. Also contact the Friends of Indiana Dunes at the Visitor Center, Indiana Dunes National Lakeshore, P.O. Box 166, Beverly Shores, IN 46301.

Although the primary features of this protected area are the dunes along the Lake Michigan shore, farther inland are various additional habitats—marsh, bog, and woodland. The ancient glacial advances and retreats shaped the landscape in this region, which is part of the funnel for migrating birds, especially warblers and shorebirds. A great variety of warblers fly through in May: blue and golden-winged, Nashville, northern parula, yellow, chestnut-sided, magnolia, Cape May, black-throated blue, black-throated green, Blackburnian, prairie, palm, bay-breasted, blackpoll, cerulean, black-and-white, American redstart, hooded, Wilson's, and Canada. Some of these stay over to nest. Especially beautiful are the scarlet tanagers, which can be seen in spring and summer. Other spring birds to observe are ducks, sandpipers, and raptors, including ospreys and sharp-shinned, Cooper's, red-shouldered, and rough-legged hawks. In the woodland areas, white-eyed, yellow-throated, Philadelphia, and red-eyed vireos as well as 6 species of woodpeckers can be found. Of special interest for western birders are the red-headed and red-bellied woodpeckers. The seashore and park are perfect stopovers for western business persons traveling through the Chicago/South Bend area. Do not miss the heron rookery and a scheduled tour to Pinhook Bog.

CREEKWOOD INN
Route 2-35 at Interstate 94, Michigan City, IN 46360, (219) 872-8357

Creekwood Inn maintains the ambience of a charming country home, which is no surprise when you consider that in the 1930s it was the country home of Lawrence Robrock. Large hand-hewn wooden ceiling beams on the main floor were preserved from an old area toll bridge by Dr. Robrock. The inn retains the interesting touches of the original owner, although it has been refurbished and expanded. The main floor of the original home has been converted into a cozy parlor. It is the perfect setting for an Agatha Christie novel, complete with high tea served in the late afternoon.

Any time, day or night, you will not go hungry at the Creekwood Inn. Begin the day with a continental breakfast featuring homemade breads, fresh fruit, and coffee. While away the lonely hours until teatime. On Saturday night, enjoy a romantic dinner in the private parlor of the proprietor, Mary Lou Linnens. Later, you can have a cup of hot chocolate before retiring for the evening.

Recently, a wing was added which doubles the size of the original home, while at the same time retaining the English country flavor of the architecture. The twelve large guest rooms are furnished in a medley of traditional styles. All have overstuffed chairs, one king-size or two queen-size beds, mini-refrigerators, and private baths. Some rooms have terraces and fireplaces.

If you are ready to take your leave of this delightful estate, there are myriad possibilities awaiting you. Birding, of course, is a priority at the Indiana Dunes National Lakeshore. As an alternative, you can go antiquing in nearby lakeside communties, sip some wine at the numerous nearby wineries, or in season, pick your own fruit at local fruit farms.

Rates: $95-$150; extra person $15
Credit cards: Visa, MC, AMEX, Diners
No. of rooms: 13
No. of baths: 13
Directions: Inn will send map.

Wheelchair access: Yes
Pets: No
Smoking: Yes
Senior citizen discount: Yes

GRAY GOOSE INN
350 Indian Boundary Road, Chesterton, IN 46304, (219) 926-5781

The Gray Goose Inn offers a touch of England without having to cross the Atlantic. Century-old oaks surround the inn, overlooking Lake Palomara, home to Canadian geese, ducks, and blue heron—a virtual wildlife preserve. You can enjoy this rural environment even more from the vantage point of a paddleboat; at sunset in the fall, the foliage reflects off the pond and highlights a family of ducks that grace the lake.

Breakfast may start with cranberry or orange muffins and fruit topped with a yogurt sauce. The entrée will usually be one of the co-owner's own concoctions: Italian bread, covered with spinach, mushrooms, tomatoes, poached egg and a Benedict sauce.

The owners, Tim Wilk and Charles Ramsey, divide their innkeeper duties. They have have owned the Gray Goose for seven years. They are antique collectors, and their impressive collection is evident throughout the house. An antique full four-poster canopied bed graces the Master Suite, which has a fireplace and mahogany furniture. The Palomara Chamber, named for its splendid view of the lake, is decorated in pale yellows with Hunt prints, brass fixtures, and fresh flowers.

Wilk and Ramsey have created a birding wonderland. "The geese are a big draw," Tim explains to me as we sit sipping tea on the back porch overlooking the lake. "They stay all year and people love to feed them." Some birders rent the entire inn for their groups.

The Gray Goose is very conveniently located for birding at the Indiana Dunes National Lakeshore. For those who have had their fill of birding, if that is possible, there are plenty of other attractions nearby. You can enter a Dorothy Look-Alike contest at the Oz Festival, do some serious antiquing in Chesterton, go hiking or horseback riding, or just stroll around the grounds with Nick and Sadie, the resident dogs.

Rates: Single $75; double $85; extra person $15
Credit cards: Visa, MC, AMEX, Discover
No. of rooms: 5
No. of baths: 5

Wheelchair access: No
Pets: Sometimes
Smoking: Limited
Senior citizen discount: On weekdays only; 10% off room rate

Directions: From Chicago I-80/90, go east to exit 31, then left on Route 49 to Indian Boundary. From Chicago I-94, go east to exit 26A, then right on Indian Boundary.

THE HUTCHINSON MANSION INN
220 West 10th Street, Michigan City, IN 46360, (219) 879-1700

This inn near the Indiana Dunes National Lakeshore Wildlife Refuge is a step back in time. The Hutchinson Mansion evokes the leisured elegance of a more gracious period, an era of gaslamps and horse-drawn carriages, of iced tea on the veranda, of croquet and long skirts, lace and ruffles.

The original mansion, built in 1876 by William Hutchinson, lumber baron, financier, mayor, state senator, and world traveler, was a glorious house in its day. Now restored to its former grandeur, the mansion is furnished with antiques and reproductions. High-beamed, decorated ceilings and beautiful stained-glass windows abound throughout the inn.

There are six guest rooms: the Jenny Lind Room, with its unusual four-poster queen-size bed, is a corner room that overlooks the mansion's gardens; the Tower Suite offers an 1850 octagon post mahogany Gothic bed, stained-glass windows, and a separate sitting room; the Servant's Quarters has a queen-size white and gold iron bed, a private porch, and an interesting turn-of-the-century original bath; or if you want to blend the best of old and new, try the luxurious Carriage House suites, each with whirlpool baths.

You can wander around the mansion exploring its many nooks and crannies or relax in the parlor and the library with its ample supply of books and games. You can forget the twentieth century and lose yourself in the mansion's gardens with some tea or lemonade.

When you want to return to the real world, there is plenty to do in the Michigan City area. You can tour historic buildings, shop the famous Lighthouse Place Outlet Mall just 3 blocks away, charter a fishing vessel, visit a nineteenth-century farmstead, bicycle the scenic backroads, go sledding and skating in nearby parks, see a play (the Canterbury Theatre is only two blocks away), enjoy the woods on horseback, or go canoeing in the summer or ice fishing in the winter.

Rates: $80-$132.50 (plus tax) double occupancy. For single occupancy, deduct $10. Off-season and midweek rates are $10 less. Rates for holidays and special events may vary.
Credit cards: Visa, MC

No. of rooms: 10
No. of baths: 10
Wheelchair access: Yes
Pets: No
Smoking: Limited
Senior citizen discount: No

Directions: Exit 39 from I-80/90 (Indiana Toll Road). Take Route 421 north for 8 miles to 10th Street. Turn left onto 10th Street. One and a half blocks to the inn on the left. Or exit I-94 at exit 34. Take Route 421 north 4 miles to 10th Street. Turn left onto 10th Street. One and a half blocks to the inn on the left.

Muscatatuck National Wildlife Refuge

NEAREST AIRPORT: Louisville, Kentucky; Indianapolis, Indiana; Cincinnati, Ohio.

LOCATION: Midway between Indianapolis and Louisville in southern Indiana. The refuge is 4 miles east of Seymour, off Highway 50. From Indianapolis, drive south on I-65 to Seymour. From Louisville, drive north on I-65 to Seymour. From Cincinnati, drive west on I-275 to Highway 50 to the refuge entrance, 4 miles from Seymour.

CONTACT: Refuge Manager, Muscatatuck National Wildlife Refuge, R.R. 7, Box 189A, Seymour, IN 47274. (812) 522-4352.

BEST BIRDING: March and November for migrating waterfowl and the first week of May for migrating shorebirds and warblers.

TOURS/WORKSHOPS: Contact refuge manager.

Established only recently in 1966, this is Indiana's only wildlife refuge. The 7,700-acre refuge has mild winter, fall, and spring seasons but is humid and hot in the summer. The Muscatatuck River forms the southern boundary of the refuge, aiding in the maintenance of water requirements for the 3,000 acres of forest, grasslands, and croplands. Wood duck habitat is excellent, and this species is abundant year-round. Other year-round residents are American black ducks, hooded mergansers, yellow-crowned night herons, green herons, red-shouldered hawks, barred owls, red-headed and red-bellied woodpeckers, Carolina chickadees, tufted titmice, and field sparrows. Springtime, as usual, presents ample opportunity to observe new birds. At this time, look for least bitterns, little blue herons, ospreys, pectoral sandpipers, American woodcocks, olive-sided flycatchers, great crested flycatchers, sedge wrens, wood and gray-cheeked thrushes, and 30 species of warblers. Thousands of waterfowl use the ponds and waterways during this time of year, as the water levels are managed to feed the spring and fall migrants.

THE LANNING HOUSE
206 East Poplar Street, Salem, IN 47167, (812) 883-3484

The Lanning House offers a wonderful night's sleep and a delicious southern Indiana breakfast for bird-watchers, genealogical researchers, history lovers, and antique buffs.

The inn (ca. 1873) was built by a local dentist, Azariah Lanning. Innkeeper Jeanette Hart now owns and operates the Lanning House in conjunction with the

Stevens Memorial Museum, which is notable for its John Jay Center, Pioneer Village, and professional assistance offered in its excellent genealogical library.

The dining room of the Lanning House is furnished almost entirely with pieces owned by Mrs. Hart's parents. In the parlor are quality reproductions of Queen Anne and Chippendale furniture accented with lithographs of Midwest birds, needlepoint, and crewel.

The four bedrooms are decorated in a variety of styles. Down on the Farm is the name of the front bedroom, which features white iron beds used by Mrs. Hart and her brother when they were growing up. The Lindley bedroom on the first floor contains lovely antique pieces belonging to the museum, including a four-poster canopy cherry bed. The room is named for Mrs. William Lindley, a nineteenth-century Quaker woman who christened her new hometown in Indiana after her native Salem in North Carolina.

If you are traveling with a birding group, you might consider renting the 1920s Annex, which was built in the Arts and Crafts style. Well-designed, clean-lined, oak built-in cabinets and a simple brick and oak fireplace dominate the living and dining rooms.

Rates: $30-$50
Credit cards: No
No. of rooms: 7
No. of baths: 3 private, 4 shared
Wheelchair access: No
Pets: No
Smoking: No
Senior citizen discount: 10%
Directions: From I-65, take the Scottsburg exit to S.R. 56 west to Salem (20 miles). From S.R. 37, pick up 60 east to 56, to the stoplight in Salem. From the south, I-65 to Hamburg, then take 60 north to Salem. The Lanning House and Museum is 2 blocks east of the square.

MORGAN'S FARM
R.R. 2, Austin, IN 47102, (812) 794-2536

Morgan's Farm is a bed and breakfast on 100 acres of rolling countryside in southeastern Indiana. All you have to do at this country estate is enjoy walks in the woods or have a swim in the pool. You can commune with nature or chat with the various animals on the property, such as the buffalo, peacocks, swans, and horses.

The rural estate was built in 1939 by Elsinore and Jack Morgan. The Morgan family founded Morgan Foods, Inc., in 1901. The company is still operating as a family-owned business. The spacious rooms at Morgan's Farm still contain many original furnishings and memorabilia.

Morgan's Farm is a great jumping-off place for exploring southern Indiana. There is wonderful birding at Muscatatuck National Wildlife Refuge. It is just 30 minutes to historic Madison on the Ohio River, 60 minutes to scenic, rustic

Brown County and Nashville, Indiana, 30 minutes to Clifty Falls State Park, and 10 minutes to Hardy Lake.

You can go spelunking in nearby caves or crew your own riverboat. Children are welcome at Morgan's Farm.

Rates: Single $55; double $80
Credit cards: MC, Visa
No. of rooms: 4
No. of baths: 4 (entire house can be rented for groups if willing to share bath)

Wheelchair access: Yes
Pets: No
Smoking: Limited
Senior citizen discount: No

Directions: I-65 – exit 34 to Austin, Indiana; 2 miles east on Highway 256, north side of road.

Morgan's Farm

IOWA

DeSoto National Wildlife Refuge

NEAREST AIRPORT: Omaha, Nebraska.

LOCATION: Along US 30 between Blair, Nebraska, and Missouri Valley, Iowa, along the Missouri River 25 miles north of Omaha.

CONTACTS: Refuge Manager, DeSoto National Wildlife Refuge, Rt. 1, Box 114, Missouri Valley, IA 51555. (712)-642-4121.

BEST BIRDING: October and November. Although the refuge grounds are closed to visitation from December through February to minimize disturbance to wintering eagle, waterfowl, and resident game populations, there are good viewing opportunities from the DeSoto Visitor Center.

TOURS/WORKSHOPS: Wildlife films on Saturdays and Sundays at 11:00 a.m., 1:30 p.m., and 2:45 p.m. Contact refuge manager for a calendar of events.

DeSoto National Wildlife Refuge's primary purpose is to serve as a stopover for migrating ducks and geese. In a typical year, 200,000 snow geese utilize this 7,823-acre refuge as a resting and feeding area during the fall migration. Peak populations of 125,000 ducks are common on the refuge during that time also, as well as an assortment of warblers, gulls, and shorebirds. Bald eagles follow the geese into the area, with many of them wintering on the refuge until March. Bald eagle numbers on the refuge may reach as many as 120.

Spring offers less spectacular concentrations of returning geese and ducks; however, large numbers of migrating shorebirds and warblers are visible at this time. One of DeSoto's management programs involves the restoration of sand-bar habitat to attract nesting piping plovers and nationally endangered least terns.

During the summer months, wood ducks may be seen in ponds throughout the refuge. Woods, fields of native prairie grasses, and multiflora rose hedges along refuge roads attract a variety of songbirds, including tufted titmice, cedar waxwings, Bell's vireos, chestnut-sided warblers, blue grosbeaks, and indigo buntings. Deer, coyotes, cottontails, raccoons, opossums, and fox squirrels are also frequently seen in the refuge. Backwater areas of DeSoto Lake and several wetlands serve as habitat for beaver, muskrat, and an occasional mink.

In addition to the varied wildlife found here, DeSoto National Wildlife Refuge is home to the buried remains of the steamboat *Bertrand* and an exhibit of artifacts found in the boat. Such steamboats played a vital role in our nation's westward expansion.

APPLE ORCHARD INN BED AND BREAKFAST
R.R. 3, Box 129, Missouri Valley, IA 51555, (712) 642-2418

The Apple Orchard Inn is located on 26 beautiful acres of apple orchards. The three comfortable bedrooms, each with adjoining baths, have a quaint 1930 decor. Breakfast features an old-fashioned country breakfast with home-baked breads made with home-ground flour and fresh jams, jellies, and apple butter. If you reserve ahead, you can get gourmet country dinners.

Great views of the Iowa countryside await you at John and Electra Strub's hillside apple orchard, located in the rich loess hills and apple land of Iowa.

You can discover Iowa's quiet country charm by walking or bicycling along country roads. Only a short distance from DeSoto National Wildlife Refuge, at the Apple Orchard Inn you can take advantage of the natural beauty of rural Iowa.

Rates: $55 double
Credit cards: Visa, MC, AMEX, Discover
No. of rooms: 3
No. of baths: 3
Wheelchair access: Very limited
Pets: No
Smoking: Restricted area
Senior citizen discount: No
Directions: I-29 to exit 75 – 5 miles; east on Highway 30 to Welcome Center; left 1 block to Apple Orchard Inn.

HILLTOP BED AND BREAKFAST
R.R. 3, Box 126, Missouri Valley, IA 51555, (716) 642-3695

Hilltop Bed and Breakfast is a farm B&B located in the rich loess hills and apple orchards of Harrison County, Iowa, above the beautiful Boyer Valley. You can relax in this tranquil environment or play Dr. Doolittle by going for walks and talking to the farm animals.

There are two comfortable, air-conditioned bedrooms with queen-size beds and private baths. On cold winter evenings, genial hosts Theresa and Merle Kenkel will join you around the fireplace. In the summertime, feel free to use their patio and grill. Save some time after birding to relax in the hot tub.

After your full country breakfast, head for nearby DeSoto National Wildlife Refuge where every season brings a new variety of birds. Antique browsers are in luck, for you are just 4 miles from the Missouri Valley Antique Mall, one of the largest antique shops in the Midwest.

Rates: Single $40; double $49; extra person negotiable
Credit cards: Visa, MC
No. of rooms: 2
No. of baths: 2
Wheelchair access: Yes
Smoking: In restricted areas
Senior citizen discount: No
Directions: 4 miles northeast of Missouri Valley, call the inn for directions.

Mark Twain National Wildlife Refuge, Big Timber Division

NEAREST AIRPORTS: Moline, Illinois; Burlington, Iowa; Iowa City, Iowa.

LOCATION: Approximately 10 miles south of Muscatine, Iowa, on Louisa County Road X-61 (the great River Road). Muscatine is about 38 miles west of Moline, Illinois, on US 80, and 47 miles north of Burlington, Iowa, on US 61. From Iowa City, drive east 32 miles on US 80 and then 18 miles south on Highway 38 to reach Muscatine.

CONTACTS: Refuge Manager, Louisa Division, Mark Twain National Wildlife Refuge, RR 1, Box 75, Wapello, IA 52653, (315) 523-6982; or Refuge Manager, Mark Twain National Wildlife Refuge, Suite 100, 311 N. 5th Street, Quincy, IL 62301, (217) 224-8580.

BEST BIRDING: Spring and fall. Nearby birding areas include Louisa Division, Mark Twain National Wildlife Refuge, approximately 25 miles south of Muscatine on Louisa County Road X-61, and Keithsburg Division, Mark Twain National Wildlife Refuge, approximately 1 mile north of Keithsburg, Illinois, on Highway 17.

TOURS/WORKSHOPS: Contact the refuge manager or the Muscatine Chamber of Commerce for information on local outfitters.

This 3,376-acre refuge is a complex of backwater sloughs and bottomland timber, including several islands. For access to the backwater sloughs, marshes, and islands of the refuge, a boat is essential; a concrete boat ramp is available.

Bald eagles are often seen along the river channel and around Otter Island; their numbers often peak during the first week of December and again in February. Several species of woodpeckers, including the pileated, can be observed and are known to nest on the refuge.

Large concentrations of migrating waterfowl use the refuge from October through November and from March through April. The most common of these are mallards, pintails, wigeons, scaups, teals, and shovelers. One of the refuge's main goals is to maintain and improve habitat for nesting wood ducks. Herons and egrets are also common throughout the summer.

Fall raptor migration usually peaks around late October. Warbler migrations usually peak around mid-May and include Nashville, chestnut-sided, magnolia, black-throated green, Blackburnian, bay-breasted, blackpoll, black-and-white, and mourning.

Other species that may be seen on the refuge year-round are squirrels, raccoons, muskrats, beavers, mink, opossums, skunks, and coyotes.

FULTON'S LANDING
1206 E. River Drive, Davenport, IA 52803, (319) 322-4069

Fulton's Landing is a newly renovated bed and breakfast on the banks of the Mississippi. You can watch the barges go through the locks while having your morning coffee on one of two porches overlooking the river.

This majestic old house, built in 1871 by Ambrose Copperwaithe Fulton, is listed in the National Register of Historic Places. It offers a choice of five bedrooms. There are two large rooms on the riverside, both with queen-size beds, antique furnishings, and private baths. A third large room is in the middle of the house and is furnished with antiques and a private bath. The two smaller rooms share the old, original marble bathroom.

Innkeepers Pat and Bill Schmidt will offer you a full breakfast before they send you off to nearby Big Timber Division. At this refuge, by the way, a boat for access to the backwater sloughs and marshes or the islands is a must.

Rates: $55-$100 (doubles)
Credit cards: Visa, MC
No. of rooms: 5
No. of baths: 4
Wheelchair access: No
Pets: Yes
Smoking: No
Senior citizen discount: No
Directions: Located on River Drive 1 mile east of downtown Davenport; 1½ miles west of I-74 exit; 1 mile east of downtown Brady Street exit, I-80.

RIVER OAKS INN
1234 E. River Drive, Davenport, IA 52803
(319) 326-2629, (800) 352-6016

The River Oaks Inn, located on scenic River Drive, offers elegance along the Mississippi. This interesting home, built in the 1850s by Abner Davison, combines Italianate, Victorian, and Prairie architecture and is on the National Register of Historic Places, as are the gazebo and carriage house.

The house is situated on a rolling tract that still shows evidence of the original carriage drive. The ornate gazebo near the front of the house is a lovely place to have coffee and enjoy the view.

There are five guest bedrooms. The River View Suite features a king-size bed, sun porch, and dressing room. The Mississippi Room has a queen-size bed, window seat, and lovely river view. The cozy Ambrose Fulton Room has a double bed and overlooks the back garden. The Mary Crowe Suite has a queen-size four-poster bed, a parlor with working fireplace, and a queen-size sleeper. Enjoy a full breakfast served in the formal dining room, on the deck, or privately in your own suite.

If you're faxing life lists to birders across the country, you are in luck as River Oaks has a fax machine and copier available.

Head out to Big Timber Division for some spectacular birding. Be advised that you need a boat for access to the backwater sloughs, marshes, and islands.

Rates: $49-$175 **Wheelchair access:** Yes
Credit cards: Visa, MC **Smoking:** Restricted
No. of rooms: 8 **Pets:** No
No. of baths: 7 **Senior citizen discount:** 10%
Directions: 2 miles off I-74; about 4 miles off I-80; 1 mile off Highway 61.

KANSAS

Quivera National Wildlife Refuge

NEAREST AIRPORTS: Hutchinson and Great Bend, Kansas.

LOCATION: Approximately 28 miles east of Hutchinson on 4th Street. From Great Bend drive south 22 miles on US 281, then east on County Road 636 13 miles to the refuge entrance.

CONTACT: Refuge Manager, RR #3, Box 48A, Stafford, KS 67578. (316) 486-2393.

BEST BIRDING: Spring and fall. The best viewing is along the scenic tour route and the wildlife drive. While in this area, you may also want to visit Cheyenne Bottoms Wildlife Area 7 miles northeast of Great Bend.

TOURS/WORKSHOPS: Contact refuge manager for special activities.

Although Quivira National Wildlife Refuge is managed primarily for migrating waterfowl, the varied plant communities created by the melding of the relatively lush eastern vegetation with that of the more arid west results in a haven for many other birds common to both eastern and western North America.

In spring and fall, the refuge acts as a staging area for from 100,000 to over 300,000 ducks, geese, American white pelicans, gulls, shorebirds, and other migrants. Endangered whooping cranes may also visit the refuge briefly as they travel through the flyway. Some of the rarer species you may encounter at these times are common loons, tundra swans, Ross's geese, merlins, red knots, buff-breasted sandpipers, Sprague's pipits, mourning warblers, and Henslow's sparrows. A colony of endangered least terns uses the salt flats at the north end of the refuge as nesting habitat. Snowy plovers, American avocets, black-necked stilts, Bell's vireos, and yellow-breasted chats also nest on the refuge.

Bald and golden eagles winter on the refuge from November until March. In addition, northern goshawks, snowy owls, Bohemian waxwings, and snow buntings are rare winter visitors.

Other wildlife frequently seen on the refuge are white-tailed deer, black-tailed prairie dogs, beavers, raccoons, badgers, and coyotes.

Much of the refuge is open to hiking, and two photography blinds are available on a first-come, first-served basis.

INN AT THE PARK
3751 E. Douglas, Wichita, KS 67218, (316) 652-0500, (800) 258-1951

The Inn at the Park has one of the most interesting decorating schemes I have encountered at a bed and breakfast. Owners Kevin Daves, an architect, and Greg Johnson, a contractor, remodeled the house into 11 suites. They worked with 27 local designers to convert each suite into a unique living area with bedroom, sitting area, and bath. Therefore, each room has its own unique personality and design.

In the main hall, you will be inspired by a Queen Ann settee covered in a rich, rose-colored damask. The second-floor landing is the focal point of the house with its expanse of original beveled glass work and richly upholstered banquette.

The Art Nouveau ambience of Suite 1 reflects a style popular at the turn of the century. The curved, flowing lines are reflected in the antique cabinet in the entry, the wall coverings in the bedroom and bathroom, the Tiffany reproduction sconces, and the custom-made armoire and stained-glass windows.

Suite 2, Yesterday's Suite, draws you into the ambience and graciousness of the nineteenth century. Strong color and design is softened by feather-light fabric, Battenburg lace, and downy pillows. The room invites you to lay your straw hat aside, loosen your tie, and take a seat in the shafts of sunlight at the window as you enjoy a cup of tea and a bite of cake.

You will have to explore the other rooms on your own, but all are interesting. With such a comfortable place to stay, you will have even more energy and enthusiasm for your birding at Quivira National Wildlife Refuge. It is a bit of a drive, approximately 80 miles, but worth it.

Rates: $75-$135
Credit cards: Visa, MC, AMEX, Discover
No. of rooms: 11
No. of baths: 11
Wheelchair access: Yes
Pets: No
Smoking: Two rooms only
Senior citizen discount: No
Directions: Take the Hillside exit from US 54, head north.

PEACEFUL ACRES
Rt. 5, Box 153, Great Bend, KS 67530, (316) 793-7527

If you want to get away from the hustle-bustle of city life, nothing could be more idyllic than Peaceful Acres. Not only can you get some much needed R&R but you will be in the perfect location to visit Cheyenne Bottoms Wildlife Area and Quivira National Wildlife Refuge. Cheyenne Bottoms is one of the most important inland staging sites for migratory shorebirds in the Western Hemisphere.

Peaceful Acres is a comfortable sprawling old farmhouse, with two bed-rooms on ground level and a possible third one upstairs. B&B guests share a bathroom. A farmhouse breakfast is served.

Children are welcome at Peaceful Acres. They will enjoy the farm animals and the sturdy swing set and teeter-totter. You can take them to the town of Lindsborg with its Swedish shops and museums, or visit Dodge City and see the famous Boot Hill.

Rates: Single $25; double $30; extra person $5

Credit cards: No

No. of rooms: 2 (possible 3rd)

No. of baths: 1 for bed and breakfast

Wheelchair access: 2 steps

Pets: Yes

Smoking: No

Senior citizen discount: No

Directions: From Great Bend north edge or 24th Street, north on Washington Street to dead end (4 miles); 2 miles west, ¼ mile south.

WALNUT BROOK BED AND BREAKFAST
R.R. 3, Box 304, Great Bend, KS 67530, (316) 792-5900

Walnut Brook Bed and Breakfast advertises itself as a "storybook getaway." The brochure reads like a whimsical children's book and is so charming, I quote from it verbatim:

"If Johnny Town-mouse and country Timmy Willie were to walk off the pages of the children's storybooks and enter the land of Ah's in Kansas, we would hope for them to find the same wonderment at Walnut Brook Bed and Breakfast. Even Johnny Town-mouse needed a change of scenery to the peace-ful burrows by the riverbank; to peep at the throstles and robbins on the lawn and see the garden and the flowers. That's Walnut Brook! We invite you to take part in the refreshment of a storybook getaway—the luxurious breakfasts by the friendship garden or dining in the cottage breakfast nook. Unwind in the spacious family room in front of the warming fireplace or lounge on our wicker decor in the enclosed greenhouse patio. Enjoy the alive atmosphere of music, or take a quiet stroll along the brook and vine-covered lane. There's a map of a discovery treasure nature hunt and the fresh tarragon, the daffodils, and the hollyhocks to smell. You can pet the lambs in the meadows or take a horseback ride on the country home acreage.

"Johnny Town-mouse would even be pleased to find the pleasantries of the city with Timmy Willie in the country—the spacious above-ground pool, sauna and gym, TV, video, cable, soothing steam radiator heat and central air-condi-tioning. We feature a gift shop of original arts and crafts by family and friends. In the evening, we offer complimentary refreshments and home-baked cinna-mon raisin bread. Breakfasts run the gamut from full country to gourmet."

Your own birding fairy tale will continue when you visit nearby Quivira and Cheyenne Bottoms, major inland staging sites for migratory shorebirds in the Western Hemisphere.

Rates: Single $50; double $65; extra person $5 (children 8 and up)

Credit cards: No

No. of rooms: 3

No. of baths: 3

Wheelchair access: No

Pets: Yes, horse stabling—$10

Smoking: Outside only

Directions: 2 miles north of Great Bend from 24th and Main to first blacktop road; turn right (east) ½ mile from Highway 281 on NE 30th Road; left before bridge, go ¼ mile north; turn left before bridge again onto the inn's private land.

KENTUCKY

Clyde P. Buckley Wildlife Sanctuary, National Audubon Society

NEAREST AIRPORT: Lexington, Kentucky.

LOCATION: One hour west of Lexington. Take Route 60 west past Versailles (route swings north). Just after milepost 4, turn left on Steele Road. Turn right at the fork, then right again when the road forms a T intersection. At the Millville School ball park, make a left turn and continue for 1 mile. Turn right at Germany Road. The sanctuary is on the left about 1¼ miles.

CONTACTS: Clyde P. Buckley Wildlife Sanctuary, 1305 Germany Road, Frankfort, KY 40601, (606) 873-5711; Audubon Society of Kentucky, P.O. Box 22378, Lexington, KY 40522-2378.

BEST BIRDING: Spring and fall.

TOURS/WORKSHOPS: The sanctuary accepts groups of up to 75 persons (there is a fee); there are tours and programs for individuals with sufficient advance notice. There is also an intern program in nature interpretation, wildlife management, and general sanctuary operations. Of special interest are the guided excursions into the forest at night to observe the adaptations of both birds and animals. For related field trips, contact the Audubon Society of Kentucky. There is an interpretive center at the sanctuary and self-guided trails. The grounds are closed Mondays, Tuesdays, and holidays.

Enjoy the old South feeling of this enchanting region as you drive to the sanctuary, whose goal is to preserve and promote the growth of native flora and fauna and to provide an active environmental education program. Tim Williams, Sanctuary Manager, is an enthusiastic and knowledgeable host.

The sanctuary's 275 acres, which are in the transition zone for northern and southern plants and animals, include ponds, fields, and mixed mesophitic forests. The varied habitat attracts birds year-round but especially during the spring and fall migrations. During spring in the wooded areas you should be able to observe Kentucky, Connecticut, and prairie warblers as well as palm warblers with their rusty caps along the field edges. Throughout the area you can hear the songs of and see orchard and Baltimore orioles, rusty blackbirds, scarlet and summer tanagers, and northern cardinals. Other birds that can be frequently seen are rose-breasted, evening, and blue grosbeaks, indigo buntings, and American goldfinches. Be sure to go to the Marion B. Lindley Bird Blind for undetected viewing of the feeding station. Other flora and fauna featured and studied here include butterflies, fish, honeybees, turtles, snakes, wildflowers, and grasses.

ROSE HILL INN BED AND BREAKFAST
233 Rose Hill, Versailles, KY 40383, (606) 873-5957

The Rose Hill Inn, nestled in the magnificent Bluegrass region of Kentucky, is steeped in history. Built in the early 1800s, it is one of Versailles' original estates. The inn is rumored to have been a hospital during the Civil War and a campground for both North and South. Rose Hill is only fifteen minutes from the Clyde P. Buckley Wildlife Sanctuary.

If you want to try your wings at touring Versailles, innkeepers Mark and Kathy Mattone Miller suggest visiting Henry Clay's Home in Ashland, the famous horse farms, Keeneland Race Course, the Lexington Children's Museum, the Shaker Village in Pleasant Hill, Bluegrass Railroad Museum, Old Fort Harrod, or the State Capitol in Frankfort.

Avid exercise buffs will want to use the wooded fitness course at Big Spring Park, directly behind the inn. Antiquers will enjoy browsing in the many shops just a block from the inn.

Whatever you decide to do, you are certain to have a rosy time.

Rates: $69-$89
Credit cards: Visa, MC, AMEX, Discover, Diners
No. of rooms: 4
No. of baths: 4
Wheelchair access: Yes
Smoking: Restricted
Pets: No
Senior citizen discount: 10%
Directions: About 12 miles from Lexington. Easy access to the Bluegrass Parkway and Route 60.

SHEPHERD PLACE
31 Heritage Road, Versailles, KY 40383, (606) 873-7843

At this old Kentucky home, owners Martin and Sylvia Yawn offer a multitude of activities and services. You can even commission Sylvia to hand-knit a sweater from yarn you select. And you can meet the sheep who might contribute to your sweater and the pet ewes, Abigail and Victoria.

You might want to just lounge around this charming pre-Civil War home, built ca. 1815. You can relax in a spacious, beautifully decorated bedroom with private bath or plan your next day's outings while sitting in the parlor. There is plenty of Southern hospitality at Shepherd Place, such as turn-down bed service and a delicious home-cooked Kentucky breakfast.

The Yawns have bushels of brochures and menus and plenty of ideas to help you plan the rest of your stay in the Bluegrass region. First of all, you will want to go birding at the Clyde P. Buckley Wildlife Sanctuary. Afterward, you can visit Shakertown, where weavers, smiths, and woodworkers display their skills in an 1839 restored village, or maybe take a ride on the winding Kentucky River in a paddleboat.

Do not forget that you are in prime horse country, so why not tour the picturesque homes of such Derby winners as Seattle Slew and Secretariat? If you are a member of the horsey set, you will want to visit the 1,000-acre Kentucky Horse Park, which includes a theater, a museum, a track, barns, and hundreds of horses.

Rates: Single $60; double $65; triple $70 (all include full breakfast)
Credit cards: Visa, MC
No. of rooms: 2
No. of baths: 2
Directions: Inn will send map.

Wheelchair access: No
Pets: No
Smoking: No
Senior citizen discount: Yes

SILLS INN BED AND BREAKFAST
270 Montgomery Avenue, Versailles, KY 40383
(606) 873-4478 , (800) 526-9801, Fax: (606) 873-4726

Tony Sills is a Southern gentleman who enjoys sharing his Victorian inn with visitors. The Sills Inn Bed and Breakfast is a 1911, three-story restored inn. The 6,000 square feet are filled with family heirloom Kentucky antiques. The staff is happy to help with your travel plans, restaurant reservations, and other needs. A full gourmet breakfast is served on fine china, crystal, and lace in the formal dining room.

Sills Inn is replete with Bluegrass country charm and grace. It is fun to relax on the wraparound porch in a wicker rocking chair or to step inside and hear tunes played on the old Victrola.

Guests are invited to fix themselves a snack in the fully stocked guest kitchen.

You will have sweet dreams whichever bedroom you choose. The Victorian Suite recalls a lost era of elegance with its Eastlake burl queen-size bed, adjacent sitting room, and sunken master bath with a double Jacuzzi.

The Oak Room features a splendid view of stately oak trees from the queen-size family heirloom bed. You can take a bubble bath in the deep claw-foot tub in your own private bath. In the Hunt Room, you can feel the Kentucky tradition of the fox hunt as the pictures above the twin beds come alive. The private bath has an antique sink.

The first thing you will want to do in the area, of course, is go birding at the Clyde P. Buckley Wildlife Sanctuary. If time permits, Tony will be happy to tell you what sights to visit in the Bluegrass country. He might suggest Midway, a delightful town surrounded by graceful horse farms. Or perhaps a walk through Versailles, a town filled with Victorian architecture and horse lovers. If antique browsing is your passion, you should visit Woodford County with its cozy antique shops.

If history beckons you, visit the Pisgah Church, established in 1784 as the first Presbyterian church west of the Allegheny Mountains, or the Jack Jouett House. Captain Jouett, a Revolutionary War hero, was known as the "Paul Revere of the South."

Rates: $55-$89
Credit cards: Visa, MC, AMEX, Discover, Diners
No. of rooms: 10
No. of baths: 10

Wheelchair access: Yes
Smoking: No
Pets: No
Senior citizen discount: No

Directions: 7 miles west of the Lexington airport in downtown Versailles.

LOUISIANA

Jean Lafitte National Historical Park and Preserve, Barataria Division

NEAREST AIRPORT: New Orleans, Louisiana.

LOCATION: The Barataria unit of the park is 15 miles south of New Orleans via US Business 90 to Route 45 south to the visitor center. Part of the unit borders Lake Salvador; this division has the most variety of birds.

CONTACT: Jean Lafitte National Historical Park and Preserve, 423 Canal Street, Room 210, New Orleans, LA 70130, (504) 589-3882. Barataria Division: (504) 589-2330.

BEST BIRDING: Fall, winter, and spring. There is still good birding in the summer, but insects are much more bothersome; take insect repellent in all seasons.

TOURS/WORKSHOPS: Contact refuge manager or the Orleans Audubon Society in New Orleans.

The watery delta of the Mississippi, a mysterious place sometimes shrouded in mists, may look inimical to life, but the swamps, lakes, bayous, flooded bald cypress forests, levees, and marshlands of Barataria support a complex ecosystem, with fish, crustaceans, and over 250 species of birds. This peaceful and fragile environment can be traversed on over 8 miles of walking trails and boardwalks. The cooler seasons of fall and winter offer a good variety of species for observation. According to *A Bird Finder's Guide to Southeastern Louisiana*, by Dan Purrington, Al Smalley, Gwen Smalley, Ronald J. Stein, and James Whelan (New Orleans: Orleans Audubon Society, 1982), the most productive trail for birding is the Bayou Coquille Trail, although all of them are good. Commonly seen are great and little blue herons, great egrets, and tricolored and yellow-crowned night herons. Other waders include white, white-faced, and glossy ibis. Broad-winged, sharp-shinned, and red-tailed hawks migrate through the preserve, some staying for the winter. Gulls, terns, and shorebirds will be seen around the lake habitat.

In this climate, moderate for most of the year, there are numerous interesting permanent resident species, including painted buntings, boat-tailed grackles, blue-gray gnatcatchers, pileated woodpeckers, barred owls, royal terns, king rails, red-shouldered hawks, and wood and mottled ducks. The balmy spring months (as opposed to the very hot and humid summers) bring out wide-winged anhingas and sprightly purple gallinules as well as an increased population of warblers and songbirds; of special interest are golden-winged warblers, blue-winged warblers, northern parulas, magnolias, and Swainson's warblers.

DAUPHINE ORLEANS HOTEL
415 Dauphine Street, New Orleans, LA 70112
(504) 586-1409, (800) 521-7111

The historic Dauphine Orleans Hotel allows you to participate in "You Are There." It is 1815 and the drums of General Jackson's army, bound for the Battle of New Orleans, echo from the walls of the French Quarter. Better yet for those who are connoisseurs of the feathered creatures, it is the early 1820s, and you are visiting the Creole cottage where John James Audubon is painting his *Birds of America*. As a matter of fact, the Audubon Room, now the main hotel meeting room, is the very cottage where the famous naturalist painted.

The Dauphine Orleans Hotel is comfortable and luxurious. Picture yourself arriving as the hospitality begins: cocktails and appetizers in the Bagnio Lounge, the spot on which a Jazz Age bordello once thrived.

Your beautifully appointed room includes a well-stocked mini bar, hair dryer, and cable television. While you are out feasting at one of New Orleans' splendid restaurants, the Dauphine Orleans Hotel staff is turning down your bed and leaving a treat on your pillow.

Next morning, you can laze over your ample continental breakfast while you read your complimentary paper. Before or after birding at Jean Lafitte National Historical Park and Preserve, take a dip in the outdoor swimming pool.

A favorite feature is the guest library. The hotel encourages you to take your unfinished library book with their best wishes.

There are many activities in the Big Easy, but for me, the main sport, after birding, is restaurant hopping. There are so many excellent eateries there is not a moment to lose.

Rates: Single $110-$150; double $120-$160; extra person $15
Credit cards: All major
No. of rooms: 109
No. of baths: 109
Directions: Inn will send map.

Wheelchair access: Yes
Pets: Yes
Smoking: Yes
Senior citizen discount: 10%

LAFITTE GUEST HOUSE
1003 Bourbon Street, New Orleans, LA 70116
(504) 581-2678, (800) 331-7971

The Lafitte Guest House is as much New Orleans as Blanche DuBois, beignets, and voodoo queens. You will get the New Orleans feeling of hospitality when you are served wine and cheese in the parlor. After all, food, drink, and charm is what the city is all about.

The house is filled with fine antiques and paintings collected from around the world. A step into the spacious entrance parlor of this fine old French manor building is a step back in time or, perhaps, into your own fantasy. New Orleans, with its carnival atmosphere, is truly a city of make believe.

No guest at Lafitte Guest House will have to worry about being comfortable. All 14 rooms are carpeted and have either queen- or king-size beds. They are decorated in period furnishings, many with original black marble mantels over the fireplace and crystal chandeliers. The most popular rooms seem to be the ones with the four-poster beds with full or half testers.

You can participate in the local color in the morning by enjoying your continental breakfast on your own private wrought iron balcony where you can watch artists walking their canvases to famed Jackson Square. For a more intimate setting, you might want to try the beautiful private courtyard.

The staff is informal but efficient. They keep a book of menus and will help you pick the perfect restaurants, whether you want morning coffee and beignets, red beans and rice, or etouffée.

Rates: $85-$165
Credit cards: Visa, AMEX, MC, Discover
No. of rooms: 14
No. of baths: 14

Wheelchair access: Yes
Pets: No
Smoking: Yes
Senior citizen discount: AARP

Directions: In the French Quarter—30 minutes east of airport.

THE PRYTANIA INN
1415 Prytania Street, New Orleans, LA 70130, (504) 566-1515

Yankees looking for Southern hospitality in a historic setting need search no further. Built in 1852 as a private home with slave quarters, the Prytania Inn was converted to a full-service guest house in 1984.

Fortunately, in the process, original hand-carved cornices, medallions, and plaster work remained undamaged, as did the twin black marble mantels that enhance the 140-year-old double parlors. All make a charming, authentic backdrop for the white wicker furniture collection.

Draped canopy iron bedsteads, replete with muffled dusters, are reminiscent of Civil War days.

Breakfast is served in the inn's courtyard on tables laden with seasonal fresh flowers. Enjoy the eggs Benedict or other equally delectable choices of the day.

Rates: $35-$55, breakfast additional $5 each
Credit cards: Visa, MC, AMEX, Discover
No. of rooms: 34
No. of baths: 34
Wheelchair access: Yes
Pets: Yes
Smoking: Yes
Senior citizen discount: Ask

Directions: 17 miles southeast of airport; I-10 to St. Charles exit; 1 block south of exit.

TERRELL HOUSE
1441 Magazine Street, New Orleans, LA 70130, (504) 524-9859

In the words of the old jazz tune, "You'll know what it means to miss New Orleans," if you stay at the Terrell House. This is the real New Orleans, from the exquisite furniture to the location on Magazine Street where the locals shop and eat. The furniture in rooms 1 and 3 are New Orleans-made pieces from the studio of Prudent Mallard, the French-trained craftsman whose workshops on Royal Street were patronized by the city's elite in the 1840s and 1850s.

Built by Richard Terrell, a New Orleans cotton merchant, the Terrell House is today an inn with antebellum grace. You will enjoy the marble fireplaces, gaslight fixtures, Oriental carpets, antique chandeliers, and a fabulous courtyard.

The Terrell House looks well loved and cared for because it is. The present owner, Fred Nicaud, loves to scout all over the globe for antiques that will shine in his showplace. His pièce de résistance is a delightful collection of children's bedroom furniture, which looks perfect in its new home in the parlor.

The original carriage house has been converted to four guest rooms, each furnished with period antiques. All open onto or overlook the courtyard. The servant's quarters, located over the kitchen, is the most unusual of the rooms and features brick walls, hardwood floors, Oriental carpets, and an ornate period bed.

Southern hospitality abounds in this gracious mansion. A continental breakfast is served in the dining room, and in the evening, you are invited to a hospitality hour in the parlor or in the courtyard.

The location is an appealing feature of the Terrell House. Originally known as Faubourg Ste. Marie, the Lower Garden District is the oldest purely residential neighborhood outside the French Quarter. Many of the homes were built during the height of the Greek Revival craze of the 1820s to 1850s. Magazine Street, also called the Street of Dreams, is the real New Orleans. You will enjoy strolling its avenue and browsing in the antique shops, art galleries, jazz clubs, and restaurants. This is the Big Easy at its best.

Rates: $60-$110; special event rates $150-$175
Credit cards: Visa, MC, AMEX
No. of rooms: 9
No. of baths: 9
Directions: 14 blocks from the French Quarter, 3 blocks from St. Charles Avenue.

Wheelchair access: No
Pets: No
Smoking: Yes
Senior citizen discount: 10%

Sabine National Wildlife Refuge

NEAREST AIRPORTS: Lake Charles and Baton Rouge, Lousiana.

LOCATION: Part of the "Creole Nature Trail," this refuge, the largest of the refuge complex, is located in the far southwest coastal area along the Texas border. To reach refuge headquarters from Lake Charles, drive I-10 west to Route 27, then south about 25 miles. From Baton Rouge, drive 125 miles west on I-10 to Route 27 south, then follow the directions above. Other nearby birding areas are Rockefeller Wildlife Refuge, Lacassine National Wildlife Refuge, Cameron Prairie National Wildlife Refuge, and Holleyman-Shealy and Henshaw bird sanctuaries. Although you can only reach it by boat, there are accommodations at Little Pecan Island Nature Conservancy.

CONTACT: Sabine National Wildlife Refuge, 3000 Main Street, Highway 27, Hackberry, LA 70645. (318) 762-3816.

BEST BIRDING: Year-round, with the greatest concentrations of waterfowl in the winter and the greatest diversity of species in spring and fall.

TOURS/WORKSHOPS: Wildlife Festival, second week in January; Marshland Festival, weekend following July 4; Blessing of the Fleet, first weekend in August. For information about festivals, contact Cameron Parish Chamber of Commerce, P.O. Box 590, Cameron, LA 70631. (318) 775-5222. Contact the wildlife refuge for sponsored naturalist programs.

The warm, moist breezes off the Gulf of Mexico cycle through the lakes, woods, and marshes of the refuge and the surrounding shores and bayous of Cameron Parish. Although this is a gentle landscape, listen for the scrape of leathery skin on sand as the alligators move languorously from the water to muddy banks. Winter is moderate here along the Mississippi Flyway; it attracts abundant snow geese, mottled ducks, gadwalls, lesser scaups, hooded mergansers, olivaceous cormorants, white and white-faced ibis, clappers, and king and Virginia rails.

Some of the year-round residents in this benign climate are great egrets, little blue herons, tricolored herons, roseate spoonbills, black vultures, purple gallinules, gull-billed, Caspian, and royal terns, black skimmers, loggerhead shrikes, and seaside sparrows. In the spring, look for warblers and shorebirds, including black-bellied plovers, black-necked stilts, marbled godwits, long-billed curlews, whimbrels, short-billed dowitchers, laughing gulls, and gull-billed and royal terns. Warblers generally seen migrating north are Tennessee, northern parula, chestnut-sided, cerulean, bay-breasted, blackpoll, prothonotary, Kentucky, hooded, and Canada. Overall, 250 bird species use the more than 140,000 acres of the refuge.

TOMMY'S MOTEL AND CABINS
Holly Beach, LA 71269, (318) 569-2426

One thing I have discovered in researching this book is that birds do not always congregate in places where there is a wide range of bed and breakfasts. Sabine National Wildlife Refuge is such a place.

The most individualistic accommodation I could find in this area is Tommy's Motel and Cabins. It is not fancy, but the cabins, 200 feet from the Gulf of Mexico, are clean and air-conditioned. All the cabins have kitchenettes, so you can prepare your own meals. Nearby is a clean beach offering good swimming. There is excellent crabbing and fresh- and saltwater fishing. If you want to bring your camper along, there are camper spots on the beach with hookups.

Rates: $35-$70
Credit cards: No
No. of rooms: 7 cottages, complete kitchen
No. of baths: 7

Wheelchair access: 3
Pets: Small only, housebroken
Smoking: Yes
Senior citizen discount: No

Directions: 10 miles west of Lake Charles via I-10. Take Sulfur exit at Highway 27 and drive south to the Gulf.

Roseate spoonbills

MAINE

Acadia National Park

NEAREST AIRPORT: Bangor, Maine.

LOCATION: On Mount Desert Island off the southeast coast of Maine. Drive southeast from Bangor on US 1 about 26 miles, then south on Highway 3 about 13 miles until you reach Hulls Cove Visitor Center on the island. Bar Harbor, near the park entrance, can be reached via ferry from Yarmouth, Nova Scotia, Canada. Reservations are required.

CONTACT: Superintendent, Acadia National Park, Bar Harbor, ME 04609. (207) 288-3338.

BEST BIRDING: Year-round.

TOURS/WORKSHOPS: Many are organized by the park service and by the Downeast Chapter of the Maine Audubon Society, P.O. Box 539, Bar Harbor, ME 04609. Be sure to take a side trip to the Wendell Gilley Museum of Bird Carving in Southwest Harbor.

Straddling the northern and temperate zones and formed by receding glaciers, Mount Desert Island and Acadia National Park consist of valleys with lakes, creeks, forested mountains, rocky shores, and rich tidal flats. With 300 bird species, 122 of them breeding on the island, this is an excellent place to spend considerable time. (Plan ahead; the area is crowded in the summer.) In January, February, and March, you can usually see dovekies, thick-billed murres, razorbill, and black guillemots. Northern fulmars, brants, common eiders, old-squaws, purple sandpipers, and black-legged kittiwakes are also easily seen in winter. In April, May, and June, there is an abundance of American black ducks, black scoters, surf scoters, white-winged scoters, red-necked phalaropes, tree swallows, winter wrens, Swainson's thrushes, and great black-backed gulls.

June, July, and August are the months of the warblers. Acadia claims to be the warbler capital of the United States, with 21 wood warblers nesting in the park. Both Leach's and Wilson's storm petrels are also abundant in summer, as are numerous shorebirds. In addition, look for the sharp-tailed sparrows, rose-breasted grosbeaks, scarlet tanagers, pileated woodpeckers, and manx, sooty, and greater shearwaters. Fall, depending on the winds, is a good time for hawk watching, and it is good news that an adult pair of peregrine falcons raised three chicks here in 1991.

BLACK FRIAR INN
10 Summer Street, Bar Harbor, ME 04609, (207) 288-5091

The Black Friar Inn is a delightful place to stay when visiting Acadia National Park. One charming aspect of this bed and breakfast is how beautifully the owners incorporated architectural features from old Bar Harbor mansions into the newly rebuilt B&B. The pub was a private library. The wicker-furnished sun room has cypress and tin walls that came from a Maine church. There are also beautiful woodworks, mantels, and bookcases that speak of a bygone era on Mount Desert Island.

Each bedroom is nicely furnished with a Victorian or country flavor. Period antiques, fresh flowers, and soft carpeting add a nice warm touch to the room. Rooms with shared or private baths are available.

The cheery sun room is where a bountiful breakfast is served. Cinnamon buns, homemade breads, and muffins are regular features. Entrées could be Belgian waffles, surprise French toast, or omelets with breakfast meats. After a full day of birding at Acadia, you will enjoy afternoon tea and refreshments.

Owners Barbara and Jim Kelly are a font of information about Acadia and Bar Harbor. Ask them about guided kayaking and fly-fishing programs or how to find the best antique shops. They are interesting subjects themselves. Over afternoon tea, they'll explain how they got into the bed and breakfast business.

Rates: $85-$105; single person $5 less
Credit cards: Visa, MC
No. of rooms: 6
No. of baths: 6
Wheelchair access: No
Pets: No
Senior citizen discount: No
Directions: From Ellsworth, take Route 3 to Bar Harbor to Cottage Street (second left off Route 3 by blue bike shop).

GRAYCOTE INN
40 Holland Avenue, Bar Harbor, ME 04609, (207) 288-3044

Graycote, a beautifully restored nineteenth-century Victorian cottage in Bar Harbor, is an elegant summer home. The airy front porch has lovely white wicker furniture and green plants. You will enjoy leisurely evenings in the parlor, basking in front of the fire and partaking of refreshments.

The large bedrooms are complete with private baths, cozy fireplaces, pleasant sun porches, and balconies. All rooms have lace-canopied king- or queen-size beds.

A leisurely breakfast is served on the sun porch with its cool ceiling fans. You will be served on china and crystal an array of baked muffins, peach cobbler, apple dumplings, raspberry crunch, fresh fruits, toast, juice, and freshly brewed coffee. Sip your coffee and plan your day. Of course, you'll go birding at

Acadia National Park. While there, enjoy hiking or horseback riding, bicycling, or walking along sandy beaches. You might also want to explore the grandeur of Mt. Desert Island or take the short five-minute walk to the village of Bar Harbor with its many shops and restaurants.

Your hosts, Joe and Judy Losquadro, can tell you where to sail, golf, fish, take nature tours, or go whale watching.

Rates: $80-$140 double occupancy; $195 suite for 2 couples
Credit cards: Visa, MC
No. of rooms: 12
No. of baths: 12
Directions: Inn will send map.

Wheelchair access: Yes, to the Carriage House Suite
Pets: No
Smoking: No
Senior citizen discount: No

NANNAU-SEASIDE BED & BREAKFAST
Lower Main Street, P.O. Box 710, Bar Harbor, ME 04609-0710
(207) 288-5575

Nannau-Seaside B&B was built in 1904 as a summer cottage and is now listed on the National Register of Historic Places.

The parlor and living room are cheerful, welcoming spots and on cool days offer a crackling fire. The living room, with its books, magazines, and television, is the perfect place to kick your shoes off and relax. The rest of the interior is furnished eclectically with an emphasis on the English. The bedrooms provide magnificent ocean views. Both guest rooms on the second floor feature fireplaces and private baths.

Breakfast, served from 8:00 to 9:30, is buffet style and bountiful. You might have fruit salad, homemade bread, poppyseed cake, muffins, bagels, homemade granola and pancakes, or French toast or eggs.

After birding at nearby Acadia National Park, come back home for afternoon tea. Innkeepers Ron and Vikki Evers will tell you how they got into the bed and breakfast business. "Years ago, on a hike we saw this magnificent house and decided we wanted to buy it. We moved in and thought the place was enormous for just the two of us. We did all the restoration work, except the plumbing, ourselves." After staying at this charming cottage by the sea, you will be glad the Evers took that important walk years ago.

Rates: Double $75-$125; extra person $15
Credit cards: Visa, MC
No. of rooms: 4
No. of baths: 4
Directions: On Route 3 one mile south of Bar Harbor down the inn's long driveway (²⁄₁₀ mile) in Compass Harbor.

Wheelchair access: No
Pets: No (owners have a small dog)
Smoking: No
Senior citizen discount: No

Great Wass Island, The Nature Conservancy

NEAREST AIRPORT: Bangor, Maine.

LOCATION: Off the northeast coast of Maine, midway between Acadia National Park and the Canadian border at Lubec. From Bangor, drive south and east on US 1 about 55 miles to Route 187, then 10 miles to Jonesport. From Jonesport take Route 187 through Beals Island to the causeway to Black Duck Cove on Great Wass Island. Other Nature Conservancy islands in the Archipelago: Mistake Island, Crumple Island, the Man Islands, Black Island, Little Hardwood Island, Mark Island, and Knight Island.

CONTACT: The Nature Conservancy, Fort Andross, 14 Maine Street, Suite 401, Brunswick, ME 04011. (207) 729-5181.

BEST BIRDING: Spring and fall.

TOURS/WORKSHOPS: Contact the Nature Conservancy, especially for short-term volunteer opportunities.

The Nature Conservancy guidebook describes the Great Wass Archipelago as being "in an unusual oceanic microclimate, where islands are colder and more moist than on the mainland, yet are buffered from the year-round temperature extremes of the interior." The coast bogs on Great Wass Island are thousands of years old, and the interior of the island has one of the largest stands of jack pine in Maine. Spruce and fir forests combine with bogs and exposed granite shores to provide a relatively pristine and varied habitat. Since this is a marine environment, you can expect to see common and king eiders, old-squaws, and black, surf, and white-winged scoters. Also, look for the dovekies, common and artic terns, common and thick-billed murres, razorbills, and black guillemots. Ospreys and bald eagles hunt and breed here, perching atop the high trees. Other raptors seen in sizable numbers are harriers, goshawks, and broad-winged, red-tailed, and rough-legged hawks.

Palm warblers nest in the forests, as do chestnut-sided, magnolia, Blackburnian, and black-throated green warblers. Both black-capped and boreal chickadees are much in evidence, courting and nesting in the interior of the island. In the fall (August), which is cool, wet, and windy, black-legged kittiwakes and alcids are common, along with great black-backed, ring-billed, and Bonaparte's gulls. The weather is as varied as the flora and fauna in this region, so be prepared for different conditions.

THE GUTSY GULL
P.O. Box 313, Machiasport, ME 04655-0313, (207) 255-8633

At the Gutsy Gull, you will see and hear gutsy gulls all around and awaken to the sound of seagulls and the sight of skittering sandpipers. This fun B&B will put you in just the proper mood for birding at nearby Great Wass Island.

Nestled in the rural beauty of a seacoast village, the Gutsy Gull offers its guests a gorgeous view of the Machias Bay, the gracious charm of a nineteenth-century Victorian sea captain's home, and the modern conveniences of a contemporary bed-and-breakfast inn.

You can relax outdoors on the manicured ground or in Chaucer's Quarters, the library. Or maybe you would like to take an appetite-building walk to nearby Fort O'Brien State Park, exercise on the inn's cross-country ski machine, or indulge yourself in the relaxing hot tub.

Breakfast may be served al fresco near the Manhattan Garden, by the fireplace in the Captain Cates room, or in the elegant comfort of the Victorian parlor. Hosts Alvin Bowker and Larry Payne are good cooks and list among their full-breakfast specialties Belgian waffles, fresh fruit crepes, pain perdu, and blueberry buttermilk pancakes.

If you bring along your bicycle, your hosts will recommend a number of beautiful day trips along their unhurried coast. Give them advance notice and they will fix you a box lunch to take along.

The G2, as the owners playfully call it, is a special place. In this unspoiled region of the world, let them spoil you.

Rates: Single $50-$55; double $50-$65; extra person full rate per room
Credit cards: Visa, MC
No. of rooms: 5
No. of baths: 3 (full)

Wheelchair access: No
Pets: No
Smoking: Outside only
Senior citizen discount: No

Directions: From BIA, follow Route 1A to Ellsworth, then Route 1 to Machias. At the foot of the hill by the University of Maine at Machias, bear right and follow Elm Street to Route 92 (past the Maine Wild Blueberry Company on the left) into the village of Machiasport (approximately 4 miles from UMM). The Gutsy Gull is located on the right across from the old Machiasport Canning Company.

MOOSE-A-BEC HOUSE
P.O. Box 274, Jonesport, ME 04649, (207) 497-2607

Charlene and John Bjorn invite you to share their nineteenth-century saltwater farm overlooking Moose-A-Bec Reach, home port to a flotilla of lobster, fishing, and pleasure boats. This pleasant hostelry is conveniently located just a few hundred feet from the marina, which is also the departure point for boats taking sightseers to Machias Seal Island for puffin watching. Moose-A-Bec is a convenient place to stay when birding at Great Wass Island.

The house documents record guests from the 1800s, when the majority arrived by boat and the others by horse and/or carriage. The Bjorns regret they can no longer accommodate your steed, but there is otherwise ample parking as well as deep-water mooring. Indeed, the facilities are considered a haven for seafarers—the proverbial port in the storm—with easy access to the marina, shipyard, and local stores for provisions and marine outfitting. Also within an easy drive are the following splendid wildlife areas: Acadia National Park, Campobello Island, Moosehorn Wildlife Sanctuary, and Quoddy Head State Park.

As for Moose-A-Bec House itself, two spacious bedrooms share one and a half baths. There is a library and a living room (with cable television), and the porch overlooks quiet gardens and the active harbor. The barn is equipped with a basketball hoop, tennis table, and the type of treadmill that a vacationing businessman does not shudder to see. A hearty breakfast is understood. After all, island-hopping and puffin-watching can be invigorating work!

Rates: $55
Credit cards: Visa
No. of rooms: 2
No. of baths: 1¼

Wheelchair access: No
Pets: No
Smoking: No
Senior citizen discount: No

Directions: Northeast of Bangor, a 1 hour 45 minute drive. From the junction of Route 1-A and Route 187, drive 10 miles into Jonesport.

CLARK PERRY HOUSE
59 Court Street, Machias, ME 04654, (207) 255-8458

Many people choose to stay at the friendly Downeast Victorian bed and breakfast, the Clark Perry House, when birding at Great Wass Island. A large lawn for games and a private patio for relaxing complement the gardens to make your stay as comfortable outside as in.

This lovely Victorian home has a sitting room with piano, books, and puzzles. The ticking of the grandfather clock will remind you of an era when life had a slower pace. There are three comfortable guest rooms, one with twin beds, one with a queen-size bed, and one small and cozy, just right for the single traveler.

After a full breakfast, head for Great Wass Island where wildlife is plentiful. Osprey nest and bald eagles regularly feed and roost on the preserve. Boreal bogs and spruce forests sustain nesting palm warblers, Lincoln sparrows, boreal chickadees, and spruce grouse.

Rates: Single $39-$49; double $45-$55; extra person $10
Credit cards: Visa, MC
No. of rooms: 2 double, 1 single
No. of baths: 1
Directions: Inn will send map.

Wheelchair access: No
Pets: No
Smoking: No
Senior citizen discount: No

ROSE MARIE'S MOTEL
Box 21, Beals, ME 04611-0021, (207) 497-2430

How could you not like a man who names his motel after his granddaughter? "It seemed the natural thing to do," said Duane Carver, owner of the motel named in honor of his four-month-old granddaughter. "Fishermen honor their wives, children, and grandchildren by putting their names on boats, so when it came to naming the motel, I just named it for Rose Marie."

The first motel on Great Wass Island is the perfect, not to mention the only, place to stay on the island. This reasonably priced, six-unit motel is the ideal location when visiting the Nature Conservancy's Refuge on Great Wass Island. "This is a photographer's, hikers, and of course, birder's paradise. There's great whale watching. People will discover that Beal's Island isn't just a fishing town," relates Carver, himself a lobster fisherman. "We just want to provide a service for those people who want to spend a few days or longer enjoying the natural and beautiful environment and ocean scenery."

"Tell your readers that the two main islands serve as a bird and animal wildland. Most of the surrounding islands not only add to the natural beauty but make for some of the best eagle nesting areas you could ever imagine. Besides birds, there are seals, porpoises, and whales."

Duane Carver's natural enthusiasm for his island is enough to make you want to visit. "Our Nature Conservancy has an abundance of birds, deer, moose, and raccoon because of the abundant food supply from the various heaths and marshes located on the islands. I've taken all this for granted for so many years and hope people from all over this nation can come year after year to enjoy some of the beauty I'm just beginning to appreciate. I hope for many years we can serve the public to the treat of a lifetime."

Rates: Single $45; double $50; cot $5 (June 1st-Labor Day); single $35; double $45; cot $5 (off-season)
Credit cards: Visa, MC
No. of rooms: 6
No. of baths: 6
Wheelchair access: Yes
Pets: Controlled, excellent chance to walk pets
Smoking: Yes
Senior citizen discount: 10% for citizens over 62 during summer season
Directions: 14 miles from Route 1 in Columbia Falls; 1 mile from Jonesport-Beals Bridge.

Common murre

MARYLAND

Blackwater National Wildlife Refuge

NEAREST AIRPORTS: Salisbury and Baltimore, Maryland; Washington, D.C.

LOCATION: From Salisbury, Maryland, drive west on Highway 50, 35 miles to Cambridge, then south 12 miles via Highways 16 and 335 to the refuge. From Baltimore, take Highway 2 south and east across the Chesapeake Bay Bridge to Highway 50 south to Cambridge, about 65 miles. From Washington, D.C., drive east and north on Highway 50/I-595 across the Chesapeake Bay Bridge and down to Cambridge and the refuge, about 85 miles.

CONTACTS: Refuge Manager, Blackwater National Wildlife Refuge, 2145 Key Wallace Drive, Cambridge, MD 21613. (301) 228-2677.

BEST BIRDING: Between mid-October and mid-March for waterfowl.

TOURS/WORKSHOPS: Contact refuge manager.

Surprisingly, an abundance of wildlife exists near urban Washington, D.C., and Baltimore, just across Chesapeake Bay, in the tidal marshes, open waters, and dense woodlands of the Blackwater National Wildlife Refuge. Although natural habitats of the open refuge have been threatened by surrounding urbanization, the Chesapeake Bay region is still home to three endangered species, the bald eagle, the delmarva fox squirrel, and the peregrine falcon, during annual migrations. The recovery of the bald eagle on the bay and in the refuge has been phenomenal, and it now represents 20 percent of the eastern bald eagle population. Peak time for viewing the eagles is October through December, when migrants increase the resident flock. In January, they build their nests, and by June, the fledglings are out. Ospreys hatch in June and fledge in August.

Up to 25 species of warblers are seen in the spring migration along with numerous shorebirds and terns, such as Caspian, common, Forster's, least, and occasionally a black. Ducks and raptors are in greatest abundance in fall. At that time, you can observe the sharp-shinned and Cooper's hawks and occasionally both red-shouldered and broad-tailed hawks as well as merlins, kestrels, harriers, and golden eagles. Also look for Henslow's sparrows, sharp-tailed sparrows, and seaside sparrows—all of which have nested at the refuge.

COMMODORE'S COTTAGES BED AND BREAKFAST
215 Glenburn Avenue, Cambridge, MD 21613, (410) 228-6938

The Commodore's Cottages, complete with the Brannock Maritime Museum, is a treat for ancient or modern mariners. The museum, containing the lifetime collection of owner Earl Brannock, is a fascinating gallery of watermen's lore and folklife. Browse through the archives and pictures documenting the Chesapeake Oyster Wars, the bloody feuds between Marylanders and Virginians that persisted until the early part of this century. It is James Michener's novel, *Chesapeake*, come to life.

If lush gardens are more your mileu, you will enjoy Shirley Brannock's magnificent yard. Birders will have a field day watching bluebirds, tufted titmice, baby cardinals, and a variety of songbirds perched in Shirley's large aged oaks and magnolia willows. As for me, I was happy to perch on the tree swing, curled up with a good book.

Shirley, an art teacher in the public schools for thirty-one years, has decorated her cottages with her charming artwork, much of it, bird subjects. The Cottage, which accommodates five, features contemporary decor with just a touch of the sea. Shirley describes it as a gracious suite in a garden setting. There is a complete kitchen, fully equipped, a bedroom with twin or king bed, a bed/sitting room with a queen-size bed, a tile bath with a shower, and color television, telephone, and air-conditioning.

The Carriage House accommodates two or more in a cozy, country setting. It includes a bedroom with twin canopy beds, a spacious living/dining room with double hide-a-bed, a complete, fully equipped kitchen, a tile bath with shower, and a color television, telephone, and air-conditioning. Residents of both cottages are served a continental breakfast of fresh fruit, homemade muffins, juice, and coffee.

If you have done your quota of bird-watching at the Blackwater National Wildlife Refuge and are ready for more outside activities, the Brannocks have plenty of suggestions. Shirley is a tour bus leader on the Eastern Shore. Some touring ideas include a visit to the Old Trinity Church in Cambridge for a recreation of a 1700 church service, a walk on the river shore, exploring quaint fishing villages, bicycling on country roads, shopping for antiques, eating good seafood, fishing, and watching the crabbers and oystermen unload their catch.

Rates: Single/double $75-$85 (plus 9% tax); extra person $10; midweek winter discount for a stay of 3 days or more
Credit cards: Visa, MC
No. of rooms: 2 private cottages
Directions: Inn will send map.

No. of baths: 1 bath each
Wheelchair access: 1 yes, 1 no
Pets: No
Smoking: Will tolerate but not preferred
Senior citizen discount: No

GLASGOW INN BED AND BREAKFAST
1500 Hambrooks Boulevard, Cambridge, MD 21613, (410) 228-0575

The grounds of Glasgow Inn Bed and Breakfast provide a peaceful birding retreat. You can meander around the seven acres at dusk and gaze at blue herons, egrets, geese, and swans. This is the ideal place to stay while birding at Blackwater National Wildlife Refuge.

If it should happen (perish the thought) that any in your party are not bonafide members of the binocular and bird book set, they might be content with the historical aspects of the Glasgow Inn and Cambridge. Louise Lee Roche, one of the pleasantly eccentric innkeepers, can tell you in wonderful detail the story of slave Harriet Tubman who lived on a nearby farm. She can also relate exactly which parts of James Michener's *Chesapeake* were written about Cambridge. The Glasgow Inn, which was built in 1760, is on the National Register of Historic Places.

This sense of history was what got Roche and Martha Anne Rayne interested in opening a bed and breakfast in the first place. "I love America and wanted to hold onto our heritage," Louise explained while serving a hearty breakfast of sausage and apple baked in pie crust and grape/orange juice. "I had a yen to save an old house. This desire was strengthened by the Bicentennial in 1976. Martha Anne and I looked at historic homes from Kennebunkport, Maine, down to Beaufort, South Carolina. But we kept coming back to Cambridge. I love the Eastern Shore. It's so peaceful and tranquil."

Together the two former teachers totally restored the eighteenth-century brick and clapboard Georgian plantation manor, furnishing it with family heirlooms. The entire inn is beautifully appointed. Among the nicest features are the colorful homemade quilts in every bedroom. The two innkeepers lovingly made every quilt and even have a quilt hanging in the statehouse in Annapolis.

Roche says that she loves having birders stay with her. "Birders are the best guests. They are so sensitive and tuned in to where they are. They walk around the acres and take time to see what is around them. Birders look with eyes that see and ears that hear."

Rates: Private bath Mon.-Thurs. $85, Fri.-Sun. $100; Semi-private bath Mon.-Thurs. $80, Fri.-Sun. $90
Credit cards: No
No. of rooms: 7
No. of baths: 5
Wheelchair access: No
Pets: No
Smoking: No
Senior citizen discount: No
Directions: Cambridge is on Route 50. The inn is 1.8 miles from Route 50.

LODGECLIFFE ON THE CHOPTANK
103 Choptank Terrace, Cambridge, MD 21613, (410) 228-1760

Water and history buffs will enjoy Lodgecliffe on the Choptank. The gracious, turn-of-the-century country home is perched on a beautiful bluff overlooking the wide expanse of the lower Choptank River. "The river is everchanging," says Sarah Richardson, the sprightly 80-something owner. "It's more alive than the mountains. The water is constantly changing. It's really choppy one minute, then suddenly it's very tranquil. You can go boating, sailing, be in regattas, go crabbing. And the sunsets are my favorite feature."

Richardson comes by her love of water naturally. Her late husband, a merchant marine captain, supervised the S.S. *United States.* "We covered the coastline of the United States—Seattle, San Francisco, Alaska, Hawaii. But we always wanted to come back to Cambridge. We've owned this house since 1946."

Richardson started the bed and breakfast nine years ago after her husband died. The family home makes a comfortable inn. Many of the rooms face the river. There are two bedrooms furnished with antiques, both with semiprivate baths. The breakfast is continental.

The innkeeper, known as Aunt Sarah, especially likes birders. "Most of my guests go to Blackwater, but you can just step outside to see birds. My guests have spotted more than 63 species of birds right in my front yard."

Richardson thinks of her guests as friends. "Every night I write a log about each and every guest. I keep a scrapbook of the letters they send me. They're like my family."

Rates: Single $60 (plus $5.40 tax); double $65 (plus $5.80 tax); extra person $10
Credit cards: No
No. of rooms: 2
Directions: Inn will send map.

No. of baths: 1
Wheelchair access: No
Pets: If trained
Smoking: On porch only
Senior citizen discount: No

Eastern Neck National Wildlife Refuge

NEAREST AIRPORTS: Salisbury and Baltimore, Maryland; Washington, D.C.

LOCATION: An island refuge at the mouth of the Chester River in upper Chesapeake Bay. Driving east across the bay bridge, the island refuge will be on the north side, opposite Love Point. From the bay bridge, drive east on Highway 30 to the junction of Route 213, then north to Chestertown; from Chestertown, take Route 20 north to Rock Hall; from Rock Hall, drive south on Route 445 to the refuge, about 55 miles from the east end of the bridge.

CONTACT: Refuge Manager, Eastern Neck National Wildlife Refuge, Route 2, Box 225, Rock Hall, MD 21661. (301) 639-7056.

BEST BIRDING: Fall, winter, and spring.

TOURS/WORKSHOPS: Contact refuge office.

Large numbers of migrating waterfowl find this island a perfect stopover. More than 2,000 acres of swamps, hedgerow, woodlands, beaches, shoals, marshes, and open fields attract both freshwater and sea ducks. In October, you can probably see both black ducks and old-squaws as well as white-winged scoters, tundra swans, scaups, buffleheads, and Canada geese. Look also for wood ducks, teals, gadwalls, black scoters, hooded mergansers, and ruddy ducks. Overhead, raptors and migrants are plentiful, including ospreys, bald eagles, black vultures, broad-winged hawks, red-shouldered hawks, and "sharpies." Try to spot royal, Caspian, and least terns at this time, along with barred owls, common barn owls, whip-poor-wills, red-bellied woodpeckers, wood thrushes, scarlet tanagers, bobolinks, and rusty blackbirds. Spring is a good time for shorebirds; however, they are also fairly abundant in summer and fall, with numbers peaking during migration.

Spring birds include veeries, gray-cheeked thrushes, numerous species of warblers, cedar waxwings, orchard orioles, ruby-throated hummingbirds, Virginia and king rails, ospreys, and bald eagles. Year-round you will be able to find mute swans, wood ducks, American black ducks, black vultures, northern bobwhites, least sandpipers, American woodcocks, fish crows, and Carolina chickadees.

BRAMPTON BED AND BREAKFAST
25227 Chestertown Road, Chestertown, MD 21620, (410) 778-1860

Getting to the Brampton Bed and Breakfast can be half the fun. Driving through Kent County in season, you can see migrating Canada geese, ducks, and swans and a variety of other wintering waterfowl in fields and sanctuary ponds. The area is a birder's paradise. The historic nineteenth-century bed and breakfast is located between the Chester River and the Chesapeake Bay in the heart of the Atlantic Flyway. From the Brampton B&B, you can bike over to the Eastern Neck National Wildlife Refuge.

Innkeepers Michael and Danielle Hanscom firmly believe that attention to detail and personal service are important, and it is their desire to make guests feel at home. They succeed admirably at this task: the rooms are extremely comfortable, with high ceilings and long windows that let in wonderful streams of sunlight and look out over farms, fields, and, of course, birds.

Danielle, who was born in Switzerland, is a natural-born innkeeper. Many of the lovely down comforters and pillows on each guest bed were custom made to coordinate with the antiques and heirloom family pieces. Most of the five bedrooms have fireplaces or Franklin stoves and offer king, queen, or twin beds.

Breakfast is a bounty of wonderful treats. You might have fresh hot lemon ginger muffins followed by a stack of blueberry pancakes or perhaps Lob Scouse, a German dish composed of scrambled eggs, scallions, bacon or ham, and vegetables. Other hard-to-resist goodies are hot sticky buns and orange-chocolate muffins.

Should it be of interest, and if you have enough time left after birding at Eastern Neck, the Hanscoms will point you in the right direction for antiquing, fishing, and crabbing.

Rates: $90-$150; extra person $25   **Wheelchair access:** Yes
Credit cards: Visa, MC   **Pets:**
No. of rooms: 8   **Smoking:** No
No. of baths: 8   **Senior citizen discount:** No
Directions: 1 mile south on Route 20 from Historic Chestertown, on Maryland's Eastern Shore.

THE INN AT MITCHELL HOUSE
8796 Maryland Parkway, Chestertown, MD 21620, (410) 778-6500

The Inn at Mitchell House is a warm and charming place to recharge city batteries. Innkeepers Jim and Tracy Stone offer gracious hospitality reminiscent of a bygone era. Their six-bedroom inn, with parlors and numerous fireplaces, provides a casual and friendly atmosphere. On Fridays and Saturdays, you are in for a special treat. At 7:00 p.m., the inn offers secluded dining. The scrumptious feast includes complimentary wine. Nestled on ten rolling acres, surrounded by woods and overlooking Stoneybrook Pond, the Inn at Mitchell House is a bird-watcher's utopia.

Depending on the season, you may be awakened in the morning by bird-song or migrating geese. At sunset, sighting white-tailed deer or a red fox or on rare occasions getting a glimpse of a soaring eagle add to the scene. It is the perfect cure for city blues.

The inn is a pleasant, seven-mile drive from Chestertown, a charming colonial town steeped in history. You are close to Eastern Neck National Wildlife Refuge, known for its wonderful birding. If time permits, you can go boating, fishing, crabbing, bicycling. Nearby Annapolis is a delightful place; I highly recommend a tour of the Naval Academy.

Rates: $75-$95
Credit cards: Visa, MC, Discover
No. of rooms: 5
No. of baths: 5

Wheelchair access: No
Pets: No
Smoking: Yes
Senior citizen discount: 20%

Directions: From the north: from the Delaware Memorial Bridge, take Route 13 south to Route 301; connect with Route 291 west to Chestertown; turn right on Route 20 south to Tolchester and Rock Hall (7 miles); turn right onto Route 21 (3 miles on right). From the west: from the Chesapeake Bay Bridge, take Route 50/301; bear left onto 301 north, then left onto Route 213 north and continue through to Chestertown. From there, turn left onto Route 291

The Inn at Mitchell House

west. Continue west for one-half mile, then turn right onto Route 20 south, drive 7 miles, then turn right onto Route 21 (3 miles on right). Via water (Chesapeake Bay): head for Tolchester Beach Marina (20 miles north of Bay Bridge). Reservations for transient boat slips are advised (410-778-1400). Phone ahead for complimentary transportation from the marina to the inn.

THE WHITE SWAN TAVERN
231 High Street, Chestertown, MD 21520, (410) 778-2300

The White Swan has been a landmark in Chestertown since pre-Revolutionary War days. Not far from the great Eastern cities, it is unexpectedly quiet, elegant, and lovely. It is a place for those who treasure serene streets, birdsong mornings, perfect service, and the grace of New World traditions.

The White Swan was beautifully restored beginning in 1978. The inn is named for the slipware "charger" (a large bowl) found among the 70,000 shards discovered during an archaeological dig behind the inn. A little museum holds the charger and gives details about the dig and the inn's restoration and past.

You will feel that you are back in colonial times in the tavern room, where you can play games of chess, checkers, and backgammon. The bedrooms are furnished with the colonial ambience in mind and have appropriate names: the Thomas Peacock Room, which is perfect for bird-watchers; the Wilmer Room; the John Bordley Room; and the Sterling Suite. The T. W. Eliason Victorian Suite leaves colonial times behind and salutes the Sovereign of Britannia. All rooms have full private baths.

Rates: $85-$135; extra person $25   **Wheelchair access:** Yes
Credit cards: No   **Pets:** No
No. of rooms: 6   **Smoking:** Yes
No. of baths: 6   **Senior citizen discount:** No
Directions: Chestertown is in Kent County on Maryland's Eastern Shore; take Routes 13 and 301 south from Wilmington, to 291; from Annapolis, cross Bay Bridge on 50/301, continue on 301 to 213 to Chestertown.

Cape Cod National Seashore

NEAREST AIRPORT: Boston, Hyannis, and Provincetown, Massachusetts.

LOCATION: From Boston, drive south on Highway 3 and connect with US 6. Headquarters is in the town of Wellfleet, about 90 miles from Boston. From Hyannis, drive east and north on Highway 6 for 24 miles, and from Provincetown, drive south on Highway 6 for 15 miles. Ferry service from Boston to Provincetown is available in the summer only. There are two visitor centers with interpretive materials: Salt Pond, at Route 6, Eastham, and Province Lands, at Race Point, Provincetown.

CONTACTS: Superintendent, Cape Cod National Seashore, South Wellfleet, MA 02663, (508) 349-3785. Or Wellfleet Bay Wildlife Sanctuary, P.O. Box 236, off West Road, South Wellfleet, MA 02663. This sanctuary is run by the Massachusetts Audubon Society: (508) 349-2615. Visitor center numbers are Salt Pond, (508) 255-3421; and Province Lands, (508) 487-2156.

BEST BIRDING: Spring and fall. Be sure to take a side trip to Monomy Island for coastal birds in late summer.

TOURS/WORKSHOPS: Many are provided through the Cape Cod Bird Club, Massachusetts Audubon Society, and Wellfleet Bay Wildlife Sanctuary.

Curving around Cape Cod Bay like the toe and bell of a court jester's shoe, Cape Cod National Seashore consists of 40 miles of sandy shorelines, dunes, tidal flats, woods, fields, and marshes. The abundant crabs and other marine life throughout the area provide ample food for migrating birds. Shorebirds are numerous from March through October; black-bellied, semipalmated, and piping plovers as well as American oystercatchers, spotted sandpipers, whimbrels, godwits, red knots, sanderlings, and dunlins can all be observed. In the fall, you might be able to see ruddy turnstones, Baird's sandpipers, stilt sandpipers, short- and long-billed curlews, red-necked phalaropes, parasitic jaegers, lesser golden-plovers, pectoral and white-rumped sandpipers, and quite a few terns, such as the roseate, common, arctic, Forster's, least, and black.

There are large concentrations of waterfowl in the area from January through April and from September through December, although you will be able to see numerous species year-round. Common migrating birds are Brant's, American black, and canvasback ducks, greater and lesser scaups, common eiders, old-squaws, black, surf, and white-winged scoters, and mergansers. Through patient observation you might also see great cormorants, Eurasian wigeons, king eiders, harlequin ducks, and Barrow's goldeneyes. Year-round residents offer excellent birding: mute swans, common loons, northern bob-whites, ruffed grouse, American woodcocks, great black-backed gulls, and black-legged kittiwakes.

THE INN AT DUCK CREEKE
Box 364, Wellfleet, MA 02667, (508) 349-9333

The Inn at Duck Creek, nestled in five woodsy acres, attracts abundant bird life to its Duck Pond, tidal creek, and salt marsh. The inn is a convenient location from which to explore the magnificent Cape Cod National Seashore and the Audubon Sanctuary.

Its 25 rooms, spread through three buildings, are all decorated to preserve the simple charm of the past circa 1800. Here you can read, relax, spend lazy days, and enjoy a delicious continental breakfast.

When your evening appetite demands attention, you can walk across the drive to Sweet Seasons or the Tavern Room Restaurant and Lounge. The former overlooks the rush bordering the pond. It features not only original art, soft music, and candlelight but culinary delights such as seafood bisque, chilled soups, and international appetizers as well as entrées made from native fresh fish, shellfish, and lobster. Steak, lamb, and pasta, also on the menu, are all prepared by the chef-owner.

The Tavern Room Restaurant and Lounge is a more appropriate spot for casual dining. Enjoy live music and great chowders and seafood; have a drink at the unusual bar made from a collection of period door and marine charts while you rub elbows with the locals.

The village of Wellfleet has excellent art galleries, shops, and old houses where you can hunt for antiques. The fine natural harbor beckons fishermen, boaters, windsurfers, and, of course, wonderful birds.

Rates: Double $50-$80; extra person $12
Credit cards: Visa, MC, AMEX
No. of rooms: 25
No. of baths: 21
Wheelchair access: No
Pets: No
Smoking: Yes
Directions: From the Cape Cod Canal, take Route 6 50 miles to Wellfleet. First "Wellfleet" exit is Main Street; 500 yards to inn.

THE PARSONAGE
202 Main Street, P.O. Box 1501, East Orleans, MA 02643
(508) 255-8217

The Parsonage is an eighteenth-century vicarage that has been authentically restored and converted into a charming, romantic inn. Each of the seven guest rooms is decorated with country antiques in a way that is consistent with your comfort and pleasure.

The Parsonage is conveniently located for visits to the national seashore, state parks, lake swimming, tennis courts, and golf courses. Just a short stroll away from the inn, you can see the migrating harlequin ducks and eiders. If bicycling is your passion, the paths that crisscross the Cape and wend their way through forests, sand dunes, and glacial ponds may prove irresistible. For the less athletic, there are art galleries and antique shops on the Old King's Highway.

Elizabeth Brownes, the Kenyan-born, English-raised innkeeper, offers continental breakfasts in the sun-filled dining room on the brick patio, on clear days, or in your room if you want pampering.

The scones with Devonshire cream are wonderful wherever you choose to eat them.

In the parlor, at day's end, Brownes will delight you with live classical music concerts featuring works by Mozart, Chopin, and Liszt. Her husband, Ian, an accountant and former medical group executive director, will enjoy chatting with you as he serves complimentary hors d'oeuvres.

Rates: Summer (June-Sept.) $65-$85; fall (Oct.-Nov.) $55-$75; spring (Apr.-May) $55-$75; winter (Dec.-Mar.) $60-$70
Credit cards: Visa, MC
No. of rooms: 7

No. of baths: 7
Wheelchair access: No
Pets: No
Smoking: No
Senior citizen discount: No

Directions: From Boston, take Route 3 south. From central Massachusetts, take Route 495 south. From Providence, take Route 195 east. Cross Cape Cod Canal and take Route 6 to Exit 12 (Route 6A), Orleans. Bear right onto Route 6A, make first right onto Eldredge Park Way. At second set of lights, turn right onto Main Street. The Parsonage is 1 mile on left.

THE PENNY HOUSE INN
Box 238 Route 6, North Eastham, MA 02651
(508) 255-6632, (800) 554-1751

B uilt in 1751, the gable-roofed Penny House Inn has served as a family home over the years. It has been converted, restored, and refurbished into an authentic country inn.

Each room is a blend of antiques, collectibles, and wicker furniture. In a 240-year-old dining room with the original wide-planked flooring and beamed ceilings, you will be served a full country breakfast. The inn's parlor/living room, sun room, or outdoor garden/patio is a lovely place to relax, socialize, and unwind from your birding activities. Tea is served there every afternoon.

The area has magnificent bird-watching, whale watching, daily ferry rides to nearby islands, dune and seashore tours, sailing, and fishing. Students of history will find the town of Eastham, settled by Pilgrims in 1644, fascinating. Three *Mayflower* passengers are buried in Cove Cemetery. The oldest wind-driven grist mill on the cape is one of many interesting landmarks to be found.

Rates: Winter $60-$90; spring $65-$100; summer $80-$115; fall $75-$95; extra persons $15
Credit cards: Visa, MC, AMEX, Discover, Diners, Carte Blanche
No. of rooms: 10
No. of baths: 10
Wheelchair access: No
Pets: No
Smoking: Limited
Senior citizen discount: No

Directions: Follow the signs for Cape Cod over the Sagamore Bridge. Go past exit 12 and around the rotary at Orleans heading north toward Eastham and Provincetown. The Penny House Inn is 5 miles beyond the rotary on the left and across from the Nauset Marsh Nursery. Look for the sign of hospitality—"The Gold Pineapple."

The Penny House Inn

THE WHALEWALK INN
220 Bridge Road, Eastham, MA 02642, (508) 255-0617

It is just a ten-minute drive from the unspoiled beaches of Cape Cod National Seashore to the three acres of lawn and meadowland that serve as home to the Whalewalk Inn. The main house, a Greek Revival built for a whaling captain, became a farm before being converted to the elegant inn it is today.

The light, airy rooms of the main house, barn suites, and cottages are done in hues of rose, blue, or soft peach. Antique furnishings, carefully collected, have been brought from as far away as France, England, and Denmark. With charm and imagination, the owners have transformed a former chicken coop into an enchanting honeymoon hideaway.

Your day may start with breakfast in the garden patio featuring such delights as Grand Marnier French toast, apple walnut raisin crepes, blueberry pancakes, home-baked bread, and fresh fruits of the season.

Obligatory activities, of course, are bird-watching and bird-watching followed by more bird-watching. Optional activities include whale watching, cycling, golf, tennis, fishing, and swimming. If you choose to just rest and relax, your hosts, Carole and Dick Smith, will see to your every comfort. Complimentary hors d'oeuvres are served by the fireplace at cocktail hour.

Rates: $90, $105, $120, $150 (all rates per room)
Credit cards: No
No. of rooms: 7 + 5 suites
No. of baths: 12
Wheelchair access: Limited
Pets: No
Smoking: No
Senior citizen discount: No
Directions: Boston to Cape Cod via Route 3 to Saganion Bridge, then Route 6 to Orleans rotary. Exit rotary on Rock Harbor Road to Bridge Road. The inn is at 220 Bridge.

ALLEN HOUSE INN
599 Main Street, Amherst, MA 01002, (413) 253-5000

The Allen House, in the heart of Amherst, is an award-winning Victorian bed and breakfast. Surrounded by tall shade trees, it stands just across the road from the Emily Dickinson house. With its many peaked roofs and rectangular windows, it is one of the finest examples of Queen Anne stick-style architecture.

This more than 100-year-old, 18-room architectural gem offers five bed-chambers with private baths, all rich in Victoriana. Wallpapers designed by Walter Crane, Charles Eastlake, and William Morris add to the charm of the building's interior. Hand-carved cherrywood mantels, both original and loving-ly restored, reflect the elegance of historic period ambience. The thoughtful hosts provide guests with a complimentary collection of selected poems of Emily Dickinson.

Your hosts, Alan and Ann Zsieminski, who radiate warmth and energy as well as a deep respect and knowledge of history, provide guests with hearty New England breakfasts. Conversation over Swedish pancakes, French toast, or eggs Benedict is often flavored with the English and German accents of guests who have studied the writings of America's foremost poet. The inn's setting makes for easy access to the many colleges and universities in the area. Galleries, museums, theater, concerts, shops, and fine restaurants will surely enhance your visit to this most memorable inn.

Rates: Single $45-$85; double $55-$95; extra person $15
Credit cards: No
No. of rooms: 5
No. of baths: 5
Wheelchair access: No
Pets: No
Smoking: No
Senior citizen discount: No
Directions: Exit 19 on I-91; 5 miles east on Route 9 to Main Street, Amherst.

Emily Dickinson

Whether it is a tale of hostelry, history, or mystery, any story based in Amherst is incomplete without a reference to the town's most famous inhabitant, Emily Dickinson. Much has been written about this white-clad recluse who constructed a universe of her own in the simple setting of the home and garden where she was born and died. No more than seven of her poems were published during her lifetime. It may be that her sharp, intense images are better understood by today's contemporary reader than by anyone of her own time.

Her acute sensory skills often focused on nature, and birds, in particular, are used in metaphor and image through many of her more than 1,700 succinct poems. Most of us nod with recognition when we hear the lines,

"Hope" is the thing with feathers,
That perches in the soul,
And sings the tune without the words
And never stops—at all.

But there is so much more, including specific reference to such common garden visitors as the bat, bee, bluejay, bluebird, bobolink, crow, hummingbird, oriole, owl, Phoebe, robin, sparrow, whip-poor-will, woodpecker, and wren. "The Birds begun at Four o'clock/Their period for Dawn/A Music numerous as space" creates a familiar image for us all, as does "No ladder needs the bird but skies/To situate its wings/Nor any leader's grim baton/Arraigns it as it sings." This last is similar to "The Bird her punctual music brings/And lays it in its place/Its place is in the Human Heart/And in the Heavenly Grace," yet neither the ideas nor the allusions bore, repeat, or overlap.

Parker River National Wildlife Refuge

NEAREST AIRPORT: Boston, Massachusetts.

LOCATION: Forty-five miles north of Boston, drive US 1 to the junction with I-95. Continue north on I-95 until you reach the exit to Newburyport on Highway 1A. Headquarters is best reached from the Route 113 exit from I-95. Follow Route 1A signs to the refuge. Birding permits are required for some areas.

CONTACT: Refuge manager, Parker River National Wildlife Refuge, Northern Boulevard, Plum Island, Newburyport, MA 01950. (508) 465-5753.

BEST BIRDING: March 1 to June 7; August 1 to October 31.

TOURS/WORKSHOPS: Check with refuge headquarters.

The area consists of beaches and dunes and saltwater and freshwater marshes —a total of 4,662 acres managed for spring and fall shorebird and waterfowl migrations. Precious and protected nesting grounds help endangered piping plovers and least terns. Since this area is visited by up to 400,000 people a year, be sure to check with headquarters for regulations and restrictions since the park is closed to protect the wildlife after a certain number of people have entered. From March to June, you can observe (be sure you walk the Hellcat Swamp Nature Trail) northern gannets, wood ducks, American black ducks, common eiders, old-squaws, black, surf, and white-winged scoters, ospreys, sharp-shinned and Cooper's hawks, piping plovers, willets, sanderlings, white-rumped sandpipers, great black-backed gulls, least terns, winter wrens, and up to 32 species of warblers. Nesting species include wood ducks, gadwalls, ruddy ducks, kestrels, king and Virginia rails, willets, Wilson's phalaropes, belted kingfishers, veeries, cedar waxwings, sharp-tailed sparrows, and bobolinks.

In late August and early fall, large flocks of shorebirds and swallows pass through, and in September, the waterfowl migration begins. Look for shearwaters and storm petrels as well as lesser golden plovers, solitary sandpipers, marbled godwits, Baird's sandpipers, and American woodcocks. Other species that can be seen then are black-legged kittiwakes, common terns, dovekies, thick-billed murres, and razorbills. In winter, you should be able to see snow buntings, Lapland longspurs, horned larks, and sea ducks offshore.

THE CLARK CURRIER INN
Forty-five Green Street, Newburyport, MA 01950, (508) 465-8363

The Clark Currier house, built in 1803 by shipbuilder Thomas March Clark, typifies the three-story square home of the Federal period. It has lovely details such as window seats, decorative dentil moldings, and wide pumpkin pine flooring. Distinguishing features are the wide center hall and the elegant "good-morning staircase."

Today, every room is appointed with antiques. All have private baths and air-conditioning. You may relax in the sunny garden room, where a bountiful continental breakfast of fresh baked breads and muffins, juice, tea, and coffee is served.

Afternoon tea is served in the parlor, where you can almost hear the echoes of John Quincy Adams serenading Mary Frazier, reigning belle of the day.

Mary and Bob Nolan are delighted with their lives as innkeepers of the Clark Currier Inn. As they express it, "When we began looking for a small country inn, we were anxious to change our busy life-style of commuting to our city jobs from our suburban home. After a year and a half of traveling all over the country, searching for that special place, we were just about ready to give up when we found not only the perfect inn but a very special community."

Rates: Double $65-$95
Credit cards: Visa, MC, AMEX, Discover
No. of rooms: 8
No. of baths: 8
Directions: Inn will send map.

Wheelchair access: Yes
Pets: No
Smoking: No
Senior citizen discount: 10%

THE MORRILL PLACE INN
Two Hundred and Nine High Street, Newburyport, MA 01950
(508) 462-2808

"There is nothing which has yet been contrived by man which so much happiness is produced as by a good tavern or inn."
—Samuel Johnson

Mr. Johnson may have had Morrill Place Inn in mind when he penned these words. Morrill Place has become the innkeeper's inn. In 1985, it was the home of the Newburyport Showhouse, a decorator's showcase extravaganza. Its twelve fireplaces are frequently photographed; one was featured by Hallmark Cards for Christmas 1985.

Innkeeper Rose Ann Hunter is certainly one of the leaders in her industry. An experienced innkeeper, she conducts seminars and lectures on the hospitality industry throughout the country. The *Boston Globe, New York Times, USA Today,* and *New Woman* have quoted Hunter on her innkeeping expertise. She is executive director of Country Inns of America Corporation.

The Morrill Place reflects Hunter's good taste. Its three floors house ten guest bedrooms furnished in antiques of the period, some with canopied beds. There are summer and winter porches, a formal front parlor, and library—all open to guests of the house.

The 1806 house is rich in history. Henry Kinsman, a junior law partner of Daniel Webster, bought it in 1836. Mr. Webster was a frequent visitor here, and the halls still echo his famous speeches.

You are only five minutes away from Plum Island and Parker River National Wildlife Refuge, part of the Atlantic Flyway. In the summer, whale-watching boats depart from the inn's docks; you can refresh yourself after this activity by partaking of afternoon tea back at the inn.

Rates: Double $60-$90
Credit cards: No
No. of rooms: 9
No. of baths: 6

Pets: Yes
Smoking: No
Senior citizen discount: No

Directions: I-95 to exit 57, 2 miles east on right; corner of Johnson and High Street. High Street is Route 113.

THE WINDSOR HOUSE
38 Federal Street, Newburyport, MA 01950, (508) 462-3778

If you would like to try an English bed and breakfast but cannot afford to cross the Atlantic, try the Windsor House. Anglophiles Judith and John Harris will greet you in their authentic English outfits, feed you a Cornish breakfast and a spot of afternoon tea, and show you their display of Cornish crafts. You might expect Bertie Wooster to pop in for high tea.

Judith is an adopted Brit, while John is the genuine article; he once lived in a cottage beside King Arthur's Castle in Tintagel. Judith is writing a book about the Neolithic people of Britain in her spare time. While in England studying megalithic Cornwall, she met John, a retired senior communications officer of the Royal Navy. "We courted on the high cliffs of North Cornwall and were married in 1990. Now, together we delight in sharing the traditions of merry old England with our guests."

The fare is definitely English. Breakfast consists of a choice of eggs, turkey ham, grilled tomatoes, baked beans, mushrooms, and English muffins. Afternoon tea features a pot of tea and a selection of tea cakes and tea breads including Cornish shortbreads, scones and jam, and Lancashire biscuit cake. These are all part of your B&B price. If you crave bubble and squeak, likky pie, Cornish pasties, trifle, Christmas pudding, and the like, you will have to pay a bit more for evening meals (Nov.-May) and a full English Christmas dinner (Dec. 1-Feb. 1).

If after visiting Plum Island and the Parker River National Wildlife Refuge, you want more birding (can a birder ever have too many birds?), the Massachusetts Audubon Society offers some wonderful bird tours and cruises. Your host and hostess can give you the latest birding information.

Rates: Private double $115; shared double $90; private single $90; shared single $70; extra person $25
Credit cards: Visa, MC
No. of rooms: 6 (3 with private bath; 3 with shared bath)

No. of baths: 4
Wheelchair access: No
Pets: Yes
Smoking: No
Senior citizen discount: No

Directions: From I-95, exit 57 marked Rt. 113 Newburyport, follow Rt. 113 to right-hand turn onto High Street; follow High Street about 2 miles to traffic light (Mobile Gas Station); stay on High Street; Federal Street is the 3rd left, sign for Old South Church. The Windsor House is across from Old South Church.

MICHIGAN

Seney National Wildlife Refuge

NEAREST AIRPORT: Marquette County Airport and Delta County Airport, Escanaba, Michigan; Sault Saint Marie, Ontario, Canada.

LOCATION: Centrally located in Michigan's upper peninsula. From Marquette County Airport, drive Highway 28 east to Highway 77, then south to the refuge entrance (75 miles). From Escanaba, take Route 2 east to Highway 77, then north to the entrance (75 miles). Drive west from Sault Saint Marie, Ontario, on Highway 28 to Highway 77, then south to the entrance (88 miles).

CONTACT: Refuge Manager, Seney National Wildlife Refuge, HCR 2, Box 1, Seney, MI 49883.(906) 586-9851.

BEST BIRDING: Spring, late summer, and fall; visitor center open May 15 to September 30. Self-guided auto tour open May 15 to October 15. Nature trail open year-round. Winter cross-country skiing and snowshoeing permitted on groomed trails. Seventy miles of roads are available for bicycling, but check with the refuge for open times, maps, and restrictions.

TOURS/WORKSHOPS: Activity calendar available. Contact refuge.

Essentially wetlands, this refuge of over 95,000 acres is a tribute to good management techniques and nature's restorative ability when protected. Of this 95,000 acres, 25,000 are designated a wilderness area, which consists mostly of bogs punctuated by stands of aspen and jack pine. The wilderness area is open to hiking and nature study from August 1 to March 15, but visits require registration at headquarters. The rich mixed habitat of the remaining 70,000 acres includes marsh, swamp, bog, grasslands, and forest.

During the year, over 200 species of birds use the refuge. In the prime birding seasons, look for many common loons, American bitterns, yellow rails, tundra swans, common and hooded mergansers, ospreys, broad-winged hawks, sandhill cranes, American woodcocks, barred owls, marsh wrens, red-eyed vireos, and up to 23 species of warblers. Year-round, you can observe bald eagles, spruces, ruffed and sharp-tailed grouse, golden-crowned kinglets, red crossbills, Canada geese, and common, goldeneyed, and American black ducks. In the fall, snow geese, wood ducks, lesser scaups, sandpipers, gulls, whip-poor-wills, great crested flycatchers, tree swallows, and gray jays can be observed, as well as many of the warblers that arrived in the spring. Snow buntings are common at this time, as are rusty blackbirds, common redpolls, and purple finches.

BLANEY COTTAGES
R.R. 1, Box 55, Blaney Park, MI 49836, (906) 283-3163

If you are a practical joker, you will like Paul Oestrike's Blaney Cottages. "I really enjoy kidding. I once told a senior citizen that his room didn't have an inside toilet. When he checked out two days later, he told me he couldn't pay the bill. Had me going for a minute." Paul's guests seem to like this treatment because he gets lots of repeat business. Maybe they return every year to watch the funny, bearded man take his huge teddy bears for a ride on his motorcycle.

Or perhaps it is his homemade breakfast featuring Texas-size muffins, either banana nut, blueberry, or apple cinnamon. "I get up every morning at 5:30 to bake my muffins from scratch," said the gruff and burly man, as he puffed on a cigarette. "Then, depending on what time they want to eat, I deliver the muffins, juice, and coffee to my guests' cabins."

Other appealing features are nightly bonfires complete with bags of marshmallows for roasting, a volleyball court, a horseshoe pit, a playground for the children, and, on special occasions, a hayride.

"My repeat customers and I have a ball together. My motto for Blaney Cottages is 'Give our guests service and warm feelings and they will become our friends.'"

With very little coaxing, Paul will show a video of the before, during, and after stages of Blaney Cottages. As he puts it so succinctly, "When I bought this place, it was a dump. It had been abandoned in 1972."

The little resort is now pristine, attractive, and eminently comfortable. The cottage we called home was quite cozy with its flowered bedspread, salmon curtains, and country accessories. We enjoyed warming ourselves in front of the fireplace on a cold, rainy fall evening.

The freshly decorated private cottages all have color television, queen-size beds, and private baths. There are eleven units that will sleep 38 people. Within walking distance is the stately Blaney Inn, the last remnant of one of the largest resorts in the United States. We dined on native whitefish while hearing the stories of the glory days of the once-affluent resort.

Paul Oestrike is enjoying his new career as innkeeper. "I had a successful nursery and landscape business for twenty years. I was getting sick of the business, Detroit, and my employees. One day, I decided I'd had enough. I sold the business, packed my bags, and moved north, all in one day. I never looked back. If I had my way, I'd never leave the Upper Pennisula. My wife, Sandra, and I are spending the winters in Florida so our daughter will be in a better school. But I hate to go. I love Blaney Cottages. You can't believe the passion I have for this place."

Those guests who can tear themselves away from Paul's Playground can amuse themselves with birding at the Seney National Wildlife Refuge, golfing, fishing, canoeing, or swimming in Lake Michigan.

Rates: $35-$90   Wheelchair access: No
Credit cards: Visa, MC   Pets: Small dogs
No. of rooms: 11   Smoking: Yes
No. of baths: 11   Senior citizen discount: No
Directions: 65 miles west of St. Ignace, 70 miles east of Escanaba, 12 miles
south of Seney Wildlife Refuge.

CELIBETH HOUSE
Blaney Park Road, M-77, Route 1, Box 58 A, Blaney Park, MI 49836
(906) 283-3409

I knew I was going to like the Celibeth House when the owner, Elsa Strom, and her friend Betty showed me their antique coffin. Betty gave a long, scholarly recounting of the number of ghosts spotted in the nearly century-old house. "We decided to put all the spirits in one safe spot, so they wouldn't bother the guests." With great fanfare and austerity, Betty offers to show them to anyone who is not faint of heart. Cautiously opening the coffin, she proudly displays an impressive array of spirits in the form of four shelves of carefully arranged liqueurs.

The puckish sense of humor and love of antiques is displayed throughout the lovely, eight-bedroom house. As we sipped champagne on the front porch, I admired the view of Lake Anne Louise and the fall foliage from the vantage point of the antique black and gold sleigh. We were serenaded by the sounds of "The Cat's Meow" played on an original Thomas Edison victrola.

Our king-size bedroom was anything but antique. The electric blanket was much appreciated on the crisp fall evening. The Dutch paintings, the lace curtains, and the fresh flowers, picked from the side yard, added a cozy touch.

After birding at Seney National Wildlife Refuge on a cold fall morning, we warmed ourselves by the elegant fireplace with the intricate carved ducks on its mantel. In the evening, we took a trip down memory lane by reading an entire stack of *Life* and *National Geographic* magazines, circa 1950.

Breakfast is a leisurely affair, served continental-style from 7:30 to 10:00. We watched hummingbirds having their midmorning snack as we munched fresh fruit, orange juice, and blueberry, bran, and cinnamon muffins. The cheerful breakfast back porch overlooks the Celibeth House's 85-acre retreat.

Strom adds a great deal of charm to her bed and breakfast. A friendly Midwesterner of Swedish descent, she is clearly in her element as she entertains guests. "It's a good thing I love this business," she explains heartily. "You're married to your house. Guests are always your first priority."

Birding guests are a special priority. Elsa fixes them a "birding breakfast of muffins, rolls, and a thermos of coffee."

"There's plenty to do if you aren't a birder. The Upper Peninsula is a wilderness area, a place to come to escape crowds. We've got great canoeing, bicycling, and a shipwreck museum. And, of course, there's the historic and elegant Mackinac Island and the rustic Tahquamenon Falls State Park. I love it up here. I can't think of a prettier part of the world."

Rates: Single $40-$45; double $45-$50; extra person $10
Credit cards: Visa, MC
No. of rooms: 8
No. of baths: 7
Directions: Located on M77, 1 mile north of US 2.

Wheelchair access: No
Pets: No
Smoking: No
Senior citizen discount: No

Bald eagle

Shiawassee National Wildlife Refuge

NEAREST AIRPORT: Saginaw, Michigan.

LOCATION: Just south of Saginaw, approximately 25 miles inland from Saginaw Bay, 110 miles northwest of Detroit. From Saginaw, take I-75 south to the Bridgeport exit, then drive west 10 miles to the refuge headquarters on Curtis Road. If you are driving from Detroit, take I-75 north to the Bridgeport exit and continue as above.

CONTACT: Refuge Manager, Shiawassee National Wildlife Refuge, 6975 Mower Road, R.R. 1, Saginaw, MI 48601. (517) 777-5930.

BEST BIRDING: Spring, fall, and winter.

TOURS/WORKSHOPS: Contact refuge manager.

The Saginaw Flats are situated in a low basin where five rivers meet along the Mississippi Flyway in Michigan. The Shiawassee National Wildlife Refuge, consisting of 9,000 acres of freshwater wetlands, bottomland hardwoods, planned crops, and impoundments, is vital to the North American and Canadian management plan for increasing the black duck population, which has decreased for 30 consecutive years. During migrations, large flocks of tundra swans, snow geese, and Canada geese rest and forage in the Shiawassee refuge and the adjoining state game refuge. Here, with careful observation you can see double-crested cormorants. Also worth observing here are the colorful ducks, especially those that stay to nest, including sleek wood ducks, mallards, blue-winged teals, and red-headed and hooded mergansers. Other ducks that can be readily observed in the ponds are buffleheads and common goldeneyes. If you are at this refuge in the spring, scan the waters for the courtship displays of buffleheads.

Bald eagles are now year-round residents on the refuge but may not be seen on any one visit. Resident owls are the eastern screech, great horned, and barred. Red-bellied woodpeckers can be seen in the forested areas throughout the year, along with red-headed, downy, and hairy woodpeckers during the spring, summer, and fall; the pileated woodpecker is a rare visitor here. About 22 species of warblers pass through the refuge during spring and fall but not in large numbers. Fall is the best time to observe the shorebirds, including gulls and terns. Other wildlife you may see in the area when you pause from birding are chipmunks, squirrels, cottontail rabbits, and white-tailed deer.

BROCKWAY HOUSE
1631 Brockway, Saginaw, MI 48602, (517) 792-0746

Dani and Dick Zuehlke, owners of the Brockway House, are contented innkeepers. They loved fixing up their bed and breakfast and now enjoy serving the public. "Our goal was to restore the home to its earlier elegance, an example, if you will, of the American dream come true," said Dick, when asked about the renovation. Dani explains her philosophy of running their inn: "Sun-dried linens, home-prepared breakfasts presented on our heirloom dishes, and our sincere interest in you are the basic ingredients." The Brockway House lives up to its slogan: "A charming step back into a gentler time."

The classic atmosphere draws you back to 1864, the year the home was built by Abel Brockway, lumber baron and family man. The four-column colonial American house makes an attractive bed and breakfast. The four bedrooms are named after previous owners of the house. The Bliss Room's king-size bed and antique setting reflects the warmth of the past. A private bath featuring a galvanized tin tub with a walnut rim enhances the rustic simplicity. The Atherton Room is decorated in warm earth tones, with yards of muslin and stenciling. The brass king-size bed is graced by a log cabin quilt. There is an adjoining private Victorian bath.

The Denton Room features Quaker rails, stenciling, and toys of an earlier era. Twin antique beds display hand-loomed coverlets in rich hues of soldier blue and cream. The Jackson Room is enhanced by a queen-size bed and nautical artifacts. The rich replica wallpaper is from the Henry Ford Museum in Greenfield Village. A full bath is just across the hall.

The Brockway House Bed and Breakfast is listed on the National Register of Historic Homes. It is a nice nest while birding at nearby Shiawassee National Wildlife Refuge.

Rates: Doubles $65-$95; extra person $10
Credit cards: Visa, MC
No. of rooms: 4
No. of baths: 2
Wheelchair access: No
Pets: No
Smoking: No
Senior citizen discount: No
Directions: 5 miles west of I-75 on M46 (B&B is 1½ blocks north of M46).

HEART HOUSE INN
419 N. Michigan Avenue, Saginaw, MI 48602, (517) 753-3145

One of the Heart House Inn's previous owners was a heart surgeon who named the inn. Therefore, a majority of the inn's menu items have a healthy heart orientation. The delicious poppy seed house dressing and raspberry chicken dinner entrée were created for the inn by the dietitians of St. Mary's Hospital in Saginaw.

Included in the room rate is a healthful breakfast of juices, fresh fruit, and assorted muffins and homemade breads. You can help yourself to tea, coffee, and hot chocolate. If you decide to eat a hearty lunch or dinner at the inn, you'll receive 10% off your food bill.

Lest you think that the Heart House lives by food alone, never fear. Flapper fans will enjoy the sounds of Roaring '20s jazz and the Glenn Miller Orchestra that are piped into the dining room during the lunch and dinner hours.

Celebrate a special occasion with your heartthrob and receive a gift box of chocolate, a bottle of champagne, and two keepsake champagne glasses and fresh flowers. If you want some heart-stopping entertainment, try "Murder Never Goes Out of Style," the inn's special murder mystery dinner.

The Heart House Inn has eight guest rooms, each with a private bath, telephone, and television. Along with your continental-plus breakfast, you receive a complimentary newspaper. This is a fun place to stay while birding at nearby Shiawassee National Wildlife Refuge.

Rates: Single $50; double $55
Credit cards: Visa, MC, AMEX, Discover
No. of rooms: 8
No. of baths: 8
Wheelchair access: Yes
Pets: No
Smoking: Yes
Senior citizen discount: No
Directions: I-75/675 exit 3 to Michigan Avenue.

MONTAGUE INN
1581 South Washington Avenue, Saginaw, MI 48601, (517) 752-3939

It is easy to see why the Montague Inn was voted the Best Bed and Breakfast in the state by the readers of *Michigan Living* in 1991. It is an elegant Georgian mansion, built in 1929 by a well-to-do businessman who made products from Saginaw's sugar-beet crop. It is one of the last bastions of distinctive mansions from Saginaw's historic Grove District.

If you choose, you can take all of your meals in the delightful dining room. Dinner is quite formal. Your candlelight dinner might consist of grilled terrine of chicken with morel mushrooms and a dijon and caper sauce, a Montague Inn salad, and fresh Norwegian salmon baked in a pineapple orange butter sauce with carmelized pecans. There is a dessert menu if you still have room.

The lunch menu will tempt you with the pasta of the day, grilled tuna steak sandwich, or smoked turkey and bacon croissant with herb brie cheese, tomatoes, and lettuce.

There are 18 bedrooms to choose from, all with air-conditioning, television, and telephone, 16 with private baths. The rooms range from the pleasant to the elegant. The Campau Room is a charming interior room with a double bath that shares a bath with the Hoyt Room. The deTocqueville Room is a large, pleasant room with a king-size bed, private bath, and a nice view of the park.

If you are a gardening aficionado, you'll want to take the tour of innkeeper Kathryn Kinney's delightful herb garden. She will tell you the history and myths of herbs; best of all, you might have the good fortune to be there when she serves an herb luncheon. Food, in the final analysis, is definitely a dominant theme at the Montague Inn.

Rates: $55-$150   **Wheelchair access:** 1 room
Credit cards: Visa, MC, AMEX   **Pets:** No
No. of rooms: 18   **Smoking:** Restricted
No. of baths: 17   **Senior citizen discount:** No
Directions: 12 miles northwest of Tri-City Airport; 7 miles north of Shiawassee National Wildlife Refuge.

MINNESOTA

Felton Prairie Complex

NEAREST AIRPORTS: Fargo, North Dakota; Minneapolis/St. Paul, Minnesota.

LOCATION: Near the west central border with North Dakota. From Fargo, drive east on Highway 10 to Buffalo River State Park, then drive south on Highway 9 until you reach the gravel road at a white farmhouse on the left side of the road (this is headquarters). From the twin cities, drive I-94 west to Highway 9 (Barnsville, 216 miles), then take Highway 9 north for about 13.5 miles. Turn right on the gravel road and drive for 2 miles to the white farmhouse (headquarters) on the right side of the road.

CONTACTS: The Nature Conservancy, Minnesota Chapter, 1313 Fifth Street S.E., Suite 320, Minneapolis, MN 55414-1524, (612) 379-2134. Preserve headquarters: (218) 498-2679; Buffalo River State Park, Box 118, Route 2, Glyndon, MN 56547, (218) 498-2124. The park has a good bird list for the area.

BEST BIRDING: Spring, early summer, and fall.

TOURS/WORKSHOPS: Contact preserve headquarters or Buffalo River State Park. The park has summer programs on the natural and cultural history of the area.

Part of the last remnants of the tall grass prairies, the Felton Prairie Complex is surrounded by cultivated fields. The total area of all three protected prairies is 3,060 acres; Buffalo River State Park and Bluestem Prairie are contiguous, and the Audubon Prairie is about 20 miles east on Highway 10. Although there are at least 12 distinct habitats in the combined areas, the two major ones are wet soil prairie in the depressions and dry soil prairie in the uplands. Rare and difficult to find species are sheltered in these grasslands, including Henslow's, Le Conte's, and Baird's sparrows, marbled godwits, upland sandpipers, and Sprague's pipits. The greater prairie chicken courts and nests here. Other sparrows you may observe here are clay-colored, grasshopper, Harris's, and Savannah. Because there are aspen stands here, you can probably observe species not common to the tall grass, such as field sparrows and alder flycatchers. Also look for Lapland longspurs, chestnut-sided warblers, bobolinks, dickcissels, common yellowthroats, brown thrashers, and western meadowlarks. Rusty blackbirds and northern orioles are commonly seen as well.

In the river woodlands and upland forest, sharp-shinned, Cooper's, red-shouldered, and broad-winged hawks soar, hunt, and perch in the treetops.

Along the edges of the prairie, Swainson's hawks and prairie falcons are more at home. Although uncommon, northern shrikes may be observed in the more open areas. Other wildlife that you can observe in this grassland habitat are red foxes, badgers, coyotes, toads, and jackrabbits. Beaver are also numerous; their dams can be seen along the Buffalo River.

BAKKETOPP HUS BED AND BREAKFAST
R.R. 2, Box 187A, Fergus Falls, MN 56537, (218) 739-2915

The Bakketopp Hus, which means "hilltop house" in Norwegian, is nestled in serene woods on a Minnesota hilltop. Innkeepers Judy and Dennis Nims have employed a Norwegian decorating scheme mixed with impressive antiques. Birding begins immediately as you listen to the loons call to each other across the lake in the still of dusk.

Each of the three bedrooms has its own special charms. The Master Suite has a king-size waterbed under a skylight, with an adjoining spa surrounded by natural cedar walls. The sunken flower gardens are a visual treat. The country French guest room has a queen-size draped canopy bed and love seat. The adjoining room has a pool table, player piano, and antique furnishings. The third is a quaint country guest room with two twin beds. This bedroom adjoins a living area with vaulted ceilings, a rock wall with a fireplace, and walk-out patio facing the lakeside.

Bakketopp Hus Bed and Breakfast

Breakfast is served on elegant antique dishes in the spacious dining room that overlooks the lake. You might prefer to dine on deckside surrounded by the songbirds welcoming the day. It is the perfect sendoff to a day of birding at Felton Prairie Complex.

Rates: Single $55-$65; double $55-$85; extra person $15
Credit cards: No
No. of rooms: 3
No. of baths: 2
Directions: Inn will send map.

Wheelchair access: Yes
Pets: Inquiries
Smoking: Outside areas
Senior citizen discount: No

PRAIRIE VIEW ESTATE
Route 2, Box 443, Pelican Rapids, MN 56572, (218) 863-4321

The Prairie View Estate is a charming Scandinavian bed and breakfast on a peaceful, out-of-the-way farmstead. It is a relaxing place to stay while en route to the Felton Prairie Complex.

One of the endearing things about Prairie View is the bottomless coffee pot. Coffee will even be left at your door, on request.

I enjoyed my cozy, comfortable bedroom furnished with family heirlooms, where I could curl up with my mystery novel in the quiet living room or in the sun parlor. In the evening, I took a leisurely walk around the farmstead and played gentlewoman farmer.

In the morning, before heading out for bird-watching, you can select either a continental breakfast or full fare breakfast. Either way, the meal is leisurely, served from 7:00 a.m. to 9:30 a.m. in the country dining room or in the parlor.

Rates: Double (shared bath) $40; double (private bath) $50; single $5 less; extra person $5
Credit cards: Visa, MC, Discover
No. of rooms: 3 (2 shared bath rooms, 1 private bath)
Directions: 1 mile north of Pelican Rapids on County Road 9; then ¾ mile west on gravel road at sign.

No. of baths: 2
Wheelchair access: Yes
Pets: No
Smoking: No
Senior citizen discount: No

Audubon Center of the North Woods, Sandstone National Wildlife Refuge, Rice Lake National Wildlife Refuge

NEAREST AIRPORTS: Duluth and Minneapolis/St. Paul, Minnesota.

LOCATION: East central Minnesota. From Duluth, drive south on I-35, 60 miles to exit 191, the second Sandstone exit. From Minneapolis/St. Paul, drive directly north on I-35 about 90 miles to the Sandstone exit. The Audubon Center is approximately 6 miles from the Sandstone exit. From the exit, travel west on County road 61; make a right turn at County Road 27. Turn right at the T intersection. Drive another 3 miles on Country Road 27 past the white Lutheran church on your left until you reach the junction with Country Road 17. Here, you turn right (north) on Country Road 17. There will be a driveway on your left about 30 yards from the intersection. Turn left and continue 1 mile to the Audubon Center complex. The Sandstone Refuge, a unit of the Rice Lake Refuge, is 2 miles southeast of the Sandstone tower, off County Road 20. To visit the Rice Lake refuge, which is about a 1-hour drive from Sandstone, continue north from Sandstone on I-35 for 24 miles to Route 27 west. Then head west 25 miles on Route 27 to the junction with Highway 65 where you proceed north on Highway 65 for a few miles to the refuge entrance.

CONTACT: Audubon Center of the North Woods, Route 1, Box 288, Sandstone, MN 55072, (612) 245-2648. Refuge Manager, Rice Lake National Wildlife Refuge, Route 2, Box 67, McGregor, MN 55760, (218) 768-2402.

BEST BIRDING: Spring, summer and fall. For additional birding, you may wish to visit the Upper Mississippi National Wildlife Refuge headquartered in the city of Winona, located 90 miles south of Minneapolis/St. Paul. (507) 454-7351.

TOURS/WORKSHOPS: Contact the Audubon Center for course and workshop listings. Contact Rice Lake Refuge for programs at Sandstone and Rice Lake.

The information booklet from the Audubon Center stresses its mission to "protect, improve, and promote the enjoyment of the natural environment through formal and informal education programs and research; to assist and encourage environmental education programs, centers and careers." The center, set among 535 acres along Grindstone Lake, provides workshops and courses in ornithology, eagle and osprey studies, raptor studies, botany field studies, and National Audubon Weeks. Nonbirding programs include wolf study weekends, fishing and ecology programs, international wilderness weeks, wolf and deer studies, youth camps, and teacher training.

You can bird the beautiful center grounds as well as the nearby Sandstone National Wildlife Refuge and Fish Lake National Wildlife Refuge. Terrain in the Sandstone Unit is primarily upland forest with smaller sections of grasslands and a few areas of wetlands. Look for ruffed grouse, woodcock, warblers, and songbirds in the spring. The wooded wetland areas should yield wood ducks and other waterfowl species. At Fish Lake, the landscape is shaped by lakes, bogs, floating bogs, and marshes. In the fall, you can observe sharp-tailed grouse near the refuge's croplands and large numbers of ring-necked ducks, scaups, and mallards in the lakes.

DAKOTA LODGE
Route 3, Box 178, Hinkley, MN 55037, (612) 384-6052

The Dakota Lodge is set on nine acres near Hinkley in beautiful east central Minnesota. With a rustic exterior and a gracious interior, the lodge was designed for privacy and comfort. Converse by the fire in the living room or share a whirlpool bath by candlelight in your bedroom. Read a book from the library, work on a puzzle, or put a movie in the VCR.

There are seven guest rooms, most with private baths. They are named for obscure or defunct North Dakota towns. Medora and Kathryn have private half baths, double-size whirlpools, comfortable sitting areas, and real woodburning fireplaces. Decorated in rose tones with black accents, Medora has a light, airy feel. Kathryn, with its navy and wheat decor, is a more intimate, down-home room.

Besides breakfast, complimentary beverages are served from 2:00 to 8:00 p.m. daily.

Rates: $52-$98
Credit cards: Visa, MC
No. of rooms: 5
No. of baths: 5

Wheelchair access: Yes
Pets: No
Smoking: Yes, in designated areas
Senior citizen discount: No

Directions: From the Hinkley exit off I-35, Dakota Lodge is located 10 miles east on Minnesota Highway 48.

GIESE BED AND BREAKFAST INN
770 Aitkin Co., Rd. 71, Finlayson, MN 55735, (612) 233-6429

The Giese Bed and Breakfast Inn is a pleasant retreat into the beauty of Minnesota's lake and woodland country. It is also a convenient place to stay when visiting the Northwoods Audubon Center in nearby Sandstone.

The inn is comfortably situated among the trees on 160 acres of privately owned wood and meadowland. In spring and summer seasons, guests are encouraged to explore the walking and hiking trails amid the maple, oak, birch, aspen, and pine. Fishing, sailing, water skiing, and swimming can be enjoyed in nearby lakes. The Upper Snake River is close by and is known as an excellent canoe route for all levels of ability.

The Giese Inn is a treat in all seasons. In the fall, the leaves turn a magnificent crimson and gold, enticing everyone to relax and enjoy. Deep snow in winter gives the base for outdoor sports such as cross-country skiing and sledding. Ice fishing, ice skating, and ice sledding are also popular Minnesota sports.

The inn itself offers interesting diversions. The west wing is a gallery of collectibles including items of brass, silver, glass, porcelain, and jewelry. There are pictures, quilts, linens, craft items, and even baseball cards. Innkeepers Dan and Evelyn Peterson also own and operate a new and used merchandise store on the same premises.

Comfortable guest bedrooms and lounges occupy the upper level of the inn. Each of the four guest bedrooms has a private bath and is comfortably furnished. The queen-size beds have extra pillows and comforters. Each room has a pleasant view and two doors, one to an outer deck and one opening to an inviting lounge. Books, games, puzzles, television, VCR, and snacks by a cozy fireplace are available in the guest lounges.

You will enjoy a hearty breakfast, served each morning by the fireplace in the family dining room. It may include fruit, juice, meat and egg dishes, muffins, breads, and, of course, coffee.

Rates: Single $50; double $60
Credit cards: Visa, MC
No. of rooms: 4
No. of baths: 4
Wheelchair access: No
Pets: No
Smoking: No
Senior citizen discount: No
Directions: 1½ hours north of Minneapolis/St. Paul; 60 miles south of Duluth.

THE VICTORIAN ROSE
2230 Highway 18, Finlayson, MN 55735, (612) 572-8041

B irding begins immediately at the Victorian Rose: ducks and geese grace the pond and yard. You will enjoy the serenity of this country place and the chance to chat with the friendly innkeepers, Su and Tom O'Brien. Their inn was originally the home of entrepreneur John Oldenberg, land purchaser for the St. Paul and Duluth Railroad. It is now listed on the National Register of Historic Places.

Victoriana aficionados will enjoy the decorating themes found throughout the house. The Rose Room, with its carved walnut double bed and a matching marble top dresser, also has an iron day bed and a private bath. The Blue Room, decorated in eyelet and lace, has a double oak bed set with a shared whirlpool bath. The Green Room features a handmade quilt decorating one wall and a double oak sleighbed set; it has a shared whirlpool bath. The third-floor Victorian Suite runs the length of the house with views of the grounds, lake, and bike trail. It has a shared clawfoot country bath.

A hearty country breakfast is served either in the dining room or on the porch.

Rates: $50-70
Credit cards: No
No. of rooms: 3—open only on weekends
No. of baths: 2
Wheelchair access: No
Pets: No
Smoking: No
Senior citizen discount: No
Directions: 1½ hours north of Minneapolis-St. Paul; 4 miles west of I-35; 5 miles north of Sandstone.

MISSISSIPPI

Gulf Island National Seashore/ Sandhill Crane National Wildlife Refuge

NEAREST AIRPORTS: Gulfport, Mississippi; Mobile, Alabama; New Orleans, Louisiana.

LOCATION: Midpoint between Gulfport and Pascagoula, Mississippi, off US 90 in the city limits of Ocean Springs. A full interpretive visitor center is located here. The barrier islands of East Ship, West Ship, and Horn and Petit Bois are accessible by ferry from Gulfport and Biloxi (about a 70-minute trip) and by charter boat from Ocean Springs. The park service has full-time staff on Ship Island; the other islands are more primitive.

CONTACT: Gulf Island National Seashore, 3500 Park Road, Ocean Springs, MS 39564. (904) 932-5302. Also, Interpretation Division, 1801 Gulf Breeze, FL 32561.

BEST BIRDING: Year-round.

TOURS/WORKSHOPS: National park naturalist bayou tours, schedules at the Visitor Center. Hikes and slide programs throughout the year. Contact superintendent for workshops.

Here at the Gulf Island National Seashore in southern coastal Mississippi even the waves seem to echo the slow Southern pace as they glide toward the beaches, their swiftness tempered by the chain of barrier islands. Here where Biloxi Bay empties into the waters of the Gulf of Mexico is a habitat for the threatened brown pelican. Twelve miles off the coast, the barrier island of Horn, a twisting snake of land, is now a future nesting site for southern bald eagles. Other habitats—tidal pools, dunes, grasses, shrubs and trees, sandy shores—are an oasis for a great variety of birds, mammals, reptiles, amphibians, and marine life; many species remain here year-round.

In spring, you will certainly see snowy plovers, willets, short-billed dowitchers, great black-backed gulls, and gull-billed, royal, sandwich, and least terns. At that time, the coastal bay is filled with black skimmers, and you are likely to also see stately tricolored herons and great blue herons silently fishing. Horned grebes are common, and magnificent frigate birds and northern gannets are frequent visitors to the coastal and surrounding waters of the barrier islands. Other eastern specialties here are fish crows, Carolina chickadees, brown-headed nuthatches, wood thrushes, white-eyed and yellow-throated vireos, and Bachman's sparrows. About 24 warbler species frequent the area in both spring and fall. Interesting raptors to look for are Mississippi and swallow-tailed kites; in addition, ospreys can usually be observed, as can red-shouldered hawks.

RED CREEK COLONIAL INN
7416 Red Creek Road,Long Beach, MS 39560
(800) 729-9670 reservation only, (601) 452-3080 information

The Red Creek Colonial Inn, located on the beautiful Mississippi Gulf Coast, sits on eleven acres of fragrant magnolias and ancient live oaks. Built by a retired Italian sea captain to entice his young bride from her family's home in New Orleans, this ca. 1899 "raised French cottage" was purchased in 1971 by Dr. and Mrs. Karl Mertz and recently converted into a country inn.

"My favorite part of the inn is the front porch where I can eat boiled shrimp and crabs in the shade of magnolias, or just swing to my heart's content, enjoying a tall drink and a thick novel," says Claudia Mertz. Karl's favorite ways of enjoying the estate are "listening to rain on the metal roof, reading in front of a fireplace, or just walking around the grounds, especially in the spring."

There are many ways to take advantage of Red Creek's Southern hospitality. You may choose to play the Victorian organ. In winter, it might be nice to sit in front of any of the six fireplaces; in the other seasons, try relaxing on the breakfast porch.

There are seven bedrooms, five with private baths. Before heading out for birding at Gulf Island National Seashore, enjoy your continental-plus breakfast.

Rates: $49-$69
Credit cards: No
No. of rooms: 3
No. of baths: 3
Directions: 1.5 miles south of I-10, exit 28.

Wheelchair access: No
Smoking: On the porch only
Pets: No
Senior citizen discount: 15%

ROYAL GULF HILLS RESORT & COUNTRY CLUB
13701 Paso Road, Ocean Springs, MS 39564, (601) 875-4211

The Royal Gulf Hills Resort and Country Club offers your friends a chance to play golf while you are adding to your life list at Gulf Island National Seashore. The 18-hole championship course is first-rate.

The resort has seventy comfortable, beautifully appointed guest rooms with cable television. The Royal Gulf Hills has a restaurant, lounge, pro shop, golf instruction, pool, tennis, and game room on the premises.

Rates: $50-75, seasonal
Credit cards: Visa, MC, AMEX, Discover, Diners
No. of rooms: 70
No. of baths: 70

Wheelchair access: No
Pets: No
Smoking: Yes
Senior citizen discount: AARP

Directions: From I-10, take exit 50 south; 3 traffic lights, follow signs; 45 minutes west of Mobile Airport, 5 minutes east of Biloxi.

Noxubee National Wildlife Refuge

NEAREST AIRPORTS: Golden Triangle Regional Airport, near Starkville and Mississippi State University off US 52; Jackson, Mississippi; Birmingham, Alabama.

LOCATION: Depending on your route, the refuge is between 15 and 20 miles from Starkville. If you take Oktoc Road south from State Road 12 in Starkville, the Visitor Center is about 17 miles. Or take Route 25 south from Starkville about 12 miles to Louisville Road, then east on Louisville Road for 6 miles to the Visitor Center. From Jackson, drive north on Route 25 to Starkville on I-55 north to US 52 east to Starkville. From Birmingham, drive south on I-20 to Tuscaloosa, then west on US 82 to Starkville.

CONTACT: Noxubee National Wildlife Refuge, Rt. 1, Box 142, Brookville, MS 39739. (601) 323-5548.

BEST BIRDING: Spring and fall.

TOURS/WORKSHOPS: Contact refuge manager; many historic tours also in this area.

Land of the Chickasaw, this region of bountiful natural resources is steeped in history. The Noxubee refuge is located in the east central region of the state. Rescued from heavy erosion and managed since 1940, its habitats consist of pine forests, lakes, wooded wetlands, and creeks and rivers. This is a year-round home for the endangered red-cockaded woodpecker and the eastern wild turkey. Water birds frequent the lakes and marshes when the air turns crisp; some stop over, and some stay, including little blue herons, white ibis, wood and mallard ducks, Canada geese, hooded mergansers, and an occasional wood stork. In the shallows, the sandpipers with their small, delicate legs whisk from place to place in search of food. Among them are pectoral sandpipers, which are now common. Point your binoculars skyward to see red-shouldered hawks and bald eagles soaring along the ridges or scanning the fields for prey.

Spring's new growth and warmer breezes induce migrating birds back to the pine woods. At this time, it is easy to see yellow-bellied sapsuckers and many species of woodpeckers, including pileated, red-bellied, and red-headed, in the trees. In addition, the brown-headed nuthatch, an eastern specialty, is commonly seen on pine cones. Of the 30 possible species of warblers migrating north, be sure to look for the prothonotary, the hooded, and, of course, the pine. Larger, more colorful, and easier to observe species that you might see are the indigo bunting and the summer tanager.

CARPENTER PLACE
1280 Highway 25 South, Starkville, MS 39759, (601) 323-4669/323-3322

Going to Mississippi always transforms me to the pages of a Faulkner novel. Maybe it is the names. His Yonnapatawpha County always sounded so lyrical, so Southern, but then most of the names in Ole Miss have Faulknerian sounds. Take the birding places, for instance. You can visit Yazoo Refuge or Noxubee. It is worth going just for the names. It is also worth it for the birding, because at Noxubee, you can spot red-cockaded woodpeckers, piping plovers, bald eagles, and wild turkeys.

In nearby Starksville, the Carpenter Place is Oktibbeha County's oldest home, built ca. 1835. It has been nominated for the National Register of Historic Places. The present owners, Roy and Lucy Carpenter, are descendants of the original owners and completed restoration of the family home in early 1992.

The Carpenters are proud of their renovated home and are happy to give you a guided tour of the environs. They will show you their 140 acres, where you may see deer, rabbits, squirrels, or quail. If you like, take your line and pole and fish in their own private fishing hole. After the tour, you can enjoy a genuine Southern farm breakfast.

The house is furnished in antiques and provides all the amenities. There are two bedrooms with private baths and a two-bedroom suite above the carriage house.

Rates: Single and double $65-$95; suite $100-$150
Credit cards: Visa, MC
No. of rooms: 2 bedrooms and 2 bedroom suites
No. of baths: 3
Wheelchair access: No
Pets: No
Smoking: No
Senior citizen discount: 5%
Directions: 1.1 miles south on Highway; 12 miles on Highway 25 south.

THE STATEHOUSE HOTEL
P.O. Box 2002, Starkville, MS 39759
(601) 323-2000, Fax (601) 323-4948

The attractive Statehouse Hotel is a convenient and comfortable place to stay while visiting the nearby Noxubee National Wildlife Refuge. The Statehouse is a small, elegant hotel listed in the National Register of Historic Places. Built in 1925 as the Hotel Chester, "an elegant and up-to-date hotel," it was restored in 1985. Upon entering the lobby of the Statehouse, you will get a sense of the splendor of the Hotel Chester. Marble inlaid floors, crystal chandeliers, a baby grand piano, and antique and period furnishings carry you back to the 1920s.

The double, queen-, and king-size guest rooms and suites are elegant and beautifully appointed with four-poster beds, coverlets, dust ruffles, beveled glass mirrors, and period furnishings.

The Statehouse is not a conventional bed and breakfast, but you will not go hungry at its Waverly Dining Room. The Library, a marble and brass Empire-style bar with warm mahogany wood tones and rich colors, is the perfect place to share birding stories with your colleagues.

Rates: $48-$104
Credit cards: Visa, MC, AMEX, Discover, Diners
No. of rooms: 42
No. of baths: At least 1 bath in each room

Wheelchair access: Yes
Smoking: Yes
Pets: Only for the physically impaired
Senior citizen discount: No

Directions: From Highway 82, turn south on Jackson Street; the hotel is approximately 2 blocks from Highway 82.

LONGVIEW FARM
Route 2, Box 1294, Starkville, MS 39759, (601) 323-7737

You can complete your magnificent birding experience at Noxubee National Wildlife Refuge by relaxing in the pleasant environment of Longview Farm. You will enjoy the excitement of a working farm. At Longview, you can select next year's Christmas tree from the 15-acre Christmas Tree Farm, watch the farmhands round up the cattle and horses, and enjoy your comfortable surroundings.

Your own private residence sleeps four adults, has a private and secure entrance, and is separated from the main farm. It includes a living/kitchen area, a bedroom with a double bed, a hide-a-bed couch, a full bath, a telephone, and a color television.

Before picking up your binoculars for your morning outing, be sure to enjoy a continental breakfast of pastry or roll, cold cereal, fresh fruit and juice, coffee, and tea.

Rates: 1-2 persons, $55; each additional person $10
Credit cards: No
No. of rooms: 1 facility, sleeps up to 4 people
Directions: Inn will send map.

No. of baths: 1
Wheelchair access: No
Pets: No
Smoking: No
Senior citizen discount: No

MISSOURI

Mingo National Wildlife Refuge

NEAREST AIRPORTS: St. Louis, Missouri; Memphis, Tennessee.

LOCATION: The most direct route from St. Louis is I-55 south 4 miles to Route 67, then south for 80 miles to County Highway E. Drive east on Highway E about 20 miles, then south on Highway 51 to the refuge entrance. From Memphis, drive north on I-55 135 miles to Highway 60 west. Then drive 35 miles to Highway 51 north. The entrance is about 20 miles from the junction of Highways 60 and 51.

CONTACT: Refuge Manager, Mingo National Wildlife Refuge, Box 103, Puxico, MO 63960. (314) 222-3589.

BEST BIRDING: Spring (February and March), fall (November and December), and winter.

TOURS/WORKSHOPS: Contact refuge headquarters.

Composed of watery swamp and marshlands, with oak trees, planted crops for feeding, and nesting boxes for wood ducks and a few hooded mergansers, the 21,676-acre refuge provides a lush habitat for migrating waterfowl, warblers, and year-round residents. In winter, you can expect to see bald eagles, Cooper's hawks, red-shouldered hawks, and rough-legged hawks, wood ducks, American black ducks, barred owls, pileated woodpeckers, and Carolina chickadees. Spring warblers can number up to 34 species; nesting warblers include black-and-white, American redstart, prothonotary, Kentucky, common yellowthroat, hooded, and yellow-breasted chat.

Other frequently seen species are summer and scarlet tanagers, rose-breasted grosbeaks, indigo buntings, vesper sparrows, orchard orioles, American bitterns, black vultures, Virginia rails, pectoral sandpipers, black terns, whip-poor-wills, chuck-wills-widows, great-crested flycatchers, and tufted titmice. Fall favorites are little blue herons, greater white-fronted geese, 12 species of ducks and sandpipers, gray-cheeked thrushes, northern cardinals, Savannah sparrows, and grasshopper sparrows. The refuge is open from March 15 through September 30, with no restrictions. Nature trails are open year-round. Check in at the visitor center.

THE STUGA
912 Nooney Street, Poplar Bluff, MO 59255, (314) 785-4085

The Stuga Bed and Breakfast is an 1887 prairie-style cottage. The colorful inn is decorated in Swedish country style and is filled with a wonderful collection of Tomtes, Dala horses, and other family treasures.

The name of the bed and breakfast has an interesting origin. In 1949, owner Jonnie Moss traveled to Sweden for the first time with her parents and grandparents. One of her great-grandfathers lived in a little house next to the family home in Raneo, Norbotten. It was called the stuga. So when the Moss family decided to embark on their B&B venture in the little house next to theirs, the Stuga seemed a perfect name.

One of the delights at the Stuga is the delicious Swedish breakfast. Depending on the day or the whim of the cook, you might be offered Swedish pancakes with lingonberries or pastries with potato sausage or meatballs and Limpa bread.

The Stuga is a perfect place when you are traveling with your children or friends. If you want lots of room, reserve the whole place for your birding group.

You will enjoy this delightful inn. Any bed and breakfast whose motto is "How Swede it is" has to be fun. *Valkommen* to a touch of Sweden only 20 miles from the Mingo National Wildlife Refuge.

Rates: $40 (one double bed in each room); $80 for 2-bedroom cottage
Credit cards: No
No. of rooms: 2
No. of baths: 1
Wheelchair access: No
Pets: No
Smoking: No
Senior citizen discount: No
Directions: Traveling north or south on Highway 67, turn east on Maud Street within the city, go 10 blocks to Main Street, turn left, go ½ block to Nooney Street, turn right, 1st house on the right.

TRISHA'S BED AND BREAKFAST
203 Bellevue, Jackson, MO 63755, (314) 243-7427

Trisha Wischmann is the kind of person who makes you feel like you have known her forever. She and her husband, Gus, offer guests a special kind of hospitality—warm, relaxed, and at home. Both of the Wischmanns enjoy cooking. The wonderful breakfasts consist of hand-picked fruits, home-baked goodies, and special gourmet entrées, all served in a fashion you will always remember.

The four guest rooms are as diverse as Gus and Trisha. The Georgia Bell Peach Room, the largest chamber, features a king-size bed with bay windows, family heirlooms, and a private bath with an extra lavatory. With its four-poster bed tucked into the bay window, Millicent's Petticoats is cozy. There is an amusing lingerie collection on display. The two other rooms are called Lavender Paradise and Pink Ice. The inn offers special packages, such as the Sentimental Journey Week-End, Romantic Retreat, Relaxation Get-Away, Golf Discount Package, and Victorian Rendezvous.

Give yourself plenty of time to spend at nearby Mingo National Wildlife Refuge.

Rates: $65-$75
Credit cards: Visa, MC, AMEX
No. of rooms: 4
No. of baths: 3½
Wheelchair access: No
Pets: No
Smoking: No
Senior citizen discount: No
Directions: 100 miles south of St. Louis via I-55, exit 99; 60 miles north of Mingo National Wildlife Refuge.

Squaw Creek National Wildlife Refuge

NEAREST AIRPORTS: St. Joseph, Missouri; Kansas City, Missouri; Omaha, Nebraska.

LOCATION: One hundred miles south of Omaha, Nebraska. From Omaha, travel I-29 to exit 79 and refuge headquarters off Highway 159. From St. Joseph, drive north on I-29 40 miles to exit 79; then proceed to refuge headquarters. Kansas City Airport is an additional 40 miles south of St. Joseph via I-29. Headquarters is 5 miles south of Mound City.

CONTACT: Refuge Manager, Squaw Creek National Wildlife Refuge, P.O. Box 101, Mound City, MO 64470. (816) 442-3187.

BEST BIRDING: For waterfowl migration, February 1 through April 1; October 1 through December 1. Winter: bald eagles and other raptors. Warbler migration, May 1 to May 20.

TOURS/WORKSHOPS: Contact refuge manager.

Strategically located along the Missouri River floodplain, the refuge of 6,919 acres of man-made marshes replaces some of the lost habitat critical to migrating flocks of waterfowl and other bird species. Some 268 species take advantage of this highly managed yet beautiful and natural area. Highlight of the bird year is the fall migration, with flocks of around 200,000 snow geese and 250,000 ducks, and mid-November to January 1, when at least 300 bald eagles use the refuge. Warbler migration occurs between May 1 and May 20; check for the most likely window.

The area is rich in prey species for raptors; consequently, harriers, hawks, and eagles fly the fields in the fall and the spring, and both the red-tailed hawks and northern harriers nest here. Other fall inhabitants are Virginia and king rails, bobolinks, rusty blackbirds, Harris's sparrows, and a variety of shorebirds. In the spring, American white pelicans are abundant. Easily seen in addition to the waterfowl and shorebirds (black-bellied and lesser golden plovers are common) will be soras, yellow-billed cuckoos, red-headed and red-bellied woodpeckers, Swainson's thrushes, cedar waxwings, American redstarts, swamp sparrows, and American goldfinches. In May, warbler species can number up to 25. With luck, you may be able to sight a Henslow's sparrow here.

APPLE CREEK INN
908 Washington, Weston, MO 64098, (816) 386-5724

Apple Creek Inn is a relaxing place to stay in the vicinity of Squaw Creek National Wildlife Refuge. Take a trip back in time to a slower-paced way of life in a charming, small-town atmosphere.

The friendly hostess of the Apple Creek is Susan Keith. The inn features a private parlor with a cozy fireplace and a second-floor sitting room for reading and playing games. The downstairs guest room has a private half bath with a clawfoot tub and shower around the corner. The second floor offers a room with a private bath and an antique washstand. The remaining two rooms on the second floor share a shower bath down the hall. After birding, you can relax on the wraparound porch. A full country gourmet breakfast is served in the sunny morning room.

If you want to try your wings at other things after birding, the town of Weston is an enjoyable place for strolling. Listed on the National Register of Historic Places, Weston was founded in 1837 and boasts 22 blocks of pre-Civil War and Victorian architecture. Browse through the antique center, craft shops, bookstores, and museums. For more local color, visit local wineries and tour the McCormick Distillery.

Apple Creek Inn

Rates: Single $60-$65; double $65-$75; extra person $20
Credit cards: Visa, MC
No. of rooms: 4
No. of baths: 3
Wheelchair access: No

Pets: No
Smoking: In designated areas
Senior citizen discount: 10% Mon.-Thurs. or 10% discount for minimum 3-day stay

Directions: From the north, I-29 to exit 20, right (west) on Highway 273 to Weston. From the south, north on I-435 (west) to Highway 45 north; continue north on Highway 45 for 15 miles to Weston. Or I-29 north to exit 20 and west on Highway 273 7 miles to Weston.

BASSWOOD COUNTRY INN RESORT
15880 Interurban Road, Platte City, MO 64079
(816) 431-5556, (800) 242-2775

Basswood Country Inn Resort is a lovely getaway retreat close to the Squaw Creek National Wildlife Refuge. It is a resort for all seasons, but the beautifully secluded 73-acre country estate is particularly nice in the fall, when the golden and scarlet leaves fall into the lake and the air is crisp and fresh.

There is a genuine sense of history at Basswood. You can stay in the Celebrity Country House and immerse yourself in the past. The elegantly furnished 1,550-square-foot suite pays tribute to Harry, Bess, and Margaret Truman, who spent many hours at Basswood in the 1940s and 1950s. The living room has a queen sleeper and an old-fashioned rolltop desk. The dining room opens onto a small balcony, which overlooks the lake and adjoins a fully furnished kitchen with a dishwasher, appliances, cookware, and dinnerware. A king-size brass bed is the focal point of the master bedroom, which is decorated in country French with lots of ruffles.

Margaret's room, on the opposite end of the suite, has a queen-size bed with a television, VCR, coffee bar, and refrigerator. Both bedrooms have large private baths with Jacuzzi tubs for two, a separate shower, and large walk-in closets. The entire upper level suite is perfect for two couples, families, retreats, honeymoons, or a group of birders.

Other suites include the Bing Crosby and Rudy Vallee suites and the Mother-in-Law Cottage. Each suite includes a television, VCR, telephone, desk and lamp, refrigerator, microwave, coffee maker, dining area, and use of outdoor grills.

A simple continental breakfast of fresh baked doughnuts and rolls, juice, hot tea, and coffee is served just a few steps from your suite in the Basswood Country Store.

Rates: Single $58; double $63-$125; **No. of baths:** 8
extra person $7 · **Wheelchair access:** 1 unit
Credit cards: Visa, MC · **Pets:** No
No. of rooms: 8 (4 suites; 4 two-bed- · **Smoking:** Yes
room units) · **Senior citizen discount:** No
Directions: I-29, exit 18, east on Highway 92 3.7 miles, north on Winan Road
1.2 miles, west on Interurban Road, 1 block on left.

THE HATCHERY BED AND BREAKFAST
618 Short Street, Weston, MO 64098, (816) 386-5700

The Hatchery Bed and Breakfast is a grand old antebellum home built in
1845 and listed on the National Register of Historic Places. Innkeepers
Glen and Jolene Payne will be happy to share the interesting history of their
inn and tell you how the Hatchery got its name. The antique-filled home has a
unique charm. In the Deacon's room, you will find a Deacon's bench (ca.
1800) and a pine table (dated 1797) plus a beautiful highback hand-carved
bed. Each guest room has full private bath with a shower, tub, and fireplace.

A generous gourmet breakfast is served in the dining room. When the
weather is balmy, you might prefer to eat outside on the high upper balcony,
overlooking the town of Weston.

Before or after birding at Squaw Creek National Wildlife Refuge, browse
through the Hatchery's two rooms devoted to an antique shop or stroll out to
Glen's workshop in the back to see furniture restoration in progress. Do not
overlook Weston, which has antique shops, a doll shop, and antebellum and
Victorian architecture.

Rates: Double $68; single $75 · **Wheelchair access:** No
Credit cards: Visa, MC · **Smoking:** No
No. of rooms: 3 · **Pets:** No
No. of baths: 3 · **Senior citizen discount:** No
Directions: I-29 north from Kansas City to Platte City exit; east on 92 to 45
to yellow blinking light (sign Weston 2 miles); left on JJ to downtown area.

Glacier National Park/
Waterton-Glacier Peace Park

NEAREST AIRPORTS: Missoula or Great Falls, Montana; Lethbridge, Alberta, Canada.

LOCATION: Glacier National Park is located in the northwest corner of Montana, abutting the Canadian border. Waterton Park, across the Canadian border, is in the southeast quadrant of Alberta. The parks, though administered separately, were jointly designated as the first international peace park by the governments of Canada and the United States in 1932. From Missoula, Montana, head north on Highway 93 about 80 miles, then east on Highway 2 at the junction of Kalispell, 35 miles from the main west entrance at Apgar. If you are coming from Great Falls, Montana, you can reach the east entrance at Kiowa or Saint Mary via I-15 north 80 miles to Highway 2 at Shelby, then east 65 miles. Highways 5 or 6 out of Lethbridge, Alberta, meet at the Waterton Park entrance, about 55 miles; and Highway 2 from Fort MacLeod, Canada, will connect to either Waterton or Glacier.

CONTACTS: Glacier National Park, West Glacier, MT 59936, (406) 888-5441. Waterton Lakes National Park, c/o Waterton Natural History Association, P.O. Box 145, Waterton Park, Alberta, Canada T0K 2M0, (403) 859-2624.

BEST BIRDING: Spring, summer, and fall.

TOURS/WORKSHOPS: The park naturalists offer intensive summer programs, and the natural history associations offer field trips. Contact Waterton Natural History Association for Canada and Glacier National History Association for the United States at Box 428, West Glacier, MT 59936, (406) 888-5756. Through World Heritage, in conjunction with the Natural History Association, Native Americans also provide interpretive programs during the summer.

Sprawling across the Continental Divide, this park of glaciers, cold crystal lakes, flowering meadows, and etched peaks seems to vibrate with life. West and east of the divide are many different life zones. On the west side, warm rains produce forests of spruce, fir, and lodgepole pine; in the valleys, cedar and hemlock thrive. Alpine wildflowers are abundant in spring, although the season is short. The east side features plains, prairies, and mountains.

Alpine species are numerous in the spring and summer; white-tailed ptarmigans are common, as are blue grouse. Rufous and calliope hummingbirds share this high altitude with Clark's nutcrackers, rock wrens, hermit thrushes, Townsend's solitaires, golden eagles, gyrfalcons, and prairie falcons. In both the east and west sections of the park, you can see tundra swans, cinnamon teals, ring-necked ducks, Barrow's goldeneyes, harlequin ducks, common mergansers, northern goshawks, and ospreys.

In the spring, sandhill cranes, black-bellied plovers, black turnstones, Caspian terns, greater scaups, and buffleheads fill the wetlands. In the woodlands, you can expect northern pygmy owls, pileated and three-toed woodpeckers, and Hammond's flycatchers, as well as black-capped, mountain, and boreal chickadees.

This is high-elevation country. Although summer temperatures can reach the 90s in the valleys, the night temperature can quickly drop to the 20s. Some areas of the park are closed in the winter. Write for detailed information on what type of weather can be expected during your visit.

THE CRENSHAW HOUSE
5465 Highway 93 South, Whitefish, MT 59937
(406) 862-3496, (800) 453-2863

The Crenshaw House, just twenty-seven miles away from Glacier National Park, is ideally located for your stay. If you want to know anything about Montana, owner Anni Crenshaw-Rieker, a fourth-generation Montanan, is the person to tell you.

The Crenshaw House

Montana is a state for all seasons. A visit to the Crenshaw House during winter affords frolicking in a snowy, sparkling wonderland as well as skiing and sitting by the fireplace. This gives way to the grassy meadows, wildflowers, and blue skies of spring and summer. The vibrant foliage of fall awakens interest in hiking, floating, fishing, or just enjoying the beautiful scenery.

Crenshaw-Rieker visited several bed-and-breakfast homes while traveling in Europe. She has incorporated the best of each into her own meadow home, featuring plush carpet, two fireplaces, a family room with a bar (BYOB), and an outside hot tub.

The three bedrooms have their individual characteristics. The Remembrance Room, with private bath, was designed in a flower garden motif with cream satin and brass accents. The other two rooms share a bath. The Meadow Room is a blue and white lace room, warmed by crystal lamps. The rustic and cozy America West Room has softly muted colors.

Crenshaw-Rieker will deliver freshly brewed coffee or tea and huckleberry popovers to your room. A full breakfast awaits you in the formal dining room anytime from 7:30 to 9:30 a.m. All of this is a mere hour and a half drive from the Canadian border.

Rates: Summer $65, $80, $95   **Wheelchair access:** No
Credit cards: Visa, MC   **Pets:** No
No. of rooms: 3   **Smoking:** No
No. of baths: 3   **Senior citizen discount:** 10%
Directions: 3½ miles south of Whitefish on Highway 93; turn left, 50 feet before mile marker 124, at Crenshaw House sign. If driving north from Kalispell, turn right on second road past mile marker 124. From Glacier Park, take Highway 40 to the junction of 93, then proceed as if coming from Whitefish on 93.

DUCK INN
1305 Columbia Avenue, Whitefish, MT 59937, (406) 862-3825

Waddle we do at the Duck Inn? Quack open a bottle of Wild Duck and hightail it into the Jacuzzi room! Okay, so you hate puns, but this place is so filled with duck motifs (dishes, lamps, ironwork, upholstery) that it is hard to resist. This ten-room haven of rough cedar and glass will enchant all birders en route to nearby Glacier National Park.

The Duck Inn is a delight. Guest rooms all have private baths, fireplaces, and balconies; some overlook the Whitefish River, which teems with wildlife. The central guest conversation area establishes a relaxed ambience with its massive stone fireplace, cathedral ceiling, and decidedly comfortable furnishings.

An in-house baker assures a generous and hearty breakfast for all, with oven-fresh berry coffee cakes, pineapple muffins, and individual-sized loaves of bread.

Ken and Phyllis Adler knew their market when they located, named, and decorated this pleasant hostelry. An additional guest service provides transportation to and from the Amtrak station and the airport. The phone number is 862-DUCK. You won't soon forget it!

Rates: $79
Credit cards: Visa, MC, AMEX, Discover, Diners, Carte Blanche
No. of rooms: 10
No. of baths: 10
Wheelchair access: No
Pets: No
Smoking: No
Senior citizen discount: Not during summer season, 10% off-season
Directions: A block off Highway 93, on the Whitefish River.

OSPREY INN
5557 Highway 93 South, Somers, MT 59932
(406) 857-2042, (800) 258-2042

Innkeepers Sharon and Wayne Finney are companionable birds-of-a-feather. Being members of the Audubon Society themselves, they love to bird-watch and to talk to guests about their avocation. They even lead guided bird-watching tours. Both are native Montanans and will be pleased to share their beautiful area with you.

Their three-story, lakeside home has a panoramic view of Flathead Lake and the surrounding mountains. The well-kept lawn extends to the lakeshore, which has a gentle, pebbled beach and a boat dock. On the grounds, you will see geese, loons, grebes, and osprey. In season you can relax on the deck and watch the morning sun play on the Mission Mountains across the lake or relax at sunset in the hot tub after a day of bird-watching at Glacier National Park.

The house has four rooms, two of which share a bath; the two others have private baths. In addition, there is a rustic but new log cabin for two that overlooks the lake.

The inn serves a full western or continental breakfast with fresh strawberries, raspberries, or cherries in season. Muffins and cinnamon rolls are a house specialty, as is the delicious homemade syrup on your pancakes.

Rates: Single $80; double $85
Credit cards: Visa, MC, AMEX
No. of rooms: 4
No. of baths: 4
Wheelchair access: Limited
Pets: No
Smoking: Outside
Senior citizen discount: No
Directions: 8 miles south of Kalispell Mountain on Highway 93.

TURN IN THE RIVER INN
P.O. Box 1356, Whitefish, MT 59937, (406) 257-0724, (800) 892-2474

The Turn in the River Inn offers a relaxed and very private atmosphere combining a unique blend of European elegance and Western hospitality. Spend happy hours with binoculars and camera so that you can record waterfowl along the river and walk or ski on trails where foxes, deer, and coyotes often cross. Here, you are only 30 minutes from dramatic Glacier National Park. The scenery is stunning, and birds are abundant.

Innkeepers Judy and Don Spivey are hospitable hosts. They have designed their inn so that they can share with guests their interests in the mountains and cross-country and alpine skiing. They are also avid bikers.

The inn reflects the Spiveys' peripatetic lives. They have traveled to most of the United States and parts of Europe and the Middle East. Breakfast is often internationally inspired. Late afternoon, after birding, you can pop in for a spot of English tea or enjoy hors d'oeuvres.

The four bedrooms all have private baths. Amenities include the great room with its massive stone fireplace and music room, complete with piano. Complimentary airport and Amtrak pickup is available for those needing transportation.

Rates: $75, $85; extra person 12 or older, $15
Credit cards: Visa, MC
No. of rooms: 3
No. of baths: 3
Directions: Inn will send map.

Wheelchair access: Inn and dining room
Pets:
Smoking: No
Senior citizen discount: No

Charles M. Russell National Wildlife Refuge

NEAREST AIRPORTS: Regina, Saskatchewan, Canada; Medicine Hat, Alberta, Canada; Williston, North Dakota; Glasgow, Billings, Great Falls, and Lewiston, Montana.

LOCATION: The refuge consists of over 1 million acres and spans the Missouri River for 125 miles in the northeast quadrant of Montana. Although the refuge is in an isolated location, it offers a wonderful opportunity to enjoy northern prairie grasslands, forests, and cottonwood stands along the Missouri River. Many of our heroes and villains of western history lived and died in this area. The Lewis and Clark expedition traveled along the Missouri; these are also homelands for various Native American tribes, such as the Assiniboine, Brule, Teton, Hunkpapa and Yanktonai Sioux, Crow, and Blackfeet.

The refuge headquarters is in Lewiston. From Billings, Montana, take I-90 west to 191 north, then Highway 200 east at the junction. The total distance is about 165 miles. From Great Falls, Montana, drive Highway 200 east for about 100 miles to Lewiston. The west entrance is approximately 50 miles north of Lewiston. To reach the west unit from Canada, drive south from Medicine Hat, Alberta, on Highway 41 (US 232), then east on Highway 2 to Highway 66 or 191 south. You can reach the east unit from Canada via Regina, Saskatchewan. Drive to Moose Jaw, west on Highway 1. From Moose Jaw, take Highway 2 (US 24) to the refuge entrance, about 100 miles. From Williston, North Dakota, head west on Highway 2 to Glasgow, then south on Highway 24. These are all main arteries into the refuge; however, since it stretches 125 miles east to west, there are other accesses. Contact the manager to find your best route. The only all-weather road is Highway 191. Inquire locally about road conditions except in dry weather.

CONTACT: Charles M. Russell National Wildlife Refuge, P.O. Box 110, Lewistown, MT 59457-0110. (406) 538-8707.

BEST BIRDING: Late March to May. Sharp-tailed grouse display and nest in June.

TOURS/WORKSHOPS: Write for *The Missouri River and Russell Counties Auto Tour Guide*, Great Falls Chamber of Commerce, P.O. Box 2127, Great Falls, Montana 59403, (406) 761-4434, out of state ((800) 527-5348, for historical tours and to the refuge for specific birding tours and outfitters.

Remote and filled with a wealth of wildlife, this ribbon of the Missouri River is home to over 240 species of birds and many mammals. Once rich hunting ground for the Indian tribes that lived and passed through here, the area remains a crucial habitat. The refuge provides rookeries for white pelicans and great blue herons. Ten species of raptors nest each year in the vast acreage, including golden eagles, ospreys, ferruginous hawks, and merlins. Gray partridges are common year-round.

During the very active spring and early summer you can observe piping and mountain plovers, California gulls, Forster's and common terns, red-headed woodpeckers, Say's phoebes, dusky flycatchers, violet-green swallows, Clark's nutcrackers, American dippers, Sprague's pipits, Bohemian waxwings, northern shrikes, western tanagers, lark buntings, and clay-colored sparrows. In late June, the breaks of the river are filled with the cooing sound of thousands of mourning doves. Swainson's and rough-legged hawks, golden eagles, and occasionally a prairie falcon will be at the refuge in the fall. Also look for grouse, wild turkeys, sandhill cranes, plovers, snipes, sandpipers, phalaropes, and 5 species of owls: great-horned, burrowing, long- and short-eared, and the northern saw-whet. Piñon jays, the only flocking jay, can be seen at the higher elevations, along with mountain bluebirds.

MOTELS
near Charles M. Russell National Wildlife Refuge
Lewiston, MT 59457

There are some birding refuges where no bed and breakfasts could be found. Charles M. Russell appears to be such a place, although if I am wrong, I would appreciate hearing from you. Meanwhile, I suggest that you take your sleeping bag and tent or stay in one of the following motels:

MOUNTAIN VIEW MOTEL, 1422 W. Main Street, Lewiston, MT 59457; (406) 538-3457; $26-40.

B & B MOTEL, 520 E. Main (On Hwy 87, N of I-90), Lewiston, MT 59457; (406) 538-5496; $26-$42.

PARK INN INTERNATIONAL, 211 E. Main, Box 939, Lewiston, MT 59457; (406) 538-8721; $45-$52.

SUPER 8 MOTEL, 102 Wendell Avenue, Lewiston, MT 59457; (406) 538-2581; $32-$44.

NEBRASKA

Rainwater Basin Wetland Management District (Platte River and Grand Island)

NEAREST AIRPORTS: Lincoln, Grand Island, and Kearney, Nebraska.

LOCATION: This approximately 4,200-square-mile area of Nebraska lies within the counties of Gosper, Phelps, Kearney, Harlan, Franklin, Adams, Hamilton, Clay, Polk, Butler, York, Seward, Fillmore, Saline, Nuckolls, and Thayer. Write to the manager of the Wetland Management District for a bird list of the Rainwater Basin, which includes a list of favorite birding spots. Also ask for location maps of federal waterfowl production areas.

CONTACT: Manager, Wetland Management District, U.S. Fish and Wildlife Service, P.O. Box 1686, Kearney, NE 68848, (308) 236-5015. Grand Island Visitors Bureau, P.O. Box 1486, Grand Island, NE 68802, (800) 658-3178. Lillian Annette Rowe Audubon Sanctuary, Route 2, Box 146, Gibbon, NE 68840, (308) 468-5282.

BEST BIRDING: March and April.

TOURS/WORKSHOPS: Contact the Grand Island Visitors Bureau for dates and information on the "Wings over the Platte" celebration held annually in March. Make reservations for tours and workshops early.

This region is characterized by flat or gently rolling loess plains. Private upland areas are used extensively for agriculture. Other habitats include irregularly distributed grasslands, freshwater wetlands, and riparian areas found along drainages and small creek bottoms.

In this region, the U.S. Fish and Wildlife Service administers approximately 49 waterfowl production areas and one refuge, totaling 18,000 acres. These areas are managed primarily for the spectacular spring migration of sandhill cranes and waterfowl. Sandhill cranes congregate on the Platte River like nowhere else in the world; each spring as many as 500,000 migrate to the 40 miles of the Platte River between Grand Island and Kearney.

The best way to view these high concentrations of sandhill cranes during the day is to drive the Platte River Road between Doniphan and Kearney and observe cranes feeding in the fields. You can reach Doniphan by driving south from Grand Island on Highway 281; then from Doniphan drive along the Platte River Road west as far as Kearney. The best viewing is usually in late March when the birds have become accustomed to the traffic and are feeding on the edges of the fields.

If you are interested in watching the sandhill cranes leave their river roost in the mornings or return to it in the evenings, take the Platte River Road west to Alda Road and turn right. There are two new bridges over the river, and next to one of them is a parking area. Visitors may park there and watch the cranes departing from or approaching their nighttime roosts. The cranes take off from the river for the fields at sunrise (about 5:30 a.m.) and begin returning to the river at about 5:00 p.m. It usually takes about two or three hours for all of the cranes to return to the river in the evenings.

Large numbers of sandhill cranes usually remain in the area until the first week of April; by the second week of April, they start to leave the area. Whooping cranes begin to arrive in mid- to late April.

The Platte River serves several other migrating species as well. Peak waterfowl numbers in late March and early April may include as many as 90 percent of the total midcontinent population of white-fronted geese. Visitors may also expect to see snow geese and Canada geese, mallards, northern pintails, blue-winged and green-winged teals, American wigeons, northern shovelers, and lesser scaups.

Besides waterfowl and cranes, several shorebirds may be seen, including piping plovers and least terns. Bald eagles, peregrine falcons, and whooping cranes are other endangered species that might be seen in this area.

KIRSCHKE HOUSE
1124 West 3rd, Grand Island, NE 68801, (308) 381-6851

The motto for the Kirschke House is, "The ornament of a house is the friends who frequent it." This Ralph Waldo Emerson quote aptly describes this warm and comfortable bed and breakfast, which was built in 1902 by the prominent contractor, Otto Kirschke, as his family home.

The vine-covered two-story brick home features such architectural highlights as a windowed cupola, a turret, and stained glass windows over an open oak staircase. The vines and roses of the exterior are reflected in the guest rooms, which are accented with Victorian lace, period furnishings, and antique accessories. Masterfully blended into the Old World atmosphere of the house, the twentieth-century luxuries include a wooden hot tub in the lantern-lit brick wash house.

Innkeeper Lois Hanks is a fine cook. Her love for cooking and entertaining is reflected in both her gourmet and country cooking; meals are served elegantly on fine china, crystal, and silver. In addition to the breakfast, which is included in the room rate, you can make special dinner arrangements.

The city of Grand Island was platted by the Union Pacific Railroad in 1866; it derives its name from the 40-mile island on the multichannel Platte River. The Rainwater Basin Wetland Management District region along the Platte River between Grand Island and Lexington and from North Platte to Sutherland is a birder's delight.

Rates: Single $40; double $45-$55;   **Wheelchair access:** No
extra person $15   **Pets:** No
Credit cards: Visa, MC, AMEX   **Smoking:** No
No. of rooms: 4
No. of baths: 1; personal sinks in
rooms
Directions: In central Nebraska, just 9 miles north of I-80. Take Grand Island's west exit 312 and drive north 9 miles on Highway 281. At the Highway 30 exit, turn east, over an overpass into the city of Grand Island. Following Highway 30 east will bring you to a traffic light at Broadwell Street. Proceed east 4 blocks past the Broadwell Street traffic light. Turn north on Washington Street and go one block. The Kirschke House Bed and Breakfast is located across the street, north of the new Edith Abbott Memorial Library.

WALDEN WEST

R.R. 4, Fawn Woods Lake, Box 56, Kearney, NE 68847, (308) 237-7296

Walden West—the name implies a setting both simple and serene. Located on Fawn Woods Lake, next to the old Oregon Trail, this land was actually once part of the reservation of historic Fort Kearny. Since 1978, Ward and Norma Schrack have had a comfortable home directly on the lakeshore, in a grove of stately cedar trees punctuated with maple, mulberry, and cottonwood. This area, a former sand quarry, was developed as a retreat for family and friends.

Bird-watching at the Rainwater Basin Wetland Management District (Platte River) is great at any time, but the epic Crane Watch (late February to mid-April) is an unforgettable sight. During this annual sandhill crane migration, special arrangements can be made for private tours, blinds, and educational programs. Walden West is directly in the center of these activities.

This is a great place to relax. With a two-couple maximum occupancy (private rooms with semiprivate bath), solitude and privacy are almost guaranteed. A full breakfast is served in the conservatory, a pleasant room overlooking the water. A 16-station physical trail has been developed, and there are several miles of walking trails as well as close access to the Platte River and the Fort Kearny State Historical Park.

Rates: $50-$55   **Wheelchair access:** No
Credit cards: No   **Pets:** No
No. of rooms: 2   **Smoking:** No
No. of baths: 1   **Senior citizen discount:** No
Directions: 1 mile north of historic old Fort Kearny; 45 miles west of Grand Island, and only 1 mile south of the Platte River.

NEVADA

Desert National Wildlife Refuge Complex

NEAREST AIRPORT: Las Vegas, Nevada.

LOCATION: The Corn Creek Field Station of the Desert National Wildlife Refuge is 22 miles north of Las Vegas on Highway 95. The northernmost border of the Desert National Wildlife Refuge is the Pahranagat National Wildlife Refuge, 90 miles north of Las Vegas on Highway 93.

CONTACT: Desert National Wildlife Refuge Complex, 1500 North Decatur Boulevard, Las Vegas, NV 89108. (702) 646-3401.

BEST BIRDING: Spring and fall migrations. Additional areas to bird are the water treatment plant and the Lake Mead marina area for water birds. Always carry water when birding in desert areas.

TOURS/WORKSHOPS: Contact refuge headquarters or the Red Rock Audubon Society: (702) 293-2716.

Although this is an arid desert area, there is nevertheless an abundance of life in these refuges. The 1.5 million acres of the Desert National Wildlife Refuge—largest in the lower 48 states—support birds and other wildlife in southern Nevada. Although its mission is to protect bighorn sheep and their habitat, over 260 bird species have been observed at the refuge in diverse habitats: desert shrub, desert woodlands, coniferous forests, and spring-fed ponds. One of the best locations for observation is the area around Corn Creek Field Station. Over 60 accidentals and rare migrants have been spotted on the refuge, essentially because of its proximity to the Pacific Flyway. A few interesting examples are wood storks, snowy plovers, common black hawks, northern shrikes, Mississippi kites, and orchard orioles. Common year-round species are Gambel's quail, Say's phoebes, horned larks, scrub and piñon jays, bustits, pygmy nuthatches, blue-gray gnatcatchers, phainopeplas, rufous-sided towhees, and Cassin's finches. Spring and fall migrating waterfowl and shorebirds stop over, as do golden eagles and sometimes northern goshawks. Look also for sage and Bendire's thrashers, Grace's and Wilson's warblers, and black-throated gray and Townsend's warblers, as well as hooded, northern, and Scott's orioles.

Farther north at the Pahranagat National Wildlife Refuge, there are 5,380 acres of marshes, open waters, meadows, and croplands that attract 240 species of birds. Spring will bring eared and western grebes, tundra swans, ring-necked ducks, and common mergansers; common snipes and Wilson's phalaropes are often seen, as are northern rough-winged swallows, black-throated sparrows, and yellow-headed blackbirds. In the summer, two common warblers are the Lucy's and the yellow. Year-round, you will be able to observe great horned owls, common barred owls, and western screech-owls as well as greater roadrunners, rock wrens, ladder-backed woodpeckers, and great blue herons. In fall, the raptors are more prevalent, including ospreys, sharp-shinned ferruginous and rough-legged hawks, kestrels, and prairie falcons.

MT. CHARLESTON HOTEL
#2 Kyle Canyon Road, Mt. Charleston, NV 89124, (702) 872-5500

One does not usually think of Las Vegas, Nevada, as a logical site for either bird-watching or cozy country inns. Most of the birds you are apt to hear of in Las Vegas are three across on a slot machine. But we have got a surprise for you. The birds are terrific at the Desert National Wildlife Refuge Complex, and there actually is a hotel in the Las Vegas area that does not feature exploding volcanoes in front or caged tigers in the lobby as its main attraction.

Mt. Charleston Hotel, only minutes from Las Vegas, is worlds away in terms of a more natural environment. There is fresh mountain air and a beautiful view of Mt. Charleston. Stroll along nature paths, or take a picnic at one of the many picnic areas.

Bedrooms at the hotel are clean, spacious, and modern with lovely mountain views. You can continue enjoying those mountain views at the Canyon Dining Room, which offers international cuisine and an intimate atmosphere.

Rates: Single $64; double $74; extra person $5
Credit cards: Visa, MC, AMEX, Discover
No. of rooms: 63
No. of baths: 1 per room
Directions: North on Highway 95 to 157, turn left.

Wheelchair access: Yes
Pets: No
Smoking: Some of the rooms
Senior citizen discount: Sunday through Thursday

Cape May Peninsula, Cape May Bird Observatory, Audubon Society

NEAREST AIRPORT: Cold Spring, via Atlantic City, New Jersey; and Philadelphia, Pennsylvania.

LOCATION: Jutting into Delaware Bay and the Atlantic Ocean, this small peninsula lies at the south tip of New Jersey. Cold Spring Airport is at Cape May Point, New Jersey. From Atlantic City, New Jersey, drive south on Route 109 along the coast 40 miles, or US 9 the same distance but farther inland. If you are driving from Philadelphia, take Route 55 southeast about 50 miles to Port Elizabeth, then continue south about 30 miles on Route 47.

CONTACTS: Cape May Bird Observatory, P.O. Box 3, Cape May Point, NJ 08212, (609) 884-2736. Also, the Wetlands Institute, Stone Harbor Boulevard, Stone Harbor, NJ 08247, (609) 368-1211.

BEST BIRDING: Spring and fall.

TOURS/WORKSHOPS: Year-round, all excellent. Many activities during the spring and fall migrations. The Cape May Bird Observatory is a research and educational association that can provide useful information for your birding trip here. Contact them and the Wetlands Institute.

To say this is a good place to bird is an understatement. The Cape May peninsula and its surrounding waters boast the best birding in the United States, with good reason. The bird checklist contains 404 species, not including accidentals. The area is most noted for the warbler migration in May, when up to 34 species can be observed, many of them in good numbers; 15 species nest here. Fairly common to common warblers that stop over are the black-throated blue, Blackburnian, blackpoll, Canada, and blue-winged; uncommon species could include the Cape May, palm, bay-breasted, prothonotary, worm-eating, Kentucky, and hooded warblers.

Toward the end of May, millions of shorebirds descend on the beaches of Delaware Bay to feast on horseshoe crab eggs. Earlier in the spring, around April, it should be possible to see ruffed grouse display, as well as rails, among these, clapper, king, Virginia, and maybe a black; tricolored herons are fairly common, as are yellow-crowned night herons. The southern migration in the fall is no less spectacular, especially for raptors. The peak autumn migration, starting as early as mid-August, is in October. The diverse species that can be seen at that time are ospreys, bald eagles, and sharpies, Cooper's and red-shouldered hawks, peregrine falcons, black and surf scoters, black skimmers, royal terns, lesser golden plovers, ruddy turnstones, red knots and yellow-billed cuckoos, Swainson's thrushes, rose-breasted grosbeaks, sharp-tailed sparrows, and orchard orioles.

MANOR HOUSE INN
612 Hughes Street, Cape May, NJ 08204, (609) 884-4710

If you agree with James Boswell that "a good pun may be admitted among the smaller excellencies of lively conversation," then you will be in for a treat when you stay with Tom Snyder, owner of the Manor House Inn.

Hughes Street, where the Manor House is located, is like yesterday's main street—lined with gracious gingerbread homes and lush shade trees. Cape May can sometimes veer toward the precious and the opulent, so the Manor House Inn is a welcome change of pace with its unassuming air and comparative modesty. The inn is a spacious, three-story Colonial Revival home, iced with weathered shingles, capped with a gambrel roof, and girded in front by an old-fashioned sitting porch—a favorite hangout during the balmy days of summer. In the winter, guests can warm themselves by the cozy Victorian fireplace or explore the gaslit Cape May streets.

The Snyders are engaging, hospitable innkeepers who miss no opportunity to pamper their guests. They offer individual robes, shampoos and soaps, beach towels and tags, plus helpful information about Cape May's walking, carriage, and trolley tours. Your hosts can help you fill your day with myriad activities or leave you alone to savor the pleasures of the Manor House itself. You will want to fly away at some point to bird at Cape May Bird Observatory.

Rates: Single $55-$130; double $65-$155; rate range reflects seasonal fluctuations
Credit cards: Visa, MC
No. of rooms: 9

No. of baths: 7
Wheelchair access: No
Pets: No
Smoking: No
Senior citizen discount: No

Directions: From the zero mile mark of Garden State Parkway, follow State Route 109 south (approximately ¼ mile) into Cape May City. You will be on LaFayette Street. Follow LaFayette to Franklin Street (approximately 8 blocks), turn left onto Franklin, proceed 2 blocks to Hughes Street, turn right; 612 is 1½ blocks on the left.

THE HENRY LUDLAM INN
Cape May County, 1336 RT 47, Woodbine, NJ 08270, (609) 861-5847

The only problem with staying at Marty and Ann Thurlow's historic Henry Ludlam Inn is that they are so affable you may never want to leave to go birding. The Thurlows are such skilled raconteurs that you will probably kick your shoes off, cozy up in the sun porch, have a complimentary glass of wine, and let the spinners of yarns entertain you.

The tale of greatest interest is about Henry Ludlam himself. According to Marty, who usually has his tongue firmly planted in his cheek, "Henry's son Joseph was a pirate without a ship. But he was no fool. At night he would ride down to the bay on his donkey with a lantern around his neck. The captain, mistaking this for a buoy, would run aground. The passengers would debark, leaving Joseph to rob the ship."

As far as birding is concerned, your first step is to walk out the front door onto the gorgeous grounds. Depending on the season, you might see owls, egrets, blue herons, or cormorants. If you go canoeing on Ludlam Lake or laze contentedly in the gazebo, you are certain to have ducks as your companions.

There are ducks indoors as well—decoys of mergansers and mallards carved by nationally known decoy carvers Harry Shrouds and Anthony Hillman. The basket of binoculars and bird books, the bird statues, duck wall hangings, and duck pillows are proof positive that the Henry Ludlam Inn is a birder's milieu.

After a morning stroll around the grounds, you will be ready for breakfast. A typical presentation might start with a homemade bran muffin with cream cheese and a beautifully presented pear soaked in kir. The pièce de résistance might be French toast stuffed with cream cheese.

One of the outstanding features of the house is the woodwork. Everything, including the handsome handcarved staircase, was made by Marty, who also doubles as a cabinetmaker. Each of the five guest rooms has its own unique character, created by a blend of antique furnishings and personal touches such as antique little girl's dresses, old children's books, and an Early American drum in the Pine Room. The loft room is cedar-lined with bird carvings and a telescope.

Henry Ludlam Inn

The bedroom on the first floor is very comfortable, with a warm feather-bed, a brick fireplace complete with antique bellows, a rocking chair, and wel-coming glasses or wine and dish of sweets. The decor right outside the room included an old wooden wagon filled with teddy bears of every size and description.

As you leave the inn for a birding excursion at Reid Beach and Cape May Bird Observatory, take note of the sign in the hallway that reads, "One day in the country is worth a month in town." This apt saying might well have been written by one of the Thurlows' guests.

Rates: $75–$110; extra person $20
Credit cards: Visa, MC, AMEX
No. of rooms: 5
No. of baths: 4
Directions: Inn will send map.

Wheelchair access: No
Pets: No
Smoking: No

THE QUEEN VICTORIA
102 Ocean Street, Cape May, NJ 08204, (609) 884-8702

Cape May is a re-creation of a long-lost era of perfectly manicured yards, croquet on the lawn, boardwalks, and fresh sea breezes.

The Queen Victoria Inn, located in the center of the National Landmark Historic District of Cape May, is composed of three buildings: one in the Second Empire style, another in the Stick style, and the third in the anachronistic Queen Anne style. The historically accurate multicolor paint schemes on all three buildings are used by the Sherwin-Williams Company to illustrate its line of Victorian paints.

Breakfast is served in two dining rooms, the Queen Victoria and the Prince Albert. The buffet, which changes daily, typically includes a choice of juices, the Queen's Oats (homemade granola), freshly baked blueberry muffins, date nut, orange chocolate chip, and honey buttermilk breads, baked stuffed French toast, and fresh fruit compote with Triple Sec.

The owners of the Queen Victoria are well suited for their jobs. Joan Wells comes by her love of Victorian things naturally. She was the first executive director of the Victorian Society in America and the former curator of the Molly Brown House Museum in Denver.

Both of the Wellses know how to cater to birders. They will give you an early-bird breakfast of coffee and pastries before you head for the Cape May Bird Observatory, and there are field guides all around. Whatever time of year you visit, save some time to enjoy Cape May. Ride bikes provided gratis by the Queen Victoria and do some gingerbread-gazing of the many streets of perfect-ly restored Victorian houses, amble along the boardwalk, or take a horse-drawn carriage along the National Historic Landmark District. Browse through the many shops, especially For the Birds, the complete nature shop. An activity we enjoyed was counting the number of lace curtains in the windows. As *Travel and Leisure* pointed out, "America's lace industry should give thanks to Cape May. Almost every window is draped in the stuff."

Rates: $65-$235
Credit cards: Visa, MC
No. of rooms: 22
No. of baths: 22
Wheelchair access: 1 suite fully accessible
Directions: Inn will send map.

Pets: No
Smoking: No
Senior citizen discount: No

The Queen Victoria

Montclair Hawk Lookout Sanctuary, Audubon Society

NEAREST AIRPORT: Newark, New Jersey.

LOCATION: Near Bloomfield, in the northeast quadrant of New Jersey. From Newark Airport, take I-78 west to the junction with the Garden State Parkway. Drive north on the parkway until you reach Bloomfield exit 151, then drive west onto Watchung to Montclair. Turn right at Upper Mountain Avenue to Bradford Avenue. Then turn right on Edgecliff and go about 2/10 mile. Look for the Hawkwatch sign on the left side of the road.

CONTACT: New Jersey Audubon Society, P.O. Box 125, 790 Ewing Avenue, Franklin Lakes, NJ 07417. (201) 891-1211.

BEST BIRDING: September through November.

TOURS/WORKSHOPS: Contact the New Jersey Audubon Society.

In the midst of urban areas, where you can see the New York skyline, stands a basalt ledge on the first Watchung Mountain in the city of Montclair. The ridge's northeast to southwest direction and proximity to the coast favors a wealth of hawk flights during the autumn's southward migration. The Hawkwatch here celebrated its 35th anniversary in 1992, second only to Hawk Mountain, Pennsylvania, for continuous counts.

Early September begins with flights of ospreys, kestrels, sharp-shinned as well as some broad-winged hawks, and possibly bald eagles. As September progresses, the number of broad-winged hawks rises, and by the end of September, the flights of Cooper's, sharp-shinned, red-shouldered, and red-tailed hawks increases. In October, you will find the greatest diversity of raptor species, as merlins and peregrine falcons join the soaring throng along the ridge; red-shouldered and red-tailed hawk numbers peak at the end of the month. Although it is often cold and windy in November, the migration continues; at this time, look for golden eagles or rough-legged hawks, whose numbers will be few but whose sightings will always be thrilling.

APPLE VALLEY INN
P.O. Box 302, Glenwood, NJ 07418, (201) 764-3735

This 1831 elegantly appointed bed and breakfast in the Early American tradition is a delightful place to stay while visiting the Montclair Hawk Watch. Each of the seven bedrooms has been named in honor of an apple—the Red Delicious, Golden Delicious, McIntosh, Grannie Smith, Jonathan, Rome Beauty, and Crab Apple.

The three-acre property is beautifully landscaped, and the home itself is decorated in a country motif with American antiques. The house's main level includes the sun room, kitchen, dining room, and private quarters. During cold weather, the glass-front woodstove provides a warm glowing fire.

The second level of the house contains three bedrooms, a large parlor, and a hallway. The hall has original plaster walls that resemble marble. Two of the bedrooms and the parlor have fireplaces with the original mantels and fire screens that are wonderful examples of Early American art. The third level has four bedrooms and a large common area with comfortable places to relax, read, or socialize.

A hearty country breakfast is served each morning at 8:30, but coffee and tea are available from 7:00 a.m. until 9:00 p.m. Guests are welcome to relax in the sun room and parlor, swim in the in-ground pool, stroll in the apple orchard, enjoy trout fishing in the babbling brook, or browse the antique shops. Innkeepers John and Mitzi Durham gives tours of their old grist mill just up the brook.

Rates: $50-$60	**Wheelchair access:** No
Credit cards: No	**Pets:** No
No. of rooms: 6	**Smoking:** Commons areas only
No. of baths: 3	**Senior citizen discount:** 10%

Directions: Located at the corner of Route 565 and 517 in the Glenwood section of Vernon. Approximately 15 miles off NY State Route 17. About 20 miles off I-80.

THE MARLBORO INN
334 Grove Street, Montclair, NJ 07042
(201) 783-5300, Fax (201) 783-8709

Here is a chance to savor the timeless elegance of a first-class European hotel without having to leave the country. The Marlboro Inn, within minutes of New York City, has the added advantage of being located near the Montclair Hawk Watch.

Listed on the National Register of Historic Places, this turn-of-the-century inn is a one-of-a-kind establishment. Set like a jewel on three and a half landscaped acres, the 8 suites and 30 rooms manage to retain the warmth and charm of an intimate country inn. The tastefully decorated rooms offer plush carpeting, antiques, objets d'art, and warm muted colors. The special ambience they create will suit the discriminating taste of the birder or corporate visitor.

Serving both the public and private guests for breakfast, lunch, and dinner, chef Eric Gallanter creates epicurian delights. Warm French brie wrapped in phyllo dough, accompanied with a warm pear sauce, or penne à la vodka in a tomato cream sauce are two of ten luncheon options. For dinner, you might tempt your palate with fresh fettucini with mesquite grilled scallops and vegetables tossed with a rosemary olive oil or a seared breast of Long Island duckling in a raspberry sauce.

A complimentary continental breakfast is served in the restaurant between 7:00 and 10:00 a.m. Heartier breakfasts are also available. Breakfast in your room is just a phone call away.

Attention to details and comfort make the difference between an ordinary and memorable stay.

Rates: $95-$110
Credit cards: Visa, MC, AMEX, Diners
No. of rooms: 33
No. of baths: 33
Wheelchair access: No
Smoking: Limited
Pets: No
Senior citizen discount: No
Directions: From Garden State Parkway, take exit 151, then 2 miles to the inn.

THE JEREMIAH J. YEREANCE HOUSE
410 Riverside Avenue, Lyndhurst, NJ 07071, (201) 438-9457

The historic landmark status of the Jeremiah J. Yereance House has been dated to 1841; it was built by a local shipjoiner who worked at the shipyards that were once located along the Passaic River. The North Wing is believed to have been constructed earlier and moved to the present location around 1840. It is one of the only buildings in Bergen County of its type and vernacular style. On April 3, 1986, the house was entered onto the National Register of Historic Places. Innkeepers Evelyn and Frank Pezzolla wanted to share their lovely historic landmark with travelers who might also enjoy its newly renovated comforts and old-fashioned charm.

The guest rooms in the South Wing of the house include a front parlor with fireplace, a central hall, and a small but comfortable bedroom that adjoins the parlor and a private bath. In the North Wing of the house, there is a

Common Parlor with fireplace, a kitchen, two double bedrooms, and one single bedroom with a shared bath. The Pezzollas serve a buffet self-service continental breakfast.

Cobblestone walks and a frontyard wisteria arbor surround the tiny house. Across from the B&B is a riverside park with walking and jogging paths, bicycle trails, picnicking, and tennis. These pleasant diversions are yours when you return from the Montclair Hawk Watch, one of North America's premier hawk-watching junctions.

Rates: Daily shared bath $55-$75 suite; weekly/monthly rates available
Credit cards: AMEX
No. of rooms: 4
No. of baths: 2

Wheelchair access: No
Smoking: No
Pets: No
Senior citizen discount: Yes

Directions: Garden State Parkway to Rt. 3 east. Riverside Ave. exit to Lyndhurst, 6 miles from Garden State Parkway.

NEW MEXICO

Bosque del Apache National Wildlife Refuge, Water Canyon

NEAREST AIRPORTS: Albuquerque, New Mexico; El Paso, Texas.

LOCATION: Central New Mexico, Middle Rio Grande Valley. From the Albuquerque airport, drive south on I-25 to exit 139; go east to flashing intersection light, then south on Route 1 until you reach the visitor center on your right and the beginning of the tour loops on your left. The total distance from the airport is about 75 miles. From El Paso, drive north on I-25 to exit 139, approximately 160 miles. Water Canyon is 15 minutes west of Socorro in the drainage canyon for the Magdalena Mountains.

CONTACT: Refuge Manager, Bosque del Apache National Wildlife Refuge, P.O. Box 1246, Socorro, NM 87801. (505) 835-1838.

BEST BIRDING: Year-round, with overwintering flocks at their peak October through mid-March; mid-April to mid-June for species diversity; August for the southward hummingbird migration. Water Canyon birding (higher elevation) follows a similar schedule, but peak times are one month later. Be sure to purchase the *New Mexico Bird-Finding Guide* (New Mexico Ornithological Society) from the American Birding Association.

TOURS/WORKSHOPS: Annual Festival of the Cranes held the weekend before Thanksgiving. Contact refuge manager for other program schedules.

Famed New Mexican artist Doug West's serigraph *Rio Grande Water Serpent* captures the terrain and the spirit of the Bosque del Apache. This high desert oasis of river, cottonwoods, freshwater ponds, wetlands, and mud flats winding below the dry, sloping uplands of the Chupadera Mountains is a magnet for wildlife. As critical habitat along the Rio Grande Flyway, the refuge supports over 300 bird species throughout the year.

The flights of honking sandhill cranes overhead returning to these wintering grounds begin in October, preceded by flocks of ducks and followed by large numbers of snow and Ross's geese. Along with sandhill cranes, you can see the foster flock of endangered whooping cranes here. Wintering populations peak in January and have usually returned to their nesting areas by the end of March. On average, 14,000 sandhill cranes, 40,000 ducks, and 65,000 snow geese feed on and around the refuge through the fall and winter. In January, up to 30 bald eagles can be observed posing in the early morning sun atop the bare cottonwoods. Also look for pyrrhuloxias and green-tailed towhees behind the visitor's center at the feeding station. Ferruginous hawks and golden eagles are almost always spotted, and both black-shouldered and Mississippi kites can be observed at this time. This is a magical place in the winter; you can become transfixed by the early morning sound of these thousands of birds as they fly around with limitless horizons as a backdrop.

In April, the hummingbirds and songbirds begin to return on the southerly winds. In May, birding between dawn and dusk in Water Canyon, Bosque del Apache, and La Joya Game Refuge (all within 30 miles of Socorro), you should have a century day (100 bird species). Water Canyon is at the northernmost boundary for many of the same species found in southeastern Arizona. Red-faced warblers nest there. On the benches, delicate Inca doves are common, usually found with white-winged doves. In addition, phainopeplas nest in the historic district of Socorro, and the mulberry trees in the region feed a multitude of birds, including cedar waxwings, orioles, rose-breasted grosbeaks, summer tanagers, western tanagers, and black-throated sparrows. In the scrub, crissal and curve-billed thrashers as well as scaled quail are common; and Gambel's quail scan the land atop the snags of dead trees. Gray vireos and flammulated and Mexican spotted owls are all found in the Magdalena Mountains. Over 65 percent (340 species) of New Mexico's birds can be found within a 65-mile radius of Socorro.

CASA BLANCA GUESTHOUSE
P.O. Box 31, San Antonio, NM 87832, (505) 835-3027

Many an inadvertent observer has been turned into an enthusiastic birder after a visit to the Bosque del Apache Wildlife Refuge. The Bosque is a magical place where sight and sound hold sway. It is a must for nature-lovers, who, like the birds, are known to return each year.

The Casa Blanca Guesthouse, just eight miles from the Bosque, has two double rooms, one with private bath, one with shared bath. Two-foot-thick adobe walls keep the rooms cool in summer, cozily warm in winter. Wood-burning stoves add a nostalgic touch. The rooms are decorated with an array of Southwest and Mexican art.

Homemade continental-plus breakfasts are served. For dinner, a popular spot is the nearby Owl Bar and Cafe, said to offer some of the best green chile cheeseburgers in the world.

Rates: Single $35-$45; double $45-$55; extra person $10
Credit cards: No
No. of rooms: 3
No. of baths: 2

Wheelchair access: No
Pets: Restricted—cats reside at the bed and breakfast
Smoking: Restricted
Senior citizen discount: No

Directions: Take the San Antonio/Carrizozo exit 139 off I-25. Proceed to the blinking light at the intersection. Continue straight through intersection for one short block. Turn right on the paved road after the antique store (Montoya Street). Continue south for two blocks. Casa Blanca is on the right-hand side—a big, white adobe with blue trim and a large veranda.

THE EATON HOUSE BED AND BREAKFAST
P.O. Box 536, Socorro, NM 87801, (505) 835-1067

The Eaton House is a winning combination of history, luxurious accommodations, and birding information. Over one hundred years old, Colonel Eaton's former home is now a registered New Mexico State Historic Building. The living room has the ambience of a cozy summer porch with its white wicker furniture accompanied by just the right amount of Victoriana. You never forget you are in a bird lover's nest, since there are bird pictures and Audubon books at every turn.

My favorite bedroom, the Colonel Eaton Room, is reminiscent of a more gracious, elegant era, when butlers and ladies maids were the rule. The lace curtains, attractive wooden antique furniture, and soothing ceiling fan complement the queen-size four-poster bed.

Anna Appleby, the innkeeper, provides an Early Birder basket featuring a big thermos of coffee and pastries that you can carry along to the Bosque. Little Red Riding Hood never had it so good.

But this "snack" is just the beginning. After you have explored the Bosque sanctuary and reveled in the majesty of the whooping cranes, you can return to the Eaton House to be served a bountiful breakfast. Depending on Appleby's fancy and what is fresh from the garden, you might be served cheese soufflé with apricot topping, brioche, mixed fruit, bacon, pumpkin fruit bread, lemon poppyseed bread, and coffee or tea. Or perhaps you might find blueberry pancakes, local sausage, a fruit bowl, and fresh blueberry coffee cake. Other Appleby specialties include German walnut coffee ring, eggs with onion, Eaton House scones with crystallized ginger, and homemade preserves.

Appleby's eyes light up when she discusses birds and how she hopes to encourage ecotourism. "If people understand cycles, they won't destroy them. People have to put special things back into the world to make it special for others."

And make it special she does. With her bird books, binoculars, and personal birding field checklist, I have not been as prepared for birding since I passed my Girl Scout badge for warbling. We went to the Bosque del Apache at twilight and at dawn, and both times were spectacular. Appleby says, "Birding makes the world more beautiful." And as the sun sets on the Bosque, I have to agree with her.

Rates: $75-$105
Credit cards: No
No. of rooms: 5
No. of baths: 5
Wheelchair access: No
Pets: No
Smoking: No
Senior citizen discount: No
Directions: From Albuquerque, south on I-25 75 miles to exit 147. Brochure has detailed map and directions.

The Eaton House Bed and Breakfast

Gila National Forest, Gila River, and Surrounding Mesas and Desert

NEAREST AIRPORTS: Las Cruces, New Mexico; El Paso, Texas.

LOCATION: Southwest quadrant of New Mexico. From Las Cruces, drive west on I-10 55 miles to Deming. Take US 180 to Silver City (40 miles); then Route 15 into the Gila National Forest. Other nearby birding areas are San Simon Marsh, Red Rock, Cherry Creek Campground, the Black Range, and the Mogollon Mountains.

CONTACTS: Gila National Forest, Regional Office, 2960 North Silver, Silver City, NM 88061, (505) 538-2771. Silver City Chamber of Commerce: (800) 548-9378 (U.S. and Canada).

BEST BIRDING: Spring, summer, and fall.

TOURS/WORKSHOPS: Contact superintendent or the Chamber of Commerce. Also, the southwestern New Mexico Audubon Society: (505) 538-9672.

In this area high above the desert floor, the weather is cool and moderate in the spring and summer. Migrants and nesters find water and food with relative ease during this time. Raptors, such as goshawks, Swainson's hawks, zone-tailed hawks, and golden eagles, glide above the brown hills and forested mountains. Montezuma quail are secretive and difficult to find, but they are residents here. Also residents are flammulated, elf, and spotted, great horned, screech-, and pygmy owls. The blue colors of the many jay species compete with the brilliant New Mexico sky; among those found here year-round are Steller's, scrub, Mexican, and the flocking piñon jays. Shiny black phainopeplas with their punk-style headdresses remain here in all seasons. Search also for hooded and Scott's orioles, hepatic and summer tanagers, rose-breasted grosbeaks, and lazuli buntings. In winter, there are Lewis's woodpeckers, Williamson's sapsuckers, Clark's nutcrackers, water pipits, sage sparrows, Cassin's finches, and chestnut-collared longspurs.

BEAR MOUNTAIN GUEST RANCH
P.O. Box 1163, Silver City, NM 88062, (505) 538-2538

Tucked away in the southwestern corner of New Mexico at the gateway to the Gila Wilderness and Gila Cliff Dwellings, the Bear Mountain Guest Ranch is not only a haven for the stressed or weary but a natural encyclopedia for the mind.

Owner Myra McCormick likes to call it the second oldest bed and break-fast on the site—the first being the ruins behind the ranch, which predecessors of the Mimbres Indians built some 8,000 years ago. It is no accident that many of the finely detailed Mimbres designs are of birds. This is one of the prime bird-ing areas in the country, and Bear Mountain puts out the welcome mat for bird-ers.

The 160-acre ranch is situated at an elevation of 6,250 feet. There are 15 units from which to choose at Bear Mountain, each with private baths, and the Ranch House itself contains the two dining areas and sitting area with a large stone fireplace. This is where the action is—where guests gather around the table at meals and introduce themselves before breaking into animated conver-sation—and where visitors can sit in the comfortable sofas and compare bird notes. The Ranch House also has three corner suites, two bedrooms upstairs, and four bedrooms downstairs. In the Wren's Nest cottage, you will find a com-bination living/bedroom with one double bed and kitchenette. Coyote (and you will hear the wonderfully haunting howels, day or night) Corner cottage has one bedroom with a double bed, two single day beds in the living room, and a kitchenette. Finally, for family gatherings and friendly reunions, the Bear's Den offers five bedrooms with two beds in each, a living room, and a foyer.

There is no lack of information for the novitiate to this part of the country. McCormick has the definitive collection of magazines, including *New Mexico Magazine*, *National Wildlife*, *Audubon*, *Birder's World*, *National Parks*, *Outside*, and books on topics ranging from where to stay to roadside flora and, of course, *Peterson's Western Birds* (the 2nd ed. is her favorite). She also has copies of her *Bear Mountain Ranch Recipes* cookbook available.

As I walked out the door one morning, I heard her say to a guest, "Now, do you have all the information you need? Do you know where you're going today?" McCormick loves this area with its four gentle seasons and wants to share it with everyone. If you feel like running away to camp and feeding the birds, you know where to come.

Rates: Single with 3 meals $65/night, B&B $48/night; double with 3 meals $114/night, B&B $80/night; extra person with 3 meals $162/night, B&B $112/night
Credit cards: No
No. of rooms: 15

No. of baths: 15
Wheelchair access: Yes
Pets: Yes
Smoking: Only in guest's room and outdoors
Senior citizen discount: Yes, for guests 65 and over

Directions: From Deming, to Silver City, stay on US 180 to the 5th traffic light; US 180 forks; take right fork. Go past McDonald's. The fourth street beyond McDonald's is Alabama St. Turn right on Alabama. Drive 2.8 miles until you have crossed the first cattle guard. Turn left on the dirt road just beyond cattle guard. Drive 0.6 mile to the 2-story ranch house.

THE CARTER HOUSE
101 North Cooper Street, Silver City, NM 88061, (505) 388-5485

. The Carter House, a comfortable building with a wonderful front porch and an interesting library, is a nice place to stay while in the Gila area. Innkeeper Lucy Dilworth Nolan has a keen interest in environmentalism.

Nolan's library has a fair number of bird books, but she is quick to point out, "I am not a birding expert. For birding information, I always refer people to Myra McCormick of the Bear Mountain Guest Ranch who knows everything about the birds around here. Or if they want a bird tour, I call Ralph Fisher of Blackhawk Services. He offers great tours."

Lucy and her husband, Jim, know how to put together an attractive bed and breakfast. They have four lovely guest bedrooms, each with a bath. The names of the rooms reflect the Silver City environment: Antelope Creek, Black Canyon, Crow Canyon, and Deer Springs Room. If you need more space, there is also a two-room suite with a bath available. If you are a young or adventure traveler, you will like the Carter House's dormitory-style American Youth Hostel with its fully equipped kitchen and laundry facilities.

Enjoy wholesome and tasty foods at the full, buffet-style breakfast served in the dining room between 7:30 and 9:00 a.m.

After birding to your heart's content, take a walking tour of downtown Silver City where the Wild West will come to life.

Explore the ancient Mimbres Native American culture at the Gila Cliff Dwellings National Monument and view the world-famous black-and-white Mimbres pottery at local museums.

Rates: $50-$60; 5% discount for a stay of 2 or more nights
Credit cards: Visa, MC
No. of rooms: 5
No. of baths: 5
Directions: Inn will send map.

Wheelchair access: Yes
Pets: No
Smoking: Outdoors only
Senior citizen discount: No

NEW YORK

Fire Island National Seashore

NEAREST AIRPORT: La Guardia, New York.

LOCATION: Southeast Barrier Island to Long Island, New York. Drive east on Highway 27 to Babylon, about 20 miles from the airport, then south to Robert Moses State Park (the west end of Fire Island National Seashore). Park headquarters is at Patchogue, farther east on Highway 27. There is ferry access from Sayville and Patchogue; east end access by car is at Smith Point via the Smith Point Bridge.

CONTACTS: Park headquarters, 120 Laurel Street, Patchogue, NY 11772, (516) 289-4810. There are visitor centers at Smith Point, (516) 281-3010; Watch Hill, (516) 597-6455; Sailor's Haven, (516) 597-6183; and Fire Island Lighthouse, (516) 661-4876.

BEST BIRDING: Spring, fall, and summer.

TOURS/WORKSHOPS: Planned programs from the end of June until just after Labor Day. From the Watch Hill area, take the 2½-hour guided canoe tour of marshes and coves. Tours are limited to 12 people, and reservations are required at least one week in advance. Early morning walks led by rangers are scheduled at the Fire Island Lighthouse. Check for birding excursions at the Fire Island Lighthouse, Sailor's Haven, and Watch Hill. Contact visitor centers or headquarters for additional information.

Twenty-six miles of 32-mile-long Fire Island have been designated national seashore. The contrast between the urban megalopolis of New York and the natural refuge makes one appreciate the habitat that has been preserved. Managed by both the National Park Service and local governments, the beaches, dunes, salt marshes, and woodlands are vital stops along the Atlantic Flyway for migrating birds. The wilderness area from Smith Point west to Watch Hill Visitor Center is accessible by foot only and offers unique possibilities for birding not found in other parts of the island.

In the protected Great South Bay behind Fire Island, waterfowl float in large "rafts" as they rest and feed in spring on their way north. Horseshoe crab eggs attract multitudes of shorebirds along the coast. Least and common terns nest here, and Caspian and royal terns can usually be seen during migration. Black skimmers, with their orange bills, are common in late spring and summer. The fall raptor migration is generally quite good here, although it varies somewhat depending on the weather. Likewise, the number of species that can be seen here during spring migration is also dependent on weather patterns.

BALLYCOVE
Seven Cox's Cove Road, Westhampton Beach, NY 11978, (516) 288-6774

Ballycove is a cozy bed and breakfast in the vicinity of the Fire Island National Seashore. Overlooking Quantuck Bay, you will be only a short walk from the beautiful ocean beach. The charming village of Westhampton Beach, with its three- and four-star restaurants, movie theaters, and shopping, is only a stroll away.

Ballycove offers the Guest Room, a sunny room with private bath, king-size bed, and television. The more deluxe Bali Hai Suite features a king-size bed, whirlpool bath, stall shower, television, and refrigerator. Both rooms include a daily continental breakfast, a full weekend breakfast, ocean beach facilities, and use of the sixty-foot swimming pool.

Save plenty of time to go birding at the Fire Island National Seashore, which is noted for its large hawk migration during the fall.

This 19,578-acre barrier island off the south shore of Long Island offers excellent birding opportunities.

Rates: $100-$200 (2-night min.) **Wheelchair access:** No
Credit cards: No **Pets:** No
No. of rooms: 2 **Smoking:** No
No. of baths: 3 **Senior citizen discount:** No
Directions: Take exit 70 off the Long Island Expressway (#495). Turn right at the end of the exit ramp. Drive south to Sunrise (Route 27) and go east to Westhampton Beach exit (#63 South), County Road 31. Continue on 31 past the railroad tracks to Mill Road. Take Mill Road to Main Street, turn right on Seafield Lane, and continue to Cox's Curve Road, turn left, then take a right when you get to Cox's Cove Road. Number seven is on the right.

THE GRASSMERE INN
7 Beach Lane, Westhampton Beach, NY 11978, (516) 288-4021

For lovers of the sea, the 100-year-old Grassmere Inn building is a pleasant combination of historic ambience and modern comfort. Rooms with private or shared baths and cottages are available. Breakfasts are included.

The main street of Westhampton is within easy walking distance. Guests will discover fashionable boutiques, charming shops, quaint bookstores, antique treasures, and the renowned Guild Museum featuring outstanding contemporary artists. Restaurants feature chefs who, having interned in New York's finest culinary establishments, compete for your sea-air appetite.

Rubbing shoulders with the rich and famous who flock to the area can be fun. Those with more modest aspirations, however, might find boating in the bay and fabulous sandy beaches more alluring. Your innkeepers will be happy to prepare picnic baskets on request.

Save plenty of time, of course, for birding at the magnificent Fire Island National Seashore.

Rates: $50-$65 in season; $100-$170 Memorial Day to Labor Day
Credit cards: Visa, MC, AMEX, Discover
No. of rooms: 22

No. of baths: 16
Wheelchair access: Limited
Smoking: Restricted
Pets: No
Senior citizen discount: Yes

Directions: From the Fire Island Seashore, take Sunrise Highway (Route 27) east to exit 63, Westhampton Beach south. Three lights and left onto Mill Road. Left turn, then right to Beach Lane; 35-40 minutes drive to the seashore.

SUMMIT MOTOR INN
501 East Main Street, Bay Shore, NY 11706
(516) 666-6000, (800) 869-6363

The Summit Motor Inn is a comfortable and convenient place to stay when visiting Fire Island National Seashore. There are 42 rooms, all with double beds, private baths, and televisions. There is no restaurant at the inn, but there are many places to eat in the vicinity.

Summit Motor Inn is in a wonderful location for birding. In addition to Fire Island, within a 50-mile radius, you can bird watch at John F. Kennedy Wildlife Sanctuary, Seatuck National Wildlife Refuge, South Shore Nature Preserve, Connetquot State Park, Heckscher State Park, Robert Moses State Park, and Captree State Park.

Take a "pass ferry" to Fire Island. This 19,578-acre barrier island off the south shore of Long Island offers excellent birding opportunities. The seashore is noted for its large hawk migration during the fall.

Rates: 1 double bed $59-$69; 2 double beds $69-$79; suite $79-$89; rates are quoted for one or two persons. Extra person $10. Suite will accommodate up to 6 persons.
Credit cards: Visa, MC, AMEX, Discover, Diners, Carte Blanche

No. of rooms: 42
No. of baths: 42
Wheelchair access: Ramps on street level
Pets: No
Smoking: Yes
Senior citizen discount: No

Directions: Long Island Expressway (495) to Route 27A (Main St.), west on 27A for 1¼ miles; Southern State Parkway to exit 42 south (Fifth Ave.). Continue on Fifth Avenue to Route 27A (Main St.), make left and go 1 mile.

Iroquois National Wildlife Refuge

NEAREST AIRPORT: Buffalo, New York.

LOCATION: In the far northwest corner of New York, between Lake Erie and Lake Ontario, 30 miles east of Niagara Falls. Drive east on I-90 24 miles to Route 77/63 north, then 18 miles to Casey Road West and a few miles to the refuge headquarters. From Niagara Falls, drive east on Route 104, 30 miles to Route 63 south, past Medina to Casey Road, and then to the headquarters, 8 miles. From Batavia, take Route 63 to the refuge.

CONTACT: Refuge Manager, Iroquois National Wildlife Refuge, P.O. Box 517, Alabama, NY 14003, (716) 948-5455. Oak Orchard and Tonawanda Wildlife Management Area, Route 77, Alabama, NY 14003, (716) 948-5182. Genesee County Chamber of Commerce, 220 East Main Street, Batavia, NY 14020, (800) 622-2686.

BEST BIRDING: Spring and fall. Other nearby birding areas are the Oak Orchard and Tonawanda Wildlife management areas, Bergen Swamp, and Letchworth State Park.

TOURS/WORKSHOPS: Contact refuges for program information.

This is a landscape of rolling green hills, red barns, lakes, and woodlands in autumn glow with reds, golds, and rusts. The refuge is contiguous with the Tonawanda and Oak Orchard wildlife areas, with combined lands of 19,000 acres. This area of primarily wetlands fed by rivers, lakes, and creeks is managed for waterfowl production. Spring migration peaks with up to 100,000 Canada geese and thousands of ducks. Tundra swans are common, as are hooded mergansers, which stay to nest in the wooded wetlands. Elusive least bitterns migrate here to nest and stay through the fall. Sandpipers also can be easily observed in the fall, including spotted, upland, semipalmated, and pectoral as well as greater and lesser yellowlegs. The insect-eating black tern feeds well here.

During the warbler migration, you can see blue and golden-winged, magnolia, Cape May, and cerulean among the 27 possible species. Spring through November, you should be able to spot scarlet tanagers, northern cardinals, rose-breasted and evening grosbeaks, indigo buntings, rusty blackbirds, northern orioles, purple finches, and swamp, Savannah, and chipping sparrows. During dusk and evening birding, look for the common nighthawk and a variety of owls, including the eastern screech-owl, great horned, barred, and short-eared.

CANAL COUNTRY INN
4021 Peet Street, Middleport, NY 14105, (716) 735-7572

The Canal Country Inn is a convenient place to stay whenever you happen to be birding at nearby Iroquois National Wildlife Refuge. This historic home was built in 1831 to face the Erie Canal, one of the great engineering feats of its day. Innkeepers Wendell and Joan Smith will be happy to fill you with canal trivia such as its various nicknames, "Clinton's Folly" (DeWitt, not Bill) and "The Big Ditch," or point you in the direction of the canal towpath.

The Canal Country Inn features a beautiful hand-carved parlor with a cozy fireplace. There are four bedrooms, two baths, and a shower room. Amenities include a dock to accommodate boaters. Enjoy croquet, horseshoes, badminton, and a tree swing. Borrow the bicycle built for two from the Smiths. In the winter, try some cross-country skiing. Regardless of the activity, Joan will be glad to pack a basket lunch.

For those who have not had enough exploring at Iroquois or the Erie Canal, a trip to nearby Niagara Falls is highly recommended.

Rates: $30-$45; extra person $15   **Wheelchair access:** Yes
Credit cards: No   **Pets:** Some
No. of rooms: 5   **Smoking:** Preferably not
No. of baths: 2 full and 1 shower   **Senior citizen discount:** No
room
Directions: From Buffalo airport, take Route 78 to 31 through Lockport, through Gasport, approximately 3 miles east, turn left off 31 (north), do not go over bridge, the red brick house on the right, back from the road.

"428 MT. VERNON"
428 Mt. Vernon Avenue, Rochester, NY 14620, (716) 271-0792

You will not have to wing it when asking birding questions at the 428 Mt. Vernon bed and breakfast. Innkeepers Claire and Phil Lanzatella are birders themselves and will be happy to let you watch their backyard birds through their powerful telescope. You will be approximately an hour away from your birding destination, the Iroquois National Wildlife Refuge. But there is little lodging near Iroquois, and staying at 428 is worth driving a bit.

This building was once a nunnery for the Sisters of Mercy. It is now a beautiful area for both you and the birds. 428's two acres of grounds adjoin 155 acres of Highland Park, making a beautiful woodland for wildflowers, rare species of trees, and birds.

Phil is a professional restorer of historical properties. His own B&B is beautifully appointed with bookcases, antiques, a piano, and an original maple fireplace. Every room at 428 is carefully maintained to reflect its Victorian tradition. The seven cheerful, sunlit rooms provide an excellent relaxing environment. All guest rooms are spacious and have private baths.

Breakfast is a well-thought-out event where you check your breakfast preferences from a menu the night before. A typical breakfast might consist of scones, apple-buttermilk pancakes, homemade jams, fruits, and hot coffee.

Rates: Single $90; double $99
Credit cards: Visa, MC, AMEX
No. of rooms: 7
No. of baths: 7
Wheelchair access: Yes
Pets: No
Smoking: Yes
Senior citizen discount: No
Directions: I-90 to exit 45, 490 to Goodman, left on Goodman to Highland Park, turn right into park and follow park road, bearing right; the 428 driveway is the only drive on Park Road.

RICHARDSON'S CANAL HOUSE AND OLIVER LOUD'S COUNTRY INN
1474 Marsh Road, Pittsford, NY 14534, (716) 248-5200

I've always liked the story of Little Red Riding Hood. One of my favorite parts has Ms. Hood delivering goodies to her alleged grandmother, a.k.a. the wolf. Okay, so Granny had a personality problem. When you get right down to it, the thing I really liked was the idea of having breakfast in bed. Which is what you get to do at Oliver Loud's Country Inn.

A big basket of breakfast goodies is left on your doorstep. You can eat your muffins, croissants, fresh fruits, and jams and enjoy a thermos of hot coffee when the spirit moves you. You can hop back into bed or move out to the porch and gaze at the Erie Canal.

This charming inn is reminiscent of a scene out of a Currier and Ives print, which is not too surprising as the original New England farmhouse inn of Oliver Loud was indeed illustrated by the artists. Mr. Loud first settled the area in 1809. As a merchant, a pamphleteer, astronomer, and tavernkeeper, he was the quintessential Renaissance man.

He would no doubt be pleased with the way the inn has been restored. Quality reproduction furniture and artifacts grace the interior. The guest rooms are particularly attractive. The doors are grained in the faux mahogany popular in Loud's day; some rooms are trimmed in wallpapers reflecting the period. There are wonderfully authentic paintings that would have been displayed in a fine home during Oliver Loud's life.

After a wonderful day of birding at Iroquois National Wildlife Refuge, you will enjoy an elegant dinner at Richardson's Canal House. It is a lovely setting, and the food matches the scenery. A favorite is the broiled Norwegian salmon with pesto sauce or grilled paillard of chicken with jalapeno butter. Save room for light white-chocolate raspberry mousse. In short, indulge yourself.

Rates: $115-$145

Credit cards: Visa, MC, AMEX, Diners

No. of rooms: 8

No. of baths: 8

Directions: Call for specific directions.

Wheelchair access: Yes

Pets: References for boarding available

Smoking: Certain rooms only

Senior citizen discount: No

NORTH CAROLINA

Cape Hatteras National Seashore

NEAREST AIRPORTS: Raleigh, North Carolina; municipal airport at Greenville, North Carolina, for southern or northern entrance to the seashore and Outer Banks.

LOCATION: The southern portion of the Outer Banks extending from Manteo to Ocracoke Island. The Ocracoke Visitor Center can be reached by ferry from Swanquarter or Cedar Island, both about a 2½-hour trip (reservations required). To reach Cape Hatteras, a free ferry is available from Ocracoke Island. (The route to Swan Quarter Refuge is outlined in the Swan Quarter Refuge section.) The northern entrance can be reached by automobile. From Swanquarter, drive north on US 264 past Mattamuskeet Refuge to Manns Harbor, then east on 64 to Manteo; continue to Route 12 and the Bodie Island Visitor Center. Route 12 continues down the island chain to Cape Hatteras, about 45 miles. You can also drive to the north entrance directly from Raleigh on Route 64; or from Greenville on Highway 64 via US 17 north.

CONTACTS: Cape Hatteras National Seashore, Rt. 1, Box 675, Manteo, NC 27954, (919) 473-2111. Pea Island National Wildlife Refuge, P. O. Box 150, Rodanthe, NC 27968, (919) 987-2394.

BEST BIRDING: Spring, fall, and winter.

TOURS/WORKSHOPS: Interpretive programs provided by seashore staff from mid-June to Labor Day. These are listed in the park newspaper, *In the Park*. Contact either the seasore or the Pea Island Refuge. The Coastal Wildlife Refuge Society can be reached at P.O. Box 1808, Manteo, NC 27954.

Sweeping south from Nags Head 75 miles to Ocracoke, this thin strip of islands, deadly to merchant ships and schooners, is life to almost 400 species of birds. The fertile land and sea nurtures a complex and varied ecosystem, and abundant food, shelter, and nesting materials combine to make this area ideal for residents and migrants alike. In the changeable weather of early fall, Cory's, Audubon's, and greater shearwaters can be observed offshore. Wilson's storm-petrels and northern fulmars are also abundant at that time, especially off Pea Island. Other interesting species that are sometimes on the refuge after storms are pomerines and parasitic and long-tailed jaegers. Numerous species of sprightly shorebirds forage on the beaches in large numbers, including plovers, black-necked stilts, willets, whimbrels, Hudsonian godwits, long-billed curlews,

Baird's sandpipers, red knots, and red-necked and red phalaropes. Tern species abound at this time; even the bridled tern can be observed offshore. More easily seen are sandwich, royal, gull-billed, and Caspian terns.

During winter, after storms, it is possible to observe usually distant seabirds that have been driven in close to shore, as well as northern gannets, tundra swans, greater and lesser scaups, surf scoters, old-squaws, common mergansers, and a possible fulvous whistling duck. Winter is also the season for black-legged kittiwakes, lesser and greater black-backed gulls, and red-throated loons. Abundant winter sparrows for your life list are the sharp-tailed and seaside.

In the spring, many of the same birds can be seen as in the fall, although there are fewer warbler species. Year-round, you should be able to see brown pelicans, American black ducks, king rails, northern cardinals, fish crows, Carolina wrens, great egrets, tricolored herons, glossy ibis, and over 20 species of shorebirds, including black skimmers.

THE BERKLEY CENTER
P.O. Box 220, Ocracoke, NC 27960, (919) 928-5911

Ocracoke Island on North Carolina's Outer Banks is one of the most magical and enchanting places I have ever had the pleasure of seeing. We visited there for the first time some 24 years ago. We returned recently to find that a few humans had discovered it. Still, it remains our own special deserted island, a place as beautiful and lyrical as ever.

During this trip, my husband and I stayed at the Berkley Center, a wonderfully restored estate on the harbor of the Outer Banks fishing village. We were surrounded by 19 miles of lovely, uncommercialized beach. Not a building in sight, only breathtaking vistas. The style and pace of the Berkley Center match the mood of Ocracoke—slow, relaxed, peaceful. The weathered, shingled main house boasts an enormous square tower rising from a second-story gable. The walls of the tower room are lined with windows looking out onto Pamlico Sound and the Atlantic. With cedar paneling and wooden ceilings, the inn has a lodgelike atmosphere. Our pleasant room with a double bed and private bath was air-conditioned. Of the four remaining rooms, two have shared baths, and two have private baths.

Our continental breakfast was enjoyable and gave us energy to explore this unusual island. The innkeepers were extremely helpful and gave us advice on restaurants, sightseeing, and boat trips. They told us about the National Park Service trip, which we found to be quite interesting.

Mostly, however, we just enjoyed the magnificent birding at Cape Hatteras National Seashore, swimming in the ocean, and watching the colorful sunsets while letting Ocracoke spin its special magic.

Rates: $65-$85; extra person $10   **Wheelchair access:** Yes
Credit cards: No   **Pets:** No
No. of rooms: 10   **Smoking:** Yes
No. of baths: 9   **Senior citizen discount:** No
Directions: On the harbor adjacent to National Park Service docks.

BLACKBEARD'S LODGE
P.O. Box 298, Ocracoke, NC 27960, (919) 928-3421, (800) 892-5314

L egend has it that Ocracoke Island was once the headquarters of the fabled and notorious pirate, Blackbeard. If the romance of swashbuckling pirates and ships appeals to you, try Blackbeard's Lodge. It is alleged that although Blackbeard himself no longer lives on the premises, his spirit still haunts the place.

The lodge was built in 1936. At that time, it faced a stretch of sand that ended in the Atlantic surf; a family-style dining room, a movie theater, and guest rooms were its dominant features.

Now the stretch of "bald beach" has yielded to shrubbery and buildings. Small airplanes can no longer land on the beach and taxi to the front door of the lodge to deliver their passengers.

The old building, with its paneling and high ceilings remains, however. The lodge has private baths in all the rooms, air-conditioning, color cable television, a shady pool, and porches.

Rates: $25-65 (June 15-Aug. 31)   **Wheelchair access:** No
Credit cards: Visa, MC   **Pets:** No
No. of rooms: 27 rooms, 10 apts.   **Smoking:** Limited
No. of baths: 27   **Senior citizen discount:** Yes
Directions: By ferry, 35 minutes from Cape Hatteras; 2½ hours from Cedar Island or Swan Quarter.

THE ISLAND INN
P.O. Box 9, Ocracoke, NC 27960, (919) 928-4351

O cracoke Island has received many accolades: the Bermuda of the United States, North Carolina's Cape Cod, and the Pearl of the Outer Banks. Whatever you call it, getting there should be half the fun. The ferryboat ride is delightful. On the half-hour ride to this tiny island, the scenery is spectacular, making it virtually impossible to remember any workday worries.

A local headquarters for bird-watching at Cape Hatteras National Seashore and relaxing is the Island Inn, which offers lovely views of the harbor and spectacular sunsets. Another attractive feature is the dining room, which features island seafood. Their recipes have appeared in *Southern Living* and *Cuisine*.

All bedrooms include private baths, air-conditioning, and color cable television. You have your choice of traditional or modern rooms. The main building, built in 1901, offers traditional rooms with the ambience of a country inn. The Stanley Wahab Wing, built in 1981, contains more modern surroundings. Each room opens through a sliding glass door onto a deck adjacent to the pool area or onto a balcony overlooking the pool. The Island Inn has Ocracoke's only heated swimming pool.

Turtledoves, take note. There are special honeymoon suites. If you are traveling with a birding caravan, there is a two-bedroom cottage that accommodates four.

Rates: $30-$95 seasonal; average price $60
Credit cards: Visa, MC, Discover
No. of rooms: 35 plus cottages
No. of baths: 35

Wheelchair access: Yes
Pets: In Dec., Jan., Feb.
Smoking: Limited
Senior citizen discount: Yes

Directions: Southernmost part of natural seashore. Accessible only by ferry from Cape Hatteras, Cedar Island, and Swan Quarter or by private plane or private boat.

Mattamuskeet and Swan Quarter National Wildlife Refuge

NEAREST AIRPORTS: Raleigh, North Carolina; Municipal Airport at Greenville, North Carolina.

LOCATION: Central coastal region of North Carolina between Swanquarter and Englehard, west of Cape Hatteras National Seashore. From Greenville, drive east on US 264 to Swanquarter (72 miles) and follow signs to the refuge entrance. To reach Mattamuskeet, continue on US 264 for about 15 miles to the junction of Route 94 north and drive 1½ miles to the entrance.

CONTACT: Mattamuskeet National Wildlife Refuge, Rt. 1, Box N-2, Swanquarter, NC 27885. (919) 926-4021.

BEST BIRDING: Fall, winter, and spring.

TOURS/WORKSHOPS: Contact refuge manager.

Mattamuskeet Refuge surrounds Mattamuskeet Lake and encompasses marshes, timberlands, and croplands along its shallow shore—40,000 acres of fresh water and 10,000 acres of wildlife-supporting land. Sixteen miles south, Swan Quarter Refuge, nearly 43,000 acres, is a perfect flyway habitat, with coastal marshlands, creeks, tidal drains, potholes, and open sea. The greatest variety of species and the peak population of water birds occur in the fall and winter. Spring is the best time to observe shorebirds and warblers.

September through March, the fresh and salt waters are filled with tundra swans, Canada geese, and a great variety and quantity of ducks, including such species as wood and American black ducks, European wigeons, greater scaups, old-squaws, black, white-winged, and surf scoters, and mergansers. In the fall and winter, shift your focus from the waters to the sky and you can view numerous raptors that feed on field mice, fish, and ducks, including many ospreys, bald eagles, and sharp-shinned, Cooper's, and red-shouldered hawks. Also, be alert for peregrine falcons and merlins as well as clapper rails that frequent the salt marshes and king rails that feed in the freshwater marshes. An interesting study in contrast, delicate little blue herons and tricolored herons are also common this time of year, as are great black-backed gulls, which are frequently seen along the coastline. For an afternoon of behavior-watching along the sandy beaches and mud flats, look for the swift movements of Wilson's plovers, dunlins, short-billed dowitchers, spotted sandpipers, and least, western, and semipalmated sandpipers.

PUNGO RIVER INN
526 Riverview Street, Belhaven, NC 27810, (919) 943-2117

A pleasant place to stay on your visit to Swan Quarter National Wildlife Refuge is the Pungo River Inn. Innkeeper Fran Johnson is a gracious Southern hostess whose goal is to make you feel comfortable. She enjoys helping guests by pointing out places of interest in the area. She might suggest that you go to the Belhaven Museum or take a short drive to historic Bath, the erstwhile home of Blackbeard. She will probably show you the way to nearby antique shops and Dutch flower farms. If you fancy yourself a pedal pusher, Johnson will provide you with bikes to ride through the friendly town of Belhaven. You can cycle to nearby seafood restaurants, tennis courts, and a swimming area.

Before winging away to make use of your binoculars at Swan Quarter and Mattamuskeet National Wildlife Refuge, however, be sure to enjoy a southern breakfast featuring Fran's Oat and Honey Loaf. Later in the day, after all of your activity, return to the inn for afternoon beverages in the courtyard.

Rates: $50	**Wheelchair access:** No
Credit cards: Visa, MC	**Pets:** No
No. of rooms: 3	**Smoking:** No
No. of baths: 2	**Senior citizen discount:** No

Directions: From Greenville Airport, Highway 60 east, via Highway 264; 25 miles west of Mattamuskeet and Swan Quarter National Wildlife Refuge.

NORTH DAKOTA

Cross Ranch Nature Preserve

NEAREST AIRPORT: Bismarck, North Dakota.

LOCATION: North of Bismarck, 52 miles on Highway 83 through Washburn. Follow signs to Cross Ranch State Park. The preserve headquarters is ¼ mile south of the park entrance. From Moose Jaw, Saskatchewan, take Highways 39 and 52 south to Minot, North Dakota (239 miles), then Highway 83 south to Washburn (65 miles). The preserve is almost in the geographic center of North Dakota.

CONTACT: The Nature Conservancy, Cross Ranch Nature Preserve, HC2, Box 150, Hensler, ND 58530, (701) 794-8741. Also Cross Ranch State Park, HC2, Box 152, Hensler, ND 58530, (701) 794-3731.

BEST BIRDING: May and June. Other birding areas are Fort Lincoln State Park, Long Lake National Wildlife Refuge, Oahe Reservoir, and the River Bottom Habitat, north and south along the Missouri River.

TOURS/WORKSHOPS: Self-guided nature trails. Maps and information available at headquarters.

Bordering a free-flowing section of the Missouri River, the preserve manages 6,000 acres of prairie and floodplain forest. It protects the largest tract of forest left along the Missouri in North Dakota. Once part of a 400-million-acre prairie ecosystem, the preserve and adjoining park have kept intact some of this vast grassland, forest, and riverine ecology. The most sought after birds on the preserve are Baird's sparrows and Sprague's pipits. In early spring, look for white-fronted geese as well as wood, canvasback, redhead, and ring-necked ducks. Broad-wing, sharp-shinned, and ferruginous hawks, golden and bald eagles, and merlins catch thermals and prey over the grasslands through the spring and summer. Look also for Hudsonian godwits. Before dawn and after dusk, search for eastern screech-owls, snowy owls, and short-eared owls. Common nighthawks also abound.

In open woods, red-headed woodpeckers are numerous and nest in the spring. Also look for yellow-shafted flickers and great crested flycatchers. Abundant as well are sedge, marsh, and rock wrens and a variety of warblers. Tennessee, orange-crowned, magnolia, Blackburnian, and American redstarts and rose-breasted grosbeaks are common, and sparrows of all species feed on the expansive grasses and sedges. Look also for chestnut-collared longspurs, yellow-headed blackbirds, and red crossbills. The many habitats in the preserve, the park, and the 100 miles surrounding them are extremely rich areas for observation.

SCOTWOOD MOTEL
Highway 83, P.O. Box 1183, Washburn, ND 58577, (701) 462-8191

The Scotwood Motel is a convenient place to stay while visiting the Cross Ranch Nature Preserve. This reasonably priced motel has 25 rooms and has recently been remodeled. All the rooms have new televisions, telephones, lamps, blinds, beds and bedspreads.

Cross Ranch Nature Preserve is an unusual place as it has both ecological and historical value. Over 100 archaeological sites have been found, with some dating to 6000 B.C. Washburn is also close to Audubon National Wildlife Refuge.

Rates: Single $28.50; double $35.50; extra person $5
Credit cards: Visa, MC, Discover, AMEX, Diners
No. of rooms: 25
Directions: Inn will send map.

No. of baths: 25
Wheelchair access: Yes
Pets: $5 extra
Smoking: Yes
Senior citizen discount: No

Marsh wren

J. Clark Salyer National Wildlife Refuge, part of the Souris Loup Refuges/Des Lacs, Upper Souris, and J. Clark Salyer

NEAREST AIRPORT: Minot, North Dakota.

LOCATION: In north central North Dakota, 26 miles south of the Canadian border. From Minot, drive east on US 2 about 40 miles to Highway 14 at Towner. Then take Highway 14 north to the park entrance, about another 26 miles. From Winnipeg, Manitoba, Canada, drive west on Highway 2 (112 miles) to the junction with Highway 10 south, then take 281 south to Highway 14, which goes to the refuge entrance (about 52 miles). From Moose Jaw, Saskatchewan, refer to directions to the Cross Ranch Preserve at Minot, then follow directions above from Minot. Both Upper Souris and Des Lacs national wildlife refuges are west and north of Minot and can be reached via Highways 52, 5, and 28. The distance from Minot to Upper Souris is about 50 miles; to Des Lacs, about 65 miles. Des Lacs is next to the border with Saskatchewan at Northgate.

CONTACTS: J. Clark Salyer National Wildlife Refuge, P.O. Box 66, Upham, ND 58789, (701) 768-2548. Des Lacs National Wildlife Refuge, P.O. Box 578, Kenmare, ND 58746. Upper Souris National Wildlife Refuge, R.R. 1, Foxholm, ND 58738.

BEST BIRDING: Spring, summer, and fall.

TOURS/WORKSHOPS: Self-guided trails; contact refuges.

This was the land of the early French trappers and hunters—vast seas of grass for buffalo and lakes and rivers for beaver, ducks, and geese. By the 1930s, the grasslands were gone, and the fragile soil was eroded; and the drought of the dust bowl era further threatened wildlife along the Central Flyway. Now, how ever, this land has become productive again. Spring and fall waterfowl migra tion peaks at close to 200,000 birds; 125 species nest here, with up to 80 nests per acre on some of the protected artificial islands in the flooded marshes. In an ecosystem now managed for wildlife, birds flourish in both number and kind.

The Salyer Refuge, largest of the three Souris Loop refuges, also benefits from the protection afforded species along the Des Lacs River. Together, the three refuges provide abundant and varied habitat consisting of grasslands, lakes, sloughs, wooded creeks, meadows, open pools, and rivers. Walk along the grassland trail to observe the spring courtship flights of the Sprague's pipit. Also look for Baird's, sharp-tailed, and Le Conte's sparrows closer to the marsh area. At home here are grasshopper and clay-colored sparrows, chestnut-collared longspurs, and western meadowlarks. Courtship dances and displays on the waters attest to the good nesting habitat for 5 species of grebes. As sprays of colorful wildflowers begin to spot the prairie, gray-cheeked thrushes, mountain bluebirds, Bohemian waxwings, northern shrikes, Harris's sparrows, and all the species of longspurs and snow buntings can be seen. Look especially for the unusual plumage of the breeding male bobolink. Overall, 239 species of birds use these prairie refuges.

D OVER L BED AND BREAKFAST
Route 3, Box 187, Minot, ND 58701, (701) 722-3326

The D over L Bed and Breakfast is a convenient place to stay in the vicinity of J. Clark Salyer National Wildlife Refuge. The D over L is a working small grain farm and ranch where owners David and Mary Larson raise wheat, barley, oats, sunflowers, and feeder steers.

Pheasants, deer, and coyote make their home at the coulee beside the house. In winter, be sure to bring your cross-country skis; you can ski right from the front door of the D over L.

You will sleep peacefully as the bedrooms are in a quiet, comfortable contemporary ranch-style home.

For those not in the know, J. Clark Salyer is an important feeding and resting area for the hundreds of thousands of waterfowl that migrate through on the Central Flyway.

Rates: $35-$45
Credit cards: No
No. of rooms: 2
No. of baths: 1

Wheelchair access: No
Pets: No
Smoking: No
Senior citizen discount: No

Directions: D over L B&B is located about 4 miles south of Minot on Highway 83 and 1 mile east on County Road 14.

THE DAKOTAH ROSE
510 4th Avenue N.W., Minot, ND 58701, (701) 838-3548

The Dakotah Rose is a handy place to nest when birding at the J. Clark Salyer National Wildlife Refuge. Constructed in 1904 by two Norwegian carpenters from Minneapolis, it consists of over 6,000 square feet of handcrafted elaborate oak woodwork enhanced by stained and leaded glass windows. A Tiffany chandelier hangs in the dining room, and the third floor has a ballroom. The butler can still be summoned with a special bell system located on each floor.

The Dakotah Rose has five antique-filled bedrooms. A continental breakfast of homemade breads, muffins, fruit, freshly ground coffee, tea, and hot chocolate is served in the dining room.

Salyer is a feeding and resting area for hundreds of thousands of waterfowl that migrate and has also been developed into an important breeding ground for ducks.

Rates: $55, $45, $35 (for two: $5 for each additional person 12 years and older)
Credit cards: Visa, MC
No. of rooms: 6
Directions: Call for directions.

No. of baths: 4
Wheelchair access: No
Pets: No
Smoking: Porch only
Senior citizen discount: No

Canada goose

OHIO

Edge of the Appalachia Preserve, The Nature Conservancy

NEAREST AIRPORTS: Cincinnati, Ohio; Lexington, Kentucky.

LOCATION: Located in the southwest quadrant of Ohio. From Cincinnati Airport, take I-275 east to Highway 32, then east about 55 miles to Highway 41 south; from there, it is 15 miles to West Union (total distance approximately 90 miles). You can save about 20 miles by driving Highway 125 from I-125 directly to West Union. The main entrance to the preserves is 14 miles east of West Union off Highway 125. From Lexington, Kentucky, Airport Drive northeast on Highway 61 to Highway 41 at Marysville, then continue to West Union, a total of about 80 miles.

CONTACTS: Cincinnati Museum of Natural History, 1720 Gilbert Avenue, Cincinnati, OH 45202, (513) 287-7020; or the Nature Conservancy, Ohio Field Office, 1504 West First Avenue, Columbus, OH 43212, (614) 486-4194.

BEST BIRDING: Spring and summer.

TOURS/WORKSHOPS: Contact museum or Nature Conservancy.

An elongated strip of 5,000 acres running north and south from Highway 125 to Highway 52 bordering the Ohio River, this preserve system is situated along Ohio Brush Creek. The eight preserves that comprise the system all have colorful names: Buzzardroost Rock, Rieveschl, Lynx Prairie, Cave Hollow, Hanging Prairie, and the Wilderness. There is a good system of trails in the preserve, but be sure to check which ones are open for walks, hikes, and nature observation. The preserve area is geologically unique, untouched by the last glacial period; it consists of prairie grasslands; mature forests, including northern cedar; mixed woodlands; and plant communities from both acidic and alkaline soils. This assemblage of geologic and biologic systems promotes species diversity. You will be able to observe yellow and black-billed cuckoos, wild turkeys, great-crested flycatchers, red-eyed vireos, and scarlet and summer tanagers. Indigo buntings are common, as are rufous-sided towhees and tufted titmice. Warblers are numerous in May, including hooded, Kentucky, worm-eating, blue-winged, pine, prairie, yellow-throated, and black-and-white. You should also see Carolina wrens, yellow-throated vireos, and whip-poor-wills. Broad-winged hawks populate the mature forest areas.

THE BAYBERRY INN
25675 Street, Route 41N, Peebles, OH 45660, (513) 587-2221

The Bayberry Inn is a cheerful and friendly spot. The innkeepers, Marilyn and Larry Bagford, offer warm hospitality and Midwestern friendship. As Marilyn told me when I inquired about the rooms, "Bathrooms are shared, and smiles are free."

The rooms are cozy, comfortable, and reasonably priced. There are fresh flowers and romantic candles in your room. Children are welcome. You will enjoy your hearty, old-fashioned breakfast with homemade bread or muffins and fresh fruit, eggs, and a cup of delicious coffee or tea.

You will want to get an early start for your trip to Buzzardroost Rock. If you have not filled in your life list there, take a bird walk at the state forest near the Bayberry Inn. The kids might like visiting nearby Serpent Mound, the largest and finest snake effigy mound in North America.

Rates: $35-$45
Credit cards: No
No. of rooms: 3
No. of baths: 2

Wheelchair access: No
Smoking: On the porch
Pets: No
Senior citizen discount: No

Directions: 60 miles east of Cincinnati, about 75 miles southwest of Columbus.

THE OLDE LAMPLIGHTER BED AND BREAKFAST
P.O. Box 820, Lucasville, OH 45648, (614) 259-3002

Nestled in the picturesque foothills of the Appalachian Mountains, this lovely brick home is in the village of Lucasville, Ohio. Designed and built in 1939 by Marilyn's parents, the home has been restored by Marilyn and Gaylord Liles, innkeepers.

Each room is filled with family heirlooms and country accents. An open staircase leads from the living room to the second-floor guest rooms. On the first landing stands a grandfather clock built in 1927. The Liles will carefully explain that the clock's hands are made from saw blades. The weight is a steering wheel from a Model T Ford. The hand-painted dial features copper numerals and both calendar and second hands. The walnut case is highlighted with diamond-shaped inlays of lighter wood.

As for the accommodations, the most appealing to me is the Massie Room, which has a pink, lavender, and white color scheme and features a pretty full-size Victorian bed, a chest, dresser, and mirrored closet door. After a long day of birding at Buzzardroost Rock, you will appreciate the deluxe posturepedic mattress. All four rooms share a single bath.

In the morning, enjoy breakfast in the Brackney Room. The Liles will encourage you to play their piano or electronic organ.

Rates: $43-$48
Credit cards: Visa, MC
No. of rooms: 4
No. of baths: 1

Wheelchair access: No
Smoking: No
Pets: No
Senior citizen discount: No

Directions: 10 miles north of Portsmouth via US 23; 1 block west of traffic light in the center of town.

THE SIGNAL HOUSE
234 N. Front Street, Ripley, OH 45167, (513) 392-1640

The Signal House left its mark on history through its involvement in the Underground Railroad. A lantern, shone from a skylight in the Signal House attic, signaled to Reverend John Rankin that the waterfront was safe to transport slaves to freedom. Innkeepers Vic and Betsy Billingsley will also be happy to tell you about the two Civil War officers who lived in the Signal House.

Built in the 1830s, the Greek Italianate house features ornate plaster moldings that surround twelve-foot ceilings. There are twin parlors and period furnishings. Of course, as a birder, you will have to request the Blue Bird Riverfront Room. From the four windows overlooking the Ohio River, enjoy the view of a passing paddlewheel boat coming round the bend, the rolling hills, and the spectacular sunsets. A queen-size poster bed is a nice touch. The Country Blue Room has a full-size Jenny Lind bed and a window for river viewing. The other window overlooks the garden. Both rooms share a bath.

Enjoy a full breakfast before going birding at Buzzardroost Rock. Later in the day, explore Ripley's 55-acre historical district. View the many different architectural styles and the historic homes in the village. Go antiquing, visit the Rankin House State Memorial or the Ripley Museum, or shop at the U.S. Shoe Women's Factory Outlet.

Rates: $68–$78 (all rooms are for doubles only)
Credit cards: No
No. of rooms: 2
No. of baths: 1

Wheelchair access: No
Pets: No
Smoking: In designated areas
Senior citizen discount: No

Directions: 50 miles east on US 52 from Cincinnati. In Ripley, turn right onto Locust Street. The Signal House is on the corner of Locust and Front streets.

Ottawa National Wildlife Refuge Complex/ Ottawa, Cedar Point, West Sister Island
(the latter is closed to the public as a protected nesting area)

NEAREST AIRPORT: Toledo, Ohio.

LOCATION: East of Toledo 15 miles on Highway 2, 18 miles west of Port Clinton on Highway 2. From Canada, take the ferry from Point Pelle to Sandusky, Ohio, then take Highway 2 west 31 miles to the refuge.

CONTACT: Refuge Manager, Ottawa National Wildlife Refuge, 14000 West State Route 2, Oak Harbor, OH 43449. (419) 898-0014.

BEST BIRDING: Spring and fall.

TOURS/WORKSHOPS: Contact refuge manager.

The refuge's 8,316 acres of marsh, grasslands, and forest, the remnants of a 300,000-acre swamp on the west coast of Lake Erie, lie in both the Mississippi and Atlantic flyways. This complex is the only National Wildlife Refuge in Ohio and provides rest areas or year-round habitat for 274 species of birds. Bald eagles are here throughout the year, with increased numbers during the fall migration. Abundant in the fall are Canada geese, blue phase snow geese, wood ducks, American black ducks, and an additional 12 duck species, along with mergansers, black-crowned night herons, and tundra swans. In addition, expect to see harriers and sharp-shinned hawks.

Interesting shorebirds that can be seen here are yellowlegs, Hudsonian godwits, red knots, white-rumped sandpipers, and short- and long-billed dowitchers as well as Baird's and pectoral sandpipers. Of the many gulls, be sure to look for the great black-backed, which is common in the fall. Spring is the time for the warbler migration (note how close the refuges are to Point Pelle, Canada); you will be able to see over 26 species on their annual trek across the lakes. Other exciting birds to see during this season are rose-breasted grosbeaks, indigo buntings, scarlet tanagers, rusty blackbirds, orchard orioles, red-shouldered hawks, ospreys, Cooper's hawks, black-bellied plovers, yellow-bellied flycatchers, gray-cheeked thrushes, and swamp sparrows.

FETHER BED AND BREAKFAST
1539 Langram Road, Put-in-Bay, OH 43456, (419) 285-5511

Fether Bed and Breakfast, an 1870 house on three acres with a lovely view of Lake Erie, may be the island setting you have always dreamed about. The front lawn can by enjoyed while lying peacefully in a hammock. There is ample time later for a rousing croquet match, a quick game of badminton, or a refreshing stroll in the woods.

To get to Fether Bed and Breakfast, you will need to take a tram. The B&B is midway between the village and Miller's Ferry. There are some areas on the island for birding; other islands would require a boat. Innkeepers Eleanor and Fred Fether can give you directions to Ottawa National Wildlife Refuge.

You have your choice of four bedrooms. One has a queen-size bed and private bath; others share two baths. All bedrooms have ceiling fans. You will enjoy a full breakfast in either the dining room or the patio.

Rates: $60-$80 per couple; extra person $20 (only 1 room accommodates an extra person)
Credit cards: Visa, MC
No. of rooms: 4

No. of baths: 3
Wheelchair access: No
Pets: No
Smoking: Outside
Senior citizen discount: No

Directions: Ferries from Port Clinton, Ohio, and from Catawba Island (S.R. 53). The inn is on South Bass Island in Lake Erie.

THE ISLAND HOUSE
102 Madison Street, Port Clinton, OH 43452
(419) 734-2166, (800) 233-7307

Traditional hospitality is always in style at the historic Island House Hotel in downtown Port Clinton, Ohio. The grand old hostelry, completely renovated over the last decade, has long been the cornerstone of this friendly vacation community on the shores of Lake Erie.

The Island House is your perfect nesting spot while visiting nearby Ottawa National Wildlife Refuge. It has the charm of a picturesque inn and the comfort of a modern hotel. If you are going to the Island House with your turtle dove, take advantage of the Honeymoon Package, which includes a night in the Honeymoon Suite, champagne for two, chocolates, and a long-stemmed rose.

You will eat well at this hospitable hostelry. Enjoy the "Bounty of Ohio," including perch and walleye from the waters of nearby Lake Erie. Hearty American cooking is another Ohio tradition. After your weekend birding expedition, indulge in the traditional Sunday breakfast buffet brunch.

Ottawa National Wildlife Refuge is a major stopover point for migrating waterfowl such as trumpeter swans and canvasbacks.

Rates: $25-$175	**Wheelchair access:** Yes
Credit cards: Visa, MC, AMEX, Discover, Diners	**Pets:** No
	Smoking: Yes
No. of rooms: 39	**Senior citizen discount:** No
No. of baths: 39	
Directions: Inn will send map.	

SOUTH SHORE BED AND BREAKFAST
Water Street, Kelleys Island, OH 43438
(419) 746-2409, (513) 773-0186

How many times have you dreamed of getting away to your own special island? This is your chance. Come to the South Shore Bed and Breakfast on Kelleys Island. At South Shore, you'll enjoy the unhurried pace of the country inn experience in a lovely old house on the lakefront. The inn, which was built in 1857, was a home for quarry master Norman Kelley, the son of the island founder, Irad Kelley.

Shaded by lovely, mature trees, the house has a lake vista and a rock beach. It is convenient to the Neuman Ferry and to town. There are four bedrooms that share one bath.

Before heading off for birding at the Ottawa National Wildlife Refuge, relax with a generous continental breakfast. At this time, ask your hosts, Judy and Larry Adams for a ferry schedule.

Rates: $55-$60	**Wheelchair access:** No
Credit cards: No	**Pets:** No
No. of rooms: 4	**Smoking:** Living room only
No. of baths: 1	**Senior citizen discount:** No
Directions: 4 miles off the Marblehead peninsula, 500 feet from the Neuman Ferry dock.	

OKLAHOMA

Oxley Nature Center

NEAREST AIRPORT: Tulsa, Oklahoma.

LOCATION: Oxley Nature Center is in Mohawk Park, Tulsa, Oklahoma. From the airport, drive north on Highway 169 to the 46th Street North exit. Take 46th Street North west to the Mohawk Park entrance.

CONTACTS: Oxley Nature Center, 5701 E. 36th Street North, Tulsa, OK 74115, (918) 832-8112; Oklahoma Chapter of the Nature Conservancy, 320 South Boston, Suite 1222, Tulsa, OK 74103, (918) 585-1117; Tulsa Audubon Society, P.O. Box 2476, Tulsa, OK 74101.

BEST BIRDING: Spring. Other good birding locations in the Tulsa area are Redbud Valley Natural Area (administered by the Oxley Nature Center), 4 miles north of 161st East Avenue and I-44; the grounds of Woodland Park and the Tulsa Garden Center, at 21st and Peoria; and the Least Tern Preserve (administered by the Oklahoma chapter of the Nature Conservancy), which is the portion of the Arkansas River bed roughly from downtown Tulsa (18th Street) south to about 81st Street along Riverside Drive.

TOURS/WORKSHOPS: Contact the Tulsa Audubon Society, which hosts numerous field trips, workshops, and other activities throughout the year. Write to them for a complete listing of events. A bird list of Tulsa County is also available from the society. Also contact the manager of the Oxley Nature Center.

All of the above-mentioned areas are best during the spring warbler migration, with the exception of the Least Tern Preserve, which is best between the months of May and August when the terns are nesting and rearing their young.

The Oxley Nature Center has an interpretive center as well as several trails. The trails range from undeveloped to boardwalks and go through areas of deep woods, prairies, marshes, and lakes. Some birding blinds are available. The park is open from 8:00 a.m. to 5:00 p.m. Wednesday through Sunday, while the visitor center is open from 11:00 a.m. to 3:00 p.m. Wednesday through Sunday.

Redbud Valley Natural Area consists of a 1-mile loop trail that should be avoided in very rainy or freezing weather as it is very rugged in areas. Habitats found along this trail include rock outcroppings, ravines, caves, floodplains, stunted blackjack oak and post oak woodlands, prairie with flowers, grasses, cactus, and forests. It takes approximately 1½ hours to complete the main loop of the trail. Redbud Valley Natural Area is open from 8:00 a.m. to 5:00 p.m. Wednesday through Sunday.

Least terns start returning to the Least Tern Preserve in May to begin courtship and nesting. On the east side of the Arkansas River, immediately adjacent to the Least Tern Preserve, is a long, linear park called River Parks. The best places to see terns are from this park near 18th Street and 51st Street.

Some of the more spectacular spring species that can be seen in this area are northern cardinals, cedar waxwings, tufted titmice, blue jays, orange-crowned and prothonotary warblers, white-eyes, Bell's, solitary, Philadelphia, and red-eyed vireos, indigo buntings, dickcissels, and American goldfinches. Ospreys, Mississippi kites, bald eagles, red-shouldered hawks, and broad-winged hawks may also be found in this area.

THE LANTERN INN
1348 E. 35th Street, Tulsa, OK 74105, (918) 747-5878

Located in the historic Brookside section of Tulsa, the Lantern Inn offers the unique experience of a secluded, private Old English guest cottage, surrounded by trees. All of this is within walking distance of Tulsa's finest shops and restaurants.

The comfortable accommodations include a living/sitting room with a nice dining area, a queen-size bedroom with down comforter, a mini refrigerator and coffee maker, cable television, a private phone, a full private bath, and enclosed patio. In your room you will find a welcoming basket of fruit and pastries.

An interesting breakfast option is to have oatmeal, coffee, fruit and toast or to take a voucher for one of the nearby Brookside restaurants.

You will be near the Philbrook Art Museum and the Tulsa Garden Center. Of course, you will also try your wings at the Arkansas River Least Tern, where you will see the endangered least tern or at least their nests.

Rates: Single $85; double $90; extra person $100
Credit cards: Visa, MC
No. of rooms: 1 + sofa
No. of baths: 1
Directions: Inn will send map.

Wheelchair access: One level, no problem
Pets: Small dogs, yard fenced
Smoking: No
Senior citizen discount: 10%

ROBIN'S NEST BED AND BREAKFAST
3316 S. 72nd W. Avenue, Tulsa, OK 74114, (918) 446-8700

This five-level New England-style inn is nestled in the woods, about one and a half miles south of Tulsa's Chandler Park and five minutes southwest of downtown Tulsa.

You will feel pampered in your own nest, also known as the master suite. This deluxe suite features a queen-size four-poster bed complete with an inviting down comforter. The English decor is embellished with Laura Ashley fabrics and wallpapers. Enjoy his and hers marble vanities as well as a whirlpool tub. You will find chocolates at your bedside. Fresh flowers set a romantic tone. You can relax in the private sitting area or on the private deck overlooking the downtown Tulsa skyline and 600 acres of protected forests. The inn serves a candlelight gourmet breakfast with china, crystal, and silver.

The Robin's Nest offers complementary transportation to and from the airport.

Rates: $95
Credit cards: Visa, MC
No. of rooms: 1
No. of baths: 1
Wheelchair access: No
Smoking: No
Pets: No
Senior citizen discount: No
Directions: 20 minutes southwest of Nature Center via I-75 and Highway 244 and Highway 11; 20 minutes southwest of Tulsa Airport via I-244.

Klamath Basin National Wildlife Refuge Complex/Bear Valley, Upper Klamath and Klamath Forest, Oregon, Lower Klamath, Clear Lake, and Tule Lake, Northeastern California

NEAREST AIRPORTS: Klamath Falls and Ashland, Oregon.

LOCATION: South central Oregon. The cities of Ashland and Klamath Falls form the bottom of an equilateral triangle with Klamath Falls National Wildlife Refuge at the apex. Highway 66 connects Ashland to Klamath Falls, about a 45-mile drive, and Highway 97 is the route to Upper Klamath Lake, Crater Lake, and the national forests. Traveling south into California, take Highway 97 or 139 to reach the other three refuges comprising the complex.

CONTACT: Refuge Manager, Klamath Basin National Wildlife Refuge Complex, Route 1, Box 74, Tule Lake, CA 96134. (916) 667-2231.

BEST BIRDING: Year-round. Up to 500 bald eagles in winter (January and February).

TOURS/WORKSHOPS: Group programs can be arranged with advance notice. Contact the refuge manager or the U.S. Forest Service at Klamath Falls. (503) 883-6824.

This is an area punctuated by forests and lakes—a region of great diversity and abundance that supports over 400 species of wildlife in the protected 151,000 acres of the refuge complex. Ten ecosystems promote year-round habitation, migratory staging areas, and wintering grounds for 253 species of birds. A boat is required for observation in the Upper Klamath National Wildlife Refuge, which consists of 14,000 acres of open water and marsh. This is an excellent area for canoeing. Look for red-necked grebes, American white pelicans, surf scoters, wood ducks, ospreys, ruffed grouse, mountain quail, spotted owls, Lewis's woodpeckers, white-headed woodpeckers, dusky flycatchers, and Cassin's finches around and in this area.

In the Klamath Forest National Wildlife Refuge, you should easily be able to see blue grouse, northern goshawks, western screech-owls, northern pygmy owls, red-breasted sapsuckers, Williamson's sapsuckers, white-headed woodpeckers, Steller's jays, and Clark's nutcrackers as well as northern and loggerhead shrikes. Bear Valley, one of five eagle roosting areas, has large stands of old-growth timber.

To protect this sensitive wintering area, public access is restricted from November through March. However, you can observe birds flying in and out of the refuge from the city of Worden on Highway 97.

CHANTICLEER BED AND BREAKFAST INN
120 Gresham Street, Ashland, OR 97520, (503) 482-1919

The Chanticleer Bed and Breakfast reflects the literary characters extolled by Shakespeare and Chaucer. The inn feels cozy and snug—from the comfortable furniture, books, and fireplace in the living room to the inviting glasses of sherry. The popular bed and breakfast is one of the most romantic and desirable inns in Ashland.

The seven guest rooms are all charming. The Rosette, with its queen-size antique wrought-iron bed and private entrance off the patio, is a favorite, but each room is furnished with antiques, fluffy goose down comforters, fresh flowers, and crisp linens. Thoughtful touches are good reading lamps and imported soaps and lotions. Scripts of all the plays being performed at the Shakespeare Festival highlight the room appointments.

"Measure for measure," the breakfasts are outstanding: shirred eggs with cream, baked pears with orange sauce, blintzes, blueberry muffins, hot breads, fresh fruit and excellent coffee and teas, not to mention the ultimate luxury, breakfast in bed.

Rates: Weekends and summers $105-$190; winter $85-$130
Credit cards: Visa, MC
No. of rooms: 6
No. of baths: 6
Wheelchair access:
Pets: No
Smoking: Outside only
Directions: From the south, take Highway 5 Ashland exit 14, follow Siskiyou Boulevard; turn left on Union (Safeway on right in town); 2 blocks to Fairview Street; turn right, 1 block turn right on Gresham. From the north, take Ashland exit 19; follow signs to downtown; turn right on Gresham (Library on right); 2 blocks to Chanticleer on left.

HERSEY HOUSE
451 N. Main Street, Ashland, OR 97520, (503) 482-4563

You will expect to see marvelous birds near Ashland, Oregon, but the Oregon Shakespeare Festival offers an added reason to visit this charming, bucolic town.

The Hersey House was built in 1904, and five generations of the family have lived there. When Lynn and Gail Savage converted it into an inn in 1983, they managed to keep the Victorian charm. The present-day Herseys thought the refurbishing was so authentic that they have lent the inn family portraits of the first Herseys who lived in the house. The Hersey House offers you a chance to meander through the lovely English garden or view the Rogue Valley from the spacious front porch. The innkeepers are always available to give helpful advice. After a day of birding or barding, you'll be invited to partake in a social hour in the main parlor.

The four guest rooms are all charming. Each offers period furnishing, a queen-size bed, a private bath, and central air-conditioning. The Sunshine Terrace Room is a favorite, with its private balcony overlooking the Cascade Foothills. The Eastlake Room features an authentic Victorian bedstead, along with a nice view of Mt. Ashland.

Breakfast is a civilized affair with theater talk sprinkled between courses of juice and fruit and daily entrées such as Eggs Hersey or gingerbread pancakes with lemon curd.

Rates: Single $79-$89 double $94-$104; triple $109-$119; bungalow $120 for two; extra person $15
Credit cards: Visa, MC
No. of rooms: 4 + bungalow

No. of baths: 4 + 1½ bath in bungalow
Wheelchair access: No
Pets: No, but the inn is near a kennel.
Smoking: On porches only

Directions: 15 miles north of the California border on I-5. Guests arriving from the south, exit I-5 at exit 11; proceed along Siskiyou and Lithia Way to North Main. Guests arriving from the north, exit I-5 at exit 19, proceed into Ashland to North Main, corner of Main and Nursery.

THE MORICAL HOUSE
668 North Main Street, Ashland, OR 97520, (503) 482-2254

The magnificent scenery at the Morical House is reason enough to stay here. The 1880s farmhouse is surrounded by an acre of rose gardens, rocks, lush lawns, and forest primeval. Best of all, it has a splendid panoramic view of Bear Creek Valley and the Cascade Mountains. The completely restored house offers twentieth-century comfort and nineteenth-century beauty: it features leaded and stained-glass windows, finely crafted woodwork, and antique furniture. All five guest rooms have mountain views, private baths with brass fixtures, air-conditioning, and soundproofed walls.

Breakfast is a treat on the glassed-in sun porch with its stunning view of the Cascade Mountains. Partake of the smoothies and homemade baked goods; daily specials include such treats as Dutch pancakes and Oregon's own fruit basket of blueberries, raspberries, marionberries, and Red Haven peaches.

Between Shakespeare's theater and the theater of the wild, you can play games in the parlor, enjoy a game of croquet, or perfect your golf skills on the putting green. Take part in some convivial banter and afternoon refreshments in the parlor or sun porch.

Innkeepers Pat and Peter Dahl will be happy to tell you all about their adopted hometown before sending you off to bird at Klamath Basin Wildlife Refuge or to sightsee at historic Jacksonville or Crater Lake.

Rates: $80-$112
Credit cards: Visa, MC
No. of rooms: 2
No. of baths: 5
Directions: Inn will send map.

Wheelchair access: No
Pets: No
Smoking: No
Senior citizen discount: AARP

MT. ASHLAND INN
550 Mt. Ashland Road, Box 944, Ashland, OR 97520, (503) 482-8707

If you want to rough it in luxury, try the Mt. Ashland Inn, near the Klamath Basin Refuge Complex. The bed and breakfast is a magnificent cabin in the woods, handcrafted of cedar logs that were cut on the surrounding property. Jerry and Elaine Shanafelt are the modern-day pioneers who designed and built this mountain hideaway. Jerry's woodworking skills and design sense are obvious throughout the inn, from the log archways, stained-glass windows, and log-slab circular staircase to the delightful hand-carved mountain scenes on the doors. He even handcrafted much of the furniture.

Rock cliffs and forested slopes tower over one side of the road leading to the inn. On the other side, converging mountain ranges provide a breathtaking view. The Mt. Ashland Inn sits just two miles from the 7,500-foot summit.

This is an inn for all seasons. There is a cross-country ski trail right out the back door in the winter or a Pacific Crest Trail hike available in summer. Indoor sports enthusiasts might prefer some of the games or books in the inn's main room. Regardless of your choice, you can relax next to the large welcoming stone fireplace and enjoy some hot spiced cider.

Each of the four guest rooms upstairs offers views of Mt. Shasta, Mt. McLoughlin, or some part of the Cascades. Breakfast is a cozy affair of fresh juice, fruit, and a hearty entrée of something like puffy orange French toast.

Rates: Single $75-$120; double $80-$125; extra person $20
Credit cards: Visa, MC
No. of rooms: 5
No. of baths: 5
Directions: Take I-5 exit 6 (Mt. Ashland exit), go west about 6 miles on Mt. Ashland Road following signs to Mt. Ashland Ski Area.

Wheelchair access: No
Pets: No
Smoking: Outside only
Senior citizen discount: No

Malheur National Wildlife Refuge

NEAREST AIRPORTS: Boise, Idaho; Klamath Falls, Oregon.

LOCATION: From Boise, Idaho, drive northwest on I-84 to Payette, then west on Highway 20 about 185 miles to Burns, Oregon, and follow signs to the refuge. From Klamath Falls, Oregon, take Highway 140 east; at Lakeview, drive north, then east on Highway 395 to Burns. From Winnemuca, Nevada, take I-80, then drive north on Highway 95 about 132 miles, then west on Highway 78 25 miles to the refuge. The refuge entrance is 40 miles south of Burns, via Highway 78 to State Road 205 to Princeton.

CONTACT: Refuge Manager, Malheur National Wildlife Refuge, P.O. Box 245, Princeton, OR 97721. (503) 493-2323.

BEST BIRDING: Spring and fall. Summer for nesters.

TOURS/WORKSHOPS: Check with the refuge headquarters and the field station, (503) 493-2629. Credit courses are offered in the summer by the field station. The Annual Migratory Bird Festival is held the first weekend in April.

Although it is strange to think of Oregon having desert lands, both Oregon and Washington have extensive desert habitat in their eastern environs. The Malheur National Wildlife Refuge, located in remote eastern Oregon, is an oasis of lakes, ponds, wetlands, and riparian woodlands; it is an important staging and nesting area along the Pacific Flyway. Listed in the checklist as nesters are 130 species, including horned, eared, western, and Clark's grebes, great blue herons and great egrets, trumpeter swans, and canvasback ducks. Swainson's hawks, golden eagles, prairie falcons, burrowing owls, snowy plovers, sage grouse, and soras all use the managed areas on and around the refuge. The warbler migration, which peaks in May (call for more specific dates), follows the staging of sandhill cranes and migratory waterfowl headed north in April, including tundra swans, snow geese, Ross's geese, cinnamon teals, gadwalls, redheads, and mergansers, along with long-billed curlews, least sandpipers, and long-billed dowitchers. During the first weekend in April, a migratory bird festival is sponsored by the refuge and the Harney County Chamber of Commerce. In the fall, the flocks migrate south again, making autumn an equally good time to visit the refuge.

FRENCHGLEN HOTEL
Frenchglen, OR 97736, (503) 493-2825

The old-fashioned eight-room Frenchglen Hotel at the southern tip of the Malheur National Wildlife Refuge offers nostalgia and seclusion. As the hotel's brochure puts it, "Here at the Frenchglen Hotel we have no jacuzzi, swimming pool, color TV, or any TV for that matter! What we have to offer is peace and quiet. Leave your alarm clock at home and wake up to roosters crowing and the aroma of coffee brewing and bacon sizzling in the morning." Breakfast is served between 7:30 and 9:30 and lunch between 11:30 and 2:30. Breakfast is $2.75 to $5.75, while lunch is $3.50 to $5.00.

Later in the day, you can indulge yourself in a family-style dinner. Entrées include baked chicken and artichoke, the Frenchglen's famous pot roast served with garlicky roasted potatoes, marinated roast beef, and honey-glazed pork chops. Save room for dessert, especially when it is ice cream with hot fudge sauce, laced with Kahlua and orange liqueur. Dinner is served at 6:30 sharp. The dining room can seat only 20, so be sure to make reservations. The price: entrées cost between $9.95 and $13.95.

Rates: $42-$48
Credit cards: Visa, MC
No. of rooms: 8
No. of baths: 2

Wheelchair access: No
Pets: No
Smoking: No
Senior citizen discount: No

Directions: 60 miles south of Burns on Highway 205.

HOTEL DIAMOND
Diamond, OR 97722, (503) 493-1898

The Hotel Diamond is centrally located for birding on the Malheur National Wildlife Refuge where the bird-watching is sensational. Raptors, such as falcons, hawks, and eagles, use thermal updrafts from the Alvord Basin to soar over the rugged countryside searching for food. Golden eagles, the largest raptors on Steens Mountain, may be seen riding the wind currents along the rim. Innkeepers Judy and Jerry Santille report that there are over 200 varieties of songbirds and waterfowl at Malheur and lots of birds here at the Diamond Hotel. The John Schaff Migratory Waterfowl Festival is held the first weekend of April.

You will enjoy settling into the newly restored Hotel Diamond with its five guest rooms and two and a half baths. Breakfast is $8.00 to $13.50. The town and hotel are thought to be named after the diamond-shaped brand used by the McCoy Ranch.

Rates: $45-$55   **Wheelchair access:** No
Credit cards: Visa, MC   **Pets:** No
No. of rooms: 5   **Smoking:** Yes
No. of baths: 2½   **Senior citizen discount:** No
Directions: State Highway 205, 42 miles south, big sign, Diamond, 12 miles east.

McCOY CREEK INN
McCoy Creek Ranch, HC 72 Box 11, Diamond, OR 97722
(503) 493-2131 days, (503) 493-2440 evenings

A pleasant place to stay in this area is McCoy Creek Inn, part of a working ranch in Diamond. McCoy Creek, home to five generations of the same family, is deep in the heart of country rich with a history of settlers, Indian battles, sheepherders, and cattle barons. McCoy Creek is the perfect jumping-off spot for visiting the Kiger Mustang lookout, historic Frenchglen, and the breathtaking Steens Mountain recreation area.

The ranch itself is appealing, surrounded by its own meadows and clear streams. The three bedrooms in the main house as well as the bunkhouse are nicely furnished and have private baths.

Start your day with a full farmhouse breakfast. Let the McCoys pack you a picnic lunch to take with you on your birding expedition. After a day filled with checking off life lists at Malheur, relax with a soak in the hot tub. Enjoy a good country dinner (part of your room fee), then stroll along McCoy Creek or hike over the rim onto the gentle north face of the Steens to watch the sun set or hunker down with a book or a movie from the video library.

Bring your children along, and let them enjoy a farmhouse vacation. They will have a great time exploring the canyon, wading in the creek, or borrowing one of the inn's air mattresses and floating around. The whole family will get a kick out of feeding the ducks, peacocks, turkeys, chickens, lambs, and calves. Perhaps you would prefer to count the raccoons, badgers, beavers, and porcupines who make their home along McCoy Creek. Watch the deer come into the meadow to feed.

Observe the migratory birds that inhabit and nest in the canyon, such as Canada geese, eagles, ducks, heron, killdeer, and many others. You'll enjoy this inn; as any guest will tell you, it is, indeed, the real McCoy.

Rates: Single $55; double $75; extra   **Wheelchair access:** Yes
person $10   **Pets:** No
Credit cards: Visa, MC   **Smoking:** Outside only
No. of rooms: 4   **Senior citizen discount:** No
No. of baths: 4
Directions: Inn will send map.

PENNSYLVANIA

Mill Grove–
Home of John James Audubon

AUDUBON WILDLIFE SANCTUARY
P.O. Box 2, Audubon, PA 19407, (215) 666-5593

Mill Grove is the only true Audubon home remaining in America. This lovely estate, located in Lower Providence Township, Montgomery County, Pennsylvania, was owned for 17 years by Audubon's father, Jean, a French sea captain.

In 1804, Captain Audubon sent his youthful son, John James, to Mill Grove to supervise the estate. The young Frenchman lived here for little more than two years, but it was while at Mill Grove that he gained his first impressions of American birds and wildlife. He spent his first few years in this country roaming the wooded hills along the Perkiomen Creek and the Schuylkill River, hunting, observing, collecting, and sketching. It was during this period that he experienced the early stirrings of a fascination for wildlife that was to become his all-absorbing life interest.

Audubon was the first to portray birds and other wildlife in natural settings. His famous engravings, published between 1826 and 1838, show his innovative style in life-sized pictures of American birds.

The attic of the home has been restored to a studio and taxidermy room, depicting Audubon's working quarters when he lived at Mill Grove. While here, he developed his special method of depicting lifelike positions of freshly shot specimens. After months of attempting to attain the image of a living bird in his drawings, he hit on the idea of piercing the bird's lifeless body with pliable wire that he could bend and twist to hold the carcass in lifelike position. Success was suddenly in hand, and he depended on this method throughout his lifetime.

Seeing these stuffed birds is a little disconcerting to today's bird lovers who prefer to see their birds alive and flying. However, you can leave the taxidermy room and head outside to the lovely grounds where there are indeed birds flying and singing all around. In season, numerous species of birds may be observed, including descendants of the phoebes that Audubon studied and banded and the unique chimney swifts whose forebears nested in the same chimneys that provided warmth to the young Frenchman.

Mill Grove is open Tuesday through Saturday from 10:00 a.m. to 4:00 p.m. and Sunday from 1:00 to 4:00 p.m.; closed New Year's Day, Thanksgiving, and Christmas. No admission charge.

THE AMSTERDAM BED AND BREAKFAST
P.O. Box 1139, Valley Forge, PA 19482-1139
(215) 983-9620, (800) 952-1580

The Amsterdam lives up to its name. The elegant living room is beautifully furnished with Dutch paintings and Dutch memorabilia. Our sumptuous second-floor bedroom was decorated with Delft china, paintings of Dutch street scenes, tulips, and wooden Dutch shoes.

It is no great surprise to discover that one of the owners, Ino Vandersteur, a chemical engineer, is from Holland. Pamela, his charming and hospitable wife, is a native Philadelphian who received her chef training in the Netherlands. Her breakfasts reflect an Indonesian restaurant background. The Dutch West Indies eggs in curry sauce with a side of bacon were delicious and offered a refreshing change from standard bills of fare. A fruit compote made with brown sugar, butter, and amaretto rounded out the meal beautifully. I should add that with plenty of advance notice, Pam will produce her reknowned Indonesian rijsttafel. This dinner extravaganza consists of rice served with different sauces and other classic Indonesian foods.

Both Ino and Pam are blessed with a lighthearted, puckish sense of humor. Pam still refers to my physicist husband and me as "Einstein and the bird lady." At breakfast, she will regale you with some of the more entertaining moments of innkeeping.

There are plenty of Audubon bird books at the Amsterdam to get you in the mood to visit the nearby John Jay Audubon House. However, if you want to take the day off and indulge in some nonbirding activities, you can choose among Valley Forge National Park, Lancaster County Amish Country, Reading and Lancaster factory outlets, or the Brandywine Museum in Andrew Wyeth country. You can also relax in the Amsterdam's luxurious hot tub, followed by a cozy evening of champagne sipping.

Rates: Double with private bath $75, shared bath $65; deduct $10 for singles; 10% discount offered weekdays at the inn
Credit cards: Visa, MC
No. of rooms: 3
No. of baths: 2
Directions: Inn will send map.

Wheelchair access: No
Pets: No
Smoking: Designated areas only; guest and dining rooms are smoke-free
Senior citizen discount: No

Hawk Mountain Sanctuary

NEAREST AIRPORT: Allentown, Pennsylvania, usually via Philadelphia.

LOCATION: Eight miles west of Kempton, in the southeast quadrant of Pennsylvania. From Allentown, drive west on I-78 to the junction with Highway 143. Drive north on Highway 143 and follow signs. Be sure to also get directions from the visitor center since the signs leading to the entrance can be confusing.

CONTACTS: Hawk Mountain Sanctuary Association, Route 2, Kempton, PA 19529. (215) 756-6961.

BEST BIRDING: Fall raptor migration—mid-August through November. Open year-round.

TOURS/WORKSHOPS: Interpretive presentations spring, summer, and fall; schedule posted in the visitor center. Lectures on Saturdays in September and October. For other workshops available, contact the Hawk Mountain Sanctuary Association. Excellent news magazine and calendar of events available for members. The best time to visit is on weekdays as the area is often crowded on weekends.

North Lookout, on the Kittatinny Ridge, overlooks rolling farmland and bucolic vistas. Here amid boulders is a good place to observe some of North America's largest hawk flights on their southward migration. Part of the 2,200-acre Hawk Mountain Sanctuary, both the north and south Hawkwatch points, provide breathtaking views of an average of 24,000 raptors during the migration season. Fourteen species pass over Hawk Mountain; beginning in August, look for sharp-shinned and broad-winged hawks, ospreys, and American kestrels in small numbers. The broad-winged hawks usually peak in October, sometimes with over 1,000 a day passing through; ospreys, American kestrels, and bald eagles generally peak at that time, as well as Cooper's and sharp-shinned hawks, which can be seen along the ridges. October is the month of the greatest number of species; it is then that the flights of goshawks, golden eagles, northern harriers, peregrine falcons, and merlins are at their best, while November is the peak month for red-tailed hawks. These are all generalizations based on many years of data from the sanctuary. Each year the timing of the greatest concentrations of species varies somewhat depending on weather patterns.

GLASBERN
R.D. 1, Box 250, Fogelsville, PA 18051, (800) 654-9296

The Glasbern is a luxurious remodeled barn. Innkeepers Beth and Al Granger fulfilled a lifelong dream when they bought a magnificent, nineteenth-century, post-and-beam, German bank barn nestled in a farm meadow. Stripping the barn to its stone walls and frame, they retained its handsome hand-hewn wooden beams, richly textured shale walls, and such rustic detailing as the farmer's ladders that once led to the haymows.

They then created a spacious Great Hall, which serves as the inn's living and dining rooms. The hall is distinguished by banks of windows and by skylights scattered across the soaring, 26-foot cathedral ceiling. These windows and skylights flood the barn with light, casting abstract patterns across the geometic beamwork. It was the open, light atmosphere that inspired the name Glasbern, which means "glass barn" in Middle English.

There is a serenity to the Glasbern, a sense of the spiritual, of a stone cathedral, of peace in the countryside. On a less ethereal plane, there is also excellent French Country cooking in the dining room, on Tuesday through Saturday from 6:00 to 8:00 p.m.

Some of the guest rooms have whirlpools, fireplaces, and tubs built-for-two. In the summer, you can cool off after birding at the inn's swimming pool. At both Hawk Mountain and the Glasbern, you will feel removed from civilization and its discontent.

Rates: $80-$225
Credit cards: Visa, MC
No. of rooms: 23
No. of baths: 23

Wheelchair access: Yes
Pets: No
Smoking: No-smoking rooms available
Senior citizen discount: No

Directions: Exit 14B, from I-78, take Route 100 north, turn left at the first traffic light (Tilghma St.), continue right on north Church St., drive %10 of a mile and turn right again on Packhouse Rd. The inn is %10 of a mile down Packhouse Rd. to the right.

HAWK MOUNTAIN INN
R.D. 1, Box 186, Kempton, PA 19529, (215) 756-4224

Hawk Mountain Inn is a lovely spot. And it is the bed and breakfast closest to one of America's foremost bird-watching sites, Hawk Mountain Sanctuary.

All bed and breakfasts promise to get you away from it all; Hawk Mountain Inn really delivers. It is Pennsylvania's answer to Walden Pond, complete with a lake, a truly rural panorama, and chickens roaming all around.

With stunning views overlooking the foothills of the Blue Mountain Valley, the lovely country setting of Hawk Mountain Inn is enticing.

Owners Jim and Judy Gaffney have blended the finest European bed-and-breakfast traditions with the American accent on comfort and luxury. There is a generous pool in the backyard and a screened-in activity and dining area with bar.

Built in 1988 by the owners, the inn has eight guest rooms, each one uniquely furnished with eclectic post-Victorian pieces, including rice, pencil post, and pineapple bedsteads, matching comforters, carpeting, window accents, and armoires incorporating television units. One bedroom that particularly caught my attention has a stonework fireplace, stained-glass windows, and a Jacuzzi.

The breakfast is definitely worth getting up for. It is a true country treat of fresh eggs from the inn's own chickens, smoked bacon and country scrapple (a Pennsylvania Dutch concoction consisting of beef and pork, buckwheat flour, and beef stock), French toast or whole wheat pancakes, grapefruit or strawberries, coffee, tea, and orange juice.

On weekends, the Gaffneys serve country dinners in their charming dining room. The room is lovely with its lace curtains, pink tablecloths, fresh flowers, stone fireplace, and a variety of stuffed bunnies on the couch. Birders may enjoy a chance to lounge around before dinner reading the large collection of *Audubon* magazines.

Hawk Mountain Inn

Jim leads midweek and weekend bicycle tours, promising "cycling and scenery at their best." Bird-watchers will want to spend all their leisure time at the 2,220-acre Hawk Mountain where bald eagles, ospreys, broad-winged hawks, and other rare species have soared for centuries. Nonbirders can hike on nearby Appalachian trails, go to county fairs, cross-country or downhill ski, ride on authentic steam locomotives, or shop at Reading's famous factory outlets.

Rates: Double $90; luxury room double $130
Credit cards: Visa, MC, AMEX
No. of rooms: 8
No. of baths: 8
Directions: Inn will send map.

Wheelchair access: No
Pets: With reservations
Smoking: Yes
Senior citizen discount: No

SUNDAY'S MILL FARM
R.R. 2, Box 419, Bernville, PA 19506, (215) 488-7821

Sunday's Mill Farm, a well-preserved country place listed on the National Register of Historic Places, is only thirty minutes from Hawk Mountain, America's birding shrine. The farm, home in 1723 to German settlers, is situated on the banks of the unspoiled Tulpchocken Creek.

Guests are invited to tour the 1820 stone mill and the 1850 brick house, which is furnished with antiques and original paintings. You are also welcome to fish in the pond or creek or to walk along the tow path. Or you might prefer to relax on one of the two patios and look over your bird lists.

There are five guest rooms, a queen-size room with a half bath, a double room with a shared bath, two suites that include a twin-bedded room and a double queen-bedded room, and a suite with a European-style bath as well as an equipped kitchen and a living room. Guests in all rooms are served a full breakfast.

Rates: Single $35-$50; double $45-$60; extra person $10 cot, $7 own sleeping bag
Credit cards: No
No. of rooms: 5

No. of baths: 2 full, 2 half
Wheelchair access: No
Pets: No
Smoking: Outside only
Senior citizen discount: No

Directions: From 78, take 183 south to just past blinking light at Bernville. Turn right at large sign on left for Christmas Village, Steidelberg Country Club, and Blue Marsh Ski area. Turn right on Christmas Village Road to Station Road, turn left, cross bridge to the first house on the right. From 419, take Bernville six miles to Statikon Road and turn right to the house.

Tinicum National Environmental Center

NEAREST AIRPORT: Philadelphia, Pennsylvania.

LOCATION: One mile north of Philadelphia International Airport. Take Route 291 south from the airport; refuge headquarters is at Scott Plaza. The visitor center is on 86th Street and Lindbergh Boulevard, just north of the airport. Drive north on Island Avenue to Bertram Avenue south; then almost immediately turn right on 84th Street. Take 84th Street to Lindbergh and turn left to the visitor center.

CONTACT: Tinicum National Environmental Center, Center Headquarters, Suite 104, Scott Plaza, Philadelphia, PA 19113, (215) 521-0662. Visitor center: (215) 365-3118.

BEST BIRDING: Mid-March to May, August through mid-November.

TOURS/WORKSHOPS: Check with refuge manager or visitor center.

Tinicum Marsh, the last freshwater tidal marsh left in Pennsylvania, has been diminished from 5,700 acres in 1643 to 200 acres at present. One hundred forty-five acres were acquired in 1955; in 1972, the 1,200-acre Tinicum National Environmental Center was established. Because the marsh has been much disturbed by diking, dredging, and filling, the center's goal is to restore the former wetlands and preserve the remaining one. Even in its present state the acreage is a haven to over 280 species of birds and is an important resting and feeding area along the Atlantic Flyway during the spring and fall migrations. Thirty-five species can be observed during the spring warbler migration in the first few weeks of May. Other spring birds include bitterns, egrets, and herons, wood, black, and ruddy ducks, greater black-backed gulls, fish crows, Carolina wrens, gray-cheeked and wood thrushes, scarlet tanagers, rose-breasted grosbeaks, and indigo buntings, as well as field, white-throated, and swamp sparrows. Spring nesters that may be seen are orchard orioles, northern orioles, blue grosbeaks, cedar waxwings, common barn owls, American woodcocks, northern harriers, and black-crowned night herons. In the fall, the southern migration peaks from mid-October to mid-November with flocks of waterfowl and raptors.

THE THOMAS BOND HOUSE
129 South Second Street, near Walnut, Philadelphia, PA 19106
(215) 923-8523, (800) 845-BOND

D r. Thomas Bond built the original part of the Thomas Bond House in 1769. He, along with Benjamin Franklin, founded the Pennsylvania Hospital, the first public hospital in the United States, chartered in 1751.

Today the Thomas Bond House bed and breakfast is tastefully furnished with period furniture and accessories. The bedrooms contain twin beds, double beds, or a queen-size bed. Two accommodations are arranged as suites with queen-size beds and full-size sofa beds. These rooms have whirlpool baths and working fireplaces. All rooms have private baths, telephone, and television.

Before visiting the Tinicum National Environmental Center and Refuge, enjoy a continental breakfast on weekdays and a full breakfast on weekends. Relax in the evenings with complimentary wine and cheese.

If you want to take a piece of history with you, visit the Key and Quill Shop, located in the Thomas Bond House. The Key and Quill carries an interesting stock of reproductions of furniture and accessories found in Independence National Historical Park and other historical eighteenth-century places including Williamsburg and Charleston. The shop also carries reproductions of old maps.

The Thomas Bond House

Rates: $80–$150; extra person $15
Credit cards: Visa, MC, AMEX,
Discover, Diners
No. of rooms: 12
No. of baths: 12
Wheelchair access: No
Pets: No
Smoking: Yes
Senior citizen discount: 10%

Directions: North or south on I-45 to Philadelphia, exit signs to Independence National Historic Park. On 2nd Street south between Chestnut and Walnut; 129 South Second.

LA RESERVE
CENTER CITY BED AND BREAKFAST
1804 Pine Street, Philadelphia, PA 19103
(215) 735-1137/0582, (800) 354-8401

La Reserve is known by many as Center City Bed and Breakfast and by all as the Grand Dame of Philadelphia. This is a well-preserved, 140-year-old townhouse that reflects the elegance of Philadelphia's historic past while offering its guests a warm, cozy retreat in the hustling modern city. It is also an ideal location for visiting Tinicum National Environmental Center and Refuge.

Here you can relax, sip a glass of wine or sherry in the drawing room, play the grand piano, have breakfast in the large chandeliered dining room, or perhaps curl up with a good book from the library. There are choices of accommodations to satisfy both the senses and the wallet. The suites are on a grand scale, with a sitting area, king or queen bed, and a private bath. The bedrooms are large with double or twin beds and shared baths.

If time allows after birding at Tinicum, visit Independence Hall, the Liberty Bell, the Philadelphia Museum of Art, or the Rodin Museum.

Rates: Single $40; double $80; extra cot $10
Credit cards: Visa, MC
No. of rooms: 7
No. of baths:
Wheelchair access: Yes
Pets:
Smoking: Not encouraged
Senior citizen discount: No

Directions: Center City (Rittenhouse Square area).

STEELE AWAY BED & BREAKFAST
715 Boyer Street, Philadelphia 19119, PA (215) 242-0722

Where should you make your home in Philadelphia while visiting Tinicum? A good possibility is the Steele Away, where you can relax in the heart of Philadelphia's Mt. Airy section nestled along the Wissahickon stream and Fairmount Park. Mt. Airy's Victorian homes, situated among stately trees and flowering azaleas and dogwoods along the rolling hills, will make you forget you are in a bustling city.

Your hosts, the Steeles, an architect and a weaver, offer the warm simplicity of Scandinavian decor amid the carved woodwork of their 12-room, late nineteenth-century stone home. Guests are invited to peer into the weaver's loom room to see works in progress. Completed works are displayed throughout.

Guest accommodations consist of two large guest rooms on the sunny third floor; one features a double bed and the other twin beds. Each room has a sitting area, hand-stenciled walls, handwoven fabrics, museum prints, and lace curtains.

Breakfast is served downstairs in the formal dining room. A continental-plus breakfast is served weekdays (homemade muffins, pastries, granola, fresh fruit, yogurt, juice, cereals, coffee, and tea). On weekends, a cooked breakfast is served.

Philadelphia is an interesting region, so if you have a few extra days, you might want to visit Pennsylvania Dutch country, Valley Forge, or Bucks County. The hospitable Steeles will point you in the right direction.

Rates: Single $50; double $65 and up; extra person $15
Credit cards: No
No. of rooms: 2
No. of baths: 1
Wheelchair access: No
Pets: No
Smoking: No
Senior citizen discount: No

Directions: From Pennsylvania turnpike, take exit 25 and make immediate right after the toll booth onto Germantown Pike. Go 6³⁄₁₀ miles through Chestnut Hill into Mt. Airy. At Mt. Pleasant Avenue traffic light turn left. Go 2 blocks to Boyer St. and turn left. Go ²⁄₁₀ mile to stop sign at Mt. Airy Avenue and park on street. You will be at front entrance. Look for black lamp posts and porch swing. From airport or south of city, take Route 95 N to exit the airport; then follow signs to get on 76 W. Go 12 miles or so. Take Lincoln Drive exit, which is ½ mile after Valley Forge sign. Follow Lincoln Drive as it winds along the Wissahickon stream and up through Mt. Airy. At Mt. Pleasant Avenue, turn right (a Sunoco station is on the right corner). Go ½ mile to Boyer Street. Turn left; go to stop sign at Mt. Airy Avenue (²⁄₁₀ mile) and park on right before the stop sign. You'll see the entrance.

RHODE ISLAND

Ninigret National Wildlife Refuge Complex/Ninigret, Trustom Pond, Block Island, and Sachuest Point

NEAREST AIRPORTS: New London, Connecticut; Providence, Rhode Island.

LOCATION: Along the southern coast of Rhode Island between the cities of Westerly and Newport Beach. Block Island is almost directly south of Charlestown. From New London, Connecticut, drive east on US 1 about 25 miles to Highway 1A, then to refuge headquarters in Charleston. The Ninigret Refuge east entrance is a few miles from headquarters, west on Highway 1A. Trustom Pond, east of headquarters, is reached via US 1; take the Moonstone Beach Road exit, then drive 1 mile to Mantunuck Schoolhouse Road and to the refuge entrance. To reach Sachuest Point Refuge from the complex headquarters, drive east and north on US 1 to the junction of Highway 138. Drive east on Highway 138 past Newport. Continue east on Miantonomi Avenue, then east on Green End Avenue. Turn right on Paradise Avenue until you reach Hanging Rock Road. Turn left, then right on Sachuest Point Road to the entrance. Block Island can be reached by ferry from Galilee. From Providence, Rhode Island, take the same highways headed south. It is 45 miles to Ninigret and about 20 miles to Sachuest. Other nearby areas to bird are the Norman Bird Sanctuary in Middleton and the great swamp management area in Kingston.

CONTACT: Ninigret National Wildlife Refuge Complex, Shoreline Plaza, Route 1A, P.O. Box 307, Charlestown, RI 02813. (401) 364-9124.

BEST BIRDING: Spring and fall migrations.

TOURS/WORKSHOPS: Conducted year-round by refuge staff. Also contact the Frosty Drew Nature Center for additional programs at Ninigret: (401) 364-9508.

The south shores of Rhode Island—the ponds, marshes, sands, rocks, woods, barrier beaches, and offshore islands—are all excellent birding areas. The size of the various refuges within the National Wildlife Refuge Complex varies. Ninigret has 400 acres and 250 bird species; Trustom Pond, 640 acres and 300 bird species; Block Island, 46 acres, as well as migratory haven and nesting sites; Sachuest Point, 242 acres and 200 species. In the spring at Ninigret and

Trustom, ospreys return to nest, and woodcocks begin their courtship flights. Endangered piping plovers and least terns arrive to nest, and a barrier beach is closed for their protection. Common terns, as well as herring and great black-backed gulls, nest on the offshore islands.

The best birding times at Sachuest Point Refuge are fall and winter; spring, of course, is best for viewing songbirds. Sachuest Point is a sanctuary for thousands of tree swallows in September. Waterfowl peak in the last two weeks in November. If the winds are right, you can observe razorbills, dovekies, black-legged kittiwakes, and gannets. Additional birds that arrive in the winter are snowy owls and short-eared owls as well as possibly Barrow's goldeneyes, purple sandpipers, and sanderlings. Also look for king and common eiders, loons, grebes, ruddy turnstones, black- and yellow-billed cuckoos, and beautiful snow buntings.

MEADOWLAND BED AND BREAKFAST
765 Old Baptist Road, N. Kingstown, RI 02852, (401) 294-4168

When you arrive at Meadowland Bed and Breakfast you can start your bird-watching immediately. Stroll around the half acre of land replete with fruit trees and admire the variety of birds on the grounds and patio.

Innkeeper Linda Javarone explains her bed and breakfast philosophy: "At Victorian Meadowland, we offer you your home away from home. Here you can enjoy a stressless time and space where you go back to a period in which comfort and quality of living were embraced in old-fashioned aesthetic beauty and charm. Meadowlands interior gives you a bit of yesterday today—from a nostalgic living room with a fireplace to wicker decorated bedrooms, with quaint bathrooms and comfortable sitting rooms on each floor. On rising each morning, you will enjoy a sumptuous candlelight breakfast in our formal dining room."

The inn is open from Memorial Day to mid-October. There are four double bedrooms, a room with two twin beds, and a single bedroom with two twin bed. All share the baths.

Nonbirders can take a tour of the famous Newport mansions, explore Block Island, attend the Newport Jazz Festival, or go to the South County Hot Air Balloon Fest.

Rates: Single $55; double $65; extra room $20
Credit cards: No
No. of rooms: 6
No. of baths: 3

Wheelchair access: No
Pets: No
Smoking: No
Senior citizen discount: No

Directions: From Boston, travel I-95 south to Route 4 south, Exit 9, North Kingstown, East Greenwich. Stay on this road until you see Wickford 102.

Take this exit. Bear right off exit until you come to a traffic light. Immediately
after light, take left. This is Old Baptist Road. Meadowland is exactly 1 mile
from the beginning of the street.

MELVILLE HOUSE
39 Clarke Street, Newport, RI 02840, (401) 847-0640

The first thing guests mention about Melville House is the charming,
unpretentious personalities of the hosts, Rita and Sam Rogers. A friend
who visited told me that the Melville House could win an award as the friend-
liest B&B in New England.

During the Revolutionary War, for example, the French general
Rochambeau, in support of General George Washington, quartered some of
his troops at the 39 Clarke Street address. The Rogers keep this history alive
with their colonial decorations and Early American furnishings. The motto of
the inn is, "Where the past is present."

Graciousness is also still very much present. A glass of sherry is offered on
your arrival. You can sit in the small country living room, relaxing in Early
American rockers while enjoying a nice fire. Sam will entertain you with his
display of antique household appliances, including dough makers, coffee
grinders and cherry pitters. On rainy days, you can play some of the many
games the Rogers keep for their guests' enjoyment.

Melville House

After a buffet breakfast of granola, yogurt, homemade muffins, preserves, juice, and coffee, head for Ninigret National Wildlife Refuge to search for the yellow-breasted chat nests.

Rates: As low as $40 per night off-season to as high as $100 per night in season
Credit cards: Visa, MC, AMEX
No. of rooms: 7
Directions: Inn will send map.

No. of baths: 7
Wheelchair access: No
Pets: No
Smoking: Limited
Senior citizen discount: No

THE OLD CLERK HOUSE
49 Narragansett Avenue, Narragansett, RI 02882-3386, (401) 783-8008

A bed and breakfast that advertises itself in its brochure as "English country comfort in a Victorian setting" got my attention. Innkeeper Patricia Watkins has recently renovated the Old Clerk House, which since its construction in 1890 was the domicile of a succession of town clerks. The very English yard with a white picket fence is abloom with roses in summer. The leather sofa and chairs in the living room invite you to relax, read, watch a video, or listen to music.

You will have a wonderful night's sleep in air-conditioned comfort in large rooms with twin, double, or king-size beds—all with private baths.

Breakfast is a cheerful affair in the plant-filled sun room. You choose your menu the night before from a wide selection: fresh kiwi with lime or fresh grapefruit with strawberry sauce and a medley of muffin choices and enough entrée choices to make you want to stay several days. Breakfast is served from 7:30 to 9:30 a.m.

Rates: Single $65; doubles $75
Credit cards: No
No. of rooms: 2
No. of baths: 2
Directions: Inn will send map.

Wheelchair access: No
Pets: No
Smoking: No
Senior citizen discount: No

ONE WILLOW BY THE SEA
1 Willow Road, Charlestown, RI 02813, (401) 364-0802

O ne Willow by the Sea is a paradise for bird-watchers. You can see your feathered friends on walks along the beautiful white sandy beaches or on nature walks.

Denise Dillon Fuge, the innkeeper, is an interesting person. Inspired by the suffragists as a teenager in London, she went on to become president of

New York City's NOW chapter. She helped create the National Women's Health Network. For 31 years, she created and edited a medical journal at Memorial Sloan-Kettering Cancer Center. She is a font of information. Be certain to ask this bird woman about her owl prowls and bird migration theme weekends.

Fuge enjoys serving her special English teapot-style tea or freshly ground coffee. Her breakfasts vary, but cantaloupe with ginger, vanilla yogurt, fresh fruit, croissants, blueberry muffins, and bagels are favorites. The reasonably priced three bedrooms include such extras as thick bath sheets, extra pillows, and sundried sheets.

Rates: Single/double in season $50-$55; Single/double out of season $40-$45
Credit cards: No
No. of rooms: 4
Directions: Inn will send map.

No. of baths: 2
Wheelchair access: No
Pets: No
Smoking: On sun deck only
Senior citizen discount: No

WOODY HILL BED & BREAKFAST
330 Woody Hill Road, Westerly, RI 02891, (401) 322-0452

Woody Hill Bed & Breakfast offers quiet country living in a convenient location just two miles from the ocean. Situated on a hilltop and surrounded by rolling fields and informal gardens, the house provides a pleasant change from the usual tourist accommodations.

Innkeeper Ellen Madison, a high school English teacher who recently earned her Ph.D., has been called by many guests "a gastronomical intellectual." Her breakfast repertoire features seasonal fruit with tasty but unusual sauces, apple crisp, strawberry nut or blueberry ginger muffins; in short, anything but eggs!

Madison designed and did much of the finishing work for her latest addition. You will enjoy her efforts in the library, which has four walls of books, shuttered windows, and window seats. She has nice touches throughout, such as antiques, wide-board floors, and hand-made quilts.

There are three large bedrooms with shared baths on two floors. You will enjoy relaxing in the yard, which features a flower and herb garden, or taking a wind-down swim in the 40-foot in-ground pool.

Rates: $55-$85; extra person $10
Credit cards: No
No. of rooms: 3
No. of baths: 2

Wheelchair access: Yes
Pets: No
Smoking: No
Senior citizen discount: No

Directions: From 95 (northbound), take exit 92, turn right onto Route 2, right onto 78, left onto Route 1. Go through two lights and turn left onto Woody Hill Road (at McDonald's), ¾ mile on right, see "Madison" on mailbox or small Woody Hill Bed & Breakfast sign.

SOUTH CAROLINA

Cape Romain National Wildlife Refuge

NEAREST AIRPORT: Charlestown, South Carolina.

LOCATION: About 20 miles northeast of Charleston, 22 miles along the coast from Bulls Island to McClellanville. Drive US 17 along the intracoastal waterway to the refuge entrance via Seewee Road (the visitor center was destroyed by Hurricane Hugo). Bulls Island, 3 miles off the mainland, can be reached by the Bulls Island boat concession. Call for information and reservations: (803) 884-5523. There is a charge.

CONTACT: Cape Romain National Wildlife Refuge, 390 Bull Island Road, Awendaw, SC 29429. (809) 928-3368.

BEST BIRDING: Fall, winter, and spring.

TOURS/WORKSHOPS: Contact the refuge manager. For information about nearby Francis Marion National Forest write or call District Ranger, Wambaw Ranger District, P.O. Box 788, McClellanville, SC 29458, (803) 887-3257.

Curving around Bull Bay, the refuge lands are laced with freshwater creeks, which meander through marshes to mix with ocean tides. Bull Island remains a primitive outpost, undeveloped for human residence. Along the walking trails you can observe a great variety of birds and other wildlife in the pristine habitat of shores, woods, ponds, and live oaks.

In spring (March and April), the beaches and ponds are filled with wading shorebirds, and the forests are populated by warblers. Look for Wilson's plovers, American oystercatchers, marbled godwits, ruddy turnstones, red knots, pectoral, eastern, and western sandpipers, dowitchers, and Wilson's phalaropes. Numerous species of terns fly overhead; expect to see gull-billed, Caspian, royal, sandwich, least, and common terns. In the forests seek out the brown-headed nuthatches and a possible 22 species of warblers. At this time you may also observe summer tanagers, northern cardinals, blue grosbeaks, indigo and painted buntings, rufous-sided towhees, and orchard orioles, American goldfinches, and eastern bluebirds.

When the cooling winds of fall arrive, brown pelicans still feed offshore and approximately 23 different species of ducks begin to return. Majestic wood storks can still be seen, and the raptor population increases, including black vultures, American swallow-tailed kites, sharp-shinned, Cooper's, and red-shouldered hawks, and an occasional peregrine falcon. On Bull Island alone more than 260 species of birds have been documented.

THE SHAW HOUSE
8 Cyprus Court, Georgetown, SC 29440, (803) 546-9663

The Willowbank Marsh is an excellent place for birding and observing nature in a particular habitat. From the Shaw House in Georgetown, you are guaranteed a clear view of it through an all-glass enclosure on the side of the building. Staying here will put you in the mood for birding at Cape Romain National Wildlife Refuge and Washo Reserve. The rooms are large, and all have private bathrooms. Scattered throughout the inn are interesting samples of antique pottery.

Innkeeper Mary Shaw has an intimate knowledge of the area, including historical sites, gift shops, restaurants, and more, which she gladly shares. She also serves a complimentary Southern home-cooked breakfast that includes fresh hot bread and your own pot of coffee.

Georgetown itself has a fascinating history for buffs to enjoy. In the early 1700s, Northern European immigrants began arriving and established settlements that flourished. Many of their traditions in homes, cultural establishments, and houses of worship still exist.

The Shaw House is within walking distance of the historical district, close to marinas, golf courses, and tennis courts. It is also near Myrtle Beach, Pawley's Island, and Charleston.

Rates: Single $45; double $50; extra person $10
Credit cards: No
No. of rooms: 3
No. of baths: 3

Wheelchair access: No
Pets: No
Smoking: Yes
Senior citizen discount: 10%

Directions: From US 17, turn right if you are traveling south on Orange Street; from US 17, turn left if your are traveling north on Orange Street. At dead end, turn left, go 50 ft. to Cypress Street and turn right; last house at end of Cypress Street on left.

The Shaw House

Francis Beidler Forest, National Audubon Society Sanctuary/ The Nature Conservancy

NEAREST AIRPORT: Charleston, South Carolina.

LOCATION: In the southeast region of the state, near Harleyville, about 40 miles northwest of Charleston and approximately 70 miles southeast of Columbia, South Carolina. I-26 is the main route from either Charleston or Columbia. However, the sanctuary can only be reached via US 178 to State Road 28. From Charleston, drive west on I-26 to exit 187, then south on Highway 27 to US 78; drive west on US 78 to US 178 and follow the signs to the entrance.

CONTACT: Audubon Sanctuary Manager, Francis Beidler Forest, 336 Sanctuary Road, Harleyville, SC 29448. (803) 426-2150.

BEST BIRDING: Year-round, with most diversity in the spring and summer.

TOURS/WORKSHOPS: Contact the Audubon Society.

You may feel like a time traveler as you walk among the ancient groves of bald cypress and tupelo gum trees in the Four Holes Swamp. Here, rising out of the slow-flowing swamp waters are the last remaining virgin stands of tupelo gum trees and bald cypress in the world, some of them over 1,000 years old.

The Beidler Sanctuary has the fourth highest rank in the nation for nesting density of birds. In the spring and summer, keen observers may see anhingas, yellow-crowned night herons, white ibis, and Mississippi and swallow-tailed kites as well as beautifully masked raptors. Twenty-three species of wood warblers grace these woodlands, 11 of which nest here, including prothonotary, orange-crowned, prairie, hooded, Swainson's, and Kentucky. Also common in winter are indigo and painted buntings and blue grosbeaks, whose colors contrast intriguingly with the sparkling reds of northern cardinals. Also look for summer tanagers and orchard orioles. Permanent residents include wood ducks, black vultures, Cooper's and red-shouldered hawks, bobwhites, pileated woodpeckers, Carolina chickadees, and melodious eastern bluebirds.

THE BARKSDALE HOUSE INN
27 George Street, Charleston, SC 29401
(803) 577-4800, Fax (803) 853-0482

This restored and elegant inn was once the townhouse of George Barksdale, a wealthy Charleston planter and member of the South Carolina House of Representatives. The Barksdale House's location in the heart of the historic district gives you access to historic Charleston.

This breathtakingly beautiful establishment reflects the great care and education that has gone into the creation of unique guest accommodations. Guests may choose to stay in *chambres* whose motifs may be Oriental, French, Victorian, or Colonial. Each is a feast for the eyes and provides comforts galore.

Many quarters feature double baths, bay windows, king-size Rice bed, armoires, original arched fireplaces, crystal accessories, a pie crust breakfast table, a dry bar, whirlpool baths with showers, and charming writing tables. All are done in decorator-selected colors and fabrics.

Begin your day with a complimentary continental breakfast complete with morning paper and fresh flowers. Take this in your room or in the courtyard.

After your visit to any or all of the three nearby birding areas (Francis Beidler Forest, Washo Reserve, and Cape Romain), stop on the back porch or in the garden for afternoon tea or sherry.

Rates: $79-150
Credit cards: Visa, MC
No. of rooms: 10
No. of baths: 10
Wheelchair access: No
Smoking: Yes
Pets: No
Senior citizen discount: Yes
Directions: From airport, take I-26 to Meeting Street exit. On Meeting Street drive 11 blocks to George Street. Turn right and the inn is the fourth house on the left. Cape Romain is 35 miles north via Highway 17. The Francis Beidler Forest is 35 miles west.

JOHN RUTLEDGE HOUSE INN
116 Broad Street, Charlestown, SC 29401
(803) 723-7999, (800) 476-9741

George Washington did not sleep here, although he did breakfast here with the lady of the house in 1791. This fact alone would entitle the inn to its designation as a National Historic Landmark. But, of course, the woman's husband, John Rutledge, earned his own special place in history. He was one of the 55 signers of the Constitution and a chief justice of the Supreme Court.

The beautiful details of the building's eighteenth- and nineteenth-century architecture such as the elaborately carved Italian marble fireplaces, the original plaster moldings, the inlaid floors, and the graceful ironwork have all been authentically restored.

The inn has 19 rooms within a complex of three buildings. You can choose from among the elegant rooms done in greens and pink, the spacious suites, or, for maximum seclusion, hideaways in the two carriage houses. All rooms have color TV, private baths, and private refrigerators. The service is unsurpassed; guests may enjoy a complimentary tray of fresh pastries, juice, and coffee or tea, served in the comfort of their own room.

In the afternoon and evenings, colonial Charleston is re-created in the inn's ballroom. Wine and sherry are offered in this opulent hall where patriots, statesmen, and presidents of the past have met. The city's finest restaurants, theaters, shops, and market are all within a few minutes walk.

Rates: $110-$200; suites available
Credit cards: Visa, MC, AMEX
No. of rooms: 19
No. of baths: 19
Wheelchair access: Yes
Pets: No
Smoking: Designated rooms only
Senior citizen discount: AARP 10%
Directions: From I-26, take King Street to Broad Street, take a right. The inn is the fourth house on the right. The inn will send a map.

TWO MEETING STREET
Charleston, SC 29401, (803) 723-7322

To sit on the veranda of Two Meeting Street, a beautifully renovated 1892 Queen Anne mansion, is to enjoy the ambience of the old South. In the quiet of a late afternoon, as you chat with new acquaintances, you will want to sip sherry and savor the succulent hors d'oeuvres and peruse the scene. Here you have manicured lawns, bountiful blooming gardens, and ancient willows swaying in the breeze. In nearby Battery Park, you might witness a wedding.

The mansion itself is filled with antiques, Oriental rugs, silver, and crystal. Tiffany stained-glass windows allow the sun to cast colorful shadows on the warm oak paneling.

Guest rooms are luxurious, with four-poster and canopied beds. Period pieces add charm to the delightful decor. Although the inn is known for its museum quality, it is not a please-do-not-touch kind of place. Manager Karen Spell, daughter of the owners and herself a permanent resident, will see to it that the highest-quality personal service is given. Small kitchens on each floor permit visitors to prepare coffee or cool wine. Continental breakfasts are served.

Later in the day, dine at Magnolia's or Carolina's, two of Charleston's finest restaurants.

Rates: $95-$155

Credit cards: No

No. of rooms: 9

No. of baths: 9

Wheelchair access: One room

Smoking: No

Pets: No

Senior citizen discount: No

Directions: 25 minutes from the airport. I-26 east to the last exit, Meeting Street downtown. Last house on Meeting Street.

SOUTH DAKOTA

Samuel H. Ordway, Jr., Memorial Prairie Preserve

NEAREST AIRPORT: Aberdeen, South Dakota.

LOCATION: Situated northwest of Aberdeen in the northeast quadrant of South Dakota. From Aberdeen drive west on US 12, 19 miles to the junction with State Highway 45, then drive north on Highway 45 for 20 miles until you reach State Highway 10. Take Highway 10 west about 9 miles, and look for a small sign posted on the right side of the road. The road to the left leads to the refuge headquarters. There are seven other Conservancy Prairie Preserves in South Dakota that are open to the public.

CONTACT: The Nature Conservancy, Samuel H. Ordway, Jr., Memorial Prairie, HCR 1, Box 16, Leola, SD 57456. (605) 439-3475.

BEST BIRDING: Spring and summer.

TOURS/WORKSHOPS: Three self-guided trails of varying difficulty. Contact Nature Conservancy preserve manager for specific programs.

With 7,800 acres, the Ordway Memorial Prairie is the largest of the Conservancy Prairie Preserves in South Dakota. Formed by receding glaciers, Ordway Memorial Prairie Preserve, with pothole wetlands, swales with short and long grasses, and rolling uplands, is one of the most productive habitats for waterfowl in North America. Of the 400 potholes within this preserve, one covers 120 acres. In a year with plentiful rainfall, there are from 1,000 to 2,000 nesting pairs of waterfowl here. Look for such species as mallards, gadwalls, pintails, green and blue-winged teal, American wigeons, northern shovelers, redheads, canvasbacks, lesser scaups, ruddy ducks, and American coots. Wilson's phalaropes and black terns are also commonly seen around the potholes. Bulrushes along the edges of the potholes harbor the long-billed marsh wren, yellow-headed blackbirds, and red-winged blackbirds. Other birds of this windswept land are the common yellow-throat, American bittern, shorebirds, upland sandpipers, meadowlarks, sparrows, hawks, and falcons. The hill crests are nesting areas for the ferruginous hawk.

Along with the birds, many butterflies, moths, and insects are attracted to the wildflowers sprouting throughout the region in the spring and summer. Bison graze on the short grasses, and other mammals such as white-tailed deer, coyotes, red foxes, raccoons, and white-tailed jackrabbits are abundant.

LAKEVIEW MOTEL
R.R. 1, Box 49, West Highway 10, Eureka, SD 57437, (605) 284-2681

If you're planning to visit the Samuel H. Ordway, Jr., Memorial Prairie Preserve, the Lakeview Motel is a promising place to stay. It offers amenities similar to those you would find at a luxurious resort but at the same price as a budget motel. There are 25 large, comfortable rooms featuring color cable television, private baths, direct dial room phones, lakeside decks and patios, and a beautiful lake view. There is a lake across the street offering boating and swimming. There are six restaurants in the vicinity.

Rates: Single $23.95-$27.95; double
$31.95-$34.95; extra person $4.50
Credit cards: Visa, MC, Discover
No. of rooms: 25
No. of baths: 25

Wheelchair access: Limited
Pets: Yes
Smoking: Yes
Senior citizen discount: No

Directions: Highway 10 in Eureka—20 miles east of Highway 83, 55 miles west of Highway 281.

THE WARD HOTEL
104 South Main, Aberdeen, SD 57401, (605) 225-6100

The Ward has an intriguing past. A. L. Ward lived the South Dakota version of the Horatio Alger story. In 1884, he migrated to Aberdeen from Troy Mills, Iowa, with only five cents in his pocket. He eventually started a lunchroom that, by 1889, had turned into a good-sized restaurant. In 1894, he built the first Alonzo Ward Hotel, a three-story red brick structure, considered one of Aberdeen's most impressive buildings.

On Thanksgiving Day in 1926, his dreams went up in smoke as a fire destroyed the hotel. Not easily discouraged, Ward rebuilt the hotel in 1928; it was considered one of the finest hotels in the state. In the late 1930s, Jack Benny did a radio show at KABR, the hotel's well-known radio station.

The Ward Hotel has been beautifully restored and today is one of the premier places to stay when visiting nearby Samuel H. Ordway, Jr., Memorial Prairie Preserve.

The hotel is not a bed and breakfast, but you can get a very reasonably priced breakfast at the coffee shop. Other restaurants include the Brass Rail for specialty sandwiches or the Grain Exchange for elegant dining with complimentary appetizers.

Rates: $22-$40
Credit cards: Visa, MC, AMEX, Diners
No of rooms: 30
No. of baths: 30

Wheelchair access: Yes
Pets: Yes
Smoking: Yes
Senior citizen discount: No

Directions: 5 miles from Aberdeen Airport via Highway 12 west.

American wigeon

Waubay National Wildlife Refuge

NEAREST AIRPORTS: Aberdeen and Sioux Falls, South Dakota; Fargo, North Dakota.

LOCATION: Located in the northeast section of South Dakota, the refuge is about 78 miles east of Aberdeen, South Dakota, on Highway 12, and 130 miles north of Sioux Falls, South Dakota, on I-29. From Fargo, North Dakota, drive south on I-29 about 104 miles to the refuge.

CONTACT: Refuge Manager, Waubay National Wildlife Refuge, RR 1, Box 79 Waubay, SD 57273-9736. (605) 947-4521.

BEST BIRDING: Spring and fall migration; songbirds in summer.

TOURS/WORKSHOPS: Visitor center interpretive programs; educational programs available for groups on request. Contact refuge manager.

This is the prairie pothole region vital to the survival of our waterfowl populations. The refuge consists of 4,650 acres, and the habitats are marshes, grasslands, woodlands, and lakes. It is well named, since Waubay is Sioux for "a nesting place for birds." A nesting area for eastern bluebirds continues to support this bird's needs, and the Bluebird Trail allows access to the area. Through the year, 245 species of birds and about 12 accidentals can be observed. Five species of grebes are here in the spring: pied-billed, horned, red-necked, eared, and western. Twenty-five varieties of ducks may be observed, plus 14 types of raptors, including ospreys, bald eagles, merlins, and peregrine falcons.

Shorebirds such as willets, Hudsonian godwits, marbled godwits, short- and long-billed dowitchers, American woodcocks, phalaropes, and ruddy turnstones may be seen also. Great crested flycatchers, blue jays, and gray-cheeked thrushes are active at the refuge in spring and fall. Be sure to check for the migration window on warblers through this area. You might see the following species: Tennessee, chestnut-sided, palm, blackpoll, black-and-white, and Wilson's. White-throated and Harris's sparrows are common, songs of blackbirds and bobolinks fill the area, and orchard orioles can be easily discerned. Over 100 species of birds nest here, sharing the refuge with 37 species of mammals and 8 species of reptiles and amphibians.

GREEN ACRES BED & BREAKFAST
R.R. 2, Box 13, Lake Preston, SD 57249, (605) 983-5097

Joyce and Dave Hesby have done a wonderful job restoring this four-level 1914 house. Dave and his two sons farm the 580 acres.

The fourth floor has two double rooms and one single room, along with a sitting room. The upper floor has two double rooms and one single room with one full bath. The home has many of the original brass light fixtures, all of which have been recently restored. If you want to get into the spirit of South Dakota, choose the Dakota Room, which is furnished in blue and gold and has the state flag hanging on the wall.

Before or after the wonderful country breakfast, featuring homemade jellies and baked goods, be certain to take a tour of the country kitchen. Joyce has decorated it with unique shingles, and she has recently acquired an old cook stove from her mother-in-law.

At Green Acres, you are about an hour away from Waubay National Wildlife Refuge.

Rates: $25-$35 **Wheelchair access:** No
Credit cards: No **Smoking:** Yes
No. of rooms: 6 **Pets:** Yes
No. of baths: 1 **Senior citizen discount:** No
Directions: 150 miles south of Wauby NWR via Highway 81.

LAKESIDE FARM BED AND BREAKFAST
R.R. 2, Box 52, Webster, SD 57274, (605) 486-4430

Sample a bit of country life at this family-owned dairy farm located close to the Waubay National Wildlife Refuge. You are welcome to go on morning chores with the owners, Glenn and Joy Hagen. Or you may explore the grove, barns, and pastures.

Glenn Hagen is the third-generation owner of this family farm. His grandfather, a Norwegian immigrant pioneer, established a tree claim on the rugged, beautiful South Dakota prairie more than a century ago. He chose the spot for its fertile soil, gently rolling hills, and proximity to Waubay Lake.

The Lakeside Farm Bed and Breakfast can accommodate four or five guests. The two guest rooms are on the second floor of the farmhouse. One is furnished with a double bed and the other with twin beds. The bathroom and shower, located on the same floor, serve both guest rooms.

The reasonable rates include a hearty country breakfast. Depending on the season, any nonbirders in your group can go boating on area lakes, visit museums featuring pioneer and Native American history and art, go cross-country skiing, or attend area rodeos.

Rates: Single $30; double $40
Credit cards: No
No. of rooms: 2
No. of baths: Shared

Wheelchair access: No
Pets: Only with permission
Smoking: No
Senior citizen discount: No

Directions: 6 miles north of Webster on Highway 25, 2 miles east. Guests should call for specific directions.

THE PRAIRIE HOUSE MANOR

209 Poinsett Avenue (SD 25), DeSmet, SD 57231, (605) 854-9131

As a little girl, I wished I could somehow materialize in the pages of Laura Ingalls Wilder's *Little House on the Prairie*. Somewhat older now and a bit more realistic, I nonetheless was thrilled to find that there really is a Prairie House Manor and that it is smack dab in the center of the Laura Ingalls Wilder homestead area. I loved being within walking distance of the homes and museum. The Manor is about 70 miles from Waubay National Wildlife Refuge.

The Prairie House Manor has a variety of accommodations. In the newly restored home itself, you will enjoy the gracious living of the past with all the luxury of the present. Four units, complete with private bath, color television, table and chairs, and air-conditioning, await your selection. You can pick My Rose Garden, featuring a queen four-poster bed in a stately room with a large bath, shower, and dressing room. This is a wonderful bridal or anniversary suite. Another room is Here's My Heart. Other choices are Americana Medley, a large family room with three beds, and Chantilly Lace, an exquisite room with a large bath, shower, and dressing area. This room is perfect for a quiet restful weekend in the heartland of America.

For larger birding groups, you might consider the Lodge or the Cottage. Innkeeper Connie Cheny is a good cook, and no one goes away hungry. You will be served a full breakfast, perhaps the house favorite, French toast. You also have a choice of pancakes, waffles, and farm fresh eggs.

Rates: Single $20; double $30 and up; extra person $5
Credit cards: No
No. of rooms: 12
No. of baths: 11

Wheelchair access: Yes
Pets: Yes
Smoking: Some areas
Senior citizen discount: No

Directions: On Highway 25, just 2 blocks north of Highway 14 at the crossroads in the center of town; west side of road; big home with purple shutters and red flower boxes.

TENNESSEE

Hatchie National Wildlife Refuge

NEAREST AIRPORT: Jackson, Tennessee, via Memphis.

LOCATION: In the southwestern quadrant of Tennessee, north of Memphis. Refuge headquarters is 3 miles south of Brownsville on Highway 76. From Memphis, drive north on I-40 about 41 miles to exit 56 (Highway 76), then south as above. From Jackson, drive south on I-40 about 30 miles to exit 56.

CONTACT: Hatchie National Wildlife Refuge, Highway 76 and I-40, P.O. Box 187, Brownsville, TN 38012. (901) 772-0501.

BEST BIRDING: Spring and fall.

TOURS/WORKSHOPS: Check with refuge manager.

In this area, the Hatchie River dips into the northwest corner of preserved, forested wetlands and meanders through sloughs bordered by water-tolerant oaks. Here is a small portion of the once vast Mississippi River Delta of swamp forest habitat; 11,000 plus acres of the original 22 million acres remains protected in the refuge. The sheltered system supports breeding and nesting for little blue herons and yellow-crowned night herons, wood ducks, hooded mergansers, Cooper's and red-shouldered hawks, barred owls, red-bellied woodpeckers, great crested flycatchers, wood thrushes, blue-gray gnatcatchers, hooded, Cerulean, Cape May, and Kentucky warblers, summer tanagers, dickcissels, and orchard orioles. Spring brings northward migration along the Mississippi Flyway; birds frequently seen then include teals, shovelers, gadwalls, American black, ring-necked, ruddy and red-headed ducks, common mergansers, ospreys, harriers, broad-winged hawks, and American kestrels as well as many species of warblers heading for nesting sites farther on. Red-headed and pileated woodpeckers can be heard in the forest; tufted titmice and Carolina chickadees swarm in the trees along with eastern bluebirds and blue jays. Porcelain cedar waxwings (with a bit of yellow on their tails) are numerous, as are indigo buntings, swamp and white-throated sparrows, scarlet tanagers, and rose-breasted grosbeaks. Uncommon birds to look for in the spring and early summer are ring-billed gulls, whip-poor-wills, eastern phoebes, purple martins, brown creepers, blue grosbeaks, bobolinks, and purple finches.

HIGHLAND PLACE BED AND BREAKFAST
519 North Highland Avenue, Jackson, TN 39301, (901) 427-1472

The Highland Place Bed and Breakfast is a great place to stay when visiting the Hatchie National Wildlife Refuge. This charming bed and breakfast offers comfortable accommodations and gracious Southern hospitality. The historic old Tennessee home, built some time around 1911, offers three rooms, one with a private bath and two with a shared bath. Innkeepers Glenn and Janice Wall are happy to entertain you in their stately home. A full breakfast is served.

Rates: $45-$65
Credit cards: Visa, MC
No. of rooms: 3
No. of baths: 2

Wheelchair access: Yes
Smoking: Outside only
Pets: No
Senior citizen discount: 10%

Directions: From the intersection of I-40 and Highway 45, exit 82A, go 3.3 miles south to 519 N. Highland Avenue, parking at the rear of the building.

THE LOWENSTEIN-LONG HOUSE
217 N. Waldran, Memphis, TN 38105, (901) 527-7174

The Lowenstein-Long House has a varied and interesting history. Built in 1898 by department-store owner Abraham Lowenstein, it later became the Beethoven Music Club. After that, the house was converted into a board-

The Lowenstein-Long House

inghouse, the Elizabeth Club for Girls. The castlelike house was recently restored to its original elegance by Charles and Martha Long and their three sons.

There are three bedrooms, all with private baths and television. Enjoy your full complimentary breakfast before heading out to Hatchie National Wildlife Refuge.

Rates: Single $60-$70; double $70- $90; rollaway $10 extra
Credit cards: No
No. of rooms: 4
No. of baths: 4
Directions: Inn will send map.

Wheelchair access: No
Pets: No
Smoking: No
Senior citizen discount: 10%

THE PEACH TREE INN
1551 Skeet Road, Brownsville, TN 38012, (901) 772-5680/772-9369

The Peach Tree Inn is a convenient place to stay when visiting the Hatchie National Wildlife Refuge. This bed and breakfast with its pleasant country setting offers private, comfortable accommodations. There are four rooms, all with private baths. A continental breakfast is served, and lunch and dinner are served on request. After birding, you can take a dip in the Peach Tree Inn's swimming pool.

Rates: Single $40; double $45
Credit cards: Visa, MC
No. of rooms: 4
No. of baths: 4
Directions: Exit 56 on I-40 (56 miles east of Memphis).

Wheelchair access: Yes
Pets: No
Smoking: Preferably not
Senior citizen discount: No

Great Smoky Mountains National Park

NEAREST AIRPORTS: Knoxville, Tennessee; Asheville, North Carolina.

LOCATION: In the southeastern quadrant of Tennessee and the western part of North Carolina. From Knoxville, Tennessee, drive south on US 441 about 54 miles to the Sugarland Visitor Center. From Asheville, North Carolina, drive I-40 west to Highway 19 west, then turn north at Cherokee to the Oconalufte Visitor Center. You can drive across the park from Cherokee to Gatlinburg on the Newfound Gap Road. Some roads inside the park are closed in the winter.

CONTACT: Great Smoky Mountains National Park, Gatlinburg, TN 37738. (615) 436-1200.

BEST BIRDING: Spring and fall; summer in the higher elevations.

TOURS/WORKSHOPS: Naturalist tours are regularly scheduled in the summer by the park staff. Check with superintendent. You can also get information from the Great Smoky Mountains Natural History Association, 115 Park Headquarters Road, Gatlinburg, TN 37738. Be sure to purchase *Birds of the Smokies* by Fred Alsop from the association for excellent local information and a checklist.

Great Smoky Mountains National Park was once the land of the Cherokee—mountains and valleys, waterfalls and creeks, ferns and wildflowers, birds, deer, and bear. Later, it became a land of small farmers, timber companies, quilts, moonshine, and fine mountain music. Now over 200 species of birds use the park, and a considerable number nest here, including yellow-crowned night herons, black vultures, sharp-shinned and Cooper's hawks, ruffed grouse, northern bobwhites, American woodcocks, barred and saw-whet owls, and red-cockaded, red-bellied, and red-headed woodpeckers. Up to 22 species of wood warblers have nested here also, among them golden-winged, chestnut-sided, black-throated-green, pine, worm-eating, and Canada. If you want to bird by color, you should easily be able to see northern cardinals, rose-breasted and blue grosbeaks, indigo buntings, rufous-sided towhees, rusty blackbirds, orchard and northern orioles, purple finches, red crossbills, summer and scarlet tanagers, and ruby-throated hummingbirds.

The park actively manages endangered species. Fourteen young peregrine falcons were raised and released in the park; in addition, the park staff is working to enhance the nesting habitat for red-cockaded woodpeckers. Ongoing programs for the red wolf, Indiana bat, Appalachian aven (a wildflower), and smoky madtoms (a fish) are directed by the park.

BUCKHORN INN
2140 Tudor Mountain Road, Gatlinburg, TN 37738, (615) 436-4468

Buckhorn Inn is a unique country inn offering serene seclusion and a reminiscence of early Gatlinburg. The 30 acres of quiet walkways, meadows, and woodland are particularly welcome. You can start your bird-watching immediately on your walk around the pond, which is graced with ducks and geese.

At Buckhorn Inn, you will be only a mile from the northern boundary of Great Smoky Mountains National Park. In addition, you will have a magnificent view of Mount LeConte.

The inn itself includes a large room with a massive stone fireplace. A Steinway grand piano is the centerpiece of a sitting area where shelves, filled with books, line the wall. There are large picture windows along the south wall of this great room that face the ever-changing panorama of the mountains.

Upstairs, there are five comfortable, intimate rooms, all beautifully furnished with antiques and artwork. Three of the rooms have spectacular views of the Smoky Mountains. All of the rooms and cottages have private baths, and all are air-conditioned.

Private guest cottages nestled in the woodlands near the inn have porches for catching the evening breeze. All have a living room with a fireplace and a bedroom.

A delicious breakfast is included in your room price. If you have the time, you can enjoy dinner here, too. The inn has always been famous for its fine food, all of which is home-cooked daily. The tempting dinner possibilities include Chablis cheddar soup, pesto chicken with basil cream sauce, accompanied by rice pilaf, salad, and a refreshing dessert of fresh strawberries, honey, and cream.

Rates: Single $80-$250; double $95-250; extra person $20
Credit cards: Visa, MC
No. of rooms: 12
No. of baths: 15
Directions: Inn will send map.

Wheelchair access: Yes
Pets: No
Smoking: Only outside some of the cottages
Senior citizen discount: No

LECONTE LODGE
250 Apple Valley Road, Sevierville, TN 37862
(615) 429-5704, Fax (615) 429-5705

Leconte Lodge is literally head and shoulders above all the other hostelries in Great Smoky Mountains National Park. Perched high atop Mount LeConte at an altitude of 6,593 feet, the only access to the lodge entails hiking the moderately strenuous trails. You will have a choice of five trails to the lodge, the shortest and steepest being Alum Cave Trail. A hiker in reasonably good condition can make this five-and-a-half-mile trek in approximately four hours.

Birders are hardy creatures and the hike to LeConte can be half the fun. An occasional bonus on one of the trails, Trillium Gap, is to overtake a llama pack train carrying fresh supplies to the lodge. Do not be surprised if a tame boomer squirrel noses around at your feet or if a meandering black bear crosses your path. Be sure to enjoy a concert of birds warbling in the bushes. The opulent and incredibly diverse flora and fauna along the way are fascinating, so allow ample time so that you will still arrive early enough to explore the lodge area before the 6:00 p.m. dinner hour.

Located in the middle of the half-million-acre Great Smoky Mountains National Park, LeConte Lodge is the only place in the region where a visitor can sleep overnight on a mountaintop in a snug permanent structure, with hot and hearty meals on tap. The lodge has a capacity of fifty guests per night, housed in either rough-hewn cabins or group sleeping lodges. The cozy cabins are furnished with upper and lower double bunk beds, making them ideal for two couples or a family of four to five persons. The lodges sleep from ten to thirteen each. There is no electricity. The mellow glow of kerosene lamps lights your accommodations, and it is recommended that you pack flashlights in your gear.

There is plenty of food available at this rustic spot, beginning with the coffee or hot chocolate that awaits you on arrival. At the family-style dining room, you will be served tasty and nourishing dishes. Best of all, you'll be surrounded by the sounds of nature, especially lovely bird calls.

Rates: $56.50 per person—Modified American Plan
Credit cards: No
No. of rooms: 15
No. of baths: Bathhouse, 4

Wheelchair access: No, hike-in only
Smoking: Yes
Pets: No
Senior citizen discount: No

Directions: 1 hour from Knoxville. Highway 441 south to Gatlinburg, then 9 miles to trailhead at Alum Can Bluff. Moderate to strenuous 5½-mile hike to the lodge. Open late March through mid-November only.

TENNESSEE RIDGE INN
507 Campbell Lead Road, Gatlinburg, TN 37738, (615) 436-4068

The Tennessee Ridge Inn is a magnificent spot, literally on top of Old Smoky. The Hollanders traveled the world for years, sampling hotels and inns of every description. In the Far East, Europe, and the islands, they found the special qualities that make visits memorable and that define luxury. They put all these extras into their own inn.

In all respects, they have done a good job. After an exhilarating day of birding at Great Smoky Mountains National Park, the deluxe setting is especially welcome. Here you can enjoy magnificent views, crackling fires, a kitchen full of tantalizing aromas, sunsets, and the chatter of distant woodpeckers.

The bedrooms are lovely and luxurious. All have private baths and two-person whirlpool tubs. Most have southern views embracing the grand scale of the mountains. Four rooms have working stone fireplaces; five have private balconies. If you can tear yourself away from your room, there is a nice swimming pool.

The Tennessee Ridge Inn will put you close to great birding as well as recharge your batteries. There is something very seductive about the Smokies as they change from muted blues to glowing crimson, shades of gray, then to distant blacks. The Hollanders claim that the Smokies "change people's souls." There's something to that.

Rates: $115-$135
Credit cards: Visa, MC, AMEX, Discover
No. of rooms: 5
No. of baths: 5
Directions: Approximately 1 mile from the center of town.

Wheelchair access: Yes
Smoking: On porch only
Pets: No
Senior citizen discount: Off-season discounts of 20%

Aransas National Wildlife Refuge

NEAREST AIRPORTS: Corpus Christi, Texas; San Antonio, Texas.

LOCATION: Two-thirds of the way down the gulf coast from Sabine, Texas, the northern tip. Also known as the Texas Costal Bend, in addition to Aransas the birding area includes Rockport/Fulton, Corpus Christi, and the outlying barrier islands and rookeries. From Corpus Christi, drive northeast across Corpus Christi Bay to Highway 35. Continue northeast on Highway 35 past Fulton/Rockport to Route 774 east and to Route 2040 south to the refuge entrance. Charter boat service is available to the outlying islands and small bays. Contact Chamber of Commerce.

CONTACT: Refuge Manager, Aransas National Wildlife Refuge, P.O. Box 100, Austwell, TX 77950, (512) 286-3559. Chamber of Commerce, P.O. Box 1055, Rockport, TX 78382, (800) 242-0071 Texas; (800) 826-6441 out of state.

BEST BIRDING: Year-round; most popular times are winter and spring.

TOURS/WORKSHOPS: Commercial tours available; for information about bird festivals, contact the Chamber of Commerce. For workshops led by naturalists, contact the refuge.

Jutting between Aransas and San Antonio Bay, the Blackjack Peninsula is ringed by tidal saltwater marsh. Inland, the grasslands, live oaks, redbay thickets, and blackjack oaks thrive on the sandy soil; interspersed throughout are shallow ponds and sloughs. The coastline here is situated directly in the migration path to and from South America. It is the end point of the southern migration of the only remaining flock of whooping cranes. The winter specialty is the whooping crane; spring, the migration of songbirds; summer, wood storks and painted buntings; fall, shorebirds and waterfowl. Because of its location, the seasons at the refuge are as follows: spring is from March through May; summer, June and July; fall, August through October; and winter, November through February.

No matter what time of year you visit, you should be able to observe tricolored herons, reddish egrets, roseate spoonbills, black-bellied whistling ducks, mottled ducks, black-shouldered kites, white-tailed hawks, and crested caracaras. Also look for greater prairie chickens, Wilson's plovers, long-billed curlews, marbled godwits, short- and long-billed dowitchers, and laughing gulls. Other residents are gull-billed, royal, sandwich, and black terns. In the grass and brush, you may see golden-fronted woodpeckers. Even northern cardinals are common here. To obtain information about the variety of birds here, write for the Aransas checklist of over 385 species, almost 500 species if the surrounding regions are included.

THE DIAL HOUSE
306 West Oak Street, P.O. Box 22, Goliad, TX 77963, (512) 645-3366

You will not go hungry at Dolores Clarke's Dial House. Clarke is an excellent cook and loves to see her guests eat. Our "dainty" evening snack consisted of homemade eggnog, pecan pie, and German chocolate cake. The made-from-scratch breakfast was so filling we did not eat dinner that evening. At breakfast, she served fresh fruit, ham, cheese and mushroom crepes with a bechamel sauce, sausage, scrambled eggs with picante sauce, potatoes, and biscuits. After we had finished this delicious groaning board of delights, she asked why we had not eaten the cinnamon roll or the oat bran muffins.

This seventy-five-year-old entrepreneur is reason enough to visit the Dial House. She could be a character out of a Western movie. As she fixed us our evening snack, she entertained us with her colorful life story. "Each time I got rid of a husband, I built onto this house that I inherited in 1955 from Aunt Alice Dial. It's a big house," she said, with a laugh, "so you can see I've had my share of husbands. Four to be exact."

"After one failed marriage, I inherited my husband's cattle business. I just loved being a cowgirl. Even enjoyed castrating those bulls. I got so good at the whole cowboy business that cowboys came to the bank where I worked and asked me questions about their cows."

Clarke is a woman of many talents. You will probably first encounter her in her lush, impressive garden. The old-fashioned front porch is a great spot for curling up with a book and a glass of homemade lemonade.

My favorite room was the Doll Room, a charming collection of Clarke's childhood porcelain dolls. The intricate dresses have all been lovingly made by the innkeeper. We slept well in our large bedroom, comfortably cooled by an air-conditioner and a ceiling fan. Each of the five bedrooms has its own bath. The entire house is peppered with interesting touches, such as hand-painted china and antique furnishings.

"I'm no birder," Clarke told me right away, "but I sure do like them. I'll fix them early breakfasts, and I give Audubon members a 10% discount." So plan to stay several days or longer when birding at Aransas National Wildlife Refuge.

Rates: $55-$65   **Wheelchair access:** Yes
Credit cards: Visa, MC   **Smoking:** No
No. of rooms: 5   **Pets:** No
No. of baths: 4   **Senior citizen discount:** No
Directions: 70 miles northwest of refuge via Highway 77-A to the junction
with Highway 59. Turn left on Highway 59, 6 blocks to Oak Street.

HOTEL LAFITTE
P.O. 489, Seadrift, TX 77983, (512) 785-2319

The infamous Bonnie and Clyde are said to have spent the night at Hotel Lafitte. They had good taste; this renovated 1909 railroad hotel is a bastion of hospitality and uniqueness. As you walk into the bed and breakfast you will be offered a choice of wine from three kegs in the parlor. In the evening, in the pretty parlor, old-fashioned sundaes are served. After a busy day of birdwatching at Aransas National Wildlife Refuge, you might just be in the mood for sitting on the veranda overlooking San Antonio Bay and rocking your cares away.

The guest rooms facing the bay have a lovely ocean view and some whimsical touches. For example, in room 5, there is a flapper dress of the 1920s hanging on the armoire. In room 6, an antique wedding dress is neatly displayed. Love birds, take note: there is a honeymoon suite with a rose satin bedspread, an inlaid-wood card-table set, a Jacuzzi, and two chaise longues.

Innkeepers Frances and Weyman Harding serve a hardy breakfast of quiche or ham-and-egg casserole along with fruit, juice, bran muffins, and coffee. For seafood specialties after your birding activities, try Barkett's, the Hardings' very own restaurant.

Rates: Shared bath $55; private $65;   **Wheelchair access:** Yes
suites $85-$95   **Pets:** No
Credit cards: Visa, MC   **Smoking:** Yes
No. of rooms: 10   **Senior citizen discount:** No
No. of baths: 6½
Directions: Highway 185 from Victoria, 30 miles.

Santa Ana National Wildlife Refuge

NEAREST AIRPORT: Brownsville, Texas.

LOCATION: In the lower Rio Grande Valley, bordering Mexico, the wildlife corridor that includes the Santa Ana refuge extends from Laguna Atosca National Wildlife Refuge on the east coast above Brownsville and along the Gulf of Mexico to Falcon Reservoir on the west. From Brownsville, drive west on US 83 to Alamo, then south on Route 907 to US 281, then east on 281 to the visitor center (total distance about 60 miles). You can also drive west on US 281 directly from Brownsville to the refuge.

CONTACT: Refuge Manager, Santa Ana National Wildlife Refuge, Rt. 2, Box 202A, Alamo, TX 78516. (512) 787-3079 or (512) 787-7861.

BEST BIRDING: Spring and fall.

TOURS/WORKSHOPS: Contact refuge manager.

Just north of Santa Ana, the great Mississippi and Central flyways converge. This 2,000-acre remnant of the once-vast thorn forest of the lower Rio Grande is a major resting and staging area for migrants, and the U.S. Fish and Wildlife Service is attempting to procure additional land to expand the protected habitat for birds as well as for mammals, reptiles, and amphibians. Year-round look for an outstanding variety of species, including least grebes, black-bellied whistling ducks, hook-billed kites, common black and Harris's plain chachalaca, Inca and white-tipped doves, common pauraques, buff-bellied hummingbirds, ringed kingfishers, Couch's kingbirds, brown-crested flycatchers, great kiskadees, green jays, long-billed thrashers, tropical parulas, olive sparrows, and bronzed cowbirds. In the cooler winter months, green jays are even more abundant, as are groove-billed anis in the spring and summer. White-tailed and zone-tailed hawks are observed a few times each season. The checklist at this small but important refuge records 377 species.

THE ROSS HAUS
P.O. Box 3306, Harlingen, TX 78551, (512) 425-1717

As you enter Harlingen's city limits, you may spot a flock of red-crowned parrots. This would be a perfect introduction to the nearby lush Santa Ana National Wildlife Refuge.

The Ross Haus is a cozy place to stay while birding at Santa Ana. Innkeepers Darrel and Grace Johnson have created a warm, quaint atmosphere for their bed and breakfast in the Rio Grande Valley.

You will have a choice of bed and breakfast or renting rooms by the day or week. The spacious accommodations include a fully equipped kitchen (microwave, coffee maker), a living/dining room, a bedroom with a queen-size bed, and a bathroom with tub and shower. Television, linens, iron, and ironing board are also included. Amenities also include a laundry room, covered parking, and public telephone.

The bed and breakfast includes a continental breakfast basket (coffee, tea, fresh fruit, a decanter of varied juices, and a plate of pastries).

Rates: Daily $65; weekly $260
Credit cards: Visa, MC
No. of rooms: 4
No. of baths: 4
Wheelchair access: Yes
Smoking: No
Pets: No
Senior citizen discount: No

Directions: 5 minutes south from Valley International Airport, near the center of town; 40 minutes east of the Santa Ana National Wildlife Reserve and west of Laguna Atosca; 30 minutes north of Brownsville.

Yellow-crowned night-heron

Bear River Migratory Bird Refuge

NEAREST AIRPORT: Salt Lake City, Utah.

LOCATION: North central Utah, along the shores of the northeastern corner of the Great Salt Lake, near Brigham City and Ogden, about 30 miles south. From Salt Lake City, drive north on I-15 to Brigham City (55 miles), then west to the old headquarters. The refuge is being rebuilt after total destruction in the mid-1980s from the rising waters of the lake. At present, the 12-mile auto tour loop is open with views of marsh, mud flats, and open pool habitats. New material on the refuge and an updated bird list are being prepared, so contact the headquarters for the latest update on conditions.

CONTACT: Refuge Manager, Bear River Migratory Bird Refuge, 866 South Main, Brigham City, UT 84302. (801) 723-5887.

BEST BIRDING: Fall and spring.

TOURS/WORKSHOPS: Contact refuge headquarters.

After the refuge is expanded and rebuilt, with additional water impoundments and dikes, this extensive marsh and upland oasis will once again attract and support the large numbers of birds for which it has been famous. Until then, expect smaller numbers of the same species to be found here. Fall migration begins early, with waterfowl arriving in August. In the past, the refuge supported up to half a million birds in October. Elegant whistling swans are visitors; and snowy egrets, snow geese, and white pelicans create a blanket of white along the waters and shores. Cinnamon, blue, and green-winged teals can usually be seen together. Colorful mergansers, redheads, and ruddy ducks are among the 25 species of ducks that may use the refuge. Many raptors also frequent the refuge, including rough-legged hawks, prairie falcons, and bald eagles. Baird's and least sandpipers are common, as are marbled godwits. Black-necked stilts and Wilson's phalaropes as well as regimented lines of California and ring-billed gulls can be seen along the shores.

BRIGHAM STREET INN
1135 East South Temple, Salt Lake City, UT 84102, (800) 364-4461

The comforts of two worlds come together in the unique appeal of the Brigham Street Inn. It combines the personal aspects of a bed and breakfast with the standards and service of a luxury hotel. Located in a graceful and historic mansion, the inn is much more than a place to spend the night; it is, in itself, an elegant destination.

Everything about this handsome hostelry reflects the careful attention of its owners, architect John Pace and his wife, Nancy. As patrons of the arts, the Paces first determined to save the building from demolition; they cooperated with 12 interior designers who worked to lend each room an individual and comfortable style. Numerous awards and special recognition have resulted from this effective association, but the real rewards go to the guests who visit here. The grand parlor contains a piano that is equally grand. The golden oak woodwork and beveled glass reflect the polish and manners of turn-of-the-century elegance. The two-and-one-half-story red brick Victorian showcase was built in 1898 for Walter Cogswell Lyne. Philanthropist Lyne lived a rags-to-riches real-life story, the abandoned child who went from drugstore errand boy to successful wool broker.

The nine guest rooms all have private bath, telephone, and television; some offer wood-burning fireplaces. The main floor common rooms provide ample space for personal or professional meetings. The continental-plus breakfast includes fresh fruit and fresh breads, served in a blue and white dining room.

Rates: $75-$150
Credit cards: Visa, MC, AMEX, Discover, Diners
No. of rooms: 9
No. of baths: 9
Wheelchair access: No
Pets: No
Smoking: Yes
Senior citizen discount: No
Directions: Approximately 2 miles east of the Morman Temple in downtown Salt Lake City.

CENTER STREET
169 E. Center, Logan, UT 84321, (801) 752-3443

At the Center Street bed and breakfast, you can enter a variety of intriguing worlds. Would you like to see the Pyramids? Then enter the Egyptian Suite, where Osiris and Queen Nefertiri are seated in a beautiful Egyptian sunrise landscape painted on the walls. Around the queen-size bed are gold-leafed pillars, a mirrored wall, a King Tut canopy, papyrus paintings, and a black panther. Two gold cobras fill the pink mother-of-pearl tiled Jacuzzi.

Perhaps something a bit more medieval might suit your fantasy. Then try the Castle of the Purple Dragon, where gray castle rock turrets hold marble statues. Through the rock tunnel lies the master bedroom with fireplace, Italian tile, Persian rug, furs, canopied queen-size bed, and Michelangelo-style celestial beings painted on the ceiling. A mounted purple dragon's head, an original brass rubbing of an English knight, and the lion's head that fills the Jacuzzi complete the medieval touch.

Feel like playing Captain Hook? The Pirate's Paradise with a sunken pirate ship resting on the ocean floor may be to your liking. This suite has giant aquariums and a beautiful underwater reef visible through cannonball holes in the ship's wall. The Jacuzzi with the skull and crossbone tile and the pirate's flag on the queen bed complete the picture.

There is Space Odyssey, with its dark blue walls covered with billions of stars, planets, and nebulas showing vivid colors with nighttime black lighting. The bathroom is inside a silver spaceship. Water from the mouth of the star god, Jupiter, fills the Jacuzzi—a wonderful place to spend a night with your favorite alien. Among the other suites are Aphrodites's Court, Ice Fantasy, Penthouse Suite, Arabian Night's Suite, Jungle Bungalow, and Victorian Suite.

Rates: $43-$146
Credit cards: Visa, MC, AMEX
No. of rooms: 13
No. of baths: 12
Wheelchair access: Yes
Pets: $5 extra
Smoking: No
Senior citizen discount: No
Directions: Go to middle of town on Main Street; turn east on Center Street; 2 blocks up on left.

PINECREST BED AND BREAKFAST
6211 Emigration Canyon Road, Salt Lake City, UT 84108
(801) 583-6663

Whether you are a fan of Robert Redford or a follower of Brigham Young, you'll find something to like at the Pinecrest Bed and Breakfast. Redford stayed in this rustic guest house; Young first entered what was to become Salt Lake City at Emigration Canyon where the bed and breakfast now stands.

There is something for the Hollywood buff, too. The large iron gates leading to the inn were installed in the 1930s by a Hollywood actor who owned the estate at the time and bought the gates from Paramount Studios.

Even if you could care less about any of the above, you will no doubt enjoy the luxury and hospitality the Pinecrest offers. The living room looks like an elegant ski lodge with its rich cherry wood paneling and woodwork, wine velvet couches, grand piano, and large stone fireplace.

There are a variety of guest rooms. A favorite is the English Library Bedroom, with its king bed, full bath with a large marble tub, and a spectacular view. There is a wonderful collection of Zane Grey short stories and a vintage radio that plays Burns & Allen, Jack Benny, and Glen Miller. Another nice room is the Holland Blue Room with antiques from Holland, wooden shoes, queen bed, and white wicker furniture. The bath has a shower with beautiful jet black tile. From this room, you have a quick exit to the various trails that traverse the property.

A full breakfast of banana-sour cream pancakes, French raspberry crepes, or omelets is served in the dining room overlooking the trout pond and formal gardens. The beautiful grounds are home to a variety of songbirds.

Rates: $70–$175
Credit cards: Visa, MC, AMEX
No. of rooms: 6
No. of baths: 6

Wheelchair access: No
Pets: No
Smoking: No
Senior citizen discount: No

Directions: 6 miles east of Salt Lake City on a secluded 6-acre estate.

Ouray National Wildlife Refuge

NEAREST AIRPORT: Vernal, Utah.

LOCATION: South and west of Vernal along the Green River in the northeast section of Utah, bordering Colorado. From Vernal, take US 40 west to Route 88 south and proceed to the refuge entrance just north of Ouray, approximately 26 miles.

CONTACT: Refuge Manager, Ouray National Wildlife Refuge, 1680 W. Highway 40, Room 1220, Vernal, UT 84078. (801) 789-0351.

BEST BIRDING: Spring and summer for migration and nesting; fall for migration.

TOURS/WORKSHOPS: Contact refuge manager.

The Green River, filled with the melting snows of the Wyoming Mountains, enriches the marshlands and creeks of the Ouray Refuge. Amid harsh desert land, this oasis of cottonwood trees and wet bottomlands abounds in the spring with ducks, geese, and cranes passing through, many staying to breed. The dry uplands are a perfect nesting area for mallard, gadwall, and pintail ducks and cinnamon teals. In addition, redtail and ruddy ducks hatch and raise their young among the cattails and bulrushes of the marshes. Rookeries of great blue herons and double-crested cormorants are nestled high in the cottonwood trees in the Johnson bottoms and other wooded areas. Sandhill cranes as well as an occasional whooping crane rest and feed here before continuing north or south.

Look for yellow-headed blackbirds shining in the marshland reeds, and listen for Lewis's woodpeckers and songbirds in the wooded areas; Virginia's, Townsend's, and Magillivray's warblers are the western specialties here. Green-tailed towhees and lazuli buntings rustle in the undergrowth. Numerous raptors are also here in spring, fall, and winter, including northern harriers, Swainson's and Cooper's hawks, and golden eagles. Bald eagles commonly winter here.

BEST WESTERN ANTLERS
423 West Main, Vernal, UT 84078, (801) 789-1202

Best Western Antlers is a comfortable and convenient place to stay when visiting the Ouray National Wildlife Refuge. This is a very nice, clean motel; our large room had a comfortable king-size bed. There is a well-run Denny's restaurant next door. A nice new feature of the motel is the hot tub and exercise room.

Rates: $35-$63 depending on season
Credit cards: Visa, MC, AMEX, Discover, Diners
No. of rooms: 49
No. of baths: 49

Wheelchair access: Yes
Pets: No
Smoking: Yes
Senior citizen discount: Winter, fall, and spring

Directions: On Highway 40; 330 miles from Denver and 170 miles from Salt Lake City.

White pelicans

VERMONT

The Barre-Montpelier Area

NEAREST AIRPORTS: Berlin Corners between Montpelier and Barre, Vermont; Burlington, Vermont.

LOCATION: Central Vermont. From Burlington, drive approximately 35 miles south on I-89 to the city of Montpelier. Barre is 8 miles south of Montpelier on Highway 302.

CONTACT: Vermont Institute of Natural Sciences, Woodstock, VT 05091, (802) 457-2779. Central Vermont Audubon Society, P.O. Box 1112, Montpelier, VT 05602. A copy of *A Guide to Bird Finding in Vermont* by Walter G. Ellison (Vermont Institute of Natural Sciences) can be ordered from the institute.

BEST BIRDING: Spring and fall.

TOURS/WORKSHOPS: Contact the Vermont Institute of Natural Sciences or the Central Vermont Audubon Society. Other good birding spots nearby are Mount Mansfield from May 30 to July 5; Dead Creek Wildlife Management Area; and the Missisquoi National Wildlife Refuge, which is 1½ miles north on the edge of Lake Champlain.

Because the Montpelier-Barre area lies between the Green Mountains and its eastern foothills, it contains bird species common to both habitats. Within Montpelier, Hubbard Park, which is bounded by State, Elm, and Terrace streets, is a good spot for observing spring and fall migrations of flycatchers, thrushes, vireos, and warblers. To see water birds, drive to Berlin Pond; a spotting scope will be needed here, because much of the area is a protected watershed. The Thurman W. Dix Reservoir in Barre is more accessible, and during migration, you should see common loons, horned and red-necked grebes, and common, hooded, and red-breasted mergansers.

For forest birding, drive northeast from Montpelier on Highway 2 to Plainfield and the Groton National Forest. At Owl's Head within the forest, look for ruffed grouse, yellow-bellied sapsuckers, rose-breasted grosbeaks, and red-breasted nuthatches as well as warblers during peak migration. South of Owl's Head is Kettle Pond, where you will find hermit and Swainson's thrushes, ruby and golden-crowned kinglets, and many warbler species. Autumn birding is especially good at Molly's Fall Pond, which is about 1½ miles from the forest.

Walter G. Ellison's *Guide to Bird Finding in Vermont* is invaluable for its descriptions of the birds and birding locations in the Montpelier-Barre area.

CHERRY TREE HILL BED AND BREAKFAST
Cherry Tree Hill Road, East Montpelier, VT 05651, (802) 223-0549

You will revel in the simple charms of country living with a stay at Cherry Tree Hill Bed & Breakfast. This completely restored Dutch-roofed farmhouse is a delightful place to stay when birding in the Barre-Montpelier area. The fifty acres of fields and meadows surround five landscaped acres of gardens and fruit trees accented by panoramic views of the Green Mountains.

Guests are invited to browse through the fiber studio, which features handmade jackets spun from wool raised on the premises. Guests are also welcome to visit the sheep and horses. The road-weary may wish to refresh themselves in the heated pool with spa or to enjoy a sunset. In the cooler seasons, a crackling fire in the large fieldstone Count Rumford fireplace beckons all comers.

Individually decorated guest rooms feature naturally finished maple or wideboard pine floors, handwoven rugs, and original plaster moldings.

For birding groups, the spacious poolside cottage is perfect. It overlooks the Winooski Valley, offers extra privacy, and is available for groups wanting to stay longer.

Breakfast, served in the solarium among fragrant herbs and cascading water, provides breathtaking mountain views. Fresh baked breads and homemade granola accompany farm fresh quiches that are specialties of the house.

Rates: Single $45; double $75; extra persons $30
Credit cards: Visa, MC
No. of rooms: 8
No. of baths: 5
Wheelchair access: No
Pets: No
Smoking: No
Senior citizen discount: No

Directions: On Cherry Tree Hill Road, accessible from either the city of Montpelier or the village of East Montpelier, along Route 2. From Montpelier, take Main Street to Towne Hill Road, turn right, and drive 3 miles; the bed and breakfast is on the right. From East Montpelier Village, take Route 2 west 1 mile, turn right onto Towne Hill Road, drive 1 mile to the junction of Towne Hill Road, and Cherry Tree Hill Road, and turn right. The bed and breakfast is the next farm on the right.

THE INN AT MONTPELIER
147 Main Street, Montpelier, VT 05602, (802) 223-2727

Two stately historic buildings of the early 1800s have been combined to create the Inn at Montpelier. Both buildings are classically Federal in design and as is typical of New England architecture, have acquired additions through the years. The extravagant wraparound Colonial Revival porch added to the yellow building is a prominent landmark in a row of gracious townhouses built originally by the founders of the city.

Innkeepers Maureen and Bill Russell consider guests' comforts and requests their main concern; the large, inviting porch, perhaps the finest in the state, is a symbol of that special kind of hospitality. Great care has been taken to retain the architectural details; the Greek and Colonial Revival woodwork, the ten fireplaces, gracious front staircases, and glass-fronted china cupboards have all been preserved. Along with your essential bird book and journal, you may wish to bring a brief treatise on Early American architecture.

The inn is part of Montpelier's National Historic District. Every guest room is unique, although each has a private bath, telephone, television, and air-conditioning. The modern amenities are complemented by fine antiques and reproductions. There are choices of king, queen, and twin beds, and many rooms have fireplaces.

Guests are encouraged to enjoy the comfortable living room or common room. You can play cribbage or backgammon by the hearth in the game room or enjoy a bit of solitude in the upstairs plant-filled sun room. The dining room, with its marble fireplace and adjoining breakfast room, offers a fine continental breakfast daily. The pantries provide coffee and rolls for early or late risers and a variety of refreshments throughout the day. Evening dining features an à la carte menu of light fare that will be appreciated by the gourmet.

Outdoor and cultural activities abound, with seasonal activities that, like migratory birds, can be anticipated with a glance toward the calendar.

Rates: Double $98-$143; deduct $10 for single
Credit cards: Visa, MC, AMEX, Diners, Carte Blanche
No. of rooms: 19
No. of baths: 19
Wheelchair access: No
Pets: No
Smoking: Yes
Senior citizen discount: No
Directions: I-89, exit 8 to Montpelier, go straight through 4 lights, at 4th turn left onto Main Street, at 147 Main Street.

THE NORTHFIELD INN
27 Highland Avenue, Northfield, VT 05663
(802) 485-8558, Fax (802) 485-7946

Snow birds and bird-watchers will find an honest welcome at the Northfield Inn. This handsome, turn-of-the-century house sits high on a hill overlooking the village of Northfield and the campus of America's first private military college, Norwich University. The town itself is framed by scenic mountain backdrops that are home to the ski resorts of Stowe, Sugarbush, and Mad River Glen; all of this is just minutes from the state capital of Montpelier. This is a very convenient place to stay when birding at the Barre-Montpelier Area.

The inn contains 25 rooms of restored Victorian elegance, with porches and gardens that rival the visual pleasures of the interior appointments. Eight rooms, including two suites, are available, all with private baths; one even features a clawfoot tub. You can choose brass, carved, and four-posters from among the queen-size beds. Two parlors, a library, a game room, and a dining room with a spirit-lifting fireplace all cater to guest satisfaction.

Innkeepers Aglaia and Alan Stalb also provide a hearty, old-fashioned breakfast for their guests, with menus that include crepes, stuffed French toast, German apple pancakes, eggs Benedict, soufflé, or stuffed omelets. Traditional high tea is served in the afternoon. Snacks are available for the inveterate nibbler, and dinners for special events may be arranged in advance.

Rates: $55-85; suites $135-$150
Credit cards: Visa, MC
No. of rooms: 12
No. of baths: 8

Wheelchair access: No
Smoking: No
Pets: Local kennel
Senior citizen discount: No

Directions: 10 minutes from Montpelier via I-89, exit 5; 1 hour from Burlington Airport.

The Springfield Area

NEAREST AIRPORT: Springfield, Vermont.

LOCATION: East central, close to the New Hampshire border.

CONTACT: Vermont Institute of Natural Science, Woodstock, VT 05091, (802) 457-2779; Ascutney Mountain Audubon Society, P.O. Box 191, Springfield, VT 05156. A copy of *A Guide to Bird Finding in Vermont* by Walter G. Ellison (Vermont Institute of Natural Sciences) can be ordered from the institute.

BEST BIRDING: March 30 to December 1.

TOURS/WORKSHOPS: Contact the Institute of Natural Science or the Ascutney Mountain Audubon Society.

The Springweather Nature Area, administered by the Ascutney Mountain Audubon Society, is a major birding location. From the center of Springfield, follow Routes 106/11 northwest to the junction where the routes divide. Take Route 106 north about 2.5 miles and turn right onto a paved road signaling the North Springfield Dam. Cross the causeway over the dam, and turn left onto a paved road that parallels the lake and continue 0.6 mile to the entrance sign. In the spring, there will be large numbers of waterfowl and shorebirds as well as osprey and belted kingfisher. The best location for migrant warblers is beyond the parking area where up to 20 species may be seen in the thick second growth woodland. Nesting species include American kestrels, ruffed grouse, great crested flycatchers, and blue-gray gnatcatchers. Well over 150 species of birds have been recorded by the Ascutney Mountain Audubon Society in the area.

Mount Ascutney is ideal for observing the bird species in the mountains of Vermont. To reach Ascutney State Park, from Springfield, take Route 11 east to Route 5 where you will head north. Drive past Route 131 at the traffic light and proceed another 1¼ miles; bear left to the entrance of the park. In the park you should see barred owls, pileated woodpeckers, least flycatchers, wood and hermit thrushes, warblers, and white-throated sparrows; from the higher points, observe hawks, turkey vultures, and northern ravens.

Other good birding places around Springfield are the Springfield Meadows for waterfowl and raptors, the Springfield Airport for hawks and sparrows, and the north end of the village of Weathersfield Bow for small migratory land birds.

A Guide to Bird Finding in Vermont by Walter G. Ellison is my source for describing the birds and birding locations in the Springfield area.

GWENDOLYN'S
P.O. Box 225, Perkinsville, VT 05151, (802) 263-5248

Enjoy the ornate, romantic, and flowery atmosphere at Gwendolyn's, a wonderful bed and breakfast. Standing on the veranda of this mansard-roofed five-room guest house, you can hear the rush of Black River Falls, which generated power over a century ago for the old Perkins mill. Step over the threshold into a spacious foyer. Open French doors invite you into a formal dining room where a leisurely gourmet breakfast is served with antique china, fine linens, and always fresh flowers. The innkeeper's culinary training is exhibited in scrumptious muffins, intriguing egg dishes, and a French toast with geranium sauce. Evening hors d'oeuvres have proved so popular that patrons have been known to cancel dinner reservations.

The inn features a curved wooden staircase and authentically captured bedrooms. Lace tablecloths, wicker furniture, patterned upholstery, swagged material headboards, and window drapery all attest to the knowing eye of a former decorator schooled in the selection of fabric, color, and texture.

After settling in, you might stroll through the garden, walk to the village general store, bicycle to one of the town's seven original covered bridges, or take a short drive to cross-country skiing areas, marked trail hiking, historic sites, gourmet restaurants, antique shops, or summer theaters. Birders can flock to the nearby Ascutney Mountain Audubon Society in Springfield.

Rates: $50-$92	**Wheelchair access:** No
Credit cards: Visa, MC	**Pets:** No
No. of rooms: 5	**Smoking:** Yes
No. of baths: 4	**Senior citizen discount:** 10%

Directions: From I-91, take Springfield exit 7, follow Route 11 west to 106 north, continue approximately 4 miles; 106 makes a right-hand turn, Gwendolyn's is about 2.5 miles on the left.

HARTNESS HOUSE
30 Orchard Street, Springfield, VT 05156, (802) 885-2115

Birders who scan the sky looking for familiar sights have nothing on Governor James Hartness, owner of the Hartness House almost 100 years ago. He too looked skyward, leading him to develop what was the first 600 power turret equatorial telescope in the country. Still in working condition, it stands on the front lawn of the mansion. On clear nights, you are invited to the underground museum to gaze at the stars through his remarkable invention.

A spacious living room adorned with fluted pilasters, carved beams, and a majestic mahogany fireplace is a pleasant place for visitors to gather and get acquainted. A gracious foyer leads to a grand staircase curving up to 11 stately bedrooms. Two converted carriage houses contain an additional 34 rooms.

The formal dining room offers an elegant yet comfortable atmosphere. The Hartness House serves a full menu at moderate prices for breakfast, lunch, and dinner. The tavern is a place to unwind at the close of the day or to enjoy some entertainment.

The Hartness House is central to both winter and summer activities. In winter, there is skiing and ice-skating in nearby lakes. Summertime features swimming, boating, fishing, golfing, hiking, and biking.

The hotel has a heated swimming pool, lighted tennis courts, and 32 acres of woods for strolling. Your birding destination, the Ascutney Mountain Audubon, is close by.

Rates: $65-$105
Credit cards: Visa, MC, AMEX, Diners
No. of rooms: 43
No. of baths: 43
Wheelchair access: Yes
Pets: No
Smoking: Certain rooms
Senior citizen discount: No

Directions: From I-91, take exit 7, go 3.5 miles into the center of town, turn right at the second light, and follow the signs to Hartness House.

THE INN AT WEATHERSFIELD
Route 106 (near Perkinsville), Weathersfield, VT 05151-0165
(802) 263-9217, (800) 477-4828, Fax (802) 263-9219

The good news about the Inn at Weathersfield has been circulating for nigh onto two centuries. An 1811 advertisement describes it as an intimate eighteenth-century country inn nestled at the base of Hawks Mountain, in a "quiet dreamy village where the magnates of the city love to come for rural rest and repose." Prominent ever since, the property has seen many uses. It was originally built by Thomas Prentis, Revolutionary War veteran, as a four-room farmhouse on 237 acres of wilderness. Its colorful history includes homestead and farm, station on the Underground Railroad, stagecoach stop, home for elderly ladies, and since 1961, an inn, now known as the Inn at Weathersfield.

Situated at the end of a maple-lined drive, the inn boasts a picture view from every window. Ten guest rooms, a bridal suite, and a family suite—all with private bath, eight with working fireplaces—are furnished with period antiques. Seven public rooms are similarly decorated; one includes a 4,000-volume library and a collection of antique bottles.

Guests are initially greeted with a view of an open hearth with beehive bake oven, used on winter holidays for an eighteenth-century dining experience. For those more interested in contemporary fare, an internationally recognized menu is presented in the appropriately appointed, historic dining room/library. "A Little Night Music" to accompany dinner is provided by innkeeper Ron Thornburn, a musician of some reputation.

Rates: $175-$210, including a meal plan (MAP + high tea)
Credit cards: Visa, MC, AMEX, Discover, Diners
No. of rooms: 12
No. of baths: 12
Directions: Call for specific directions.

Wheelchair access: Yes
Smoking: Not permitted in guest rooms, restricted in public rooms
Pets: With prior permission
Senior citizen discount: No

VIRGINIA

Chincoteague National Wildlife Refuge and Assateague National Seashore

NEAREST AIRPORTS: Norfolk, Virginia; Salisbury, Maryland.

LOCATION: Situated at the south end of Assateague Island, a barrier island on the Atlantic coast of Virginia and Maryland. From Norfolk, Virginia, drive north on US 13 to its junction with Route 679. Continue on Route 679 to Route 175 until you reach the refuge entrance. The total distance is about 70 miles. From Salisbury, Maryland, drive south on US 13 about 28 miles to Route 175 and the refuge entrance.

CONTACTS: Refuge Manager, Chincoteague National Wildlife Refuge, P.O. Box 62, Chincoteague, VA 23336, (804) 336-6122. Also Tom's Cove Visitor Center, National Park Service, (804) 336-6577.

BEST BIRDING: Spring, fall, and winter.

TOURS/WORKSHOPS: National Wildlife Refuge open house during Thanksgiving week. Many naturalist programs through both the park service and the National Wildlife Refuge. Contact headquarters.

Both Chincoteague and Assateague islands are barrier islands off the shores of Virginia and Maryland. The Virginia area is more restricted, since the refuge is managed primarily as a migratory bird habitat. Here you will find sandy shores, tidal flats, fresh- and saltwater marshes, shrubs, and pine forests for the more than 300 species of birds. Large numbers of species winter in this region, including red-throated and common loons, herons, tundra and mute swans, brants, snow geese, and more than 20 species of ducks. In the fall, look for the tricolored herons, glossy ibis, northern bobwhites, clapper rails, lesser golden and piping plovers, whimbrels, godwits, western and least sandpipers, dunlins, pectoral sandpipers, and 25 other possible sandpiper species, including an occasional Baird's sandpiper. Black skimmers are common, as are fish crows. You should also be able to observe rose-breasted grosbeaks, scarlet tanagers, indigo buntings, sharp-tailed sparrows, seaside sparrows, and orchard orioles.

Ospreys and piping plovers nest here in the spring. Nesting areas are restricted, so always check in with the visitor center. Other nesting species are peregrine falcons, Virginia rails, American oystercatchers, willets, American woodcocks, and chuck-wills-widows as well as pine, prairie, and black-and-white warblers. The numerous species of terns that fly through the area in the spring are gull-billed, Caspian, royal, sandwich, common Forster's, least, and, in rare instances, black terns, which are seen more frequently in summer.

THE GARDEN AND THE SEA INN
P.O. Box 275, New Church, VA 23415, (804) 824-0672

The Garden and the Sea Inn is the creation of two Washington, D.C., escapees, real estate attorney Jack Betz and interior decorator Victoria Olian. They sampled the inns and restaurants in the south of France before opening their own inn.

The inn's two guest rooms are furnished with a mixture of antiques, mostly Victorian, and have touches like wall sconces and stained glass. One room has a wonderful wicker sleigh bed and the other a bed of lacquered wrought iron. Both have romantic Victorian baths.

A large front room is used to display pottery, paintings, and other art for sale. There is a wide porch stocked with rockers.

A complimentary continental breakfast and afternoon tea come with your room. An extra charge will bring you a wonderful dinner. House specialties include grilled fresh fish with herbs and lemon butter, bouillabaisse, and scallops with sautéed cabbage and parsley.

The innkeepers enjoy music and art and host a number of chamber music dinner-concerts and art shows throughout each season. They will also be glad to direct you to Chincoteague National Wildlife Refuge, a mere fifteen minutes away.

Rates: Single $75; double $135; extra person $15
Credit cards: Visa, MC, AMEX, Discover, Diners
No. of rooms: 5 (large)
No. of baths: 5 (3 with whirlpool tubs)
Wheelchair access: No
Pets: No
Smoking: Restricted to public areas
Senior citizen discount: No
Directions: From Washington, D.C.: Route 50 east to Salisbury; Route 13 south from Salisbury; 1½ mile south of Maryland line turn right onto Route 710. Inn is 300 yards on right.

MISS MOLLY'S INN
4141 Main Street, Chincoteague, VA 23336, (804) 336-6686

There is something about an island that can be so magical, so poetic, so filled with possibilities. One of the most memorable is Chincoteague Island, complete with the magnificent birding retreat found at the Chincoteague National Wildlife Refuge.

I have had many happy visits at Chincoteague, staying at Miss Molly's Inn. The house has a rich history. In 1886, J. T. Rowley, then known as "The Clam King of the World," built a charming Victorian home on Chincoteague Island. His daughter, "Miss Molly," was one of the island's best loved citizens, and she lived in the house until the age of 84. While writing *Misty*, about the famous ponies of Chincoteague, Marguerite Henry stayed in this grand old building. In fact, the plot of *Misty* was worked out while she rocked on the front porch with the original Miss Molly.

The rooms are appropriately named Miss Molly's Room, Marguerite Henry Room, Captain Jack's Room. Other rooms are named after colors, Red, Yellow, and Green. There is a choice of king-size or double room with a private bath or twin beds with a shared bath.

There is a charming traditional English afternoon tea as well as a full breakfast. You will want to return time and again to this island retreat.

Rates: $69-$135   **Wheelchair access:** No
Credit cards: No   **Smoking:** No
No. of rooms: 7   **Pets:** No
No. of baths: 5 with private, 2 shared   **Senior citizen discount:** No
Directions: From Salisbury, 1 hour south on Highway 13; from Norfolk, 2 hours via Highway 13 north.

YEAR OF THE HORSE INN
600 South Main Street, Chincoteague Island, VA 23336, (804) 336-3221

Chincoteague Island is one of the truly charming places around. With the wild ponies romping virtually everywhere, it brings to mind the beloved children classic, *Misty*, which was written on this very island.

A convenient place to stay when visiting this birding hot spot is the Year of the Horse Inn, only five minutes from Chincoteague National Wildlife Refuge. A rambling, Colonial-style structure built in the 1940s, the inn is just a tad less than 20 feet from Chincoteague Sound. Three of the guest rooms, all with private entrances onto the balcony, overlook the water. All rooms have private bath, color cable television, central heat, and air-conditioning. Enjoy the water view and spectacular sunsets from your own balcony.

The Year of the Horse is a birder's delight as well. During breakfast on the balcony, one might see a hundred brants, a few industrious oystercatchers, a gaggle of snow geese, and a few cormorants. During wine at dusk, do not be surprised to see a great blue heron land on a nearby pylon.

The spotless guest rooms are simple but comfortably furnished and feature wall-to-wall carpeting, light and colorful fabrics, some antiques, and private baths. One room has a full kitchenette; a two-bedroom apartment is also available.

The Year of the Horse, Chincoteague's first bed and breakfast, is a perfect nesting spot to roam the 16 miles of undeveloped beach and enjoy large pure stands of loblolly pine, all manner of waterfowl, and Assateague's famous herd of wild ponies.

Rates: $75-$95 in season; $65-$75 off-season
Credit cards: Visa, MC
No. of rooms: 5
No. of baths: 4
Directions: Inn will send map.

Wheelchair access: No
Pets: No
Smoking:
Senior citizen discount: No

Shenandoah National Park

NEAREST AIRPORTS: Charlottesville and Richmond, Virginia; Washington, D.C.

LOCATION: This long park snakes along the Blue Ridge Mountains for over 80 miles in the northwest quadrant of Virginia—from Front Royal in the north to Rockfish in the south. From Richmond, drive west on I-64 to Charlottesville, about 55 miles; continue on I-64 to the south entrance at Waynesboro. From Washington, D.C., drive west on I-66 to the north entrance at Front Royal. Highway 81, Skyline Drive, traverses the length of the park.

CONTACTS: Shenandoah National Park, Route 4, Box 348, Luray, VA 22835, (703) 999-2229. Also, the Shenandoah Natural History Association at the same address, (703) 999-3582.

BEST BIRDING: Spring, fall, and summer.

TOURS/WORKSHOPS: Many; contact park headquarters.

The Shenandoah Valley and the Blue Ridge Mountains have long been noted for their beauty and celebrated in song. Shenandoah evokes the mists of the valleys and the hardwood forests of the mountains. The overlooks and side trails along the Appalachian Trail, which follows the ridge (and skyline drive), are rewarding places to bird. The park naturalist, Jerry Lindsay, especially recommends Gravel Springs (milepost 17.6), Stony Man Nature Trail (milepost 41.7), Limberlost Trail (milepost 43), Big Meadows (milepost 51), and South River Falls Trail (milepost 62.8). Under a restoration program, the park has released young peregrine falcons to the wild each year since 1989. The best place to observe them is near Hawksbill Mountain.

In the spring, you can hear a symphony of bird sounds along the wooded trails as the warblers and songbirds migrate through and nest within the protected forest. Their bright colors stand out against the neutral tree branches; look for the yellows and golds of Blackburnian, Canada, and magnolia warblers and common yellowthroats, or the blues of northern parulas and blue-winged warblers. You should also be able to spot chestnut-sided and bay-breasted warblers. Overall, there are more than 200 species of birds on the park's checklist. The park environment also supports an abundance of other wildlife and more than 250 types of wildflowers. Park and trail guides can be purchased from the Natural History Association.

JORDAN HOLLOW FARM INN
Box 375, Stanley, VA 22851, (703) 778-2209/778-2285

Virginia is horse country, and if you would like to do a little riding with your birding, Jordan Hollow Farm Inn is the place for you. Innkeeper Marley Beers is an accomplished horsewoman who leads guests on trail rides. Depending on your skill level, you can take a gentle beginner ride or join the advanced treks into the mountains.

The innkeepers are reason enough to visit this inn. Marley was a Washington, D.C., consultant the day she fell in love with the farm and its dilapidated house. Jetze Beers was a nautical engineer whose work took him around the world. They met in Monrovia, West Africa. It was love at first sight. Today, Jetze speaks his native Dutch along with German and some French to guests from foreign countries.

The Beers have created the inn and have done a masterful job. Guests have a choice of lodgings. There is Arbor View Lodge, a vine-covered lodge surrounded by a sun deck that offers serious porch sitters a lovely view of the meadows or mountains. It has 16 rooms with private baths, decorated hand-made furniture, and country artifacts.

The Mare Meadow Lodge is a hand-hewn log lodge nestled in a quiet meadow. It has four guest rooms, all with whirlpool bathtubs, fireplaces, cable television, private porches, and a common room for guests. The rooms are attractively decorated with a generous collection of carefully chosen artifacts. The lodge is surrounded by pastures where horses can be seen peacefully grazing.

The rates at the inn are based on the Modified American Plan, which means that breakfast and dinner are included. The dinner, served in the Farmhouse Restaurant, features a homey, hearty, slightly exotic blend of what Marley calls "country cosmopolitan—a little bit French with an unsuspected touch of African."

Jordan Hollow Farm Inn is an elegant place to stay when birding at Shenandoah National Park.

Rates: $140-$180 (includes breakfast and dinner for 2 people)
Credit cards: Visa, MC, Discover, Diners
No. of rooms: 21
No. of baths: 21
Wheelchair access: Yes
Pets: No
Smoking: Yes
Senior citizen discount: No

Directions: From Washington, D.C., take I-66 west to exit 13 (Front Royal and Linden). Continue on Highway 55 into Front Royal. At third traffic light, turn left on Highway 340 south. Arrive in Luray after approximately 24 miles. From traffic light in Luray, proceed for 6 miles on Highway 340 south. See Exxon service station on left, and after 0.1 mile turn left on 624. At next stop sign, turn left on 689 and cross bridge. After 0.5 mile, make a right on 626. The inn's entrance is on right within 0.25 mile.

THE RUFFNER HOUSE
Box 620, Route 4, Luray, VA 22835, (703) 743-7855

The Ruffner House is a historic manor in the foothills of the Blue Ridge and Massanutten mountains. It was built more than 200 years ago by Peter Ruffner, the first settler of Luray. It is now elegantly restored and features period antiques. There are four comfortable bedrooms with private baths. If you are traveling with a larger birding group, try the Cottage.

Enjoy a hearty, home cooked country breakfast in the antique-filled dining room. After a day at Shenandoah, cool off in the swimming pool or feed carrots to the magnificent Arabian horses pastured on the grounds. Sip a cool drink on the outdoor porches while gazing at the beautiful mountains. During cooler weather, enjoy the pleasure of reading a book in front of the cozy fireplace.

Rates: $40-$125
Credit cards: Visa, MC
No. of rooms: 8
No. of baths: 6
Wheelchair access: No
Smoking: No
Pets: No
Senior citizen discount: Yes
Directions: 70 miles west of Dulles Airport; at the intersection of Highway 340 and Route 211.

WAYSIDE INN
7783 Main Street, Middletown, VA 22645, (703) 869-1797

To walk into the Wayside Inn is to find yourself suddenly back in the eighteenth century. The past gently echoes throughout this elegantly restored inn.

You can almost hear the stagecoaches approach the original Wilkerson's Tavern along Old Black Bear Trail. You can imagine the peaceful respite after the Civil War, when the inn welcomed postbellum guests as Larrick's Hotel. The tradition expanded in the early 1900s with the addition of a third floor, graceful wings, and its present name. Today, guests who stop by the Wayside step back two hundred years.

Each of the 22 guest rooms and suites is uniquely decorated with rare antiques, fine art, objets d'art, and an interesting potpourri of memorabilia. You will find four-posters with canopies, cannonball and acorn carved detailing, and French Provincial and Greek Revival period pieces. If you fall in love with one of the inn's antiques, you will be pleased to know that all of the inn's furnishings are available for purchase.

Historic good taste is the specialty of the inn, with authentic regional American cuisine served in seven antique-filled dining rooms. You may savor peanut soup, spoon bread, and country ham in the Lord Fairfax Room. You may prefer a variety of game, seafood, and homemade desserts in the Old Slave Kitchen, Portrait Dining Room, or your choice of other picturesque settings.

This historic inn is an excellent place to stay when birding at Shenandoah National Park.

Rates: $65–$125
Credit cards: Visa, MC, AMEX, Discover, Diners
No. of rooms: 24
No. of baths: 24

Wheelchair access: Yes
Pets: No
Smoking: Yes
Senior citizen discount: 10%

Directions: At the crossroads of I-81 and I-66; on Route 11, in Middletown (exit 302).

WASHINGTON

Nisqually National Wildlife Refuge Complex

NEAREST AIRPORT: Seattle/Tacoma International Airport, Washington.

LOCATION: Located at the southern end of Puget Sound, on the delta of the Nisqually River, the refuge can be reached from I-5 about 55 miles south of the airport. The nearest city is Olympia. Take Exit 114 on I-5 to the entrance and headquarters.

CONTACT: Refuge Manager, Nisqually National Wildlife Refuge, 100 Brown Farm Road, Olympia, WA 98506. (206) 753-9467.

BEST BIRDING: Fall migration and winter.

TOURS/WORKSHOPS: Contact refuge manager for listings. Self-guided nature trails. Twin Barns Education Center available for groups by reservation.

Flowing into Puget Sound, the Nisqually River forms a rich estuarial habitat of fresh- and saltwater marshes and ponds, mud flats, dense woodlands, grasslands, and cultivated croplands. Overlooking the delta, the mixed wood forests are a prime perching place for bald eagles and ospreys as they scan the waters for fish. One of the largest remaining Washington state estuaries left undisturbed, the delta has been a part of the protected refuge since 1974. The variety of habitats attract a great diversity of bird species. In the salt marshes and mud flats, the shorebirds, gulls, ducks, and herons dine on small crustaceans and worms; the quiet freshwater marshes and grasslands sustain and protect migratory waterfowl. Raptors, soras, bitterns, woodpeckers, and owls frequent the surrounding woodlands, while songbirds are attracted by blackberries and crab apples along the creeks.

Of the more than 200 species of birds using the refuge, waterfowl and shorebirds dominate the fall and winter months. Abundant species at this time are red-throated and common loons, green-winged teals, mallards, pintails, American wigeons, greater scaups, surf scoters, and hooded, red-breasted, and common mergansers. Some of the birds you can see skittering along the edges of the water are greater and lesser yellowlegs, killdeer, western, least, Baird's, and pectoral sandpipers, dunlins, short-and long-billed dowitchers, and common snipes. Other specialties are common murres, pigeon guillemots, marbled murrelets, and rhinoceros auklets. Other wildlife you will enjoy observing here at various seasons are snowshoe hares, beavers, chipmunks, red foxes, coyotes, river otters, and Columbia blacktail deer. Offshore, look for whales, seals, and sea lions.

BRITT'S PLACE
4301 Waldrick Road S.E., Olympia, WA 98501, (206) 264-2764

Britt's Place is a place to sidestep life's fast pace, a place of quiet solitude, friendly conversation, or quiet reflection. It is also a convenient spot to stay when visiting Nisqually National Wildlife Refuge. You will see birds at Britt's Place. As innkeepers Theo and Virginia Britt explain, "Our mild climate, rural solitude, and abundance of wetlands and forested hills bring a continued changing of bird hosts."

There is one guest room with a private bath; after a peaceful night's sleep, you will awaken to the smell of freshly brewed coffee. The inn's generous breakfast menu has gained quite a reputation. They have one couple who comes every summer from Stuttgart, Germany, maybe for the breakfast but as they put it, "to rejuvenate here."

After birding at Nisqually, swim, fish, or canoe on a peaceful lake surrounded by Washington's beautiful evergreens. Enjoy a spectacular view of Mount Rainier or a quiet evening by a roaring fire. Britt's Place is ideally situated for taking in everything that Washington has to offer. The bed and breakfast is equidistant from Seattle, with its famous coffee bars and Pike Place Market, and Washington's two national parks, Mount Rainier and Olympic National Park.

Rates: Single or double $70/night; extra person $15
Credit cards: No
No. of rooms: 1
No. of baths: 1
Directions: Inn will send map.

Wheelchair access: No
Pets: Conditional
Smoking: No
Senior citizen discount: No

HARBINGER INN
1136 East Bay Drive, Olympia, WA 98506, (206) 754-0389

Let the Harbinger Inn take you under its wing when you are visiting Nisqually National Wildlife Refuge. You will find its warm, informal atmosphere to your liking.

There is a continental breakfast. You can enjoy complimentary late afternoon tea or cookies, or just sit and contemplate the water. You are encouraged to borrow books from the library for night reading.

You might want to choose the Blue Heron Suite, which has a double bed, a sitting room, turn-of-the-century antiques, a private bath, and nice views. The Coral Room, Victoria Room, and Cloisonné Room, all with shared baths, have pleasant appointments and great views.

Rates: $55-$80
Credit cards: Visa, MC, AMEX
No. of rooms: 4
No. of baths: 3

Wheelchair access: No
Pets: No
Smoking: On porch only
Senior citizen discount: Yes

Directions: 10 minutes from Nisqually National Wildlife Refuge. Take I-25 south to exit 105-B, then 2 miles east of exit; 50 minutes south of Seattle/Tacoma Airport.

Bittern

Olympic National Park

NEAREST AIRPORTS: Seattle/Tacoma International Airport; Port Angeles, Washington, on the Olympic Peninsula; Victoria, British Columbia.

LOCATION: The northwest corner of Washington, bordering Canada via the Strait of Juan de Fuca. The park entrance is on Highway 101 just a few miles from Port Angeles. Ferry from Victoria, BC, to Port Angeles, Washington. Drive from Seattle-Tacoma International Airport, skirting Puget Sound on Highway 5 south to Highway 101 north, through Olympia and Shelton to Port Angeles (about 150 miles). From Portland, Oregon, drive north on Highway 101; various entrances to the park start at Quinault, about 200 miles away.

CONTACTS: Olympia National Park, 600 East Park Avenue, Port Angeles, WA 98362, (206) 452-4501; the checklist from the Northwest Interpretive Association, (206) 553-7958, is excellent.

BEST BIRDING: January to April and September to December. You will still be able to bird well in the summer. Another good birding location is Dungeness National Wildlife Refuge near Port Angeles on the Olympic Peninsula.

TOURS/WORKSHOPS: Heron Cove Tours: (206) 866-9575; also check with park manager for additional information.

Surrounded by the Pacific Ocean and Puget Sound, this is a land of striking contrasts. The great variety of habitats here support an unusual diversity of bird species as well as marine life. Here there are sandy, muddy, and rocky shorelines, rain forests, prairie oak and savanna, marshes and bogs, shrubs and thickets, riparian forests, and lakes and rivers. From January to April, the marine and shoreline habitat is filled with loons, red-necked grebes, Brandt's and pelagic cormorants, great blue herons, tundra and trumpeter swans, greater and lesser scaups, harlequin ducks, old-squaws, Barrow's goldeneyes, bald eagles, peregrine falcons, blue and ruffed grouse, black oystercatchers, black turnstones, surfbirds, mew gulls, pigeon guillemots, and ancient murrelets. During the same time of year farther inland in habitats such as prairie/oak savannas, forests, freshwater lakes and rivers, and croplands, you should be able to observe tundra and trumpeter swans, marbled murrelets, snowy owls, spotted owls, gray jays, Bewick's wrens, American dippers, varied thrushes, northern shrikes, and Steller's jays. If you are at this park in the fall, expect to see the same species. During the summer, look for black-footed albatross, pink-footed, flesh-footed, and sooty shearwaters, northern fulmars, fork-tailed and Leach's storm-petrels, ospreys, golden eagles, Caspian terns, Cassin's and rhinoceros auklets, tufted puffins, black and Vaux's swifts, pileated wood-peckers, Pacific slope flycatchers, warblers, sparrows, and finches.

GLEN MAR BY THE SEA
318 North Eunice, Port Angeles, WA 98362, (206) 457-6110/457-4686

To prepare yourself for the beauties of Olympic National Park, begin your adventure with a stay at Glen Mar by the Sea. The spacious living room provides a view of Port Angeles Harbor and the lights of Victoria across the Strait of Juan de Fuca. Watch the graceful sailboats ply the waves as you sit beside the cozy fireplace or play an inspiring tune on the grand piano. This is a relaxing place to stay while birding at Olympic National Park.

Allow hostess Glenndia Witherow to pamper you with tea or coffee served from an antique tea cart in nineteenth-century china cups; you can also enjoy the same indulgence in the privacy of your room. Hearty breakfasts feature Glen Mar egg dishes, fresh fruit specialties, and other delicacies served in the dining room or on the patio overlooking the water.

Glen Mar by the Sea offers four bedrooms, all with private baths and all boasting spectacular views of either the water or the mountains. The Hideaway is the most secluded room and features a king-size bed and a double whirlpool bathtub. Children ten years of age and older are welcome; arrangements will be made for your pet at the nearest pet hotel; and a smoke-free environment is provided for the comfort of all guests.

Rates: $80-$97.50; extra person $15
Credit cards: Visa, MC
No. of rooms: 4
No. of baths: 4

Wheelchair access: No
Pets: No
Smoking: No
Senior citizen discount: No

Directions: Follow 101 through Port Angeles to N. Eunice Street. Turn north. It is the last place on the left overlooking the water and Port Angeles Harbor.

LAKE CRESCENT LODGE
National Park Concessions, HC 62, Box 11, Port Angeles, WA 98362-9798
(206) 928-3211

Staying at National Park lodges often reminds me of being at summer camp. The surroundings are gorgeous, but accommodations tend to be on the rustic side. For example, the deeply blue, glacier-cut Lake Crescent provided many hours of tranquillity. Lake Crescent Lodge, however, is the old-fashioned variety, typical of many in our national parks. The lobby recalled WPA days, with its wonderful log-burning stone fireplace.

At Lake Crescent Lodge, my husband and I stayed at the twin-bedded motel addition. We had beautiful views of Lake Crescent, but our temporary domicile was not as cozy as some of the bed and breakfasts where we had been staying. The old-style gracious rooms in the lodge, with polished wood floors and paneling, are more elegant.

The historic fireplace cottages looked like the most interesting places to stay at Lake Crescent. They were built in 1937 for Franklin Roosevelt, while he was exploring the area and considering the peninsula for a future national park.

Meals are served in the sunny dining room, with views of the garden through large windows. Specialties include salmon, Quilcene oysters, and Dungeness crab Louis.

From the lodge, it is a comfortable walk by well-kept trails to Marymere Falls in a rain forest setting but a more rugged hike to the top of Storm King Mountain. At the breathtaking Olympic National Park, you might see common murres, pigeon guillemots, marbled murrelets, rhinoceros auklets, and tufted puffins.

Rates: $65-$166
Credit cards: Visa, MC, AMEX, Diners
No. of rooms: 52
No. of baths: 47

Wheelchair access: Yes
Pets: Yes, $5 per pet
Smoking: Yes
Senior citizen discount: No

Directions: 20 miles west of Port Angeles, just off Highway 101.

LAKE QUINAULT LODGE
P.O. Box 7, Quinault, WA 98575, (800) 562-6672

Situated in the midst of one of the few rain forests in North America, Lake Quinault Lodge offers the rare opportunity to blend the pure, pristine beauty of nature with modern conveniences. You can sense the natural wonders of the beautiful Olympic National Forest in the main lodge, the fireplace rooms, or the 35 new lakeside rooms of the lodge. There is plenty to do at the lodge. Stroll through the rain forest trails, canoe on the lake, or take a dip in the heated pool. Save plenty of time for birding at the Olympic National Park, however, because it is one of the prettiest places in the country.

The lodge retains a high degree of cheery, comfortable prewar charm. The spacious lobby calls out for you to sit by the fireside. Settle into a wicker chair or settee, and admire the big brick fireplace with its gleaming brass andirons, polished hearth, and real logs. From here, you can see the startingly blue Lake Quinault.

One of the reasons the lodge is anything but rustic is that it is privately owned rather than being operated by the National Park Concessions. Your choice of accommodations include the main lodge with its simple cedar-plank walls, period furniture, and old-fashioned clawfoot bathtubs. In the new annex, rooms are positively luxurious, with wall-to-wall carpeting, big sofas, queen-size beds, and full baths. All of these have balconies or patios with lakeside view.

The dining at Lake Quinault Lodge features Northwest regional cuisine.

Rates: $80-$210
Credit cards: Visa, MC, AMEX
No. of rooms: 92
No. of baths: 92
Wheelchair access: Yes
Pets: Certain areas only
Smoking: Designated areas only
Senior citizen discount: No
Directions: I-5 south to Olympia, west to Aberdeen. In Aberdeen pick up 101 north. Lake Quinault Lodge is about 42 miles north of Aberdeen on the South Shore Road.

KALALOCH LODGE
HC 80, Box 1100, Forks, WA 98331, (206) 926-2271

Perched on a bluff overlooking the Pacific Ocean, Kalaloch Lodge is considered by many to be the most scenic, all-inclusive resort in Olympic National Park. Built in 1953, the lodge has retained the charming characteristics of an oceanside fishing village but has added all the modern conveniences to make one's stay carefree and enjoyable.

A variety of accommodations allow a choice of several vacation styles: the main lodge (8 guest rooms plus dining room, lounge, coffee shop, reading room, and gift shop), authentic log cabins (roomy kitchenette facilities and Franklin-style fireplaces), and Sea Crest House (3-room suites that open onto an ocean-view deck).

Superb Northwest Coast cuisine is available at every meal. Kalaloch Lodge specialties include hearty, homemade clam chowder, omelets stuffed with oysters and smoked salmon, and a tempting Northwest blackened salmon.

There are guided tours of magnificent Olympic National Park in addition to whale-watching, beachcombing, and, of course, birding of both rain forest and ocean species.

Rates: $55-$125
Credit cards: Visa, MC, AMEX
No. of rooms: 40 cabins, 18 hotel rooms
No. of baths: 58
Directions: On Highway 101.
Wheelchair access: Yes
Pets: Yes
Smoking: Yes
Senior citizen discount: No

San Juan Islands National Wildlife Refuge and Skagit County

NEAREST AIRPORT: Seattle-Tacoma International Airport, Washington; there are also commuter flights to Orcas Island; however, if you wish to have automobile transportation, it is better to rent a car at the airport and take the ferry across to the islands. There are also airports located in Victoria, Sidney, and Vancouver, British Columbia. Best access is by boat from Anacortes or Friday Harbor.

LOCATION: An archipelago of three major islands surrounded by many smaller ones, the San Juan Islands are at the north end of Puget Sound, a Paul Bunyon step to the mainland, to Victoria and Vancouver, British Columbia, or to the Olympic Peninsula. The three large islands are Lopez Island, San Juan Island, and Orcas Island. From Washington State, take the Washington State Ferry at Anacortes for the cruise to the islands, which takes a little over an hour. Direct ferry service is also available from Sidney, on Vancouver Island. Some of the archipelago is closed to the public for the protection of the wildlife. Check regulations before planning any trips.

CONTACT: San Juan Islands National Wildlife Refuge, c/o Nisqually National Wildlife Refuge Complex, 100 Brown Farm Road, Olympia, WA 98506. (206) 753-9467.

BEST BIRDING: Spring and fall for migrations; summer for nesters (although there is more tourist traffic then). A copy of *Birding in the San Juan Islands* by Mark G. Lewis and Fred A. Sharpe (Seattle: Mountaineers, 1987) will enhance your visit.

TOURS/WORKSHOPS: Contact National Wildlife Refuge; also Washington Department of Wildlife, 600 North Capitol Way, Olympia, WA 98504, (206) 753-5700; The Nature Conservancy, (206) 728-9696; Moran State Park, Orcas Island, (206) 562-0990.

Isolation from the mainland has saved the San Juan Islands from the encroachment of civilization. Here you can still experience the wildlife that was once abundant in this area of the Northwest. Habitats include forests, meadows, springs, shorelines filled with small invertebrates that can feed millions of birds, and the nearby Skagit River, which is filled with salmon and trout. Look for bald eagle and osprey nests high on the trees; the largest concentration of bald eagles in North America flies between the San Juan Islands and the mouth of the Skagit River.

Lewis and Sharpe have defined the birding habitats of the San Juan Islands as open salt water; rocky shoreline; sandy and gravelly shoreline; mud flat; salt marsh; freshwater lake; marsh and farm pond; field; farmland or pasture; dry grassland; grassy, bald, and rocky slope; open woodland and oak savanna; dry coniferous forest, wet coniferous forest, riparian, woodland; shrubby thicket; town and garden; and aerial.

This is a perfect place to bird by habitat. Common and/or abundant birds are trumpeter swans, greater white-fronted geese, ring-necked, canvasback, and harlequin ducks, old-squaws, Barrow's goldeneyes, black oystercatchers, black turnstones, surfbirds, common snipes, pileated woodpeckers, Eurasian skylarks, varied thrushes, northern shrikes, and red crossbills. Less common but generally seen are peregrine falcons, blue grouse, ancient murrelets, tufted puffins, red-breasted sapsuckers, water pipits, and snow buntings. In addition, you can observe large flocks of shorebirds and seabirds during migration.

While here, be sure to also bird in the areas around the Skagit River, especially the Samish Flats, where you can observe many raptors in the winter. Procure a *Skagit County Bird-Watching Guide* from the Washington Department of Wildlife.

HILLSIDE HOUSE BED AND BREAKFAST
365 Carter Avenue, Friday Harbor, WA 98250, (206) 378-4730

With over 200 species of resident and migratory fowl, the San Juan Islands are a bird-watcher's paradise. A special attraction for eagle lovers is the annual bald eagle count held at San Juan every January. Visitors are invited to participate by either land or boat.

Hillside House Bed and Breakfast caters to bird-watchers. Innkeepers Dick and Cathy Robinson have located their bed and breakfast on the side of a valley overlooking Friday Harbor and have a very special pair of 200mm binoculars mounted on the deck for observation. They also have a two-story flight aviary that houses a variety of exotic game birds, along with several domestic birds. Some of the bedrooms have window seats that actually hang in the aviary.

Hillside House features seven distinctive guest rooms, most with window seats and private baths, including a very special penthouse honeymoon retreat. Enjoy country-style breakfasts, with eggs straight from the hen house, while basking in the panoramic views of Mount Baker.

The Robinsons can tell you where and how to best see birds at the San Juan Islands National Wildlife Refuge.

Rates: Double $65-$145; single $10
less; extra person $25
Credit cards: Visa, MC, AMEX
No. of rooms: 7
No. of baths: 5

Wheelchair access: No
Pets: No
Smoking: Outside
Senior citizen discount: No

Directions: From Spring Street – north on 2nd Street; follow curve of street, becomes Guard Street; ½ mile; right on Carter Avenue; Hillside House is one block on left.

MOON & SIXPENCE
3021 Beaverton Valley Road, Friday Harbor, WA 98250, (206) 378-4138

At Moon & Sixpence, every room contains a list of all the birds seen at the bed and breakfast, including the American goldfinch, rufous hummingbird, and red crossbill.

Moon & Sixpence, with views of Mount Dallas, marshes, meadows, pasture, and pond, is a classic country bed and breakfast in the middle of San Juan Island. An acre of lawn surrounds the farmhouse; sheep graze in the pasture beyond. In the weaving studio, wool is dyed, spun, and woven into fabric for the inn. Walking and hiking trails are nearby; seaside picnic sites, whale watching, fishing, boating, and swimming are also available. An option is just to find a comfortable spot on the deck and do some bird-watching.

This remodeled dairy farm, built in the early 1900s, offers accommodations in the farmhouse as well as in the outbuildings. The Olympic Chamber is the most popular room in the farmhouse because of its view of the Olympic Mountains towering in the distance. The room is furnished in antiques and features a queen bed and a shared bath. In the outbuildings, built 85 years ago, the lookout offers exposed beams, beautiful views, a private bath, and queen bed.

The name of the Moon & Sixpence derives from Somerset Maugham's description of Gauguin's discovery of place in his novel, The Moon and Sixpence, a story loosely based on the life of the impressionist painter. As Maugham himself put it, "Sometimes a man hits upon a place to which he mysteriously feels that he belongs." This bed and breakfast is just such a place for visitors.

Rates: Double $65-$105; single $10
less; no rollaways
Credit cards: No
No. of rooms: 4
No. of baths: 3

Wheelchair access: No
Pets: No
Smoking: Porch only
Senior citizen discount: No

Directions: San Juan Island, with its port in Friday Harbor, lies 80 miles north of Seattle. Take I-5 to exit 230, then Highway 20 west to Anacortes and the

San Juan ferry terminal, and board the ferry to Friday Harbor. From the Friday Harbor ferry slip, take Spring Street 2 blocks to Second, continue onto Guard Street, and bear right onto Beaverton Valley Road. The inn is about 3 miles from the ferry.

Moon & Sixpence

Willapa National Wildlife Refuge and Columbia River

NEAREST AIRPORTS: Aberdeen, Washington; Seattle/Tacoma, Washington; Portland, Oregon.

LOCATION: The southwest corner of Washington, near the Oregon border. From Aberdeen, drive south approximately 50 miles on Highway 101. From Seattle/Tacoma, drive I-5 south to Highway 4 west, around 271 miles; then take Highway 30 north and west 100 miles. Continue on Highway 101 north about 35 miles to the refuge. Other nearby areas to bird are the Julia Butler Hansen Refuge, the Lewis and Clark National Wildlife Refuge, and the Long Beach Peninsula.

CONTACT: Willapa National Wildlife Refuge, Ilwaco, WA 98624. (206) 484-3482.

BEST BIRDING: The largest diversity of species is found in the winter; the highest concentrations occur in spring and fall. Areas are closed in the summer for nesting snowy plovers. Also check Grays Harbor, just north of Willapa near the city of Aberdeen, for large concentrations of shorebirds in the spring. This refuge has an annual schedule for best viewing times; call (206) 753-9467.

TOURS/WORKSHOPS: Contact refuge headquarters.

The total lands of the various refuge units comprise about 11,000 acres. This refuge developed a rich diversity of habitats that now includes shoreline, dunes, coastal forest, coniferous forest, salt marshes, sloughs, and pasturelands. Further enriching the habitat, the Columbia River sweeps to the ocean just south of the refuge. Over 250 bird species have been recorded in this area. In winter, you can expect to see flocks of black brandts, scaups, and scoters, tundra and trumpeter swans, hooded, common, and red-breasted mergansers, bald eagles, peregrine falcons, dowitchers, and turnstones as well as sharp-tailed sandpipers. Barn, western screech-, great horned, northern pygmy, barred, short-eared, and northern saw-whet owls can all be observed at the right time and in the right habitat. Also look for varied and hermit thrushes, golden-crowned sparrows, and rufous-sided towhees. In the fall and spring, shorebirds number in the hundreds of thousands, including black-bellied and snowy plovers, whimbrels, long-billed curlews, surfbirds, red knots, sanderlings, western sandpipers, dunlins, and short- and long-billed dowitchers. Among the nesting species are cinnamon teals, great blue herons, wood ducks, bald eagles, ospreys, Virginia rails, American black oystercatchers, glaucous-winged gulls, pigeon guillemots, marbled murrelets, cedar waxwings, black-throated gray warblers, and purple finches.

THE SHELBURNE INN
P.O. Box 250, 4415 Pacific Way, Seaview, WA 98644, (206) 642-4142

The Shelburne Inn was built in 1896 as a boardinghouse and was later joined with another building by a covered passageway. The cozy common room offers coffee, current magazines, and newspapers that you can read as you sit around the stone fireplace. Handmade quilts decorate the walls and cover the beds in thoughtfully furnished rooms, most of which have private decks. The sixteen creaky-floored bedrooms are colorful, with quilts, antique furniture, and fresh flowers.

The food at the Shelburne Inn's Shoalwater Restaurant is heavenly. It bases its cuisine on an abundance of fresh, locally harvested foods. Start with smoked seafood mousse or pâté Shoalwater, then move on to the innkeeper's mussel chowder or seafood Caesar salad. The baked Columbia River Chinook salmon with blueberry mustard butter sauce is a wonderful choice for an entrée. You might prefer the grilled fillet of Columbia River white sturgeon with gingered apple, leek, and sweet red pepper cream sauce or Northwest seafood stew, an assortment of seasonal local seafood in a broth of champagne, saffron, leek, red onion, and thyme.

This repast should keep you going until breakfast, when you will feast on Shelburne scrambled eggs with shrimp, apple, and spinach or asparagus crepes with sweet curry sauce, or fried polenta with homemade sausage and Mexican eggs, or smoked salmon and watercress salmon. Any of these tasty dishes is served with fruit juice, fresh fruit, sauteed potatoes, homemade breakfast pastry, and fresh ground coffee or tea.

There is more to life than food, I have been told. The scenery surrounding the Shelburne is stunning. The peninsula, an unspoiled 28-mile stretch of wild Pacific seacoast known as the longest, continuous beach in the United States, is a natural paradise complete with bird sanctuaries, lighthouses, and panoramic vistas. Willapa Bay, just east of the inn, is a pristine haven for waterfowl.

Save some time to stroll through the inn's flower and herb garden and to visit the informal Heron and Beaver Pub with its thirst-quenching selection of Northwest specialty beers.

Rates: Single $79-$149; double $85-$155; extra persons $10; midweek off-season packages
Credit cards: Visa, MC, AMEX
No. of rooms: 15
No. of baths: 15

Wheelchair access: Yes
Pets: No
Smoking: Permitted in the pub and outdoors only
Senior citizen discount: No

Directions: From Seattle: I-5 south to Olympia, then take the Aberdeen-Port Angeles (Highway 12) exit. Follow the signs west to Montesano, then to Raymond and South Bend, and then to the Long Beach Peninsula. From Portland, take Highway 30 to Astoria or Highway 26 to Seaside, then go north on US 101 across the Astoria Bridge. Turn left to Ilwaco, then north 2 miles to Seaview.

The Shelburne Inn

WISCONSIN

Baxter's Hollow, The Baraboo Hills, The Nature Conservancy

NEAREST AIRPORT: Madison, Wisconsin.

LOCATION: Southwestern Wisconsin. Drive west and north from Madison on Highway 12, 20 miles to Sauk City. From Sauk City, drive north on US Highway 12, 8 miles to County Road C. Turn left on County Road C and continue 1½ miles to the intersection with Stone's Pocket Road. Turn right, go north for 2 miles, and park in turnout area. Other nearby birding areas are Big Woods, Devil's Lake State Park, Steinke Basin, Hemlock Draw, Honey Creek Valley, Klondike Campground, Pan Hollow, and Pine Hollow; all are in the 5-mile-wide, 25-mile-long Baraboo Hill Country.

CONTACT: The Nature Conservancy, Wisconsin Chapter, 333 W. Mifflin Street, Suite 107, Madison, WI 53703. (608) 251-8140.

BEST BIRDING: Spring and summer.

TOURS/WORKSHOPS: Contact Nature Conservancy or Wisconsin Society of Ornithology, (414) 966-1072.

Baxter's Hollow is part of Wisconsin's southern deciduous forest. This is largely a pristine area ecologically dominated by Otter Creek, stands of oak, and hickory, maple, dash, and alder thickets. Sand barrens are found in the area, along with rich riparian habitat. More than 135 species of birds have been observed here, including many nesters. All species of woodpeckers are here, and you can see broad-winged hawks, winter wrens, and gray catbirds. The endangered (in Wisconsin) worm-eating warbler and the threatened (in Wisconsin) cerulean, Kentucky, and hooded warblers are all breeders in the hollow. Other nesting species are rose-breasted grosbeaks, scarlet tanagers, northern cardinals, northern orioles, great crested flycatchers, Acadian flycatchers, veeries, blue-gray gnatcatchers, and Louisiana waterthrushes. Other warblers that can be spotted or heard are the Blackburnian and Canada. Additional species you can see are blue-winged, chestnut-sided, mourning, black-and-white, black-throated green, blue and golden-winged, yellow, and magnolia warblers as well as American redstarts. Specific locations and directions can be found in *Breeding Birds of the Baraboo Hills, Wisconsin: Their History, Distribution, and Ecology* (Wisconsin Department of Natural Resources and the Wisconsin Society for Ornithology).

THE COLLINS HOUSE
704 E. Gorham Street, Madison, WI 53703

If you are an admirer of Frank Lloyd Wright, you will want to stay at the Collins House, a classic example of the Prairie School style of architecture that was founded by Wright at the turn of the century.

The house is true to Wright's spirit with its open interior and natural woods. The leaded-glass bookcases in the Arts and Crafts style fit in beautifully with the simple lines and open spaces. The library houses more than eighty classic movies.

All the guest rooms are attractive, but a favorite is the Rosalie Peck. From the balcony of this suite, you can gaze across the five-mile stretch of Lake Mendota shoreline or enjoy the view from the comfort of your sitting room. Named after Madison's first innkeeper in 1837, the suite is trimmed in greens and golds, appropriate for showcasing its collection of furnishings from the Arts and Crafts movement.

Innkeeper Barb Pratzel has a full-time catering business, which means you will eat very well here. Sometimes you may even serve as experimental tasters for her new recipes. At breakfast, you may find such house specialties as Swedish oatmeal pancakes, chicken tarragon roulades, or potato pancakes; all these are served with home-baked breads fresh from the oven or pastries such as streusel muffins and strawberry orange coffee cake. Breakfast ends with seasonal fruits, Wisconsin cheeses, and a selection of juices.

After breakfast, head for Baxter's Hollow, an important nesting area for forest-dwelling birds. If time allows, explore Madison and the beautiful University of Wisconsin campus.

Rates: $59-$125
Credit cards: Visa, MC
No. of rooms: 5
No. of baths: 5
Wheelchair access: No
Smoking: No
Pets: Yes, limited
Senior citizen discount: No
Directions: 5 blocks east of the Capitol, on Lake Mendota.

GRANDPA'S GATE
E 13841 Lower DL, Merrimac, WI 53561, (608) 493-2755

Grandpa's Gate and country store is located in the valley of the Baraboo Bluffs, an area of natural beauty and country serenity. The inn has four guest bedroom units with private baths and air-conditioning. Grandpa himself is master chef, and you can sample his breakfasts in a spacious dining room.

The country store, on the grounds, sells antiques, crafts, and collectables. You will not want to return home without Wisconsin sausage and cheese.

You will enjoy looking for more than 134 bird species at Baxter's Hollow. If time allows, visit nearby attractions: the International Crane Foundation, known for rare birds; Parfrey Glenn, a site that offers unusual plants and rock formations; and the Circus World Museum.

At dinnertime, the Old Schoolhouse Restaurant, one-half block away, is sure to provide you with a memorable meal.

Rates: $45-$100
Credit cards: No
No. of rooms: 7
No. of baths: 7
Wheelchair access: Yes
Pets: No
Smoking: No
Senior citizen discount: No
Directions: From I-90/94, take the Merrimac exit 108, then drive on Highway 78 south about 9 miles, turn right on Highway DL (Devil's Lake), drive approximate 2 miles to Grandpa's Gate B&B on the left-hand side of the road.

PINEHAVEN BED & BREAKFAST
E13083 State Highway 33, Baraboo, WI 53913, (608) 356-3489

The Pinehaven Bed & Breakfast, surrounded by pine trees, overlooks a two-acre lake. An upper veranda and lower deck allows for good bird-watching as Jenny wrens serenade you with their sweet song.

The guest rooms offer diversity. Choices include a Victorian wicker room, a country garden room, and, for those who prefer a touch of yesteryear, an antiquity room. The Pinehaven room is done in blue and white and features handmade quilts on its twin beds. All rooms have private baths and air-conditioning. A hearty breakfast is included. A separate small cottage is a great place for family vacations. It is self-sufficient and has such amenities as electric heat, a wood-burning stove, fireplace, color television, and VCR.

The inviting scenery in the area includes not only leisurely strolls in the woods, fishing, and rowboating but such seasonal treats as sleigh rides in winter and hay rides in summer.

Rates: $55-$70; extra person $10
Credit cards: Visa, MC
No. of rooms: 4
No. of baths: 4
Wheelchair access: No
Pets: No
Smoking: No
Senior citizen discount: No
Directions: On State Highway 33, 10 miles west of I-90/94; 3 miles east of Baraboo.

VICTORIAN TREASURE
115 Prairie Street, Lodi, WI 53555, (608) 592-5199

At Victorian Treasure, you can enjoy nearby Baxter's Hollow and the architecturally compelling Taliesin at your leisure. But the Victorian Treasure is a pleasant place to visit in its own right. Built in 1897 by a Wisconsin state senator and lumber merchant, it has been lovingly restored and features many original details including gas chandeliers, pocket doors, leaded and glass windows, and a magnificent wraparound front porch. There are four unique guest rooms named after wildflowers and decorated in an eclectic and comfortable mix of antiques and collectables. All beds have dual-control electric blankets, down comforters, and four pillows, in the European style. Several of the rooms have whirlpools.

Other European traditions, such as afternoon tea, are observed here. Enjoy an evening sweet with herbal tea before retiring. Before birding at Baxter's Hollow, have a full breakfast with homemade breads and muffins as the featured specialty.

Birders often want to book the first Saturday of every month for the monthly speakers program, particularly the one on eagle watching. Other speakers include experts on history, wine-making, pottery, and art history.

Rates: $85–$110
Credit cards: Visa, MC
No. of rooms: 4
No. of baths: 4
Wheelchair access: No
Pets: No
Smoking: Limited
Senior citizen discount: No
Directions: From I-90/94, exit Highway 60 west; at Highway 113 (Main Street), continue straight 1 block; turn right on Prairie Street.

Horicon National Wildlife Refuge

NEAREST AIRPORTS: Oshkosh, Madison, and Milwaukee, Wisconsin.

LOCATION: Southeast quadrant of Wisconsin, 40 miles inland from Lake Michigan. From Milwaukee, drive northwest on Highway 41 about 35 miles to the junction of Highway 33, then east to Highway 67 north; the refuge office is off County Road Z. From Oshkosh, drive south on Highway 41 to Highway 33. Use the same directions as above from Highway 33 (about 55 miles). Take Highway 151 northeast about 41 miles to Highway 33. Head west to Highway 67, then proceed as above (approximately 60 miles).

CONTACTS: Horicon National Wildlife Refuge, Route 2, Mayville, WI 53050, (414) 387-2658. Horicon Marsh Wildlife Area, adjacent to the National Wildlife Refuge can be called at the Horicon Area Department of Natural Resources Office: (414) 485-3000. For visits to the heron rookery, call Blue Heron Landing: (414) 485-2942 or (414) 485-4663.

BEST BIRDING: Spring and fall.

TOURS/WORKSHOPS: Contact refuge office or Wisconsin Department of Natural Resources: (414) 485-3018. Ask for the Wildlife Education Specialist.

The complex of the Horicon Marsh spreads across 31,000 acres. The Horicon National Wildlife Refuge consists of more than 20,000 acres at the north end of the marsh and the marsh wildlife area of 10,000 acres at the southern end near the city of Horicon. Two hundred sixteen bird species use the marsh, upland grasses, forest, and island habitats. The best time to bird here is during the fall migration when over 250,000 Canada geese use the region as a stopover point. This number represents 25 percent of the total Mississippi Valley population of Canada geese. In addition, some 2,000 to 3,000 redhead ducks nest here. Other spring courters and nesters are great blue herons, great egrets, black ducks, ruddy ducks, northern harriers, gray partridges, sandhill cranes, common gallinules, American woodcocks, upland sandpipers, Forester's terns, ruby-throated hummingbirds, willow flycatchers, blue-gray gnatcatchers, scarlet tanagers, and indigo buntings.

Many raptors can be observed in the spring: sharp-shinned, Cooper's, red-tailed, red-shouldered, broad-winged, and rough-legged hawks as well as bald and golden eagles and ospreys. American kestrels are common year-round. In the fall, Canada geese are joined by large numbers of American bitterns, mallard ducks, blue- and green-winged teals, lesser scaups, Virginia rails, soras, great horned owls, great-crested flycatchers, cedar waxwings, bobolinks, indigo buntings, vesper sparrows, and 11 species of warblers.

THE AUDUBON INN
45 North Main Street, Mayville, WI 53050, (414) 387-5858

E ven without its winning name, this inn would be worth the stay because of its elegance and service. The guest rooms have beautifully crafted four-poster canopy beds, topped with handcrafted quilts. Brass lamps, wooden window blinds, Shaker-inspired writing desks, and whirlpool tubs complete the effect.

The inn represents the ultimate in renovation. Owner Rip O'Dwanny spent more than $500,000 in the handsome woodworking alone. The lobby features the original oak stairway with newel post and banister. Oak Brook Studios did the magnificent stained-glass windows that adorn the dining room and bar. In 1988, the cupola was designed to look identical to the original and placed on top of the building.

The bar has been called by some the most beautiful bar in Wisconsin. Bird-watchers will want to spend time there if only to see the lounge's centerpiece and ceiling, featuring the massive, hand-etched glass depiction of geese in flight over the marsh.

The dining room features four master chefs plus a pastry chef. Everything on the menu is excellent, but the Swordfish Moutarde, a charbroiled steak with a coarse mustard cream sauce and citrus segments, is a favorite. Another recommendation is Tournedos Audubon, which are grilled filets of beef tenderloin topped with shrimp and bernaise sauce.

A complimentary continental breakfast is served Monday through Friday; brunch is served on Sunday.

Rates: $69-$99
Credit cards: Visa, MC, AMEX, Discover, Diners
No. of rooms: 17
No. of baths: 17

Wheelchair access: Yes
Smoking: Limited
Pets: Yes
Senior citizen discount: No

Directions: 5 minutes north of refuge, via Highway 67 in downtown Mayville.

THE INN AT PINE TERRACE
351 Lisbon Road, Oconomowoc, WI 53066
(414) 567-7463, (800) 421-INNS

H istoric Pine Terrace mansion was a summer home for one of the two Schuttler brothers, both of whom married into the brewing families of

Anheuser and Busch. It is a charming spot to perch while birding at Horicon National Wildlife Refuge.

This estate originally included over 220 acres of forest and farmland, with numerous outbuildings. The mansion itself has been diligently restored to reflect the prestigious Lake Country "cottage" (as such second homes were called, no matter their size or affluence) of Henry and Mary Schuttler, who built it as a seasonal getaway from their Chicago-based wagon industry. The nineteen-room showpiece was constructed in 1884; in its heyday, a large Victorian flower garden and "park" (read "lawn") connected the estate with the north shore of Fowler Lake. The largest brick home in Oconomowoc, Pine Terrace is reputed to be one of the most accurately restored homes in Wisconsin and as such, is listed on the National Register of Historic Places.

Each of the thirteen guest rooms has been furnished to reflect the opulence and gracious life-style of a highly decorative arts period. The high ceilings, lavish decor, and elaborately carved woodwork are impressive, as are the modern conveniences—double whirlpool baths, television and telephones, and a new swimming pool. Rooms at the inns bear family names: Minnie, Maria, or Lillie Anheuser, Aldophius Busch, Captain Fred Pabst, and Montgomery Ward.

Breakfast includes fresh fruit, croissants, pastries, juice, and beverage. Guests may enjoy the superb views as they plan their itinerary for birding at Horicon or visiting Oconomowoc, a city surrounded by three clear lakes.

Rates: $69.50-$119.50
Credit cards: Visa, MC, AMEX, Discover, Diners, Carte Blanche
No. of rooms: 13
No. of baths: 13 (6 with double whirlpools)
Wheelchair access: Yes
Pets: Yes
Smoking: Designated area
Senior citizen discount: No
Directions: Approximately 45 miles west on Highway 94 from Milwaukee, north on Highway 67 into town; approximately 1 mile north of town, take right fork onto Usbon Road.

THE WASHINGTON HOUSE INN
W62 N573 Washington Avenue, Cedarburg, WI 53012
(414) 375-3550, (800) 554-4717

The Washington House Inn has been restored to create the countrified Victorian inn a traveler would have found 100 years ago. The first thing you encounter is a long lobby with brass chandeliers, a marble-trimmed fireplace, and antique Victorian furniture.

The guest rooms feature cozy down quilts, antiques, floral wallpaper, fancy armoires, and fresh flowers. Some of the rooms are highlighted with leaded-glass transom windows. If you are celebrating a special event or if you just want to live it up, try the deluxe quarters. Some have loft beds and fireplaces; others feature a 200-gallon spa tub.

For those in a mood to be pampered, breakfast in bed is an option. Otherwise, you can join other guests in the attractive dining room with its oak tables and chairs and white pressed-tin ceilings. In either case, enjoy home-made muffins, cakes, and breads made from recipes from an authentic, turn-of-the-century Cedarburg cookbook. Fresh fruit, cereal, juices, and coffee or tea are also available.

Cedarburg is a historic woolen mill town; the downtown area has more historic structures than any city west of Philadelphia. Innkeeper Wendy Porterfield takes pride in telling her guests all about the town. She holds court every afternoon in front of a cheery fireplace.

Rates: $59–$139; extra person $10 **Wheelchair access:** Yes
Credit cards: Visa, MC, AMEX, Discover **Pets:** Kennel available
Smoking: Yes
No. of rooms: 29 **Senior citizen discount:** 10%
No. of baths: 29
Directions: I-43 north to Cedarburg exit, left on C to Washington Avenue; right to second stoplight at the corner of Washington and Center.

WYOMING

Grand Teton National Park

NEAREST AIRPORTS: Salt Lake City, Utah, and Denver, Colorado, with continuing flights to Jackson Hole.

LOCATION: In the northwest corner of Wyoming, Jackson Hole is surrounded by the Grand Teton Mountains and the Bridger Teton National Forest. The Snake River and the Gros Ventres River bisect the valley floor. From Salt Lake City, drive east and north on I-80, then north on Highway 189. From Cheyenne, take I-80 east to Highway 191 north. From Billings, take Highway 310 south to Highway 789 south, then Highway 28 south to Highway 191 north, or Highway 789 south to Highway 26 north to 191 south. Distances are great, and you will be in higher elevations, so be sure to check the weather and road conditions.

CONTACT: Grand Teton National Park, P.O. Drawer 170, Moose, WY 83012. (307) 733-2880 or (307) 543-2467. The park is generally open May through September.

BEST BIRDING: Spring and summer, with some very special birds in the winter.

TOURS/WORKSHOPS: The park has an extensive tour and workshop schedule. Contact park headquarters. In addition, there are tours on the Snake River and Wildlife Research Expeditions through the Teton Science School in Jackson Hole. Also contact the Jackson Hole Bird Club, Box LL, Jackson, WY 83001.

Here in this region the western myth comes alive—breathtaking mountains, rivers, and valleys, with crisp, clear air and water. While the spring flowers are blooming amid the melting snow, lift up your binoculars and look for snow and Ross's geese, black-bellied plovers, semipalmated plovers, piping plovers, ruddy turnstones, red knots, Baird's sandpipers, red-necked phalaropes, Sprague's pipits, rose-breasted grosbeaks, and rusty blackbirds. Summer is the most crowded season here; however, there is an abundance of land so it is possible to take the less traveled trails to see such species as eared and western grebes, wood ducks, cinnamon teals, harlequin ducks, ospreys, Swainson's hawks, sandhill cranes, willets, Wilson's phalaropes, Caspian and Forester's terns, black-billed cuckoos, burrowing owls, common whip-poor-wills, cordileran flycatchers, red-eyed vireos, American redstarts, lazuli and indigo buntings, and orchard orioles. Most impressive, however, are the residents and winter birds.

Residents include bald eagles, northern goshawks, ferruginous hawks, golden eagles, merlins, and prairie falcons. Sharp-tailed, ruffed, and sage grouse are here year-round also, as well as many owls, such as flammulated, eastern and western screech, and long- and short-eared. Amid snows and skiers, you may see winter raptors such as gyrfalcons and rough-legged hawks. Tundra swans, trumpeter swans, snowy owls, Bohemian waxwings, Lapland longspurs, snow buntings, purple finches, and white-winged crossbills can also be observed.

FISH CREEK BED AND BREAKFAST
2455 Fish Creek Road, P.O. Box 366, Wilson, WY 83014, (307) 733-2586

At the Fish Creek Bed and Breakfast, you can luxuriate on the sun deck or soak in the hot tub while at the same time adding some new species to your life list. You may also see an occasional moose or elk; late at night, you are sure to hear the howl of far-off coyotes.

You might want to just relax at Fish Creek and enjoy the refreshing peace and quiet. There is something very soothing about the sounds of tinkling wind chimes, babbling brooks, and songbirds. If you have come for a little more activity, private fly-fishing is available at your doorstep. Owners Putzi and John Harrington will be happy to instruct you in the art of alpine or Nordic skiing and accompany you on your journey. As 40-year residents of this area, the Harringtons are well equipped to help you plan any of the myriad activities available.

Whatever you decide to do, the Harringtons will make certain that you enjoy it and feel at home at their inn. The ambience here is friendly and relaxed. The guests could not say enough about how wonderful this inn is. Several people told me that this was their second visit of the winter and they had already booked ahead for the following summer. The Harringtons have their share of foreign visitors; they are fluent in both French and German.

The breakfasts are excellent: homemade cinnamon rolls, a variety of blintzes, sourdough hot cakes, sausage and mushroom crepes with Swiss cheese sauce.

The log cabin home has an attractive rustic feeling. The three Western-style bedrooms, all with private baths, are decorated with gingham curtains, quilts, pillow shams, and pole furniture.

Rates: Double $85-$105	**Wheelchair access:** No
Credit cards: Visa, MC	**Pets:** No
No. of rooms: 4	**Smoking:** No
No. of baths: 4	**Senior citizen discount:** No

Directions: West from the town of Jackson on Highway 22, 5 miles, turn right on Second Street in Wilson, right on Fish Creek Road, 1.5 miles.

TETON TREE HOUSE
P.O. Box 550, Wilson, WY 83014, (307) 733-3233
Fax (307) 733-3233 (call before sending)

The elevating experience at the Teton Tree House begins with a ninety-five-step climb from the parking lot through the pine-scented woods to the entrance of the inn. No matter which room you choose, you will be treated to spectacular mountain views. The guest rooms are even situated in such a way that you feel as though you are on a tree limb.

You may be so busy looking out the window that you will fail to notice how attractive the guest rooms are. All five rooms have either extra-long, double, or queen- or king-size beds. Most of the rooms have private balconies; one has a window seat; another has a bidet.

The Tree House rooms may recall childhood fantasies, but the breakfasts are concocted for the health-conscious, zero-cholesterol adult contingent. You will dine on granola, fresh fruit, hot cereal, and a large selection of homemade baked goods, featuring Swedish buttermilk coffee cake, zucchini breads, blueberry, bran, or cherry muffins, and banana breads, all of which are made with whole wheat flour.

Your bird-watching could actually begin on the trilevel decks where you can observe the habits of numerous species. Later, you might borrow a book from the browsing library and sit in front of the Southwestern-style beehive fireplace. You can also luxuriate in the extra-large, seven-person hot tub.

In addition to birding at the gorgeous Grand Teton National Park, the owners, Denny and Chris Baker, can give you sage advice on mountain activities. The Bakers can steer you in the right direction for white-water float trips, scenic float trips, day or multiday canoe trips, short or long hikes, horseback or horse pack trips, rodeos, chuckwagon dinners, mountain climbing, backpacking, swimming in the hot springs pool, dory river trips, fishing trips, scenic photography trips, or a Yellowstone tour.

Rates: $85-$125   **Wheelchair access:** No
Credit cards: Visa, MC   **Smoking:** No
No. of rooms: 5   **Pets:** No
No. of baths: 5   **Senior citizen discount:** No
Directions: Teton Tree House is 3/8 of a mile from Wilson, 10 miles from the Grand Teton National Park, and 60 miles from Yellowstone.

TETON VIEW BED AND BREAKFAST
2136 Coyote Loop, P.O. Box 652, Wilson, WY 83014, (307) 733-7954

If you are you looking for a bed and breakfast that is kid friendly, look no further than Teton View. The innkeepers, Jane and Tom Neil, have two small daughters, Lynn and Rachel, who enjoy playing with visiting children. Teton View's big fenced backyard is the perfect playground. It sports a swing set, hammock, horseshoes, trampoline, sandbox, picnic table, and a barbecue for grilling hot dogs. If you want to get away from the children for a few hours, Jane will arrange baby-sitting.

Bird-watchers will find the decor of the inn charming: there are swan, duck, and goose decorations in every room. The upstairs guest rooms are the perfect place for junior birders and their parents. In a private wing, they will have their own deck and small sitting area with games, books, refrigerator, and laundry facilities.

You can have your own home away from home by staying in the two rooms that share a bath and closing off the rest of the inn. The bath has a tub, shower, and a double-sink vanity.

If you are traveling sans children, try the Grand View room. It is named for the splendid view of the Grand Tetons. It has its own bath, a brass bed with soft blue cover, pale blue Venetian blinds, and a resident calico goose.

The whole family will like the candy kisses that magically appear on your pillow; you will enjoy the basket of cosmetics in the room. Everyone will sleep comfortably on the cozy flannel sheets.

Breakfast is a family affair, with everyone sitting around a large table in the dining room. You can choose from hot and cold cereal; home-baked coffee cakes, sticky buns, or muffins; homemade granola, fresh fruit, yogurt, juice, or coffee.

Teton View welcomes pets, with prior approval. So pack up the station wagon and head west! Teton View could provide the ideal family vacation for birding at Grand Teton National Park.

Rates: $60-$90
Credit cards: Visa, MC
No. of rooms: 3
No. of baths: 3

Wheelchair access: One room, summer only
Smoking: No
Pets: Limited
Senior citizen discount: No

Directions: 7 miles south on Highway 39; 56 miles south of Yellowstone, via Highway 390 and Highway 89. Check for road closures in winter and fall.

Yellowstone National Park

NEAREST AIRPORTS: Salt Lake City, Utah; Denver, Colorado. Use the same directions as to Jackson Hole and Grand Teton National Park, then head north on Highway 191 for about 1 hour to reach Yellowstone. Commercial airline service is available year-round from Cody and Jackson, Wyoming; Idaho Falls, Idaho; and Bozeman and Billings, Montana.

LOCATION: The south entrance is about 55 miles from Jackson (see information on the Grand Tetons). At Billings, Montana, you are 165 miles west and north of the north entrance. This is the only Yellowstone entrance open year-round. Drive Highway 212 from Billings to the northeast entrance or Highway 90 west, then Highway 89 south to the north entrance. From Bozeman, drive Highway 90 east to Highway 89 south to the north entrance.

CONTACT: National Park Service, P.O. Box 168, Yellowstone National Park, WY 82190, (307) 344-7381. Be sure to check on weather conditions and dates the park is open to visitors. Weather is the determining factor at this park for any birding. To arrange for lodging inside the park, call (307) 344-7311.

BEST BIRDING: Spring, summer, and fall.

TOURS/WORKSHOPS: The park rangers have prepared extensive wildlife tours and workshops. Check at the visitor center or in the park newspaper. Schedules are not available by mail. Be sure to contact the Yellowstone Institute, P.O. Box 117, Yellowstone National Park, WY 82190, for field programs on natural history and to arrange for custom courses for groups.

Although Yellowstone National Park, with over 2.2 million acres of wilderness, is often the most crowded of the national parks in the summer, with forethought and planning, it is spacious enough for good birding any time of the year. This is the world's greatest wildlife refuge, with lush and varied terrain. Over 225 species of birds inhabit the area. Spring (March through May) brings both whistling and trumpeter swans, over 20 species of ducks, goshawks, golden and bald eagles, and possibly prairie and peregrine falcons. Ospreys are common, and great gray owls are year-round residents. Yellow-bellied sapsuckers and northern three-toed woodpeckers can be found in the proper habitats, as can dusky and Hammond's flycatchers. Gray and Steller's jays, black-billed magpies, and Clark's nutcrackers are all common in the park. In the fall, horned and eared grebes as well as Barrow's goldeneyes are often seen. Blue and ruffed grouse, white-throated swifts, mountain chickadees, dippers, and northern shrikes are also numerous. Cassin's finches, green-tailed towhees, and snow buntings will show themselves to the patient birder. For a nonbirding partner, the park offers numerous opportunities for photography, painting, hiking, or simply enjoying the wilderness.

THE IRMA HOTEL
1192 Sheridan Avenue, Cody, WY 82414
(307) 587-4221, (800) 745-IRMA, Fax (307) 587-4221, ext. 21

This is the best of all possible worlds: the Irma has fame, being listed on the National Register of Historic Places, and has known fortune; when the hotel was built in 1902, the cherrywood bar alone cost $100,000. The Irma Hotel has all this and modern plumbing, too.

The town of Cody was founded at the turn of the century by Buffalo Bill Cody and quickly developed into a thriving community that included a fine hotel for housing and entertaining important guests. This symbol of Western hospitality built of native wood and sandstone was named by Cody in honor of his daughter. The magnificent bar was crafted in France, shipped to the East Coast, brought by rail to Red Lodge, Montana, and finally delivered by wagon to Cody. It remains one of the most photographed subjects in the town, second only to the Scout statue of Buffalo Bill standing at the end of Cody's main street.

Handsomely renovated rooms that housed some of the most famous names in the history of the West are now available to you. In addition to the colonel's own room, there are others named for characters such as newspaperwoman Caroline Lockhart and Phonograph Jones. Modern baths have been carefully installed to blend with the character of the rooms, and each suite is air-conditioned. For those less steeped in the past, completely modern hotel rooms attached to the historic site are also available.

Dining is superb at the Irma Restaurant, noted for its great prime rib. The Buffalo Bill Bar and Silver Saddle Lounge in the original lobby area also offer dining and relaxing. The Governor's Banquet Room features photographs of every governor of the state of Wyoming, and they have all been to the Irma.

You are in a perfect location for birding at Yellowstone National Park. History buffs will appreciate the Buffalo Bill Historical Center, Old Trail Town, and the Cody Nite Rodeo, while the outdoor sportsperson will find his or her fill of trout fishing, white-water rafting, pack trips, and rock climbing. Buffalo Bill's Original Wild West Show may be only a nostalgic memory, but the flavor and vitality of those times still echo in the main street and in the corridors of the historic Irma Hotel.

Rates: $35-$82
Credit cards: Visa, MC, AMEX, Discover, Diners
No. of rooms: 40
No. of baths: 40
Directions: The Irma Hotel is located in downtown Cody.

Wheelchair access: Yes
Smoking: Yes
Pets: No
Senior citizen discount: No

THE LOCKHART INN
109 W. Yellowstone Avenue, Cody, WY 82414, (307) 587-6074

As a journalist, I was delighted to stay at the home of the legendary Caroline Lockhart, the *Boston Post*'s first newspaperwoman. She was a talented and colorful character who believed that one had to experience a way of life to write about it. Following an interview with Buffalo Bill Cody, during an eastern tour with his show, she decided to move to his hometown. In 1904, she wrote a series of "rip-snorting, belly-tickling" stories about Cody that appeared in the *Stockgrower* magazine.

Lockhart's spirit lives on in the Lockhart Inn. The rooms are completely furnished with antiques, including Caroline's wind-up phonograph, rocking chair, and saddle. There are modern amenities as well, such as private baths in each room, direct-dial touch-tone phones, color cable television, and individually controlled heat and air-conditioning. Other attractive features include ceiling fans, writing desks, white iron beds with crisp linens, and delicious mints on cloisonné trays.

Breakfast is a treat, as innkeeper Cindy Baldwin prepares homemade breads, biscuits and gravy, pancakes, French toast, quiche, and homemade sausage. The currants for Cindy's preserves are hand-picked.

If you are spending the day birding at Yellowstone National Park, ask Cindy to pack you one of her box lunch treats.

Rates: $50-$135
Credit cards: Visa, MC
No. of rooms: 13 and 1 cabin
No. of baths: 14
Directions: 50 miles east of Yellowstone, off Highway 15.

Wheelchair access: Downstairs
Smoking: Limited
Pets: No
Senior citizen discount: No

Canada
BRITISH COLUMBIA

Creston Valley
Wildlife Management Area

NEAREST AIRPORT: Calgary, Alberta, Canada; Spokane, Washington. If you take the route through Banff National Park in Alberta, enjoy some of the forest birding. Border crossings are at Rykers and Kingsgate (open 24 hours).

LOCATION: In the northeast corner of British Columbia, 40 miles north of Bonners Ferry, Idaho, off Highways 3A and 3, which border Kootenay Lake in Canada. The interpretation and visitor center is at the end of the area off Highway 3.

CONTACT: Supervisor, Creston Valley Wildlife Centre, Box 1849, Creston, BC, Canada V0B 1G0, (604) 428-9319; Visitor Centre, (604) 428-9383.

BEST BIRDING: Spring, summer, and fall.

TOURS/WORKSHOPS: Check with naturalist at the Creston Valley Wildlife Centre.

Nestled in a valley at the south end of Kootenay Lake, the Creston Valley Wildlife Management Area is a magical place because of its clear air, clean water, and a variety of habitats attractive to both waterfowl and warblers. Known as the "Valley of the Swans," since so many of these birds stop over each year, the area is a cooperative operated by federal/provincial and private groups dedicated to wetland management.

The spring arrivals include red-necked and western grebes, white-fronted geese and Canada geese, wood, canvasback, pintail, and ring-necked ducks, and common and Barrow's goldeneyes. Whistling swans break the ice on Duck Pond during courtship rituals; snow buntings stop over on their northern migration. Although the colors and courtship displays of the waterfowl may be compelling, do not overlook the dikes, riverbanks, shorelines, and mountainsides for sightings of golden and bald eagles, hawks, pheasants, and grouse. Ospreys as well as golden and bald eagles soar overhead with the mountains as their backdrop. The rookery of great blue herons (about 200 pairs) begins to build nests in early April. In summer, you can see the common loons, and around June, the females may be observed carrying the young on their backs. Phalaropes, sandpipers, gulls, and terns frequent the mud flats and lakes throughout the summer. The peak of the fall waterfowl southward migration usually occurs the first two weeks of October. Overall, the area has 250 species of birds. Be sure to secure a bird list and enjoy this gem of British Columbia.

GOAT RIVER LODGE BED & BREAKFAST
1108 Lamont Road, Creston, B.C., Canada V0B 1G0, (604) 428-7134

A pleasant place to stay while visiting Creston Valley is the Goat River Lodge Bed & Breakfast where you literally overlook the Goat River. You will enjoy the peaceful, nicely landscaped surroundings, complete with swimming pool. If there are love birds in your group, have them request the Honeymoon Suite. For you ordinary birds, there are suites with private baths. You will all enjoy a hearty European breakfast with hosts Gertrude and Werner Allmeritter.

Rates: $40-$65
Credit cards: No
No. of rooms: 3
No. of baths: 3
Wheelchair access: No
Pets: No
Smoking: No
Senior citizen discount: No
Directions: The brochure has a detailed map to the lodge.

KOOTENAY KOUNTRY BED & BREAKFAST
220 Eleventh Avenue North, Creston, B.C., Canada V0B 1G0
(604) 428-7494

Enjoy a little bit of country in the heart of town at the Kootenay Kountry Bed & Breakfast. This heritage house features Victorian-style rooms with private baths. A country kitchen breakfast is served in an elegant dining room.

Be sure to check out the informative Wildlife Interpretation Centre at Creston Valley where you can learn about the 250 species of birds, 55 mammals, and numerous reptiles and amphibians and plants that inhabit areas ranging from wetland to mountain communities. Enjoy wildlife movies or slide shows in the air-conditioned theater, join a naturalist on an interpretive walk, or take a canoe trip through the marshes. While hiking a dike or uplands trail, be sure to watch waterfowl foraging for food or caring for their young.

Rates: Single $45; double $55; extra person $10
Credit cards: Visa, MC
No. of rooms: 3
No. of baths: 2
Wheelchair access: Limited
Pets: No
Smoking: No
Directions: Traveling east, turn left at 11th Avenue in town, go less than 1 block, watch for sign at big white house; traveling west, turn right.

THE WEDGWOOD MANOR
16002 Crawford Creek Road, Box 135
Crawford Bay, B.C., Canada V0B 1E0, (604) 227-9233

If you want an elegant, turn-of-the-century experience on an attractive fifty-acre estate, try the Wedgwood Manor. This hideaway locale is within fifty miles of your birding destination, the Creston Valley Wildlife Management Area.

All of the large rooms are furnished with pieces from the Victorian era. Each guest room has its distinct personality, and the library lounge, living room, dining room, and front veranda provide pleasant settings for mingling with the other guests.

With only five guest rooms available, the innkeepers are able to provide the special care and attention to detail that typified a successful guest house at the turn of the century. Much of the fresh food for breakfast comes directly from the manor gardens. Evening tea, served in the living room or on the veranda, is a tradition that began with the original mistress of the house, Lucy Caroline Wedgwood, and is still a ritual you will want to enjoy every day.

You can swim in water still pure enough to drink, canoe along pristine shoreline, or fish for world record rainbow trout. There are excellent walking and hiking trails right at the inn's doorstep. There are bicycles, available free to all guests, on which to explore the local back roads. The innkeepers will give you tips on where to find wild huckleberries and mushrooms.

Love birds take note: Wedgwood Manor is the essence of romance, so you might want to consider celebrating your marriage, anniversary, or any special occasion here.

Rates: Single $69; double $89; extra person $20
Credit cards: Visa, MC
No. of rooms: 5
No. of baths: 5

Wheelchair access: No
Pets: No
Smoking: No
Senior citizen discount: No

Directions: Take Highway 3-A north from Creston 50 miles to Crawford Bay, or from Nelson, drive 20 miles east on 3-A to free car ferry at Balfour across Kootenay Lake. Watch for our Gov. Accom. sign at Crawford Bay on the highway.

George C. Reifel Migratory Bird Sanctuary

NEAREST AIRPORT: Vancouver, British Columbia, Canada.

LOCATION: The sanctuary is located 16 miles south of the Vancouver Airport and 6 miles west of Ladner. Take Highway 99 south from the airport to Highway 17. Then turn right at Ladner on Highway 10 until you reach the entrance. Ferry service is available from Victoria to the Tsawwassen Ferry Terminal; then take Highway 17 to Ladner and Highway 10. From Bellingham, Washington, proceed north on Highway 5 to Highway 99 in British Columbia; then continue north on Highway 99 until it intersects with Highway 17 and follow the above directions.

CONTACT: British Columbia Waterfowl Society, 5191 Robertson Road, Delta, BC, Canada V4K 3N2. (604)946-6980.

BEST BIRDING: The sanctuary was set up to provide a place for migrating and wintering birds using the Pacific Flyway. From mid- to late August, the shorebirds arrive. The peak time for migrating birds is in November and the Snow Goose Festival is held the first week of that month. Tens of thousands of these birds migrate from Wrangel Island, and most of them remain through March.

TOURS/WORKSHOPS: Contact the sanctuary for the exact date of the Snow Goose Festival each November and for any scheduled tours that may be available. An excellent resource for birders is the Vancouver Natural History Society, (604) 738-3177. Leave a message if you wish a return call.

Westham Island at the mouth of the Frasher River is part of the delta confluent to the Strait of Georgia. This marshy island supports Canada's largest wintering population of waterfowl. Consisting of 850 acres, the George C. Reifel Migratory Bird Sanctuary at the northwest corner of Westham Island is managed habitat for over 240 species of birds. The varied nesting species here include wood ducks, redheads, snow geese, scaups, Cooper's and red-tailed hawks, bald eagles, glaucous-winged gulls, short-eared owls, kingfishers, tree swallows, and savannah and fox sparrows.

In the winter, you can see 9 species of gulls as well as marbled murrelets, rhinoceros auklets, purple finches, red crossbills, song sparrows, horned and western grebes, and up to 20 species of ducks. Look for red-throated loons in spring, winter, and fall. Spring and fall transients (check with headquarters for the best migration window) can include Pacific and common loons, common terns, western wood-peewees, and Nashville warblers. As the winter flocks leave and spring returns, you will be able to see semipalmated plovers, wandering tattlers, whimbrels, stilt sandpipers, short- and long-billed dowitchers, violet-green swallows, and rufous hummingbirds.

Because of the sanctuary's geographic location, always be on the lookout for accidentals; there have been sightings of over 105 casual and accidental species in the Vancouver area.

THE COUNTRY GUEST HOUSE
2829-53rd Street, Delta, B.C., Canada V4K 3N2, (604) 946-9248

The Country Guest House is located in a landscape of mountain views and spectacular sunsets. It sits on a ten-acre farm, three of which are landscaped gardens and lawns. Your private two-bedroom hideaway includes a comfortable double bed, fully equipped kitchen, and living room with television and VCR. Your hostess, Tillie Enns, will bring a continental breakfast to your door. On the premises, facilities include a large kidney-shaped pool, hot tub, and horseback riding.

The birding is excellent at the George C. Reifel Migratory Bird Sanctuary. If you have had your fill and long for the excitement of a city, Vancouver is just 20 minutes away.

Rates: Single $65; double $85-$95; extra person $10
Credit cards: No
No. of rooms: 2
No. of baths: 1
Wheelchair access: No
Pets: No
Smoking: No
Senior citizen discount: 10%
Directions: From Vancouver, take Highway 99 south, through the George Massey Tunnel. Follow Highway 17 past Ladner. Turn right on 28th Avenue, travel for 2 miles to the intersection of 28th Avenue and 53rd Street, where the inn is located. From Tsawwassen Ferry Terminal, take the first left on 52nd Street, turn right on 28th Avenue. The inn is approximately ¼ mile from the corner of 28th and 53rd.

OUR HOUSE
4837 44A Avenue, Delta, B.C. (Ladner), Canada V4K 1E3
(604) 946-2628

Proprietors Carol Dillman and Irene Scarth have turned their home on a quiet residential street into an inn. Guests have access to the entire upper floor, bedrooms and a shared bathroom, a spacious dining room, and a large living room with fireplace and television. In good weather, meals are served on the patio. Special breakfast choices are available, and special diets can be accommodated on request.

While the village of Ladner, a fishing and farming community south of Vancouver, may charm you, other delights await. You will enjoy the wonderful birding at the George C. Reifel Migratory Bird Sanctuary. If time allows, you have easy access to ferries, which take you to the beautiful quaint gulf islands. Near Our House there are miles of uninterrupted dikes for walking or cycling, shopping, and several fine three-star restaurants.

Airport pick-up and delivery is available for a small fee, as is pick-up at the Tsawwassen Ferry Terminal.

Rates: Single $30; double $50; twin $50; extra person $10 (children 8 and up)
Credit cards: No
No. of rooms: 3
Directions: Inn will send map.

No. of baths: 1
Wheelchair access: No
Pets: No
Smoking: No
Senior citizen discount: No

QUAIL HOLLOW
8924 Nelson View, N. Delta, B.C., Canada V4C 7V5, (604) 583-1204

If you venture 20 miles north of the border into North Delta, British Columbia, you will discover an intimate inn that honors its native birds. Quail Hollow has two guest rooms. One, the Heron's Nest, features an authentic Laurence Bradley queen-size brass bed and is decorated in black, brass, and gray. Visitors have use of an adjacent bathroom complete with Roman tub. The Gull's Nest offers a queen-size four-poster pine waterbed and private half-bath. From its adjacent sitting room, it might be possible to hear the rush of the mighty Fraser River, whose banks welcome joggers, walkers, and bikers.

Owners Steve and Karin Shantz serve a delicious, healthful breakfast with homemade specialties.

Sometime during your stay, take the thirty-minute Skytrain into Vancouver. With its idyllic setting, temperate climate, manicured parks, and myriad restaurants, Vancouver is the San Francisco of Canada.

Rates: Single $65; double $75; extra person $15
Credit cards: Visa, MC
No. of rooms: 3
No. of baths: 2½
Directions: Inn will send map.

Wheelchair access: No
Pets: Yes, kennel facility available
Smoking: No
Senior citizen discount: No

Grand Manan Island and Machias Seal Island Migratory Bird Sanctuary

NEAREST AIRPORTS: McAdam, Frederickton, and St. John, New Brunswick, Canada; Bangor and Bar Harbor, Maine.

LOCATION: Grand Manan Island can be reached via ferry from Blacks Harbour. Machias Seal Island is accessible via private boat charters from Seal Cove, Grand Manan. There is no access to Machias Seal Island Bird Sanctuary from June 1 to July 31 each year, but birding can be done offshore from the boats. To reach Blacks Harbour from Saint John, drive east on Highway 1 to Route 778 south. From McAdam, drive south on Highway 3 to the junction of Highway 1. Continue west on Highway 1 to Route 778 south. From Bangor, Maine, take I-95 north to the Highway 6 exit. Drive east on Highway 6 until you reach McAdam, New Brunswick, Canada. The coastal drive from either Bar Harbor or Bangor is Highway 1 east to the Canadian border, then continuing on Highway 1 to south exit on Route 778.

CONTACT: Canadian Wildlife Service, Atlantic Region, P.O. Box 1590, Sackville, N.B., Canada E0A 3C0. (506) 536-3025 or (902) 426-3274.

BEST BIRDING: Spring, summer, and fall. Please note seasonal restrictions for the Machias Seal Island Migratory Bird Sanctuary.

TOURS/WORKSHOPS: Check with Canadian Wildlife Service.

Grand Manan Island lies at the mouth of the Bay of Fundy. The best birding time for this area is March through May and August through November. Fall is a good time to observe migrating accidentals. You can find a wealth of seabirds here, including petrels, shearwaters, razorbills, guillemots, and colorful, comic Atlantic puffins. Look for common and king eiders as well as oldsquaws.

From Grand Manan Island, take the tour to Machias Seal Island Bird Sanctuary. There is a time limit of three hours on the island as well as other necessary restrictions, so bird with respect. The most numerous species is the Artic tern, with about 1,900 nesting pairs, a decrease in population from the estimated 3,500 there in the 1940s. Since there are only 100 pairs of common terns, you will have to look carefully for identification. Leach's storm-petrels nest on the island but cannot be seen. This is the perfect haven for the Atlantic puffin; according to some estimates, there are as many as 900 pairs breeding on the island. A small group of razorbills (cousin to the puffin) breeds here as well. More than 100 accidentals have also been listed here. Even without landing on the island, you can observe the flocks of seabirds flying, dipping, and squawking around the shores, as well as whales, dolphins, and seals.

THE COMPASS ROSE
North Head, Grand Manan Island, N.B., Canada, E0G 2M0
(506) 446-5906, (506) 662-8570 (after May 1)

A pleasant place to stay on Grand Manan Island is the Compass Rose, a bed and breakfast consisting of two charming old houses by the sea. The bedrooms, furnished with antique pine, look out to sea. The dining room in the main house—where you will be served breakfast, lunch, afternoon tea, scones, and dinner—opens to a long deck overlooking the harbor.

Evening conversations and early morning plans take place in the sitting rooms around the Franklin stoves. The menu for the Compass Rose is homespun; it comes from local gardens, the bed and breakfast's ovens, or the Bay of Fundy (lobster, scallops, and a variety of fish).

Innkeeper Cecilia Bowden reports, "Our guests, who return regularly, are bird-watchers, artists, photographers, hikers, and kindred spirts who crave the simple life. There are meadows of wildflowers; trails along steep cliffs; picnics on secluded beaches; a boat trip to see the puffins, whales, and dolphins; or talks on the wharves with local fishermen."

Rates: $45-$55; extra person $6   **Wheelchair access:** No
Credit cards: Visa, MC   **Pets:** Yes
No. of rooms: 8   **Smoking:** One dining room only
No. of baths: 3 full, 2 half   **Senior citizen discount:** No
Directions: Turn off Highway 1 at Pennfield for Blacks Harbour, take ferry to North Head. The inn is a five-minute drive from ferry dock on the main road.

MARATHON INN
North Head, Grand Manan Island, N.B., Canada E0G 2M0, (506) 662-8144

The Marathon Inn is everything you could possibly expect of a hotel built over a century ago by a retired sea captain. It has been impeccably maintained over the years and has recently been refurbished. It still retains the charm and leisurely living of another age. Antiques and period decor complement the mood.

The rooms are sun-clean and inviting. Many of them overlook the harbor and have running water; some have private showers. In the dining room, you will be served seafood specialties cooked fresh from the ocean.

Grand Manan Island offers you an opportunity to be surrounded by the sea, unspoiled nature, and the quaint, historic charm of a beautiful maritime fishing community.

Rates: $44-$89; extra person $6   **Wheelchair access:** Yes
Credit cards: Visa, MC   **Pets:** Summer only
No. of rooms: 7 winter, 29 summer   **Smoking:** Yes
No. of baths: 7 winter, 29 summer   **Senior citizen discount:** No
Directions: Ferry from Blacks Harbour, docks in North Head; inn located ¼ mile from ferry terminal; pick-up at ferry available.

Puffin

NOVA SCOTIA

The Border Region/Amherst Point Bird Sanctuary and Sackville Waterfowl Park

NEAREST AIRPORTS: Moncton, New Brunswick; and Halifax, Nova Scotia, Canada.

LOCATION: The Border Region is situated at the head of the Bay of Fundy. From Moncton, New Brunswick, drive southeast about 28 miles on the Trans Canada Highway (Highway 2) to the cities of Sackville and Amherst Point. The Sackville Waterfowl Park is reached from exit 451 south to East Main Street, with entrances at the corner of King Street or near the Anglican Church Hall on East Main Street. From Halifax, Nova Scotia, drive north 56 miles on Highway 102 until you reach Glenholme and the junction with the Trans Canada Highway (Highway 104). Continue north, then west on the Trans Canada Highway another 56 miles until you reach the Amherst exit next to the Wandlyn Motel, then turn left toward Amherst Point. The sanctuary is located on the left-hand side of the highway approximately 2 miles from the Trans Canada exit.

CONTACTS: Wildlife Biologist, Canadian Wildlife Service, Amherst Point Migratory Bird Sanctuary, P.O. Box 1590, Sackville, N.B., Canada E0A 3C0. Use the same address to reach the Sackville Waterfowl Park, (506) 536-3025.

BEST BIRDING: Spring, fall, and summer. Very large shorebird migrations from mid-July through August, numbering in the hundreds of thousands.

TOURS/WORKSHOPS: In early August, there is an Atlantic Waterfowl Celebration, with many birding tours, natural history workshops, and wildlife art exhibits. For specific dates and information, contact the Canadian Wildlife Service. Another good source of information is the Nova Scotia Bird Society: (902) 424-7353.

It is difficult to resist the shorelines, marshes, islands, and bays of Nova Scotia and New Brunswick. With its variety of habitat and weather, this North Atlantic area has a grand medley of bird species. Part of the Chignecto National Wildlife Area, Amherst, Sackville, and the John Lusby Salt Marsh support over 200 species of birds. In addition to common waterfowl, such as scaups, scoters, and ring-necked, black, and ruddy ducks, the shorebird migration in the fall brings great black-backed gulls, Artic and black terns, black terns, whimbrels, godwits, phalaropes, and many common varieties numbering in the thousands. The spring and summer are of short duration this far north, so plan your trip accordingly. There is good habitat for hawks, owls, and songbirds. Even in winter, you can find rough-legged hawks as well as short- and long-eared owls and snowy owls.

The entire area is good habitat for observation. Do not miss these other nearby hot spots: in Nova Scotia, Brier Island, Annapolis Valley, and Cape Breton Island; in New Brunswick, Fundy National Park, Mary's Point, Cape Jourimain National Wildlife Area, and Saint's Rest Marsh. Also try to include some time on Prince Edward Island to observe the spring and fall migrations.

THE DIFFERENT DRUMMER
P.O. Box 188, 82 West Main Street, Sackville, N.B., Canada E0A 3C0
(506) 536-1291

Welcome to the Different Drummer, a spacious Victorian home located on a tree-covered rise within easy walking distance of the town center. The house is surrounded by almost an acre of lovely, shaded garden. This is a winning bed and breakfast combination of modern conveniences set in a comfortable period atmosphere. The attractive bedrooms are furnished much as they would have been at the turn of the century, and all have private baths. A large parlor and adjacent sun room are available for guests, and a hearty continental breakfast is served daily in the sunny dining room. Hosts Georgette and Richard Hanrahan encourage you to enjoy the homemade bread, muffins, local honey, fresh ground coffee, and berries in season.

Sackville is situated at the geographic center of the Maritimes in southeastern New Brunswick just a short distance from the Nova Scotia border and the Prince Edward Island ferry to Cape Tormentine. Originally settled by Acadians in the eighteenth century, it was resettled by American colonists and immigrants from Yorkshire. The old Sackville Harness Shoppe welcomes visitors, who may watch harnesses and horse collars still being made by hand for shipment to destinations all over the world. Also located in the center of town is the Sackville Waterfowl Park, your birding destination, which offers some two kilometers of boardwalks and a unique, closeup view of marsh life. A short drive takes you to Fort Beausjour (1751), a National Historic Site. From the fort, there is a panoramic view of Chignecto Bay and the vast Tantramr Marsh, now a protected wetlands bird sanctuary, which the Acadians reclaimed from the sea almost three centuries ago. Also nearby are the world-famous fossil cliffs at Joggins.

Rates: $40-$51   **Wheelchair access:** Limited
Credit cards: Visa, MC   **Smoking:** No
No. of rooms: 8   **Pets:** No
No. of baths: 8   **Senior citizen discount:** No

Directions: 10 minute walk to Sackville Park; 40-minute drive east via Highway 2 from Moncton Airport.

THE SAVOY ARMS
55 Bridge Street, P.O. Box 785, Sackville, N.B., Canada E0A 3C0
(506) 536-9790

The Savoy Arms includes in its mailings a brochure for the Sackville Waterfowl Park, just a five-minute walk from this gabled nineteenth-century home. Bill and Jean Young, your hosts at the Savoy Arms, entice you to enjoy sleeping under a French duvet and to awaken with a homemade buffet breakfast. All rooms have private baths, and the common rooms provide a piano, games, television, a special reading corner, a fireplace, a spacious deck, laundry facilities, and a resident cat (nonbirding variety, of course).

The informative Sackville Park brochure recounts that waterfowl outnumbered early French settlers here by a large margin. The Acadians named their settlement Tintamarre, or "great noise," in acknowledgment of the enormous migrating flocks. "Tantramar" now applies to the entire vast marsh, actually four major areas formed by river drainage. This was once part of an enormous salt marsh, created by tidal currents and wave action that eroded soft red sandstone and deposited mud and silt. Today, most of it is freshwater marsh, isolated from the sea, except where countless tides have broken through the dikes of early settlers. As a representative of the surrounding marshlands, the park may lead you to explore nearby wildlife areas. Your presence here, along with a large number of preservationists who also have been guests at the Savoy Arms, puts you among an important group of people who take pride in a very special natural heritage.

Rates: Single $45; double $50 **Wheelchair access:** No
Credit cards: No **Pets:** No
No. of rooms: 4 **Smoking:** No
No. of baths: 4 **Senior citizen discount:** No
Directions: On one of 2 main streets in the small town of Sackville.

Godwit

ONTARIO

Long Point Bird Observatory, National Wildlife Area, and Provincial Park and Surrounding Area

NEAREST AIRPORTS: Buffalo, New York; Toronto, Ontario; London, Ontario; Windsor, Ontario; Detroit, Michigan.

LOCATION: Jutting out from the north shore of Lake Erie, Long Point and the surrounding wildlife area are almost equidistant from Toronto, Ontario, and Buffalo, New York. From Toronto and points east and north, the main routes extend from Highway 403 to Highways 2, 24, and 59, approximately 104 miles; from Buffalo, New York, take Highway 59, which leads to the park, a distance of approximately 94 miles. London, Ontario, is the closest major city at a distance of 70 miles. The Detroit/Windsor area is about 151 miles to the south and west (Point Pelee is about 90 miles away), and Niagara Falls, Ontario, is 75 miles to the west.

CONTACTS: Long Point Bird Observatory, P.O. Box 160, Port Rowan, Ont., Canada N0E 1M0. St. Williams Headquarters: (519) 586-3531; Old Cut Field Station and Visitor Centre: (519) 586-2885.

BEST BIRDING: Be sure to take in the entire area around Long Point on Lake Erie as well as the marshes, forests, and dunes on the mainland. In May and September, the greatest number of species can be seen. The largest concentrations of waterfowl are in Long Point Bay in March and the fall. You can observe 331 species at Long Point and Turkey Point, Spooky Hollow, St. Williams Forestry Station, Hahn Marsh, and Backus and St. Washington woods on the mainland.

TOURS/WORKSHOPS: Many field trips and workshops are available from the Long Point Bird Observatory. Bird banding demonstrations are conducted daily. Long Point Bird Observatory members have first choice on facility use. Write to the Long Point Bird Observatory for a schedule.

Long Point peninsula is a place where turtles have the right of way and where birds have migrated for as many years as this spit of land has existed. The base, point, and mainland provide diverse habitats: beaches, dunes, wet marshes, meadows, and cottonwoods.

The Long Point Bird Observatory, located at the base of the spit, was established in 1960 to monitor migrant songbirds and is now involved in many studies promoting the conservation of wild birds and their habitats. Some of these many research programs are the Canadian Lakes Loon Survey, the Ontario Heronry Inventory, the Breeding Bird Survey, and the Ontario Rare Breeding Bird Program. Designated a Biosphere Reserve by UNESCO, the fragile habitat is strictly protected by both private and public owners.

Each spring you can expect to see hooded, common, and red-breasted mergansers, and Tennessee, Nashville, yellow, chestnut-sided, magnolia, Cape May, black-throated blue, black-throated green, Blackburnian, cerulean, and up to 22 additional species of warblers. American redstarts, tundra swans, red knots, ruddy turnstones, and any number of waterfowl and shorebirds can also be observed. Some migrating species pass through for periods as short as a week, so it may be wise to contact the observatory.

The sharp winds of fall bring the raptors. Broad-winged, sharp-shinned, Cooper's, red-shouldered, and rough-legged hawks all can be seen August through November, with rough-legged hawks still present in the early part of December. Peak months for variety are September and October. Be sure to request the seasonal bird list for more precise information.

BAYVIEW BED & BREAKFAST
45 Wolven Street, Port Rowan, Ont., Canada N0E 1M0, (519) 586-3413

The Bayview is a small bed and breakfast with a great view of the inner bay. Nearby is Long Point, home of North America's first bird observatory, where you will want to spend plenty of time.

Guests can expect clean, comfortable facilities and a full breakfast. Rates include a full breakfast. The Bayview, which is 1.5 blocks from the downtown area, is very private.

Rates: Single $45; double $55; 1 single bed and 1 double bed $70
Credit cards: No
No. of rooms: 4
No. of baths: 2

Wheelchair access: No
Pets: No
Smoking: No
Senior citizen discount: No

Directions: In Port Rowan, 1½ blocks from main intersection (east direction), north side of Wolven Street (situated on the Talbot Trail).

THE HARBOUR RESORT
R.R. 3, Port Rowan, Ont., Canada N0E 1M0, (519) 586-2301

The Harbour Resort is a family-run resort near Long Point Bird Observatory. Long Point is a peninsula stretching for over 20 miles into the waters between Lake Erie and Long Point Bay. People visit the area from early spring to watch the migratory birds, through the summer to enjoy the fantastic fishing until fall arrives to bring back the birds migrating south again. The Harbour Resort's facilities include cabins and efficiency units. They have their own boat ramps and docks on a main channel. Each of the units has complete facilities, which include kitchen utensils, refrigerator, and stove. Bedding is provided, but the owners ask you to bring your own towels.

There is a restaurant on the premises, and nearby are a golf course, tennis courts, and marinas.

Rates: $40-$55
Credit cards: Visa, MC
No. of rooms: 5 cabins, 2 motel rooms
No. of baths: All private, 7
Directions: 1.5 miles west of Long Point Observatory.

Wheelchair access: Motel room
Smoking: Yes
Pets: Limited
Senior citizen discount: No

THE UNION HOTEL
Box 38, R.R. 1, Vittoria (Normandale), Ont., Canada N0E 1W0
(519) 426-5568

Normandale is a serene hamlet bordered by Lake Erie, Crown land, a reforestation project, and a wildlife refuge. It is an ideal location for cycling, English-style "constitutionals," cross-country skiing, water sports, and, of course, bird-watching at Long Point Bird Observatory and Turkey Point.

The Union Hotel is a handsome clapboard building a mere 600 feet from the sandy beach of Lake Erie. It boasts a pleasant strollway along a nearby rainbow trout stream.

Originally built in 1835, this historically designated home has been immaculately restored. Exterior cladding, decorative wood detailing, cast iron latches, wide plank floors, and tin room signs are only a few of the many original features that reflect the life-style once prevalent in upper Canada. Antiques and vivid historical colors also help to recapture the hotel's original style and authenticity.

The three guest rooms offer handsome furnishings, appropriate to their distinctive names: Governor Simcoe has a delicate four-poster bed, done up in satin and lace; Joseph VanNorman is graced with a large mahogany canopy bed; John Dey Post is high Victorian from its embossed gold leaf ceiling to the Chinese carpet on the floor. Hosts Peter and Debbie Karges serve a gourmet breakfast, a meal reminiscent of the early 1800s.

Rates: Single $35-$45; double $65
Credit cards: No
No. of rooms: 3 double, 1 single
No. of baths: 2
Wheelchair access: No
Pets: No
Smoking: Upper balcony only
Senior citizen discount: No
Directions: Normandale – Main Street, northeast corner of main intersection; from Highway 24, south on Turkey Point Road (Reg. 10), east on Lake Shore Road to Normandale.

Union Hotel

Point Pelee National Park and Lake Erie Southern Shore

NEAREST AIRPORTS: Windsor, Ontario, Canada; Detroit, Michigan.

LOCATION: The park is approximately 40 miles from Windsor, Ontario, and 52 miles from Detroit. The major accesses from the United States are via the Windsor Tunnel (Highway 3) and the Windsor Bridge (Highway 3). Highway 401, the major road from London to Windsor, is the primary access from northeast Canada. Both of these roads connect to Highway 18 and the park entrance. Be sure to write the park for excellent maps and written directions.

CONTACT: Superintendent, Point Pelee National Park, RR 1, Leamington, Ont., Canada, N8H 3V4. (519) 322-2365.

BEST BIRDING: Spring (March through May) and fall (mid-July through October). The total number of species recorded is 350, and it is possible to see up to that number during each of the migration periods. Point Pelee is an incredible funnel for birds. Other areas for good observation are Hillman Marsh, Wheatley Provincial Park, Kopegaron Woods, Rodeau Provincial Park, Amherstburg, Hawk Cliff near Port Stanley, and Holiday Beach Provincial Park near Windsor. Be sure to stay on trails to preserve vegetation and spread out along the Lake Erie and Detroit River areas to reduce the pressure on Point Pelee. Practice good birding ethics, and help preserve this fragile small habitat.

TOURS/WORKSHOPS: The Visitor Centre and the park staff provide a variety of programs. For information about dates and subjects, call (519) 322-2365. During the birding seasons, call (519) 322-3371 for recorded message on bird species update.

Not far from the factories of Detroit and Windsor is Canada's southernmost national park, Point Pelee. The smallest of Canada's parks, a mere sandspit jutting into Lake Erie, it has a special blend of marsh, field, forest, and beach habitats. The magnificent spring and fall migrations funnel to the point and spread throughout the northern shores of Lake Erie from Amherst to Port Stanley. A very large number of bird species as well as monarch butterflies will pass through, stop over, and continue either north or south. Programmed by temperature and the number of daylight hours, moving by day and by night, these birds fulfill a cycle that we are privileged to observe, if not completely understand. The spring migratory flow begins in March and does not end until early June. In mid-May, up to 39 species of warblers migrate north. Pine warblers, cerulean, golden-winged, magnolia, Cape May, and bay-breasted warblers as well as northern parulas, willow flycatchers, whimbrels, yellow and black-billed cuckoos, vireos, and orioles can all be seen. Large numbers of grebes, teals, and kinglets are there in April. Possible rarities that can be observed are Louisiana waterthrushes, purple finches, and prothonotary warblers.

The fall migration can start as early as June for some species, such as the greater yellow-legs. Golden eagles, peregrine falcons, and other hawks and eagles present excellent hawk-watching opportunities in September and October. Numerous harriers, sandpipers, warblers, gulls, and terns can be seen in August; in September, the birds to look for are hawks, parasitic jaegers, and rusty blackbirds. In October, you may have the thrill of seeing thousands of black-capped chickadees, as well as snow buntings and the northern saw-whet owls.

HOME SUITE HOME
115 Erie Street South, Leamington, Ont., Canada N8H 3B5
(519) 326-7169

Home Suite Home is a pleasant place to stay while birding at Point Pelee. This turn-of-the-century home has a log-burning fireplace for cool evenings and a large in-ground pool for summer days. Innkeepers Harry and Agatha Tiessen have decorated their bed and breakfast in a Victorian and country theme.

The Tiessens offer bedrooms with private and shared bath. All enjoy plush carpeting and fine linens. Before starting your birding day, enjoy a hearty country and gourmet breakfast on the enclosed sun porch.

Rates: Single $40; double $65 (Canadian)
Credit cards: No
No. of rooms: 3

No. of baths: 3
Pets: No
Smoking: No
Senior citizen discount: No

Directions: 5 blocks south of main intersection in Leamington, 115 Erie Street South.

POINT PELEE BED & BREAKFAST REFERRAL SERVICE
115 Erie Street South, Leamington, Ont., Canada N8H 3B5
(519) 326-7169

If you are planning to visit Point Pelee, Canada's southernmost point, call the Point Pelee Bed & Breakfast Referral Service. There are 55 rooms available, including country cottage rentals and rooms with kitchenettes. Whichever home you choose, you will enjoy warm hospitality and comfortable accommodations.

Most of the homes are within five or ten minutes of your birding destination, Point Pelee National Park. They feature rooms with shared or private baths and early bird breakfasts.

Besides the 22 nearby birding hot spots, your hosts can direct you to nature trails, nature bookstores and gift shops, Jack Miner Bird Sanctuary, and Colasanti's Tropical Gardens. You are in birder's heaven here, so enjoy!

Appendix

AMERICAN BIRDING CODE OF ETHICS

We, the membership of the American Birding Association, believe that all birders have an obligation at all times to protect wildlife, the natural environment, and the rights of others. We therefore pledge ourselves to provide leadership in meeting this obligation by adhering to the following general guidelines of good birding behavior.

1. Birders must always act in ways that do not endanger the welfare of birds or other wildlife. In keeping with this principle, we will:

• Observe and photograph birds without knowingly disturbing them in any significant way.

• Avoid chasing or repeatedly flushing birds.

• Only sparingly use recordings and similar methods of attracting birds and not use these methods in heavily birded areas.

• Keep an appropriate distance from nests and nesting colonies so as not to disturb them or expose them to danger.

• Refrain from handling birds or eggs unless engaged in recognized research activities.

2. Birders must always act in ways that do not harm the natural environment. In keeping with this principle, we will:

• Stay on existing roads, trails, and pathways whenever possible to avoid trampling or otherwise disturbing fragile habitat.

• Leave all habitat as we found it.

3. Birders must always respect the rights of others. In keeping with this principle, we will:

• Respect the privacy and property of others by observing No Trespassing signs and by asking permission to enter private or posted lands.

• Observe all laws and the rules and regulations that govern public use of birding areas.

• Practice common courtesy in our contacts with others. For example, we will limit our requests for information, and we will make them at reasonable hours of the day. Always behave in a manner that will enhance the image of the birding community in the eyes of the public.

4. Birders in groups should assume special responsibilities.

• As group members, we will take special care to alleviate the problems and disturbances that are multiplied when more people are present. Act in consideration of the group's interest, as well as our own.

• As group leaders, we will:
Assume responsibility for the conduct of the group.
Learn and inform the group of any special rules, regulations, or conduct applicable to the area or habitat being visited.
Limit groups to a size that does not threaten the environment or the peace and tranquillity of others.
Teach others birding ethics by our words and examples.

The goals of the ABA are to promote recreational birding, to contribute to the development of bird identification and population study, and to help foster public appreciation of birds and their vital role in the environment.

American Birding Association
P.O. Box 6599
Colorado Springs, CO 80934
(719) 634-7736
(800) 835-2473 (U.S. and Canada)

A BIRDER'S DICTIONARY
(An Aid to Understanding Birding Jargon)

Black-belt birder—Reserved for field identification experts such as Roger Tory Peterson, Ken Kaufman, Dale Zimmerman, Cindy Lippincott, Bill Thompson III.

LBJ—"Little brown jobbie(s)"—What to call groups of single indistinct birds of indeterminate color that are tough to identify.

LGB—"Little gray bird(s)"—See LBJs.

Stick bird—Often confused with real birds. Does not count on life lists. Usually identified when binoculars are focused incorrectly.

Leaf bird—See stick bird.

Life bird—Elusive birds; bird observed and identified for the first time, and added to your life lists.

Life list—All birds seen and recorded to date in your life.

Good bird—Rare; unusual for time of year, range, continent.

Guide—Usually refers to bird identification books. Questions often heard: "Do you have *Peterson's*, *Golden*, or *National Geographic?*"

Bird Counting Terms

Abundant—Many.

Common—Lots but not many.

Uncommon—If you keep looking, you will find them.

Occasional—Right time, right place, right season, good luck.

Rare—Right time, right place, right year, and a lot of luck.

Checklist—A listing of bird species you can expect to find in the area you are birding. Having one sometimes guarantees the bird you are pursuing will not be observed.

TIPS ON VISITING BIRDING AREAS

When planning your birding trip, whether it is a short excursion or an extended regional vacation, it would be wise to contact each of the birding areas listed to check on dates and times it is open. Many places are closed during the winter. Please be aware that most national wildlife refuges still allow hunting in season. You should write for the hunting schedules if you wish to avoid birding while the hunters are out.

Since refuges, forests, and preserves are subject to the whims of nature, as we all are, you should call or write for any change in status of the refuge from floods, droughts, hurricanes, tornadoes, or earthquakes. There may also be closings due to maintenance or upgrading of facilities.

The protected areas written about here have the primary purpose of preserving both habitat and bird life; some sections may be closed to the public, especially during nesting seasons. Always abide by these restrictions and by the code of ethics of the American Birding Association.

Bibliography

Bellrose, Frank C., and Bob Hines. *Ducks, Geese and Swans of North America.* Harrisburg: Stackpole Books, 1980.

Chandler, Richard J. *North Atlantic Shorebirds.* New York: Facts on File, 1980.

Clark, William S., and Brian K. Wheeler. *Peterson Field Guide to Hawks.* Boston: Houghton Mifflin, 1987.

Corral, Michael. *The World of Birds: A Layman's Guide to Ornithology.* Chester, Conn.: Globe Pequot Press, 1989.

Heintzelman, Donald S. *A Guide to Hawkwatching in North America.* University Park and London: University of Pennsylvania Press, 1985.

Holing, Dwight. *A Guide to Nature Conservancy Preserves.* San Francisco: Chronicle Books, 1988.

Jones, John Oliver. *Where the Birds Are.* New York: William Morrow and Company, 1990.

Lotz, Aileen. *Birding Around the Year.* New York: John Wiley and Sons, 1989.

National Geographic Society. *Field Guide to the Birds of North America.* Washington, D.C.: National Geographic, 1987.

Peterson, Roger Tory, and Virginia Peterson. *Peterson Field Guide to Western Birds.* 3d ed. Boston: Houghton Mifflin, 1990.

Terres, John K. *The Audubon Society Encyclopedia of North American Birds.* New York: Alfred A. Knopf, 1991.

Index of Inns

Index of Birding Sites

We Want to Hear from You

This is an audience participation book. If there are other birding refuges or bed and breakfasts you would like to see in the next edition, I would like to hear from you. If you have any complaints about the inns I mentioned, I want to know that, too. I would also appreciate knowing what additional information you would like to see in future additions. Please send any comments to:

Peggy van Hulsteyn
1833 Arroyo Chamiso
Santa Fe, NM 87505

Peggy van Hulsteyn won the Southwest Writers Workshop Storyteller Award for Best Novel for her murder mystery, *The Last Resort*. She was awarded first place for nonfiction by the New Mexico Press Women for her book, *Mind Your Own Business*. She has published articles in the *Washington Post, Cosmopolitan*, the *Los Angeles Times, Playgirl, Miami Herald*, and *Mademoiselle*. She is also the author of *What Every Business Woman Needs to Know to Get Ahead*.

Photo credits:

pages 15, 137 and 344 – Scott Martin
pages 29, 129, 284 and 290 – John and Karen Hollingsworth
page 33 – Lois Winter, USFWS
pages 41, 269 and 309 – USFWS, Sacramento NWR
pages 46 and 50 – D. Menke, USFWS
pages 76, 159 and 226 – Davis/Lynn
page 208 – Nedra Westwater
page 229 – USFWS, Wheeler NWR
page 347 – T. Rountree

Other Books from John Muir Publications

Travel Books by Rick Steves
Asia Through the Back Door, 4th ed., 400 pp. $16.95
Europe 101: History, Art, and Culture for the Traveler, 4th ed., 372 pp. $15.95
Mona Winks: Self-Guided Tours of Europe's Top Museums, 2nd ed., 456 pp. $16.95
Rick Steves' Best of the Baltics and Russia, 1995 ed. 144 pp. $9.95
Rick Steves' Best of Europe, 1995 ed., 544 pp. $16.95
Rick Steves' Best of France, Belgium, and the Netherlands, 1995 ed., 240 pp. $12.95
Rick Steves' Best of Germany, Austria, and Switzerland, 1995 ed., 240 pp. $12.95
Rick Steves' Best of Great Britain, 1995 ed., 192 pp. $11.95
Rick Steves' Best of Italy, 1995 ed., 208 pp. $11.95
Rick Steves' Best of Scandinavia, 1995 ed., 192 pp. $11.95
Rick Steves' Best of Spain and Portugal, 1995 ed., 192 pp. $11.95
Rick Steves' Europe Through the Back Door, 13th ed., 480 pp. $17.95
Rick Steves' French Phrase Book, 2nd ed., 112 pp. $4.95
Rick Steves' German Phrase Book, 2nd ed., 112 pp. $4.95
Rick Steves' Italian Phrase Book, 2nd ed., 112 pp. $4.95
Rick Steves' Spanish and Portuguese Phrase Book, 2nd ed., 288 pp. $5.95
Rick Steves' French/German/Italian Phrase Book, 288 pp. $6.95

A Natural Destination Series
Belize: A Natural Destination, 2nd ed., 304 pp. $16.95
Costa Rica: A Natural Destination, 3rd ed., 400 pp. $17.95
Guatemala: A Natural Destination, 336 pp. $16.95

Undiscovered Islands Series
Undiscovered Islands of the Caribbean, 3rd ed., 264 pp. $14.95

Undiscovered Islands of the Mediterranean, 2nd ed., 256 pp. $13.95
Undiscovered Islands of the U.S. and Canadian West Coast, 288 pp. $12.95

For Birding Enthusiasts
The Birder's Guide to Bed and Breakfasts: U.S. and Canada, 288 pp. $15.95
The Visitor's Guide to the Birds of the Central National Parks: U.S. and Canada, 400 pp. $15.95
The Visitor's Guide to the Birds of the Eastern National Parks: U.S. and Canada, 400 pp. $15.95
The Visitor's Guide to the Birds of the Rocky Mountain National Parks: U.S. and Canada, 432 pp. $15.95

Unique Travel Series
Each is 112 pages and $10.95 paper.
Unique Arizona
Unique California
Unique Colorado
Unique Florida
Unique New England
Unique New Mexico
Unique Texas
Unique Washington (available 2/95)

2 to 22 Days Itinerary Planners
2 to 22 Days in the American Southwest, 1995 ed., 192 pp. $11.95
2 to 22 Days in Asia, 192 pp. $10.95
2 to 22 Days in Australia, 192 pp. $10.95
2 to 22 Days in California, 1995 ed., 192 pp. $11.95
2 to 22 Days in Eastern Canada, 1995 ed., 240 pp $11.95
2 to 22 Days in Florida, 1995 ed., 192 pp. $11.95
2 to 22 Days Around the Great Lakes, 1995 ed., 192 pp. $11.95
2 to 22 Days in Hawaii, 1995 ed., 192 pp. $11.95
2 to 22 Days in New England, 1995 ed., 192 pp. $11.95
2 to 22 Days in New Zealand, 192 pp. $10.95
2 to 22 Days in the Pacific Northwest, 1995 ed., 192 pp. $11.95

2 to 22 Days in the Rockies, 1995 ed., 192 pp. $11.95
2 to 22 Days in Texas, 1995 ed., 192 pp. $11.95
2 to 22 Days in Thailand, 192 pp. $10.95
22 Days Around the World, 264 pp. $13.95

Other Terrific Travel Titles
The 100 Best Small Art Towns in America, 224 pp. $12.95
Elderhostels: The Students' Choice, 2nd ed., 304 pp. $15.95
Environmental Vacations: Volunteer Projects to Save the Planet, 2nd ed., 248 pp. $16.95
A Foreign Visitor's Guide to America, 224 pp. $12.95
Great Cities of Eastern Europe, 256 pp. $16.95
Indian America: A Traveler's Companion, 3rd ed., 432 pp. $18.95
Interior Furnishings Southwest, 256 pp. $19.95
Opera! The Guide to Western Europe's Great Houses, 296 pp. $18.95
Paintbrushes and Pistols: How the Taos Artists Sold the West, 288 pp. $17.95
The People's Guide to Mexico, 9th ed., 608 pp. $18.95
Ranch Vacations: The Complete Guide to Guest and Resort, Fly-Fishing, and Cross-Country Skiing Ranches, 3rd ed., 512 pp. $19.95
The Shopper's Guide to Art and Crafts in the Hawaiian Islands, 272 pp. $13.95
The Shopper's Guide to Mexico, 224 pp. $9.95
Understanding Europeans, 272 pp. $14.95
A Viewer's Guide to Art: A Glossary of Gods, People, and Creatures, 144 pp. $10.95
Watch It Made in the U.S.A.: A Visitor's Guide to the Companies that Make Your Favorite Products, 272 pp. $16.95

Parenting Titles
Being a Father: Family, Work, and Self, 176 pp. $12.95
Preconception: A Woman's Guide to Preparing for Pregnancy and Parenthood, 232 pp. $14.95

Schooling at Home: Parents, Kids, and Learning, 264 pp., $14.95
Teens: A Fresh Look, 240 pp. $14.95

Automotive Titles
The Greaseless Guide to Car Care Confidence, 224 pp. $14.95
How to Keep Your Datsun/Nissan Alive, 544 pp. $21.95
How to Keep Your Subaru Alive, 480 pp. $21.95
How to Keep Your Toyota Pickup Alive, 392 pp. $21.95
How to Keep Your VW Alive, 25th Anniversary ed., 464 pp. spiral bound $25

Ordering Information
Please check your local bookstore for our books, or call **1-800-888-7504** to order direct. All orders are shipped via UPS; see chart below to calculate your shipping charge for U.S. destinations. **No post office boxes please; we must have a street address to ensure delivery.** If the book you request is not available, we will hold your check until we can ship it. Foreign orders will be shipped surface rate unless otherwise requested; please enclose $3 for the first item and $1 for each additional item.

For U.S. Orders Totaling	Add
Up to $15.00	$4.25
$15.01 to $45.00	$5.25
$45.01 to $75.00	$6.25
$75.01 or more	$7.25

Methods of Payment
Check, money order, American Express, MasterCard, or Visa. We cannot be responsible for cash sent through the mail. For credit card orders, include your card number, expiration date, and your signature, or call **1-800-888-7504**. American Express card orders can only be shipped to billing address of cardholder. Sorry, no C.O.D.'s. Residents of sunny New Mexico, add 6.25% tax to total.

Address all orders and inquiries to:
John Muir Publications
P.O. Box 613
Santa Fe, NM 87504
(505) 982-4078
(800) 888-7504